Praise for *HISTORY IN THE MAKING*

"Most Americans have probably relied on Christy Bowe's photography throughout their lives as she's worked to document the first draft of history as a photojournalist in the White House press corps. Through her beautiful photographs and sharply rendered anecdotes in *History in the Making*, Christy provides a close-up of the most defining and intimate moments from the past five presidencies. A marvelous achievement.

—Congressman Jamie Raskin (Eighth District of Maryland)

"Americans grow up fascinated and awed by the office of the president of the United States, and the men who served in that role. Bowe's book is an enthralling "peek behind the curtain" into what goes on in the White House—a peek only accessible to someone with a camera, press credentials, and the talent to capture history in the making."

—Congressman Andy Harris (First District of Maryland)

"Christy Bowe's photographs are sublime. With each moment captured in *History in the Making*, she shares her extraordinary talent and nearly thirty years of White House history for the benefit of generations of scholars to come."

—Marcia Anderson, Chief Publishing Officer of the White House Historical Association and Editor of *White House History Quarterly*

"I've heard it said by another photographer, 'You can take a snap. Anyone can, but a photographer makes a picture.' Indubitably. Take a look at Christy's book, and you'll see. Christy is of a special breed—able to be omnipresent, but unobtrusive, a silent creator of the record."

—Llewelyn King, Creator, Executive Producer and Host of "White House Chronicle" on PBS

"In an impressive collection of images and insights, Christy's pictures make me feel important moments, both happy and sad—those I was a bit player in, and those watched from the sidelines. An important contribution to the history of recent American presidents."

—Mary Catherine Andrews, Former President of the American News Women's Club and Special Assistant to George W. Bush for Global Communications

"Christy's images take us behind the velvet rope, revealing a unique and insightful look into both the history and the character of the presidency."

—Eric Draper, Former Chief White House Photographer and Author of *Front Row Seat: A Photographic Portrait of the Presidency of George W. Bush*

"The truly unique power of this book is the construct of Bowe's reflections of five different leaders who were in their own time the most powerful people in the world. She was never beholden to the role of an official White House photographer or personal presidential photographer. Christy is one of the fortunate few who has 'elbowed' her way and her images into the history books."

**—Mark Greenberg, Pulitzer Prize Nominee,
Former Photo Editor for *Associated Press*, and
Bestselling Author of *Obama: The Historic Front Pages*
and *Obama: The Historic Presidency of Barack Obama***

"Christy Bowe's *History in the Making* offers an intimate and refreshing perspective on the modern American presidency. Her brilliant photos capture the unique personalities of the men who occupied the office, document many of the key events of the past three decades, and offer a glimpse into the personal side of living in the White House, including first ladies and first dogs. Highly recommended!"

**—Steven M. Gillon, Senior Fellow, The Miller Center for the Study of the
Presidency at the University of Virginia; *New York Times* Bestselling
Author of *America's Reluctant Prince: The Life of John F. Kennedy Jr.*
and *The Pact: Bill Clinton, Newt Gingrich, and
The Rivalry that Defined a Generation***

"Christy has brought a whole new perspective on capturing our presidents, their families and history in the making. Technology and the people in the White House have changed, but Christy shows us that the art of composing a picture that expresses feelings and emotions does not. As news photographers we have a unique skill set to be objective. Christy is totally professional at all times, and never misses a shot."

—Melissa Young, Broadcast Photographer for ABC News

"Get to know the White House and the presidents through the experiences of a world-class photographer who is a member of the White House press corps. Christy Bowe does it again with her unique photographic talent that documents history. I love this book."

—Barry Donadio, Former U.S. Secret Service

"*History in the Making* is a must-read for those curious about the day-to-day of the most important 'office space' in the world: the White House! Getting it from a legendary firsthand observer is the real deal. . . . An important ode to women in the profession, finally!"

—Scott Mc Kiernan, CEO and Founder of ZUMA Press

History in the Making

HISTORY IN THE MAKING

A FOCUS ON FIVE US PRESIDENTS

CHRISTY BOWE

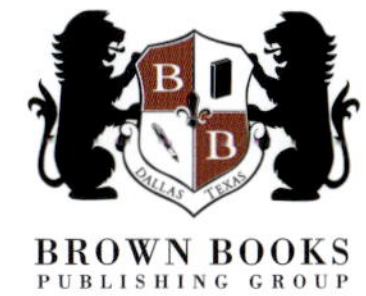

BROWN BOOKS
PUBLISHING GROUP

History in the Making: A Focus on Five U.S. Presidents

Brown Books Publishing Group
Dallas, TX / New York, NY
www.BrownBooks.com
(972) 381-0009

A New Era in Publishing*

Publisher's Cataloging-In-Publication Data

Names: Bowe, Christy, author.
Title: History in the making : a focus on five U.S. presidents / Christy Bowe.
Description: Dallas, Texas : Brown Books Publishing Group, [2024] | Includes bibliographical references.
Identifiers: ISBN: 978-1-61254-691-9 (hardcover) | LCCN: 2024939758
Subjects: LCSH: Presidents--United States--Pictorial works. | Photojournalism--United States--History--20th century. | Photojournalism--United States--History--21st century. | Clinton, Bill, 1946---Pictorial works. | Bush, George W. (George Walker), 1946---Pictorial works. | Obama, Barack--Pictorial works. | Trump, Donald, 1946---Pictorial works. | Biden, Joseph R., Jr.--Pictorial works. | LCGFT: Illustrated works. | BISAC: PHOTOGRAPHY / Photojournalism. | PHOTOGRAPHY / Subjects & Themes / Historical. | POLITICAL SCIENCE / American Government / General.
Classification: LCC: E176.1 .B69 2024 | DDC: 973.930922--dc23

ISBN 978-1-61254-691-9
LCCN 2024939758

Printed in Thailand
10 9 8 7 6 5 4 3 2 1

For more information or to contact the author, please go to
www.ChristyBowe.com.

*I dedicate this book to my faithful family, friends,
and various animals in our household who have
shown their support throughout this project.*

Table of Contents

Foreword

Politics is the making of history in real time. I have served under Republican and Democratic administrations with the President Reagan through Obama White Houses. A few highlights to my career are my eight terms as a US congresswoman (1986–2003) and four years as ambassador to the Organization of Economic Cooperation and Development in France and commissioner on the American Battle Monuments Commission. During these tenures, I have been the subject of media photographers more than most people. I recognize the importance of maintaining objectivity and considering various points of view when reporting a story. Now, as an "ex-con," I continue to appreciate how a story is told.

Over the years, I have stood at the podium and looked out at the photographers on the other side of the velvet ropes as they scanned the area with their lenses, quickly deciding what images they needed to tell the story of what was happening around them. Often it seems to have been the candid moments that speak the greatest truth.

Like myself, Christy Bowe chose a profession that was male-dominated, and we each held our own in our respective arenas. Christy is one of the few women photographers in the White House Press Corps who has captured history being made by five US presidents at the White House. She remains objective and loyal to her subjects from one administration to the next.

It is the reporters and photographers who let the public know what it is like to be present at both the small and large moments. They chronicle the constant activity that occurs inside 1600 Pennsylvania Avenue, and it is through their work that we know what is taking place in the three branches of our government.

Christy Bowe's *History in the Making* offers that intimate glimpse into the world of the White House. Within these pages she shares what she has learned while photographing our presidents and offers a look behind the scenes at the White House, capturing unforgettable, up-close moments in history with heart and humanity.

Christy has the incredible ability to seize and capture a moment as it unfolds. She is a visionary through her camera, allowing us to feel what we couldn't even comprehend in a thousand words. Her success is hard fought and hard won; success such as this requires purpose, preparation, patience, and perseverance. Christy has utilized these qualities throughout her life, whether it be through martial arts or other death-defying accomplishments.

Through her photographs in this book, I learn from and appreciate viewing the sudden, sometimes subtle shifts in attitude, personality, and reactions of the presidents she has covered over the years—flaws and eccentricities included. She captures the qualities that make them *human*.

Christy's journey has changed its course as politics has demanded. Press conferences are fewer, shorter, and often more exclusive. Access to the Oval Office has been dramatically and systematically reduced. Even in the face of all this, however, Christy's camera remains ready for rapid fire; when it's time to shoot, every second counts. You will learn from Christy Bowe's journey as she takes us, using her camera, onto the front lines of history at the White House.

—Connie Morella,
Former Congresswoman of Maryland and
US Ambassador to the Organization for Economic
Cooperation and Development in Paris

Still in the White House

I often pass tourists on my walk to 1600 Pennsylvania Avenue, then veer off to the special area that reads "White House Pass Holders Only," making me feel special. I have been walking through the northwest gates of the White House for over thirty years, and I continue to feel both humbled and honored by the experience.

Each time a uniformed Secret Service agent verifies my hard pass, I hear that click of the giant black iron gate as it unlocks, granting me entry. Next, the bulletproof door snaps open for access into the small building that houses more agents and scanning devices. I scan my pass, type in my passcode that unlocks the turnstile, and proceed through the magnetometer, which is followed by an additional detailed scan by an agent after

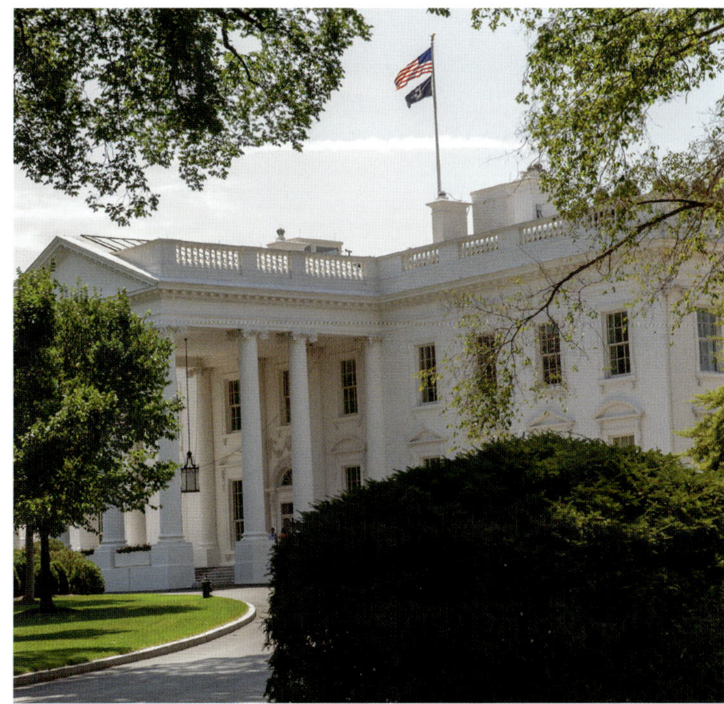

View of the northwest portico of the White House from Pebble Beach. Photo taken January 2007.

the metal in my two knee replacements predictably sets off the alarm. Meanwhile, my camera gear goes through the conveyer belt's scanner, and once I collect my equipment, I enter the White House compound. Same routine; still special. Once inside it is customary to pass by heavily armed members of the Secret Service as they patrol the grounds.

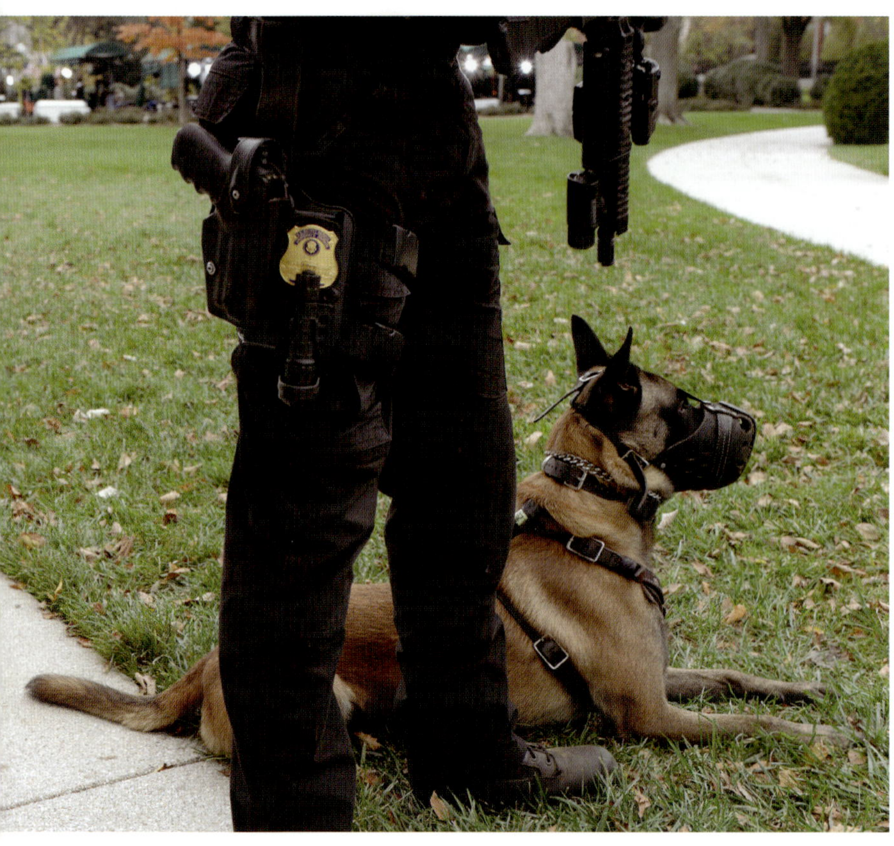

*A Belgian Malinois, a member of the
US Secret Service, and his handler look out
on the North Lawn of the White House.
November 2014.*

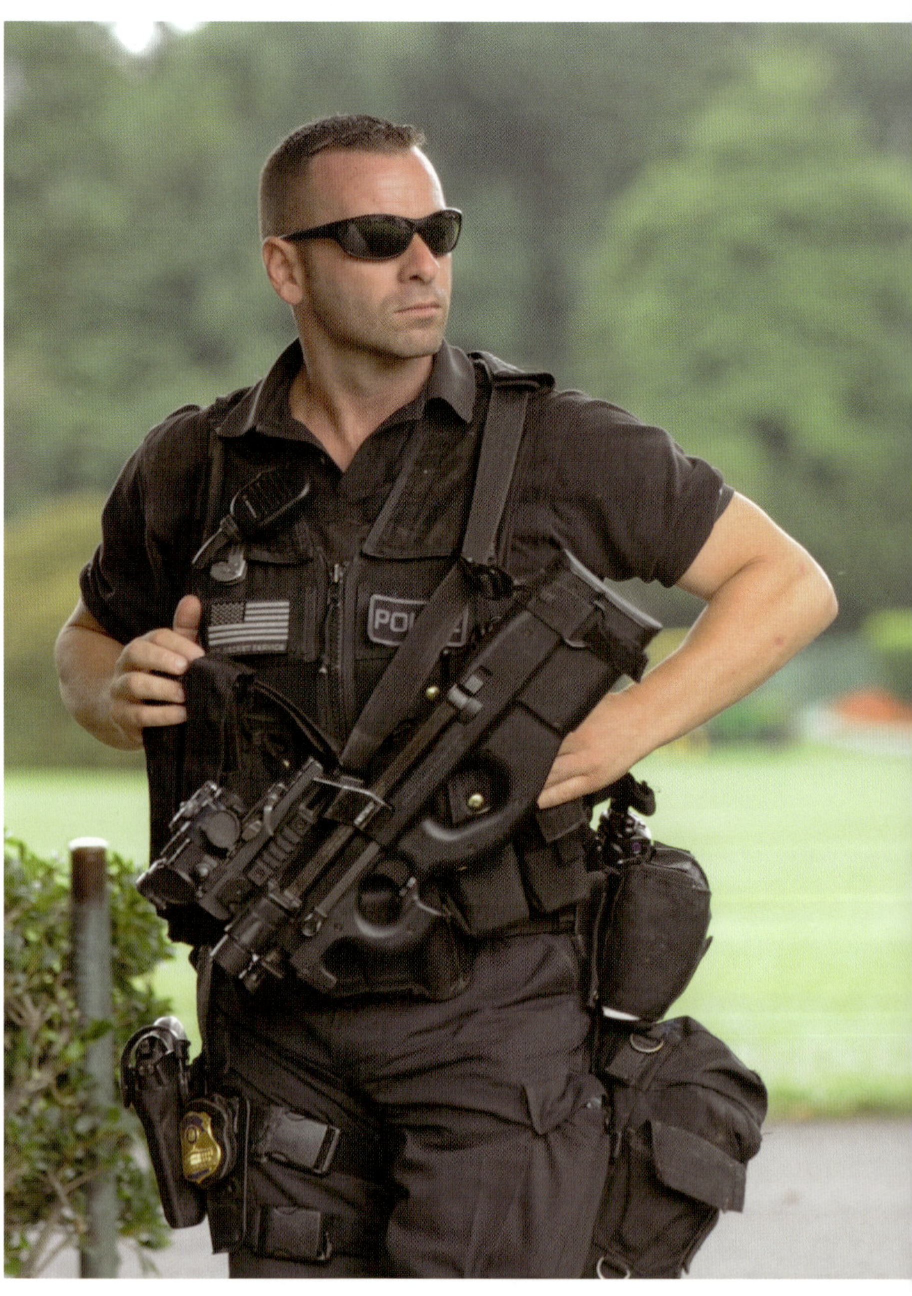

*Barry Donadio, a member of the White House
Secret Service Emergency Response Team,
patrols outside the Oval Office with his P-90
submachine gun while doing his rounds.*

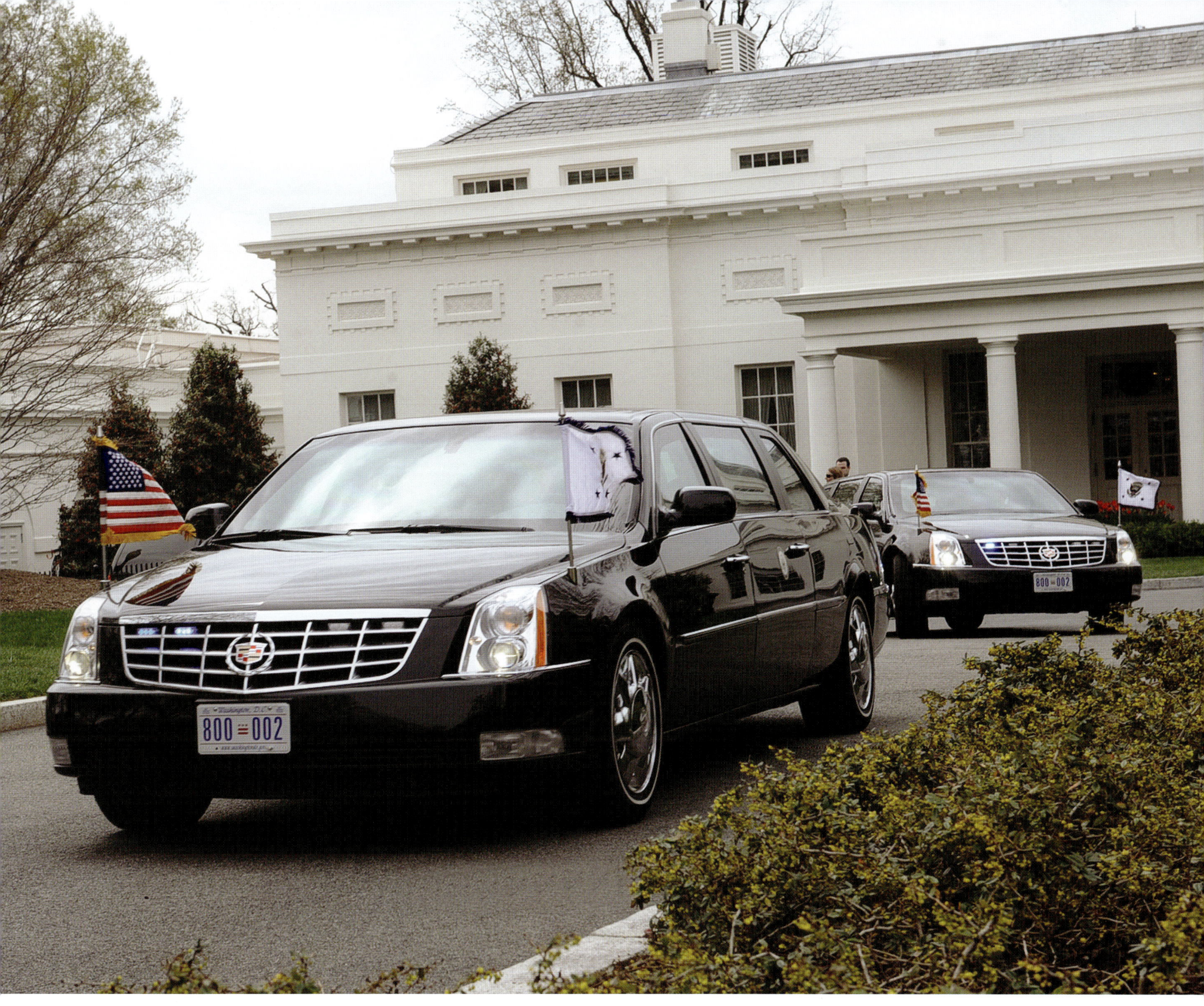

President Barack Obama and Vice President Joe Biden leave the West Wing in their respective limos. The United States presidential state car, known as "the Beast," is built to US Secret Service standards. Photo taken April 2009.

According to the White House Press Office, I'm known as a "still"—that is, a photographer with a 35mm camera, whereas a TV network photographer is referred to as a "stick" because they often require a tripod to hold up the heavy television cameras. I'm proud to say that I work alongside several women TV photographers who have been covering the White House longer than I have and are true warriors of the profession.

I have always had a strong sense of curiosity and a driving desire to be where the action is, so shooting the news was a perfect fit for me. It was on a cross-country road trip that I discovered my passion and excitement for relaying, and relating, to people the events I had just witnessed through photographs.

I later fell in love with news photography while shooting a protest rally in Washington, DC. It was there that I met a United Press International (UPI) photographer on the press truck, and he invited me—although he did not have the authority to extend the invitation—to hop aboard and join the professionals. This was a rare opportunity for any photographer, especially myself, and it ignited the fire in my belly for covering the news. That opportunity gave me a leg up in the industry, and weeks later I found myself working for UPI, acquiring my first press credential on Capitol Hill. After working at UPI, I switched over to work with reporter Sarah McClendon of McClendon News Service.

Working with Sarah was not only a great training ground but a wonderful opportunity to learn from the best, hands down. Sarah had a mindset, an attitude, and a belief system like my parents that still grounds me and guides me in my work: "No one is better than me, and I am not better than anyone else."

Working in a small news bureau, Sarah always fought to be heard and respected—a challenge that still exists today. She was the self-proclaimed "Citizen Journalist." Sarah always managed to keep a friendly attitude, but if she didn't get a satisfactory answer, all bets were off—especially when a president tried to dodge one of her questions during a presidential news conference. Presidents were actually intimidated by *her*!

When asked about Sarah, President Bill Clinton once revealed, "All of us who called on her in news conferences did so with a mixture of respect and fear, I suspect, because we would never quite know what she might say. I couldn't help but admire her spirit."[1]

Clinton was right, of course, about her inexhaustible spirit. One day Sarah and I were in a taxi, as we often were, on our way to a press conference at the White House. She always insisted on sitting up front with the

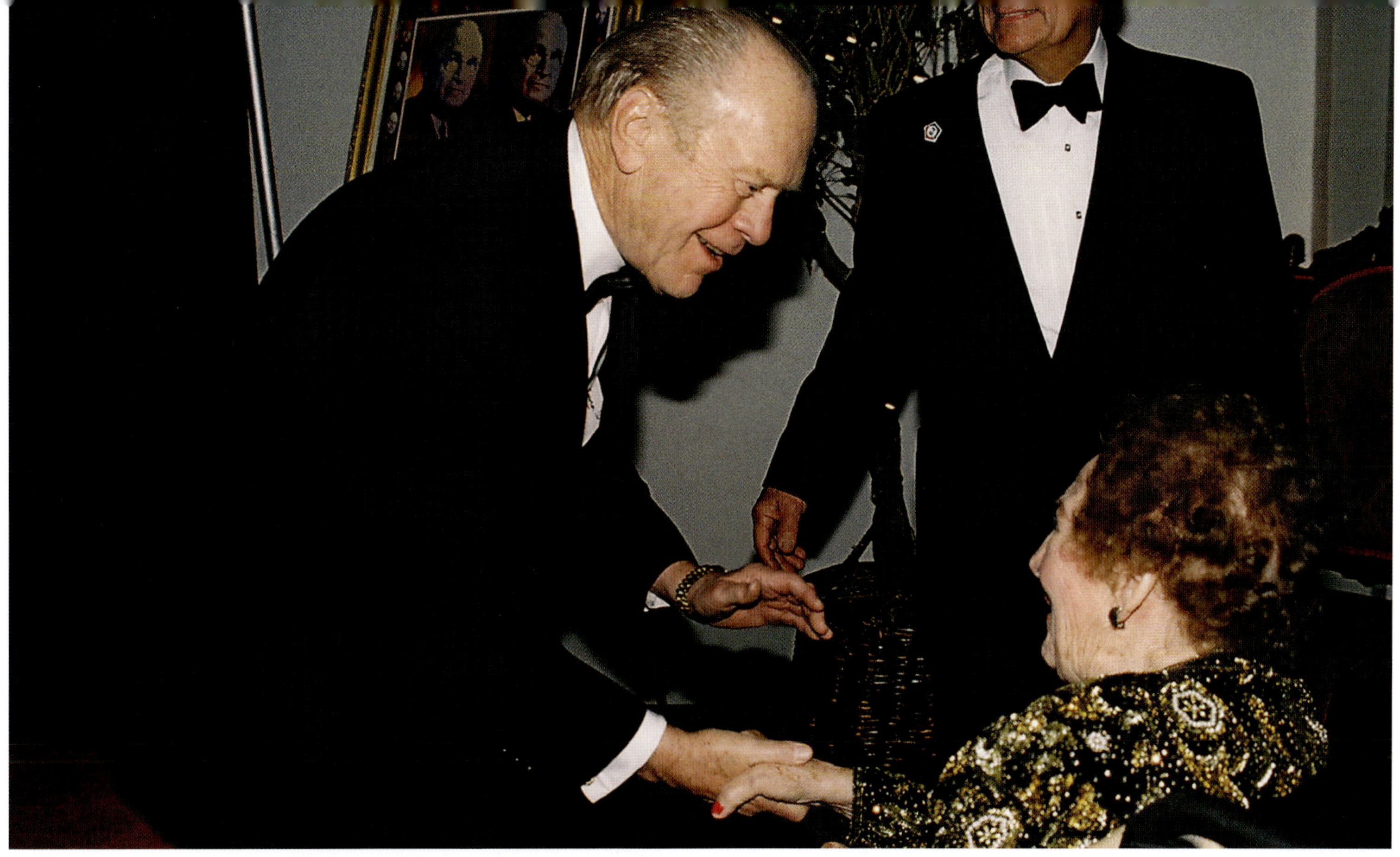

*Reporter Sarah McClendon is greeted by President Ford during a fundraiser
for the Truman Library held at the National Building Museum, May 1995.*

cab driver. Several minutes into her conversation with the driver, she leaned in and asked what he would like to ask the president of the United States if he ever had the opportunity. The cabbie responded that he would ask about a family immigration problem. Forty-five minutes later, Sarah was posing the cab driver's question to the president of the United States on national television. She *truly* was the voice of the citizens, of the little people.

Over the years I worked with her, whenever we attended various public events, everyone from White House cabinet members to movie stars would come over to say hello to Sarah—sometimes even waiting in line if they had to! At a "Roast and Toast" held in her honor by the American News Women's Club, Senator Alan Simpson (R-Wyoming) put it like this: "Sarah knows how to tell somebody to go to hell and make them look forward to the trip."[2]

I am so grateful to have learned from both Sarah as well as her friend—and competitor—Helen Thomas. Helen was a long-serving member of the press corps for over seventy years. She had seen so much history and countless events take place at the White House and was always ready to use the wisdom she gained to help others, including me. I didn't work as closely with Helen as I did with Sarah, but she was always in our same circles and made an impact that no one could ever forget. Once, Helen stood up for me when I had my pass cut during the George W. Bush administration. She began yelling at the senior press wrangler who was "thinning the herd." She let him know he had no right to prevent me from doing my job and my hard pass better be reinstated *now*. All the normal bustling in the briefing room came to a halt. You could have heard a pin drop. The wrangler turned red in the face and asked Helen to quit yelling at him, all the while backing away from her and out of the briefing room. The next day, my hard pass was reinstated.

Both of these reporters were legendary women competing in a man's world and doing it well. *Better* than well, in fact. They were kick-ass trailblazers who redefined journalistic standards and taught me enduring lessons about resilience, tenacity, and integrity. Having them on my side—and having my back—was the best insurance policy I could have asked for.

Helen was once quoted as saying Sarah "walked in where angels feared to tread. She had guts, she asked the

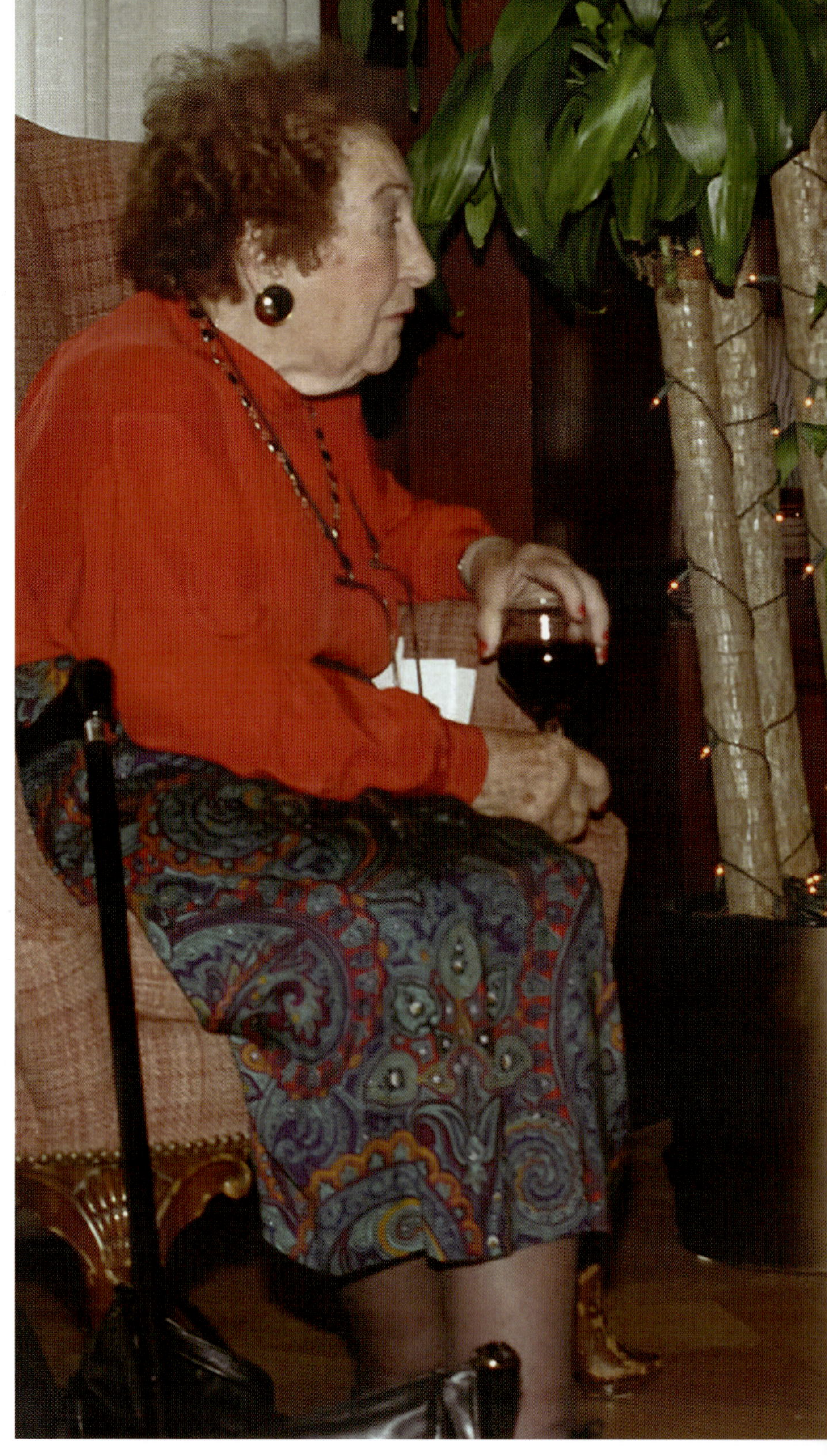

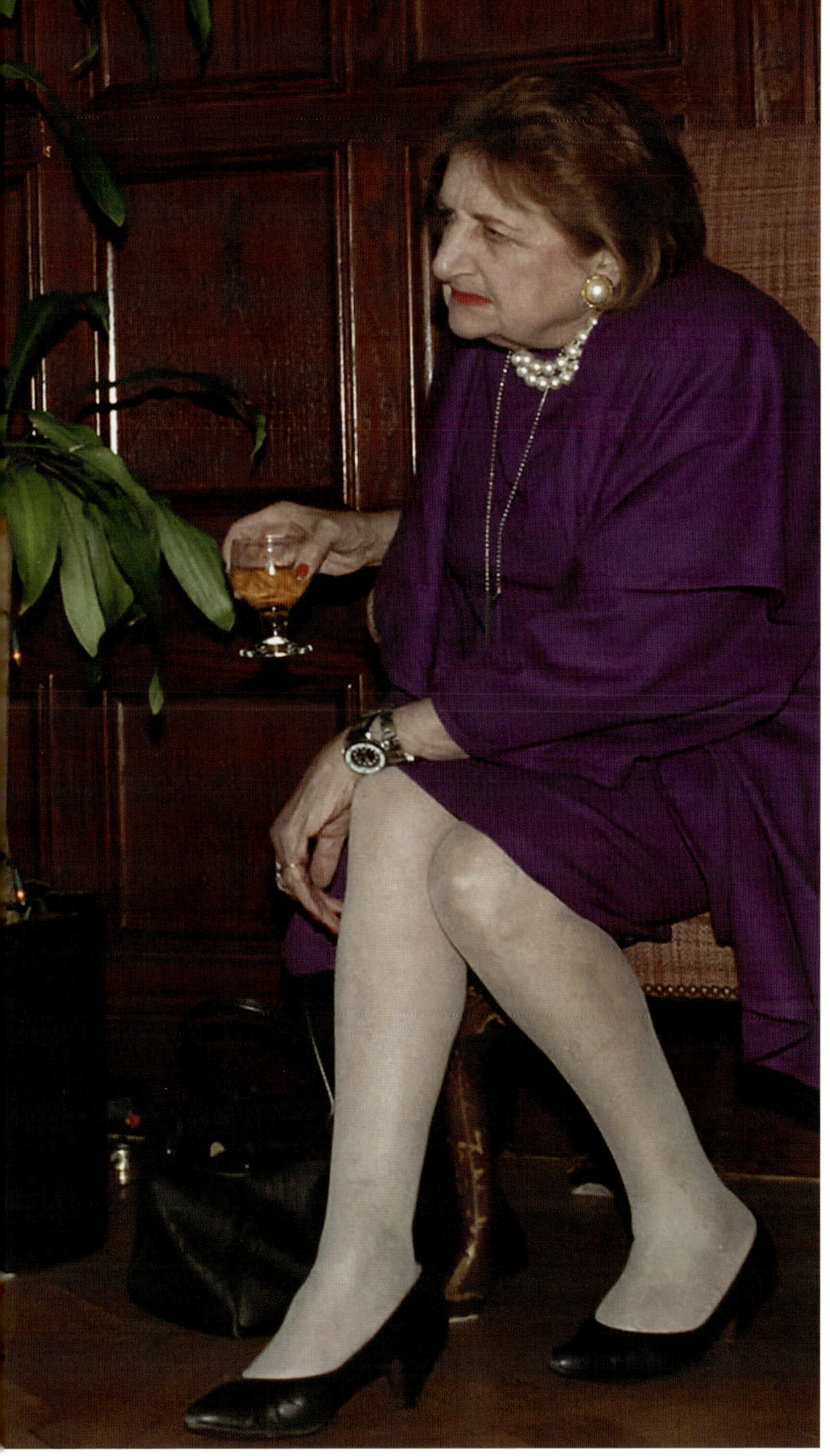

questions that should have been asked, and she asked questions for people who had no voice."[3]

Sarah always believed in giving people a hand up, and she certainly did that for me. All she ever asked in return was that I make the best of my talents, extend a helping hand to others, and to "be sure to always keep an eye on the president." Not only did I keep my eye on the president, I've kept my eye (and my lens) on five of them. They'd be happy to know that my love for both the craft and the profession has not waned one bit over the years. With encouragement from both Sarah and Helen, I started my own photo news bureau, ImageCatcher News. Both my company and I are now represented by Zuma Press and Getty Images.

The people I have met and worked with along the way have had a lasting impact on my life. Over the years, I have stood with pride, side by side and toe to toe with some of the most well-respected photographers in the country, several of whom are Pulitzer Prize winners.

Two friendly competitors who were legendary reporters, Sarah McClendon and Helen Thomas, share a drink and news tips with each other at the National Press Club in 1994.

I am most grateful to all the photographers who have given me a break and shown me respect in our ever-competitive journalistic world. Though photographers obviously work for different news outlets, we are also able to work cooperatively and respectfully to get the shots we need. Although now you will find more women photographers covering my beat in Washington, there are still many more men in the profession. I feel so grateful to be one of the women photographers covering the White House. To paraphrase Maya Angelou: "I come as one, but stand as ten thousand."[4]

Jumping out of an airplane at fifteen thousand feet and earning my first-degree black belt were also good preparation for my roller coaster career in news photography. These challenges brought out in me the courage to take chances, the commitment to follow through, and the conviction to face every challenge head on. In news photography, every day holds new challenges, and you have no choice but to step up to the plate when it is time to take a swing at capturing an important moment.

My camera has taught me to really see what's going on around me and take it all in authentically. When shooting pictures, I am concentrating on doing just that: the shot is what matters. I observe and attempt to predict what may be the one photographic moment that defines the story. Whether it's something as routine as photographing the president's arrival on Marine One (the president's helicopter) or as history-making as documenting a riot on Capitol Hill, behind the lens, getting the picture that tells the story, is what I am focused on.

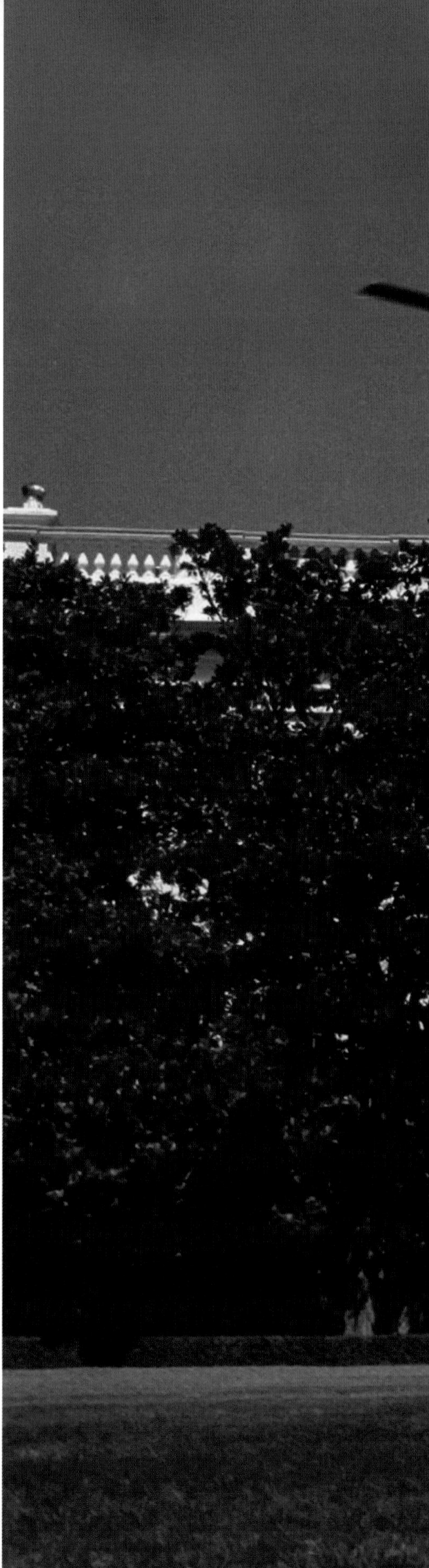

*Marine One takes off
from the South Lawn at the
White House, September 2001*

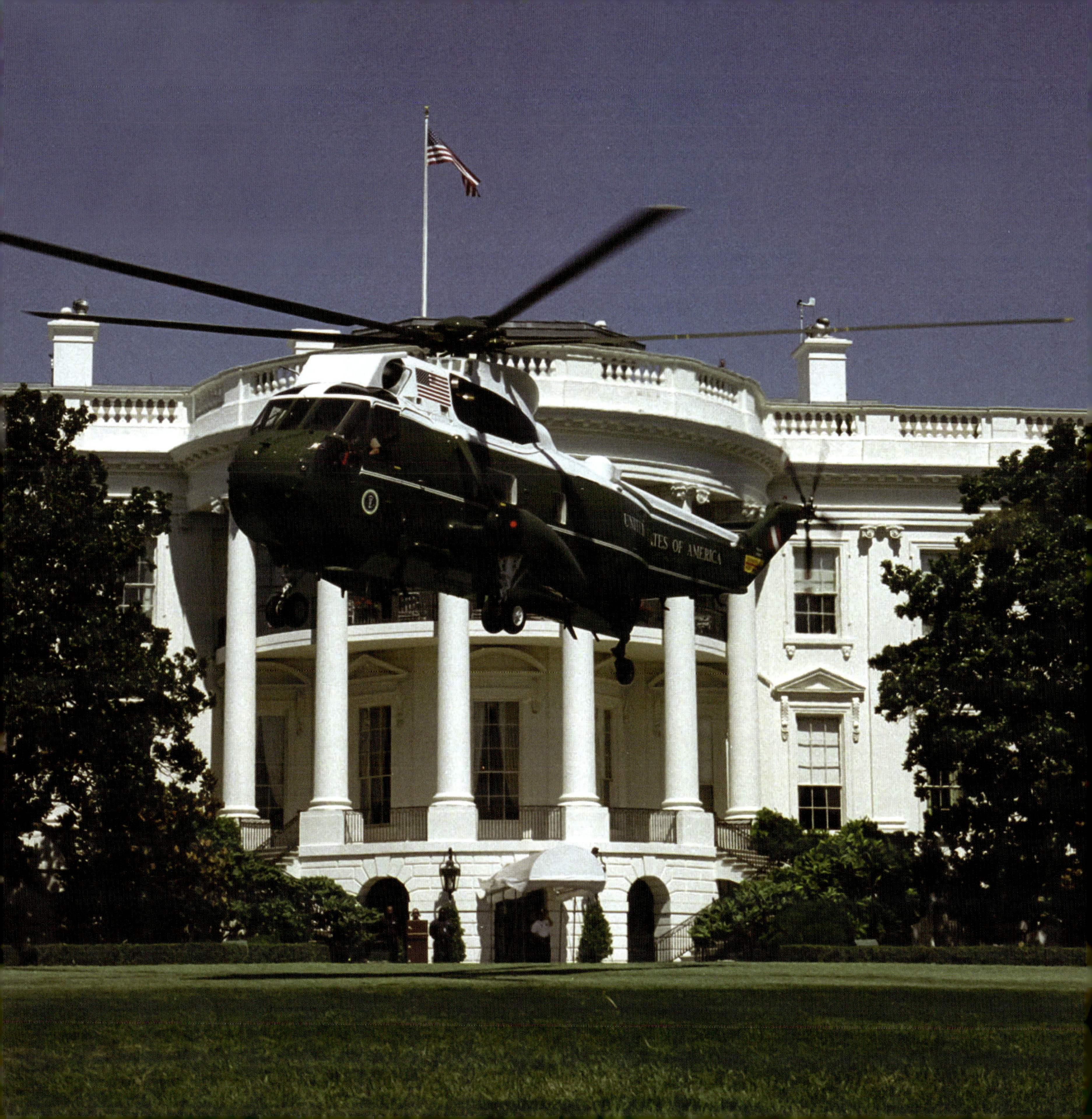

Yet it's always important to stay aware of everything around you—for the image you've come for might not be where you first expect to find it. It may actually be the reaction of someone in the crowd that says it best, even if that means gambling on the "Hail Mary shot" in heavily crowded situations (holding the camera with arms outstretched over your head, firing the shutter and praying to get a good image).

I have certainly put in my share of long hours and hard work covering the news; there's almost always something happening in our nation's capital. Sometimes it requires us small news organizations to be in two places at once. "Hurry up and wait" is the mantra of a news photographer. We can (and often do) wait hours for a photo opportunity that lasts under a few minutes. Not long ago, the pre-credentialed media spent hours waiting for Ukrainian President Volodymyr Zelensky and his wife to be greeted by President Biden and the first lady at the White House. Our photo op lasted about fifteen seconds.

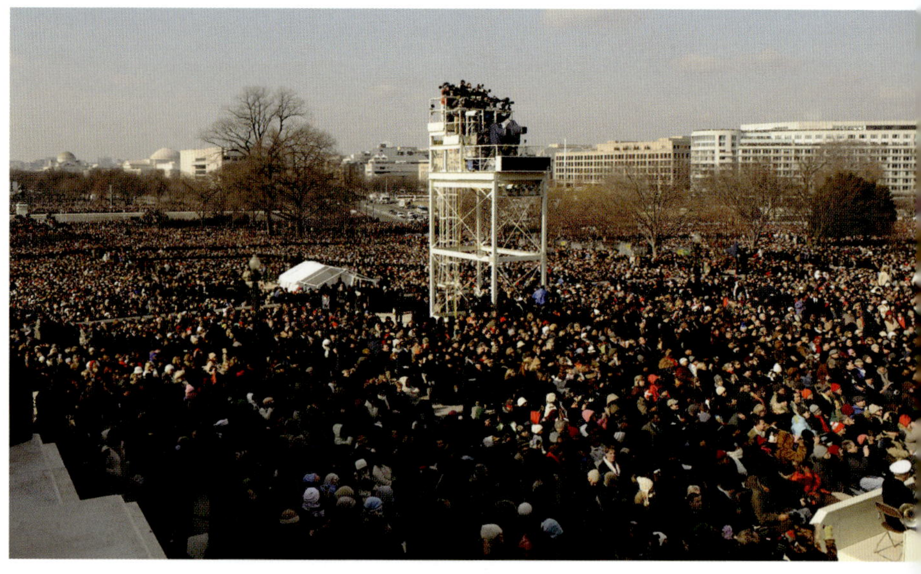

A view of the crowd from the press riser at President Barack Obama's first inauguration at the US Capitol, January 2009.

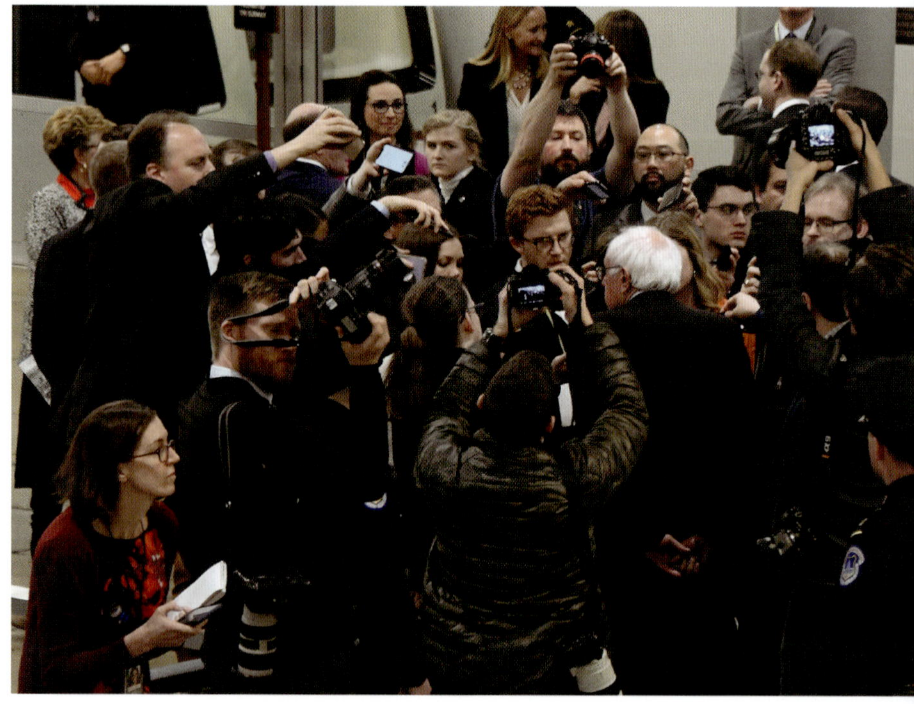

Senator Bernie Sanders is swarmed by the media as he makes his way to the Senate subway following the verdict to acquit President Donald Trump on two articles of impeachment. The US Capitol, February 2020.

I have learned many valuable lessons along the way, such as how to work in potentially violent and unpredictable situations as a news photographer. Trusting my instincts on when to flash 'em and when to stash 'em makes all the difference—that is, knowing when to flash my pass for access to officials or quickly stash my credentials under my jacket to blend into the crowd for my own protection.

I grew to understand that I needed to travel light and shoot with one camera so I could move more freely through the crowd. Sometimes I will even use my cell phone camera as a backup (after all, the cameras on smartphones today are now better than professional cameras were ten years ago).

Almost every presidential inauguration brings with it brutal weather conditions that challenge the most seasoned of photographers, as I describe in the Bush chapter of this book. Even as I write these words, I wonder how it's possible that I am heading into my ninth presidential inauguration ceremony! (I must admit, I do feel a bit cheated by the fact that several of the presidents I covered were elected for two terms, or my count would be higher . . .)

Although my company is minor, the history I witness is major. Because I have covered five administrations,

I feel fortunate to be able to provide some unique glimpses into the office of the presidency from a non-political perspective. Certainly, advances in computers, smartphones, digital cameras, and of course social media have greatly impacted the news profession. Outside of the secure venues (and often within), everyone reports and photographs now with their phones, documenting their own lives and the people around them, channeling more and more information onto the internet.

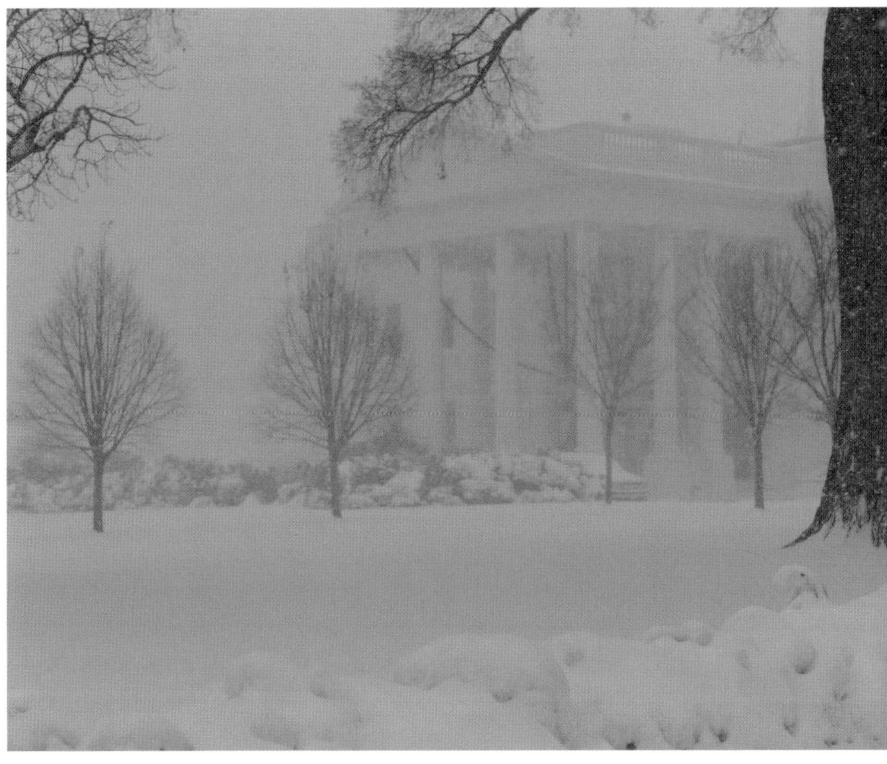

The White House under a record-breaking nor'easter that briefly cripples the US Capitol. The blizzard became known to locals as "Snowpocalypse." December 2009.

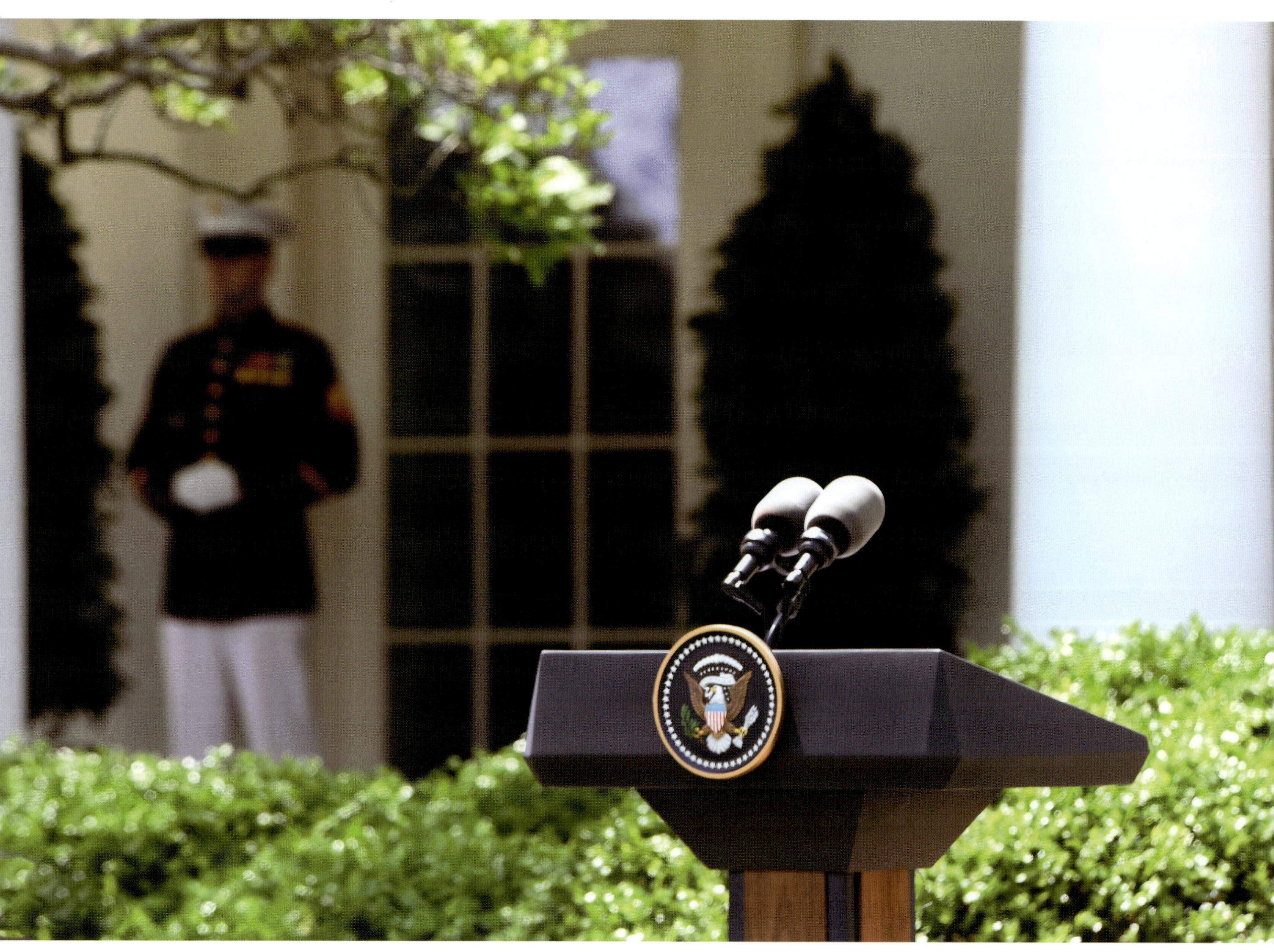

The media waits for President Biden and President Yoon Suk Yeol of the Republic of Korea to come out of the Oval Office into the Rose Garden following the arrival ceremony, April 2023.

Those who are interested in learning some of the backstories of presidential history can see these moments, captured frame by frame, as I convey a vital part of the diverse presidential narratives I've witnessed. Social media was not even around when I began my coverage! Throughout this book, you will get to experience the presidents as I have, and in my interactions with them, you will notice the steady decline in the press corps' access to the president over the years. Therefore, there are fewer stories and pictures from different perspectives to be shared from inside the White House by news photographers—perhaps at least partly the result of the intense scrutiny our presidents are constantly under. This is a very dangerous path to go down when the watchful eyes of the press are slowly being moved back further and further with each new administration.

For many years, photo ops in the Oval Office were only allowed for ten to fifteen seconds. That means photographers had to know the correct camera settings prior to entering the room. Having my camera gear ready and in place before I even entered the Oval Office afforded me more time to concentrate on positioning myself for a good angle and scanning the room for other VIPs who may also be in attendance. Thankfully, the time constraints have somewhat widened over the years, but the amount of photo opportunities has decreased.

The finite amount of one of the most precious resources we have—time—is not lost on me, especially in my line of work. I have learned the true value of what can be accomplished in a short period of time, sometimes in a matter of seconds. We also need to consider that each president has his own set of rules regarding media in the Oval Office and photographing at the White House in general.

Some may be familiar with my first book, *Eyes That Speak*, which covers different aspects of my career as a news photographer, including my experiences covering well-known newsmakers outside the White House. My new book, *History in the Making*, concentrates solely on my coverage of the White House and includes additional work that makes a deeper dive into photographing our presidents. This new book contains takeaways as seen through my own lens—the lens of one of two female still photographers who have covered five consecutive US presidents and counting.

I have certain takeaways from each POTUS. Each one brought his own style, quirks, and preferences to the White House. In this closer, more intimate view of the presidents I have covered, I'll usher us, together, into this hallowed-but-human place they live in that happens to be called the White House. In addition to my photographic work, I also have vivid memories in instances we were forbidden to lift our cameras. There are images in my *mind*—snatches of conversations, chance encounters, the witnessing of a spontaneous gesture that might not have been caught on camera—that I will share and reflect upon in these pages. I hope that my images and shared stories will paint a portrait of these leaders not just as presidents, but as people.

My coverage of five US presidents—Clinton, Bush, Obama, Trump, and Biden— has let me see, up close, the humanity that exists within the large fortress of the White House. Each of these men have one thing in common: they are all close to their families.

From my first day on the job, I've gotten to experience amazing occurrences up close. For instance, my first day covering President Clinton, I walked toward the White House Briefing Room and witnessed a bullet-riddled exterior wall, traces of an event I learned the president avoided thanks to, as we'll learn, his devotion to a particular sports event.

At the beginning of Bush '43's term in office he revealed that he had two loves: sports and family. He soon realized that he could invite sports icons he admired to the White House, and they would probably come. Being a lover of baseball and former owner of the Texas Rangers, he invited all the living Baseball Hall of Famers to lunch at the White House. The legendary players not only accepted his request but also presented him with a baseball bat signed by each of them. President Bush seemed as excited as a kid living out his childhood fantasy.

In 2001, President Bush promoted baseball and fitness by hosting T-ball games for kids on the South Lawn of the White House. Bush invited famous sports figures

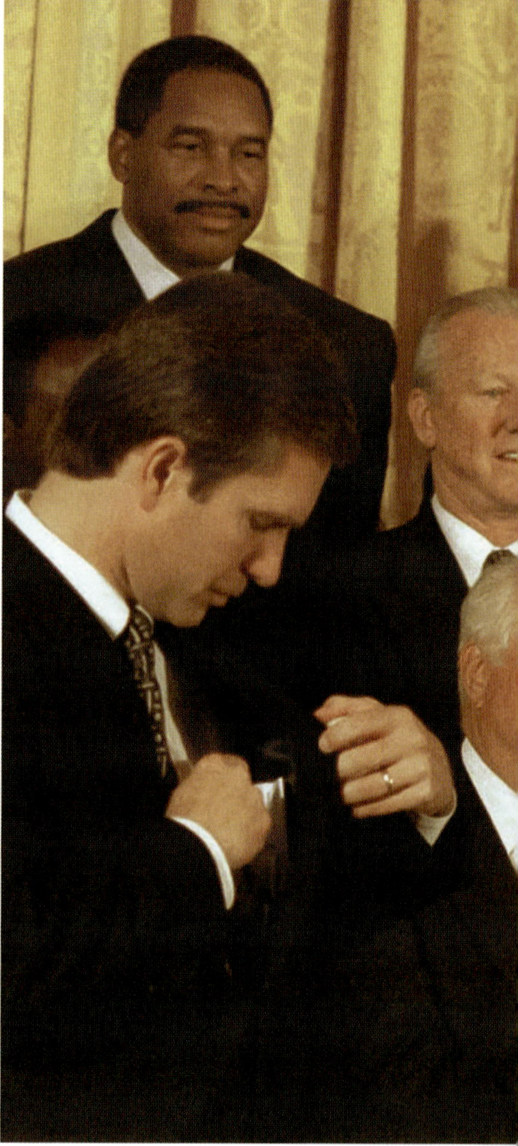

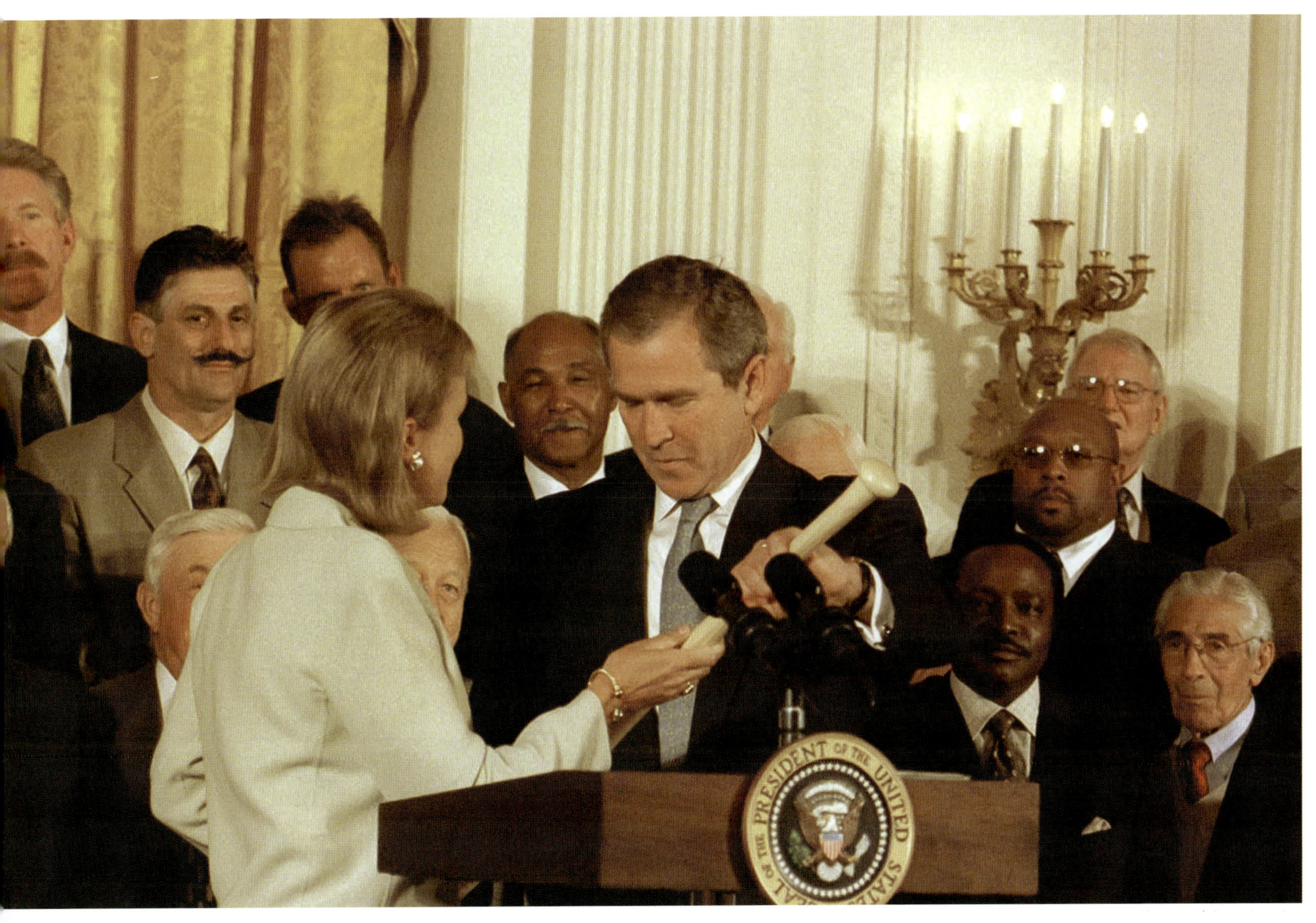

*President Bush is presented a baseball bat that is signed by all of the living Hall of Famer baseball champions
in the East Room of the White House as they celebrate the opening of the baseball season, March 2001.*

and enlisted Baseball Hall-of-Famers to coach the children, among those Cal Ripken Jr. of the Orioles. These afternoons were full of fun and friendly competition, complete with hot dogs and sodas for the kids and their families.

Just after the Sandy Hook Elementary shooting, I was in the East Room of the White House, photographing President Obama as he addressed the parents whose children had been killed. I watched him grow frustrated as he responded in tears to the family members in the emotionally charged room, telling them he wished he could do more. There were tears flowing that day—even from some of us in the press corps as we all grieved together.

President Trump single-handedly changed the format of a press conference while at the White House. Rather than hold a traditional presser for an hour or so with the media, he would stop and take questions from anyone and everyone on his way to or from Marine One. Every presidential arrival and departure became a crowded event. With the rumble of the idling engine of the helicopter behind us, Trump would talk and take questions according to his mood—totally in control. If he got a question he was not sure of or did not like, he would say he had to leave. We got the access; he was in charge.

When President Biden was vice president, he was often running behind schedule. He was, and still is, challenged to be punctual. As vice president, he would give a speech and then stop to greet people who normally would not be acknowledged by a vice president—such as those working in maintenance or even waiters—causing delays in his busy White House schedule. Now, as president, he continues to do the same. Ten months after being sworn into office, Biden bounded out of the White House with Vice President Harris onto the South Lawn as he greeted cheering members of Congress and signed the $1 trillion infrastructure bill, fulfilling one of his campaign promises.

I've captured these US presidents experiencing joy, grief, love, anger, surprise, and even remorse. I have witnessed them being both the leader of the free world and just being human. It's very different than the view most of America sees of the president, especially now. Today, there is a twenty-four-hour news cycle. When I started, our photos were transmitted an hour or more after the event had ended. Now our pictures are being transmitted around the world *as the president is speaking*.

Networks are in fierce competition. Sometimes in the rush to beat out their competitors, facts are not as closely checked because the deadlines are constant,

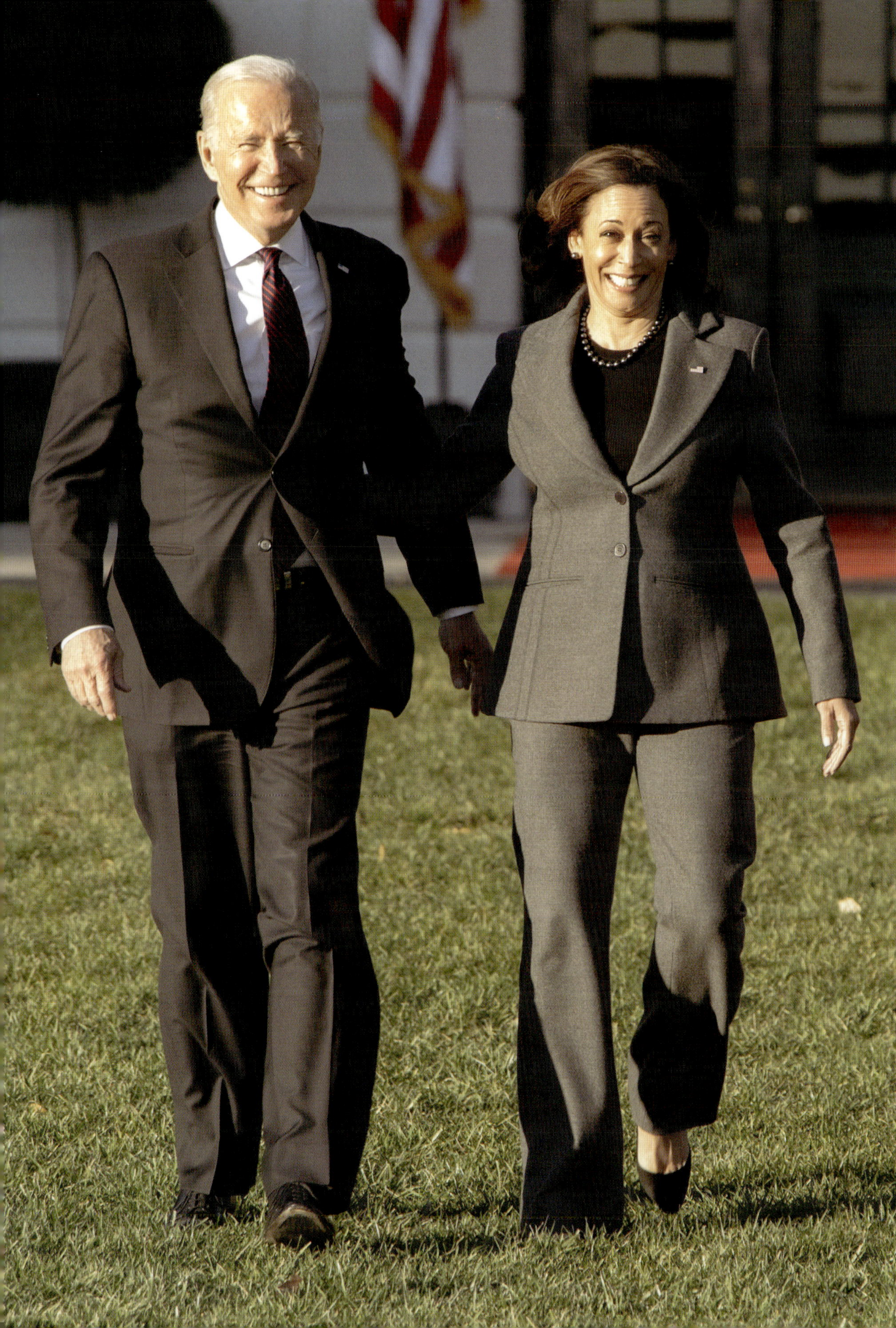

President Biden and Vice President Kamala Harris walk onto the South Lawn of the White House to greet members of Congress and sign the $1 trillion infrastructure bill, November 2021.

unlike in the earlier days of my career. Now, networks are known for broadcasting the point of view of their station, and folks typically tune in to get *their* news from *their* people who think like *they* do. I think this is a major factor in the current division our country is experiencing. During the Trump administration, I was covering one of the presidential pressers during a Marine One departure on the South Lawn, and I personally witnessed two networks broadcasting completely different versions of the same conversation.

Framing and targeting stories for certain audiences to keep up ratings are just a few problems I've seen grow throughout my career. Access to the president, for both photojournalists and the American public, is changing too. The traditions of regular, hour-long presidential press conferences where many reporters get a chance to ask questions or are granted brief Oval Office access have been steadily declining. For those of us in the press corps, each new administration comes with anticipation, touched with a hint of downright fear, that some of us will lose our precious hard passes that grant us entry onto the White House grounds. We also worry about what modifications will transfer over from the previous presidential guidelines that will affect how we provide our coverage. In the beginning of a new administration, there is a period of time—you could call it a learning curve—where photographers and reporters will discover the new guidelines set by the new press office staff, as every press office is unique. However, the one constant theme—and the one disturbing trend—throughout each changeover is the *shrinking access* to the president.

The way the president responds, his expressions, his body language, and his spontaneous gestures are all part of the story of his presidency. Different visuals and viewpoints are critical to present the story. We sticks and stills are the eyes and ears of the public, and it is our responsibility to relay what we witness.

In order to get an unbiased view of the news, I strongly believe that the public needs to watch a couple of networks with different viewpoints and then figure out their own opinion on the matter. Most people do not have the time, energy, or desire for that.

History in the Making: A Focus on Five US Presidents is an unveiling of both the professional and personal sides of our presidents through the stories I've lived and the images I've documented as a member of the White House Press Corps.

It is becoming harder for us to know who our president is, and it is becoming harder for the American people to feel connected in a way that fosters trust in our country's leadership. It is getting harder for me, as a photographer committed to showing the truth that happens within the walls of the White House, along with other members of the press corps to document history. This is needed for future generations to know the what, when, how, why, and most importantly the who of each presidency.

I challenge my readers now to buckle up and I invite you to join me behind the lens as I share some of my press corps adventures.

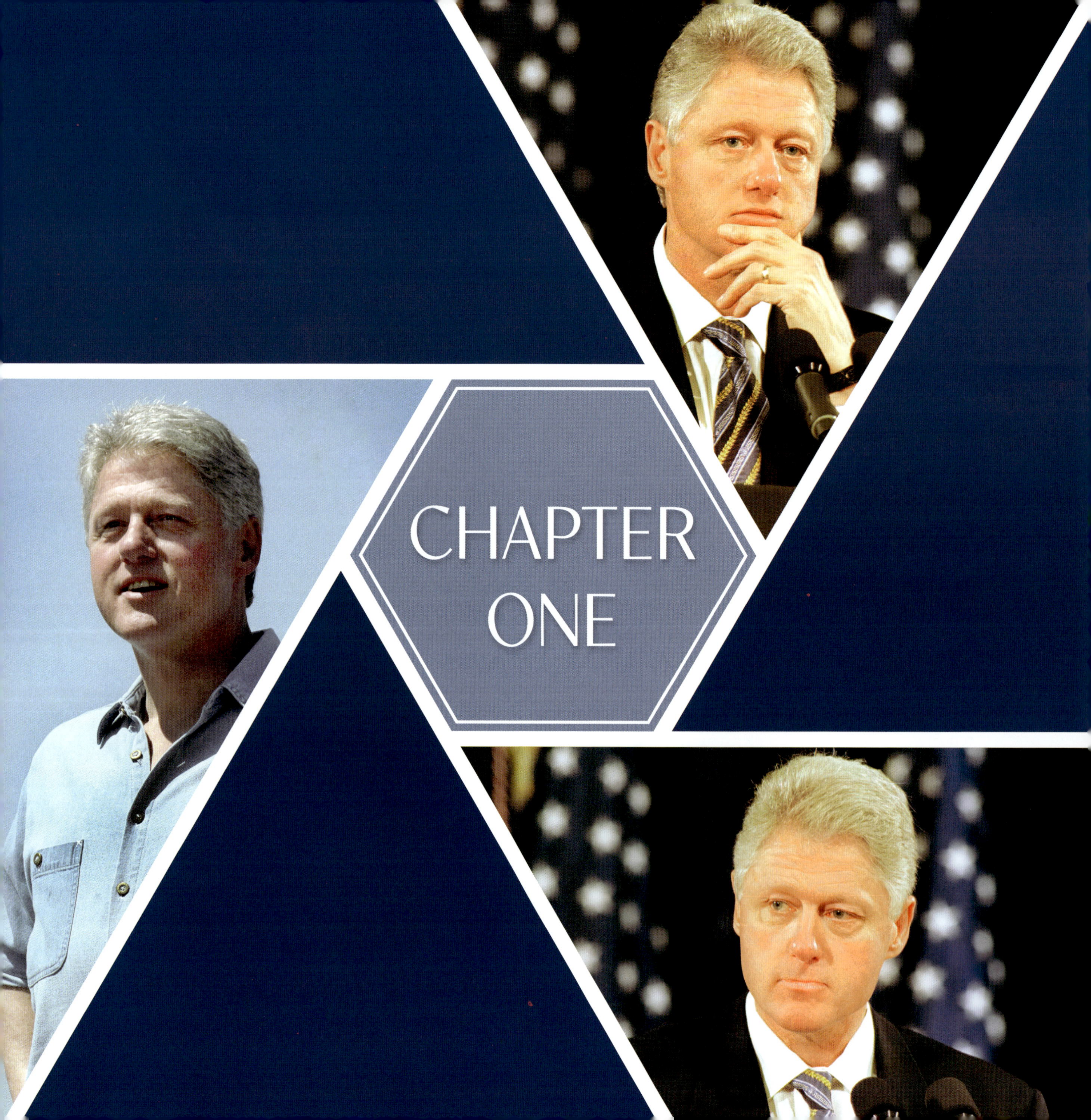
CHAPTER
ONE

PRESIDENT

WILLIAM J. CLINTON

The White House is uniquely the only place that is a museum, place of business, and private residence of a world leader. The first time I passed through the gates of 1600 Pennsylvania Avenue with my newly acquired White House hard pass was in October of 1994. I was thrilled to be "living the dream"—covering the White House. As I approached the famous briefing room, a reporter pointed out the bullet holes in the exterior wall of the building. A crazed man had gone on a shooting spree with a Chinese SKS semiautomatic rifle and opened fire on the White House from outside the northwest gate. Earlier in May, President Clinton had banned imports of that same rifle. Reportedly, the president was the only member of the first family who was home at the time.

He was watching football on TV in the private residence. He had heard the gunfire but was never in any danger. I was amazed at the amount of drama that had taken place in such a short time inside the gates of the White House.

Later during my first day's adventure, the media was escorted onto the South Lawn to hear President Clinton give remarks. Police tape and scaffolding still surrounded the old magnolia tree, awaiting repair from the small Cessna 150 aircraft that had crashed into it several weeks before. The 38-year-old truck driver who had stolen the aircraft flew it to the White House and turned off the engine mid-flight, surprising the Secret Service detail as the plane silently glided toward the mansion in the middle of the night with headlights glaring.

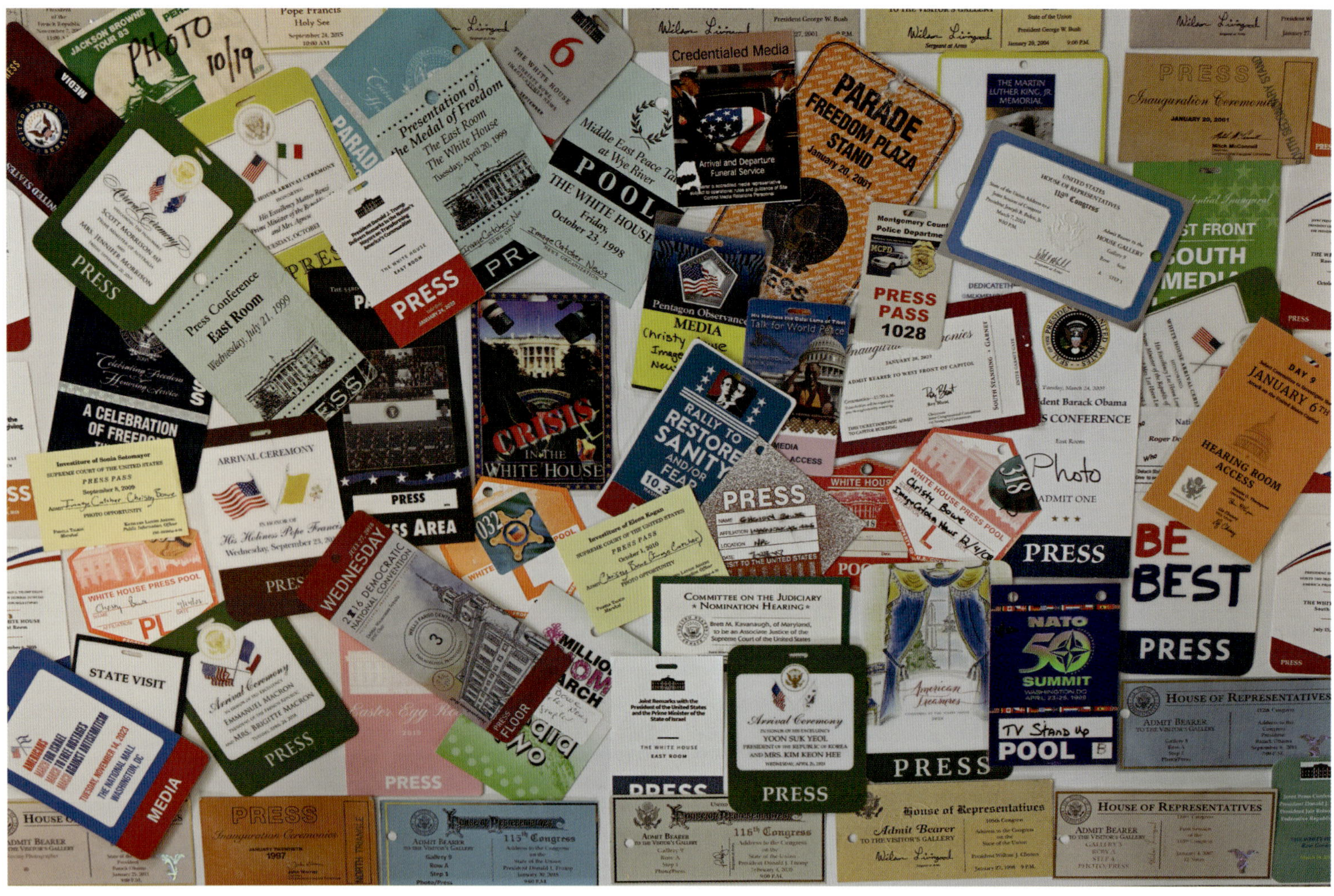

Credentials I have acquired over the years.

Apparently, the pilot was attempting to land on the South Lawn, but his path had been obstructed by folding chairs and a stage that had been set up for an event the following day. When the pilot crashed into what is known as the Jackson Magnolia tree (President Andrew Jackson had planted it decades earlier) that stood just a few feet from the White House itself, he was killed on impact. Both of these potentially catastrophic events had occurred within a few weeks of each other. I remember thinking, "What an introduction to the White House!"

I first began covering the White House during President Clinton's first inauguration in 1993. I was elated to be standing on the grounds of the US Capitol that day. All my senses were amplified. There was so much going on around me, and I wanted to capture it all. William Jefferson Clinton was soon to be known as "Eagle," the code name given to him by his Secret Service protective detail. Each president, first lady, and family member has a code name. Although it is not a big secret, I thought that was pretty cool.

Once President-elect Clinton arrived, I realized that my close-up spot, known as the triangle, was not so great for a photographer. It was closer than I had ever dreamed, but sadly, due to the bulletproof glass surrounding him, all my pictures were distorted. I was unable to use any of my images from the presidential swearing-in that day. Although disappointed, I needed to refocus on what I could capture of the event, so I turned my attention to the inaugural parade that followed. I decided to chalk it up to a learning experience and file that away in case I was ever fortunate enough to photograph another inauguration. I never imagined that I would be photographing eight more (and counting!) in the coming years.

Proudly displaying my temporary Capitol Hill credential, I moved on to test the waters with my newly acquired press pass, wandering around the parade area and taking pictures of the participants.

I managed to get other photos throughout the freezing morning and afternoon, but no more of President Clinton that day. Even though the bitter temperatures were very uncomfortable, the excitement of being on the front lines for the first time distracted me from the nasty weather and biting cold. Little did I know that over the years, I would meet and shake hands with President Clinton many times.

Clinton has the reputation for being able to make anyone he is speaking to feel special and important. I, too, found this to be true.

> Clinton has the reputation for being able to make anyone he is speaking to feel special and important. I, too, found this to be true.

I first met the president with my boss at that time, Sarah McClendon of McClendon News. I had always assumed that he was giving me some special recognition because I worked with Sarah, and I always appreciated that. Years later I requested that he sign my favorite picture I'd taken of him while he was in office. He was kind enough to return the photo with not only his signature, but a nice note as well.

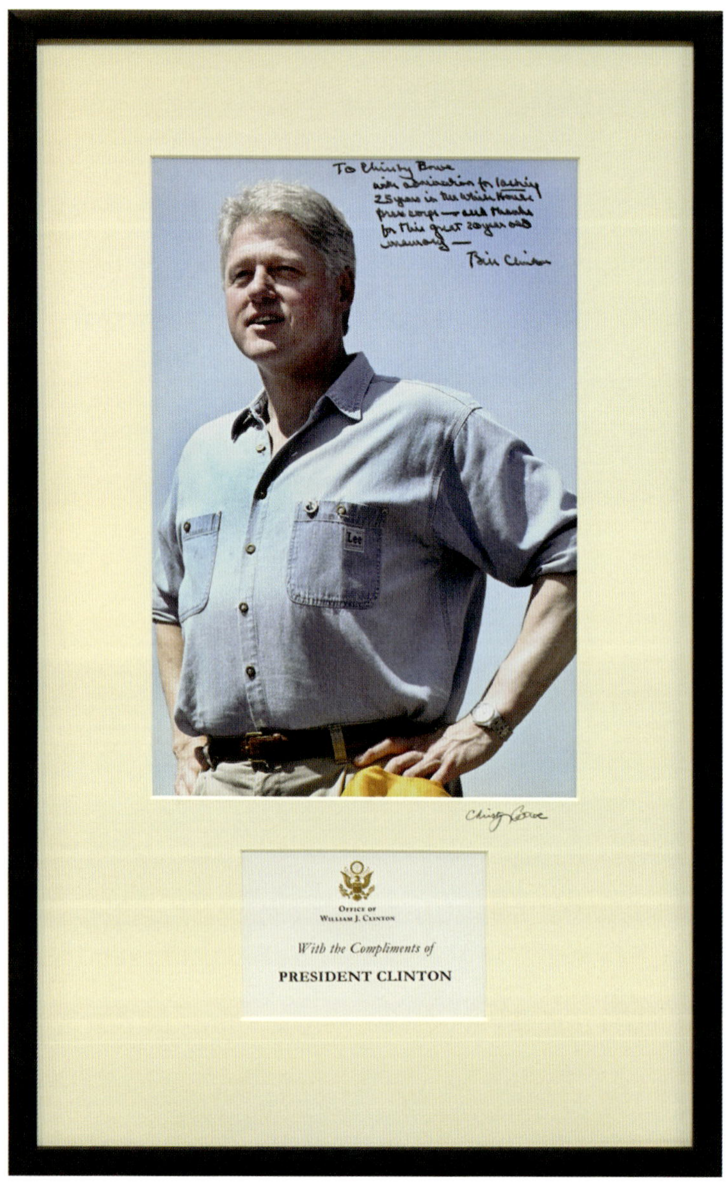

To Christy Bowe,

With admiration for lasting 25 years in the White House press corps—and thanks for this great 20-year-old memory—

Bill Clinton

In my opinion, President Clinton is one of the most intelligent of our presidents, and not only because he was a Rhodes Scholar who studied at Oxford. I myself witnessed how quick on his feet he was, whether dealing with other world leaders or navigating tough questions from the press corps. However, the Monica Lewinsky scandal was a major part of covering his presidency as a photojournalist. It had been many decades since any US president had been impeached, and the prospect of an impeachment trial was breaking news.

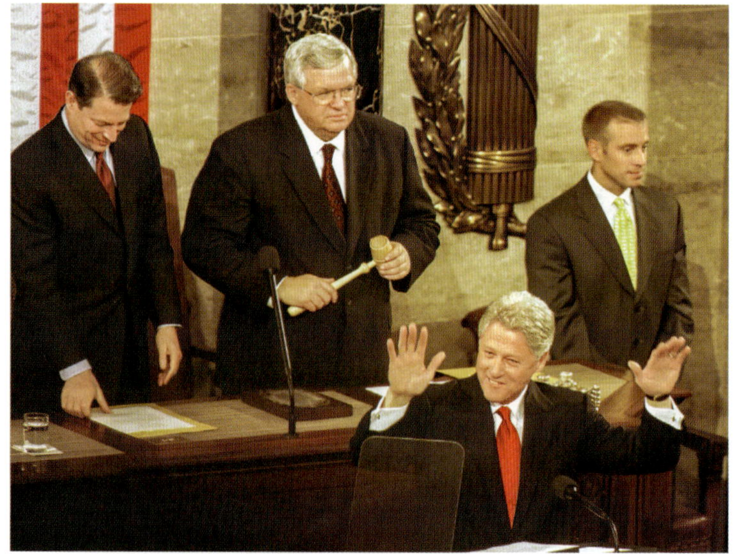

President Clinton attempts to quiet down the audience as members of Congress welcome him with a standing ovation at the start of his January 2000 State of the Union Address.

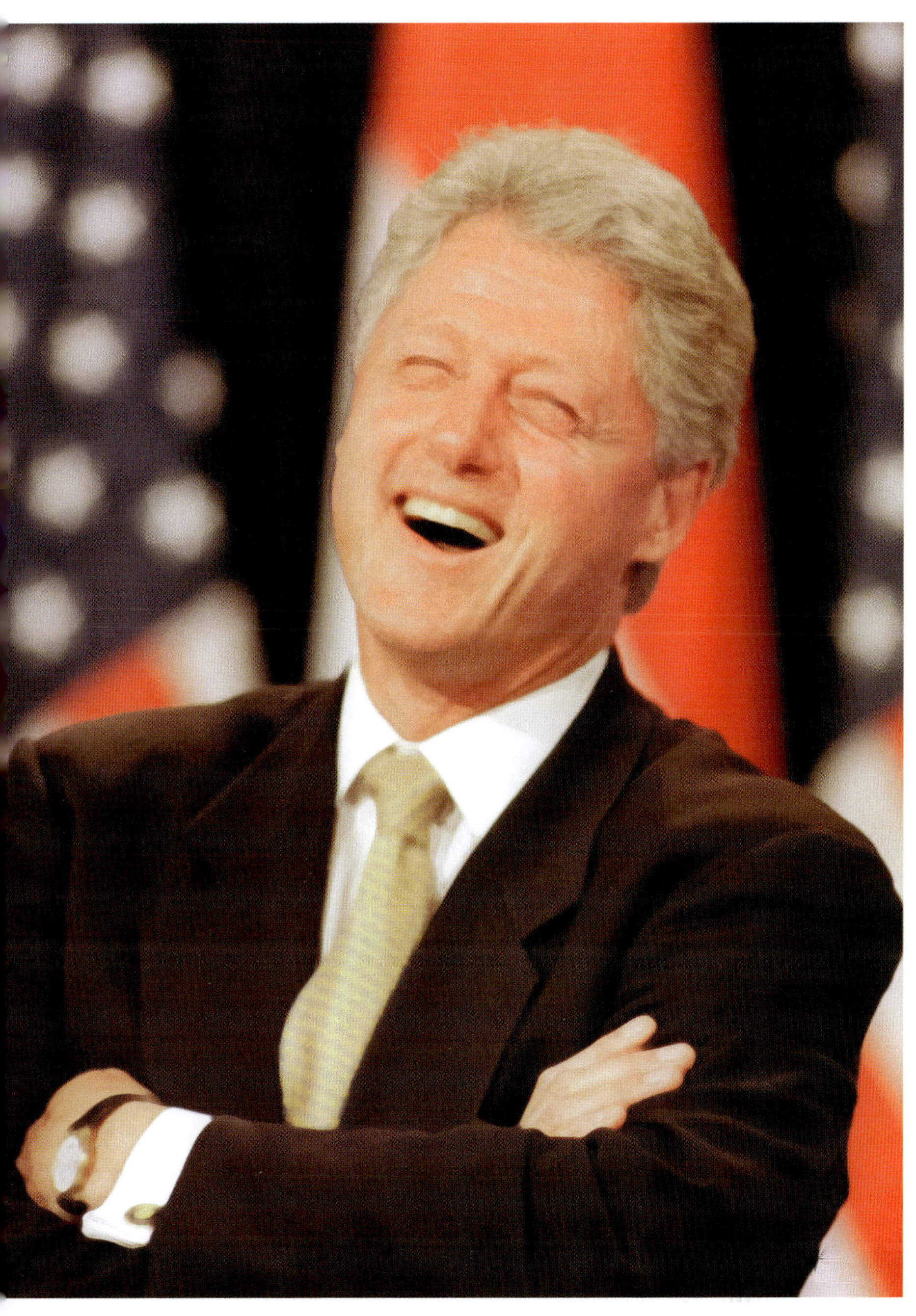

*President Clinton laughs during a joint press
conference at the State Department, July 1999.*

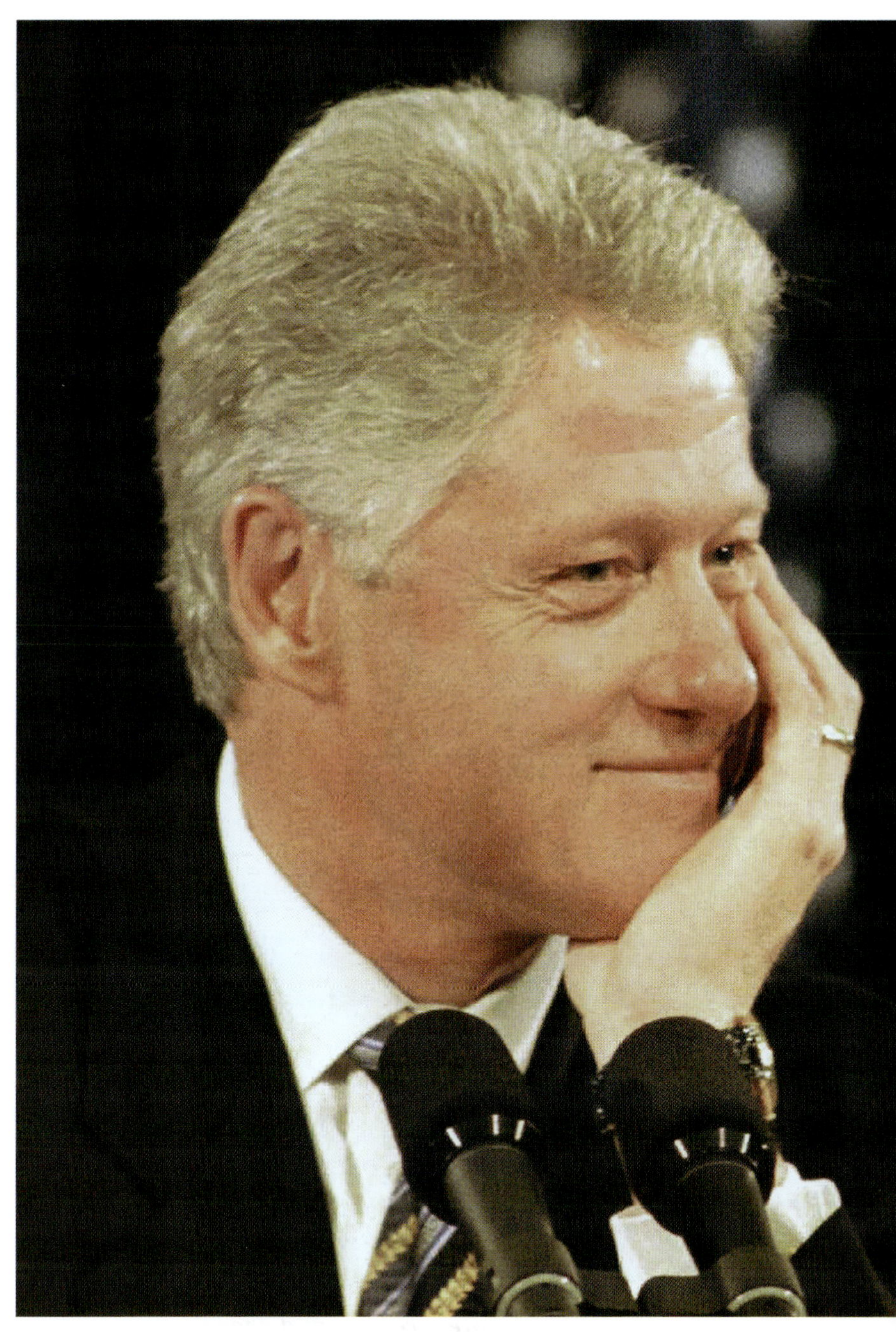

*President Clinton fields questions during his
final press conference of the millennium at
the State Department, December 1999.*

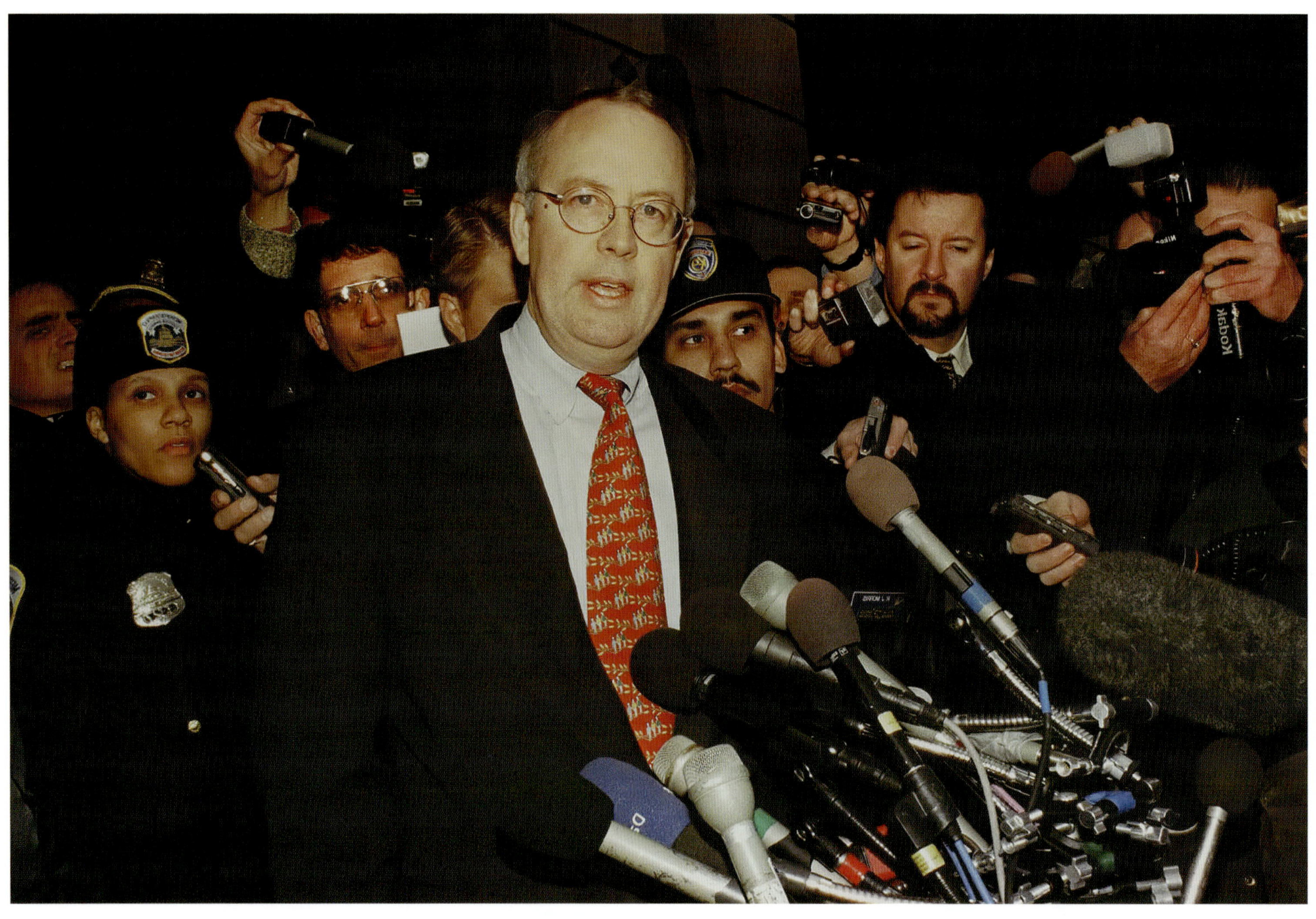

*Kenneth Starr, Independent Council, holds a press conference outside his office prior
to President Clinton's impeachment by the House of Representatives. December 1998.*

On January 26, 1998, the entire world heard (and saw) President Clinton tell reporters on national television, "I did not have sexual relations with that woman, Miss Lewinsky." Later in the press area, as various bits of information sifted into the briefing room, ABC reporter Sam Donaldson was one of the first to scoop Special Prosecutor Ken Starr's report. He read aloud to all of us that were in the briefing room the spicier details of the document in his famous voice, as if he were reciting Shakespeare.

Since I was just beginning my post at the White House, I was vigilant in my coverage of the scandal, even though my personal opinion was that this was between President Clinton, his family, and Monica Lewinsky. However, lying under oath was another matter. Once the cover-up began unraveling, it changed everything for us members of the press corps. When this rumor became news in 1998, I needed to cover the historic process unfolding before the nation. As a small news agency photographer, I had to be in several places at the same time. It was rewarding, but exhausting.

One day, I received word that special prosecutor Starr was about to make a statement to the media outside of his Washington, DC office. I waited there, embedded in the swelling crowd of photographers, TV crews, and reporters. We were roped off only by security folks keeping us pushed back, and there was not a lot of order to the mob. After waiting patiently for several hours, Starr emerged and walked right up to where I was standing near the gaggle of microphones. The crowd behind me surged forward, almost pushing me into him. I was so close that I had to keep backing up against the crowd behind me just to get him in focus with my lens. That was my first successful stakeout.

Weeks later, on the cold, early morning of December 19, 1998, I put my stakeout skills to good use once again. It was a big day at the US Capitol: Congress was voting on whether to impeach President Clinton for perjury. Many stakeout locations were set up at different places outside the Capitol because no one knew from where or whom an official statement would come. I closely watched some of the more seasoned photographers that I respected, and following their lead, eventually ended up at the southeast corner of the Capitol. After thirteen and a half hours of debate in Congress, a decision was finally announced. With a flurry of activity, everyone flocked to where I was standing.

It felt like I had won the lottery. Members of Congress paraded down the stairs with a determined stride, coming to a stop *directly in front of me.*

The news was big: members of Congress announced that they were about to cast their votes on whether to impeach President Clinton, and they apologized for what the country was about to go through. After making their brief statement they abruptly turned and proceeded back up the stairs to make their final decision.

A short time later, the reporter waiting next to me was startled as he listened to his network earpiece. He then spoke into the camera. Fox News was reporting live from the Capitol that "President William Jefferson Clinton, the forty-second president of the United States, has just been impeached by the House of Representatives." A shiver ran down my spine as I listened to breaking news being made right in front me. Only once in history had this ever happened before: President Andrew Johnson, the successor to Abraham Lincoln after his assassination, was impeached in the 1800s.

Immediately after the announcement, I knew I *had* to put it in high gear, so I rushed for the Metro. I paced impatiently as I rode the train for the twelve stops to my commercial photo lab, where the owner was waiting on standby so he could process my film with top priority. Then, I raced back to my office to scan the film and transmit the selected images to my agency in New York. Those were the days of dial-up internet, and the whole scanning and transmission process took quite a long time to get just six or eight images out.

As I was transmitting my images from my home office, I remember listening to CNN as correspondent Wolf Blitzer announced that President Clinton was about to respond to the media about the impeachment verdict.

I immediately called the White House Lower Press Office, which arranges all the media escorts, to see if the "final escort" had taken place yet. Traditionally, after a final escort, the media cannot get in or out of the area where the president will be appearing. I was told the final escort was happening *at that very moment*.

To this day, I don't think I have ever moved so fast. Even though all the odds were against me, I knew I had to at least try to make it. The Metro—again!—took what seemed like forever to get back downtown.

Once I got off, I ran the two blocks from the train station to the White House and sailed through the security checkpoint at the northwest gate. Reporters, microphones in hand, were in position and ready for action on "Pebble Beach," the area used in live broadcasts so that the north side of the White House is clearly visible in the background. I sprinted up the driveway, and finally arriving in the briefing room, flung the doors open only to find it empty. My heart dropped as I realized I had missed the final escort.

I rushed to the door to the Rose Garden, where a plainclothes Secret Service agent stood at attention with his back to me, his focus on the large crowd of media on the other side of the doorway. I pleaded with him to let me slip out, or even allow me to photograph over his shoulder. He refused. As I was pacing back and forth like a caged tiger, the doors suddenly flung open. Veteran Associated Press photographer Scott Applewhite briskly walked in with rolls of film to hand off to a courier who had just arrived in the briefing room. I had a feeling of panic as I kept thinking that this huge event was happening without me.

"What's the matter? Are you locked out?" Scott asked me with just a touch of humor in his voice.

"Yes!" I exhaled in a pleading voice. Of course, he had no authority to get me past the agent, but in that moment, I knew he was my only chance. Scott softly reminded me that I had no position in the crowded fray that had gathered outside the Oval Office in the Rose Garden. The press conference had already begun; I could even hear Vice President Al Gore speaking. I knew that all I needed was to get into the Rose Garden, a mere few feet away.

After Scott handed off his film to the courier, he turned to go back into the Rose Garden but was stopped by the same Secret Service agent who'd refused me. Scott reminded him that he had been there all day, that he was with the AP, and that he needed to get back out there to do his job.

I saw the chance and took it, following behind him so closely there were only inches separating us. I made it! With adrenaline still pumping, I surveyed the large crowd, immediately worked my way around the perimeter, and was able to maneuver up to the front, thanks to the gracious reporters who allowed me in their area. (All photo positions had been taken hours earlier.)

> "As I gathered my wits and reached into my camera bag, I found I did not need that long lens after all. I was now just two rows from the president."

As I gathered my wits and reached into my camera bag, I found I did not need that long of a lens after all. I was now just two rows from the president, and it was just about time for him to speak. Vice President Al Gore, who'd just finished speaking, moved to stand stoically behind President Clinton. First Lady Hillary looked up at her husband with what appeared to be a tear-stained face, strong in her resolve to get through this moment. That was how I saw it anyway. The amount of courage it took for the first lady to maintain a sense of dignity and pride as she stood beside her husband that day spoke volumes about her own core strength. I imagine that had to be one of the most difficult moments in her life, when both her personal and professional lives collided in front of the entire world.

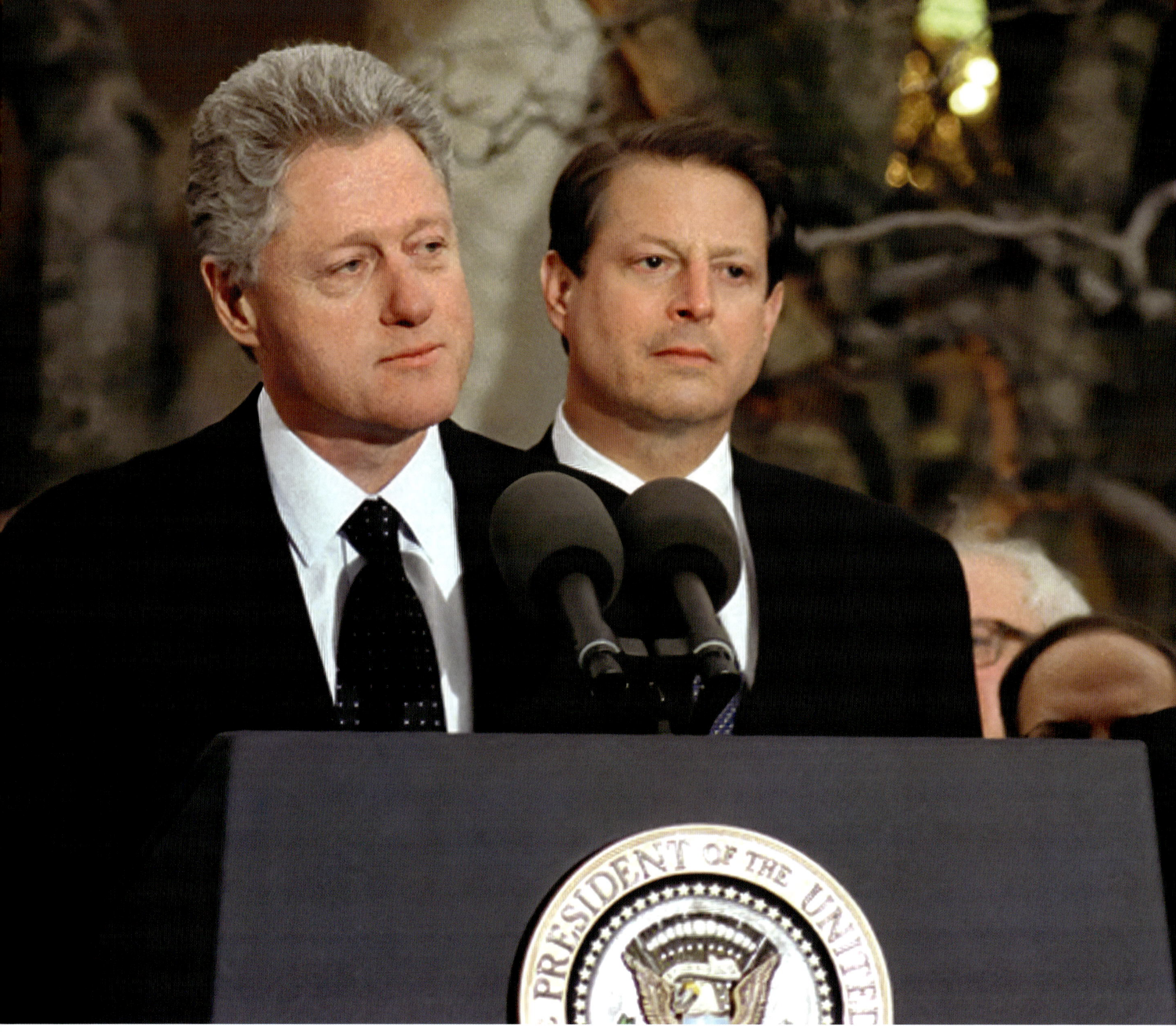

30   History in the Making

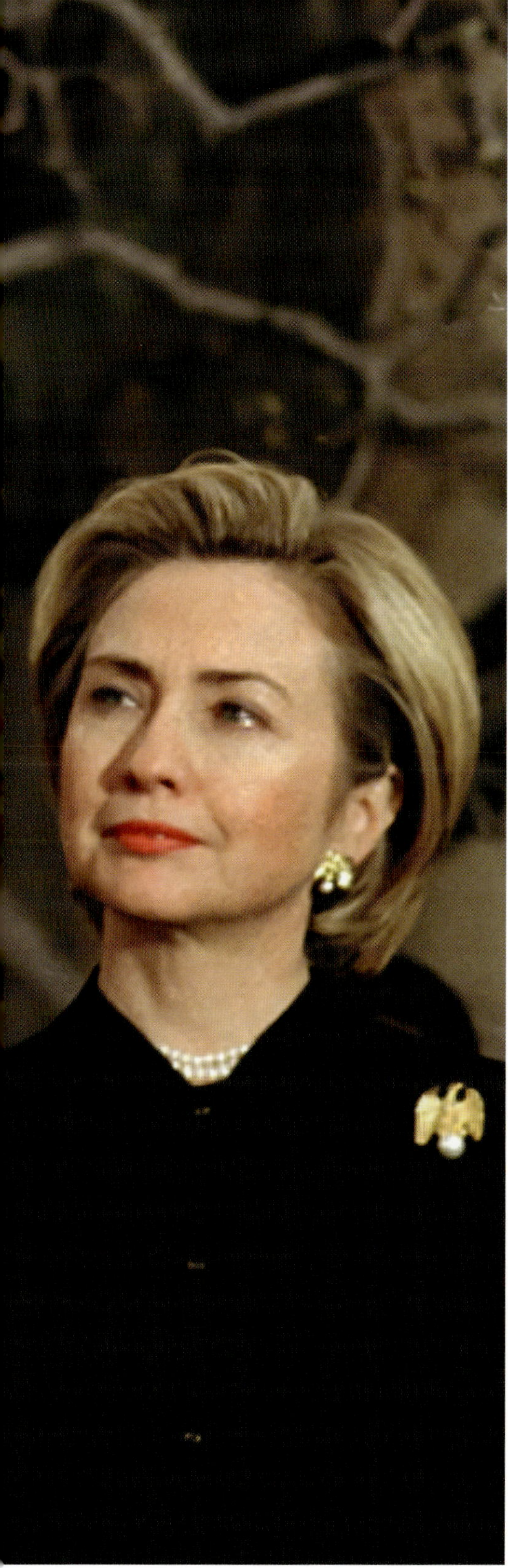

Racing home to repeat the same process I had done only hours earlier, I was grateful to have my wonderful photo lab cooperate with me and agree to stay open late to process my film. That was one long day!

On February 12, 1999, it was now the press corps' job to wait for the Senate votes to come in. You better believe that when it came time for the Senate to announce their decision, I was on top of it. I was *not budging* from the White House Briefing Room. After many hours of suspense, the Senate ended up not having enough votes to remove President Clinton from office, so we waited to see if he would make a statement. We knew there could be a couple of options: the president could either speak from the Oval Office with only one TV camera that would feed to the other networks, or he could face all of us in person.

Suddenly, someone noticed the special presidential podium being wheeled up the driveway outside of the briefing room—a sure signal that the president would be making a statement. I was so proud to be one of the first in line to enter the Rose Garden that day, standing alongside two legendary reporters, Helen Thomas and Sam Donaldson. I will never forget that moment.

A little while later, President Clinton stoically walked up to the podium and stated, "Now that the Senate has fulfilled its constitutional responsibility, bringing this process to a conclusion, I want to say again to the American people how profoundly sorry I am for what I said and did to trigger these events and the great burden they have imposed on the Congress and on the American people."[1]

President Clinton responds to his verdict of impeachment
by the US House of Representatives as Vice President
Al Gore and First Lady Hillary Clinton look on,
December 1998.

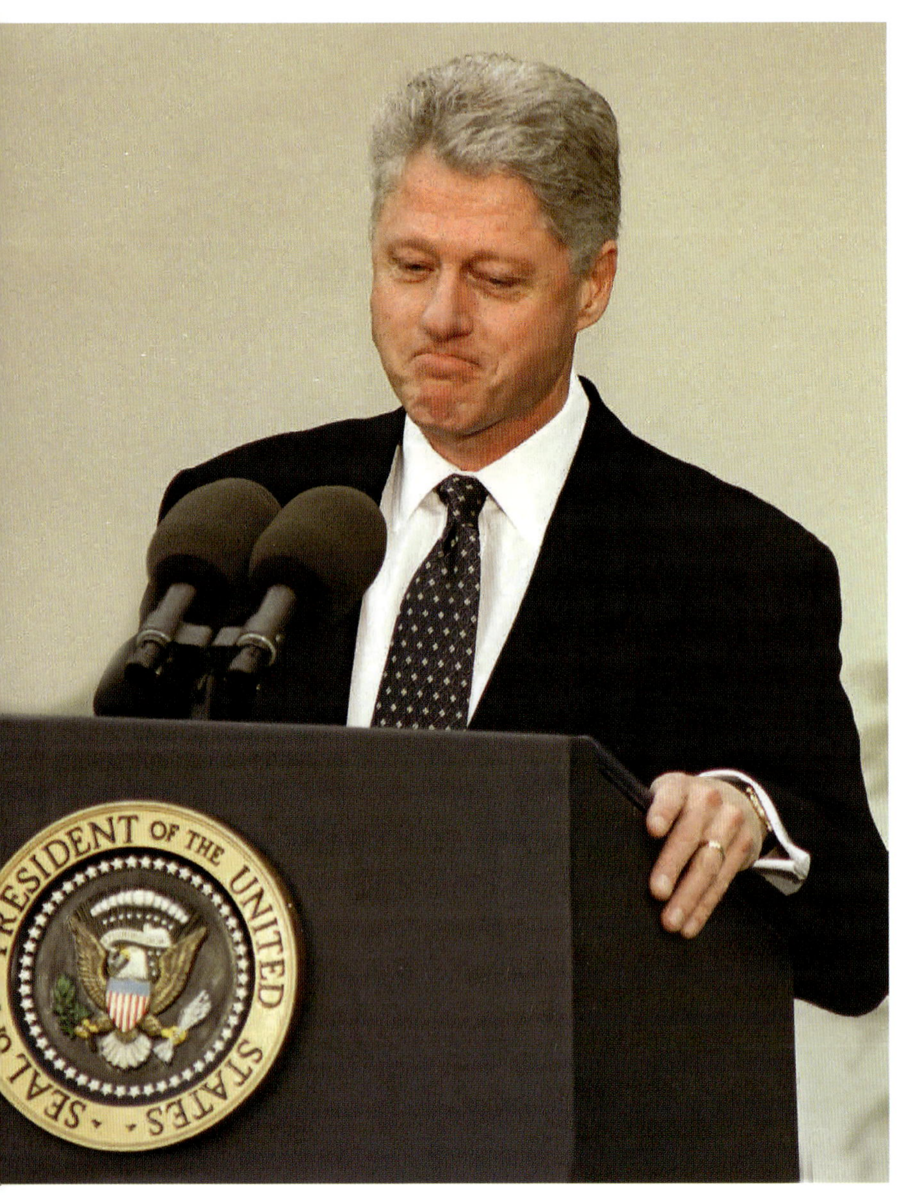

*Bill Clinton makes comments on
the end of the Senate trial over the
Monica Lewinsky scandal, February 1999.*

As he turned to walk back into the Oval Office, Sam Donaldson yelled out, "Mr. President! In your heart, sir, can you forgive and forget?" There was an audible and collective *aaahhh* from the press corps. This question covered what everyone had been feeling over the last several months during which the president's personal life had been dissected. To our amazement, the president slowly turned, walked back to the podium, and said, "I believe any person who asks for forgiveness has to be prepared to give it."[2] It was an unforgettable moment. All of us were thrilled to get a bit more time with the president.

As he was speaking, it seemed to me that President Clinton was bursting with relief; it looked as if he was doing all he could to keep himself from breaking into a dance. And in that next moment—in the 1/60 of a second when he looked down and made an "aw shucks" type of gesture—his reaction in that instant was what the media considered the "nailed-it" shot. Competing as we do, each photographer fired away. All that could be heard as he made that simple gesture was the thunder of shudders firing simultaneously. That exact moment that was captured by the various photographers there was what newspaper editors around the world selected for the front page of their papers.

Shortly after the vote, the first family headed to Martha's Vineyard for a private vacation. I was able to capture a poignant shot of daughter Chelsea walking between her two parents toward Marine One for their departure, with the family dog Buddy close at hand. Although this well-known shot conveyed a heartfelt, almost warm family image, there were many photographers that day who gave witness to the first family's struggle and deep internal pain. During the rest of his administration, I felt that the president was never quite as friendly toward the media, and our access was a bit more limited than before. Still, President Clinton did know how to forgive us photographers from time to time.

Earlier in his administration, things got a little crazy in the Oval Office. In my thirty years of coverage, only two *rare* occasions of calamity stand out in my memory, and both occurred in the Clinton White House. The first is when Secretary of State Madeleine Albright, gracefully perched on one of the two couches, was smacked soundly in the back of the head with a large camera lens during an Oval Office photo op with the president and a visiting head of state. A week or so later, one of the wire photographers backed into the president's desk and knocked several framed family pictures onto the floor.

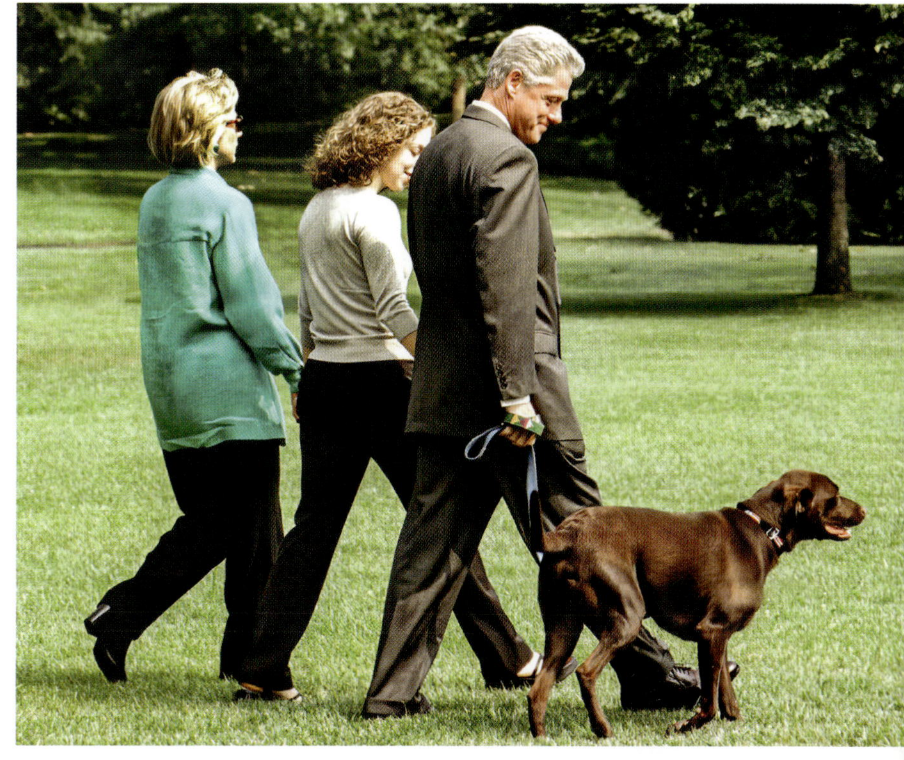

After President Clinton's historic address to the nation following the Lewinsky scandal, daughter Chelsea links up with both her parents to board Marine One en route to Martha's Vineyard.

cookout. There were even various shooting galleries with air rifles set up, which helped give the picnic a "boardwalk at the beach" vibe.

After making a few remarks and welcoming all of us to this special event, the president and first lady walked among us, their ever-vigilant protective detail always just a few yards away as we made small talk.

Everyone knew that President Clinton's administration would be a turning point in American history. He was the consummate diplomat, whether he was hosting the ever-watchful press in his backyard or uniting conflicted world leaders at the Wye River Peace Treaty.

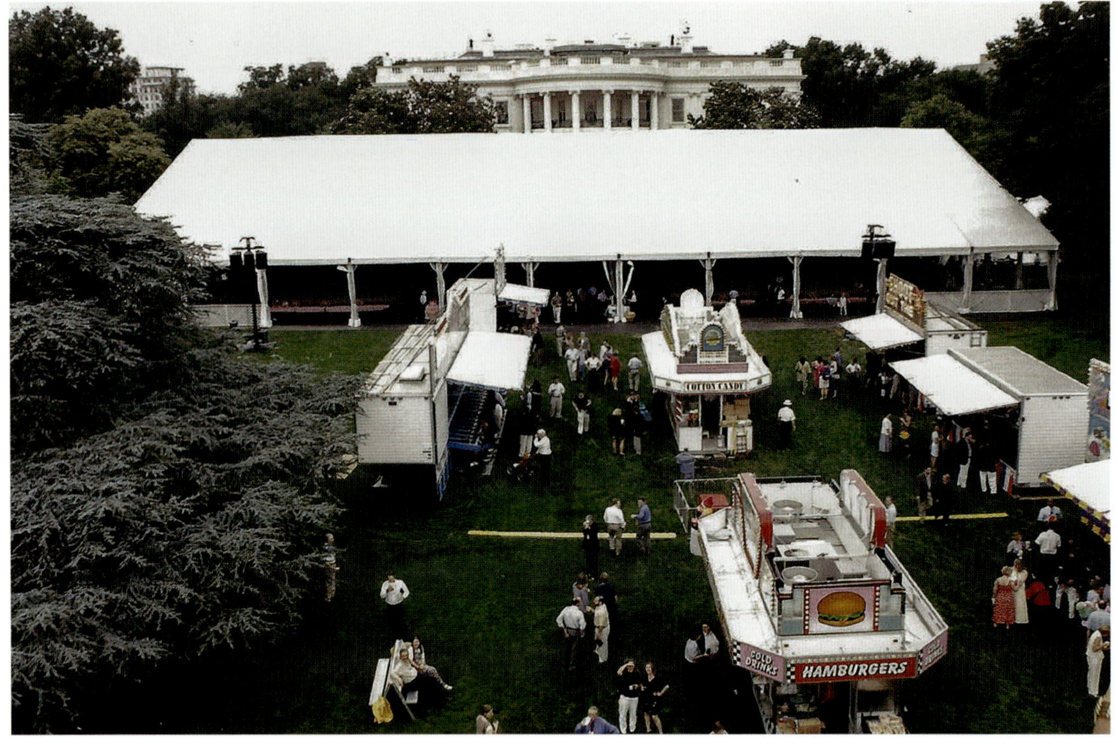

President Bill Clinton and First Lady Hillary host a surprise picnic for members of the White House press corps. They transformed the South Lawn into a carnival complete with BBQ and Ferris wheel (from which I took this picture). June 1998.

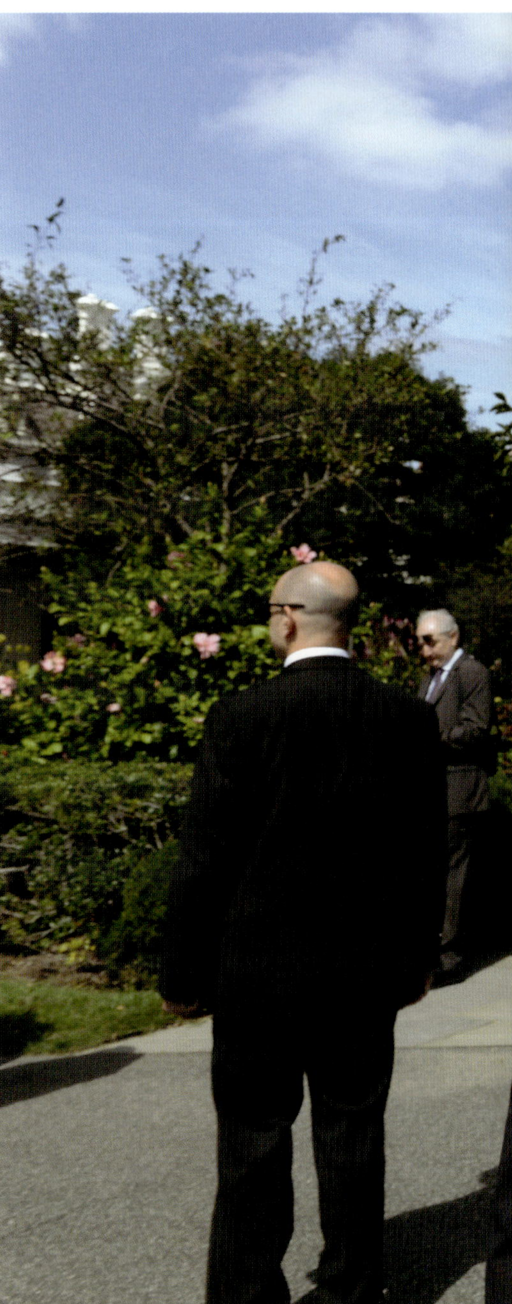

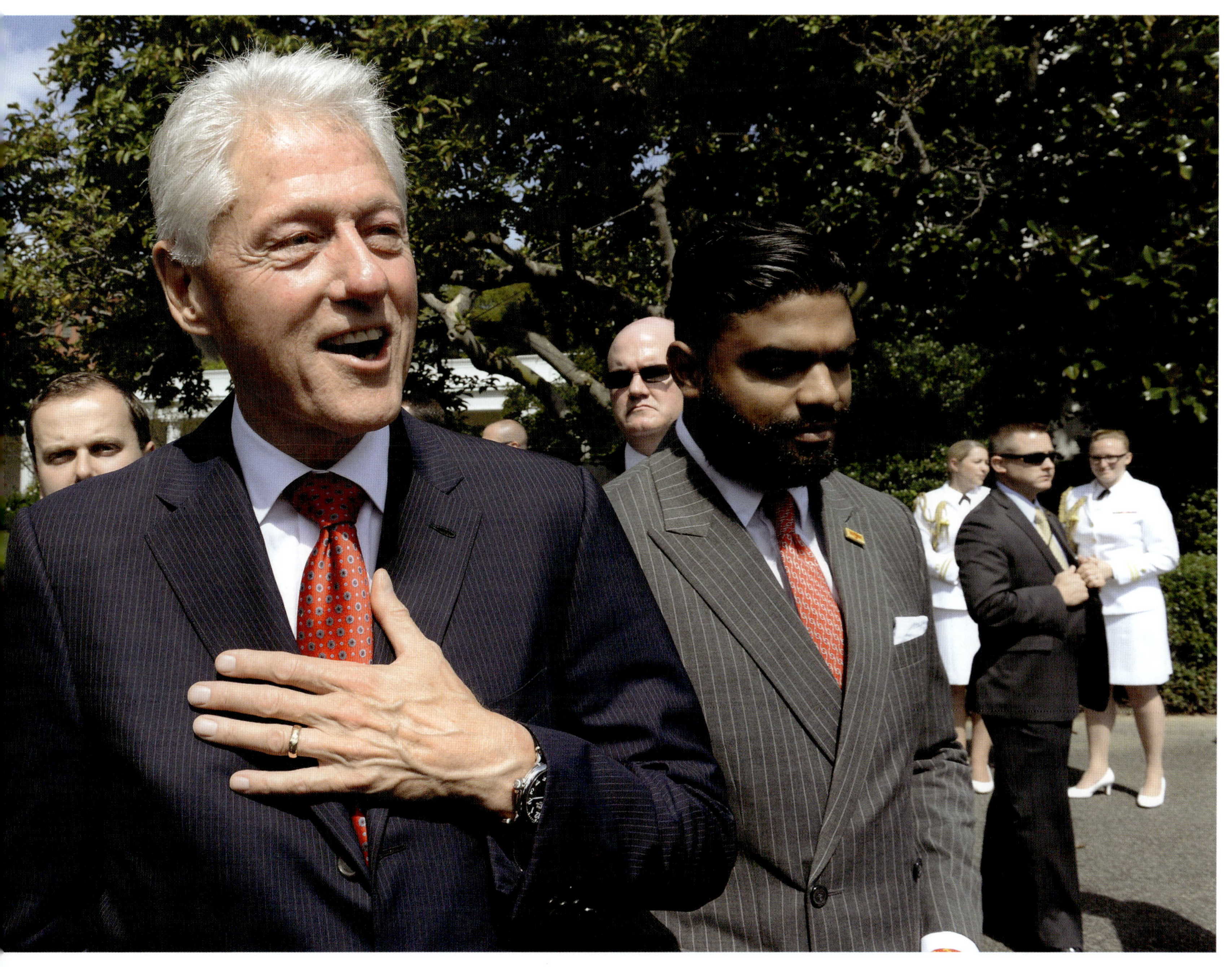

*President Clinton pauses to say hello to the media following an event celebrating
the twentieth anniversary of AmeriCorps. The White House, September 2014.*

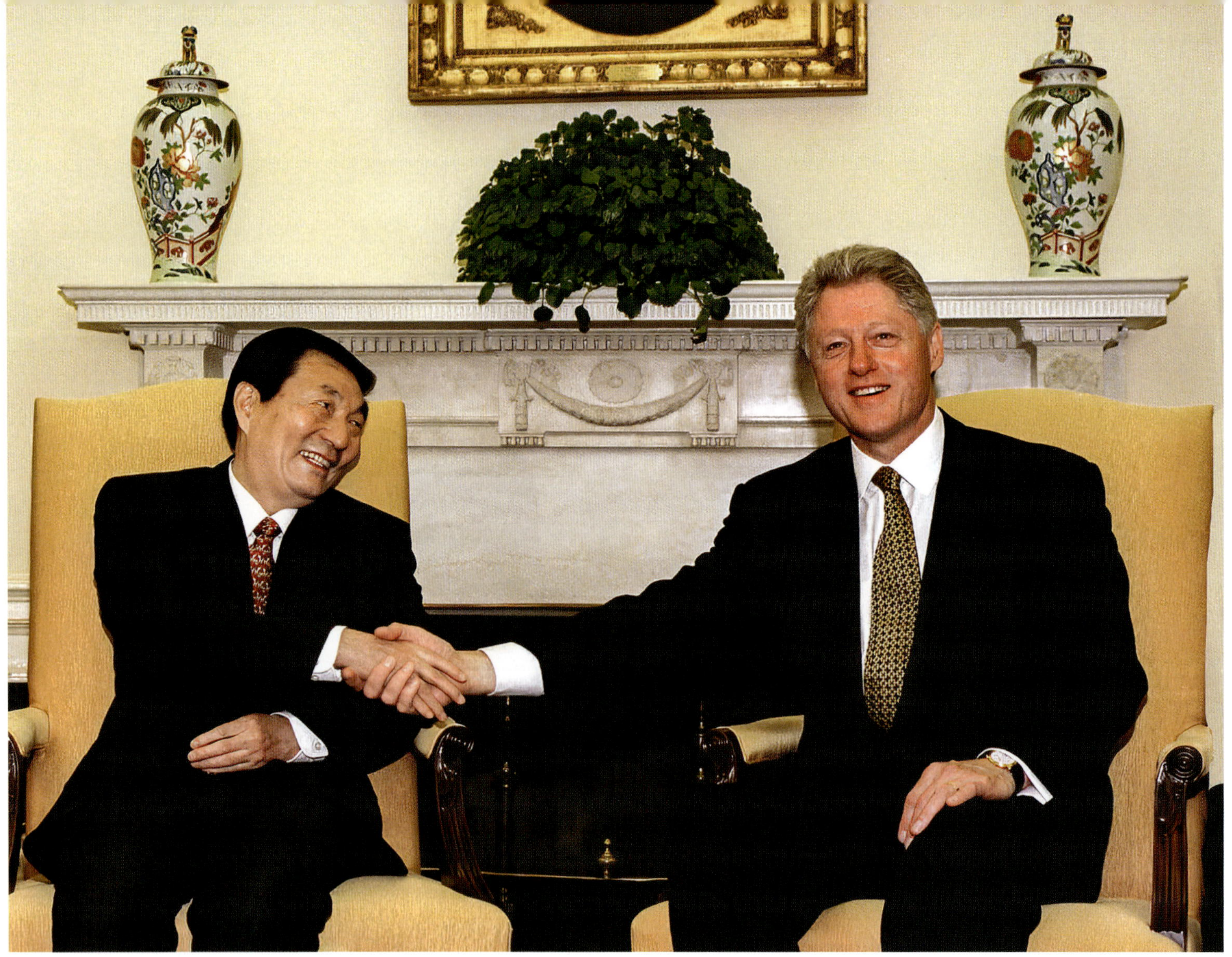

President Clinton establishes a bond with the prime minister of China Zhu Rongji in the Oval Office, April 1999.

President Clinton was also defined by his charisma. He would often charm world leaders, such as Zhu Rongji, the Premier of the People's Republic of China, as he met with him in the Oval Office.

In April of 1999, President Clinton hosted the NATO Summit in Washington, DC. That was an especially synchronized event. Twenty world leaders landed in local airports with their own security detail plus US security, endless motorcades, and the constant snarl of traffic—yet it went smoothly, overall. I was honored to have photographed the group of leaders as they posed for their "class picture" symbolizing the affair.

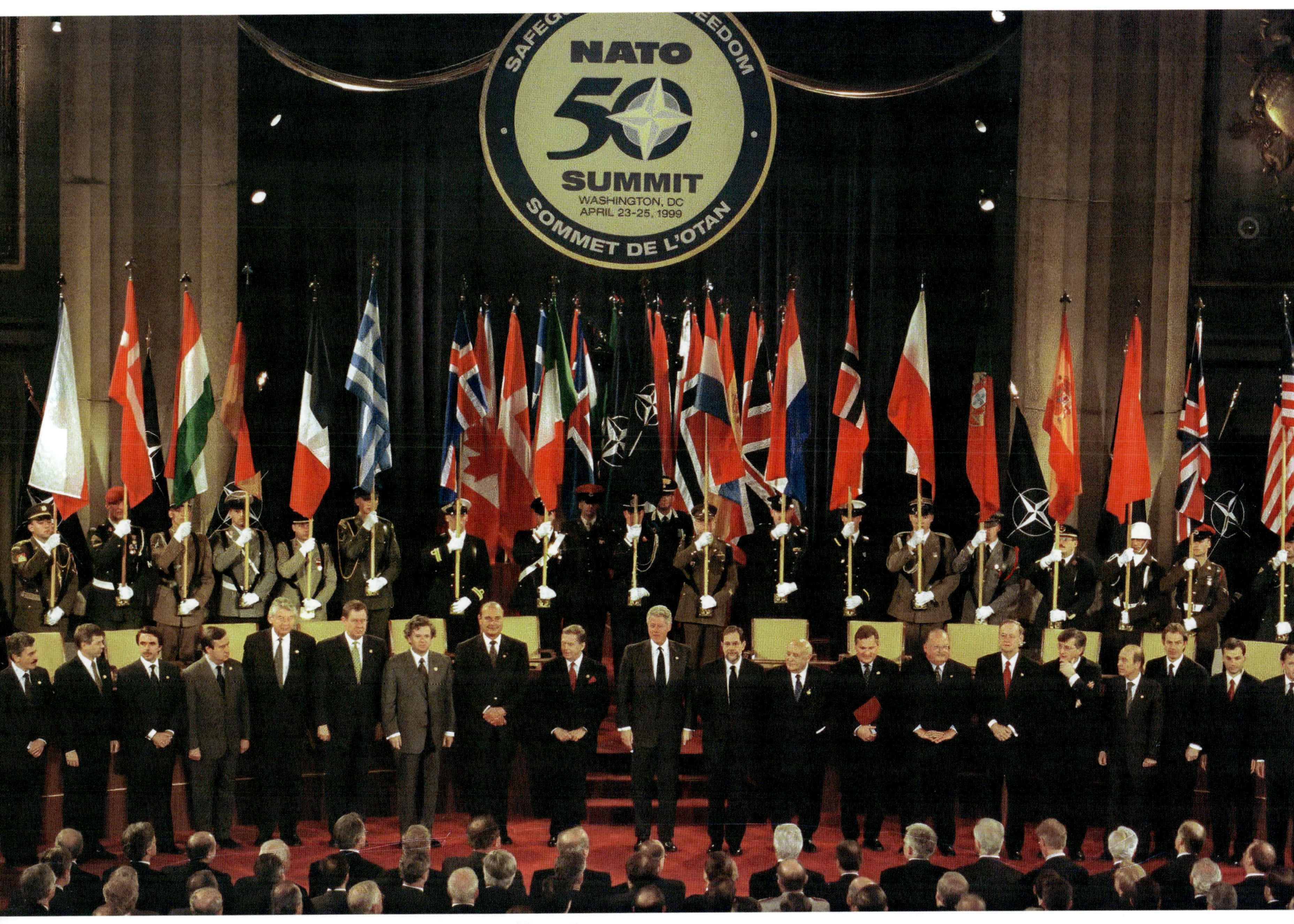

President Clinton hosts nineteen world leaders to celebrate the founding of NATO fifty years earlier.
Ronald Reagan Trade Center, Washington, DC, April 1999.

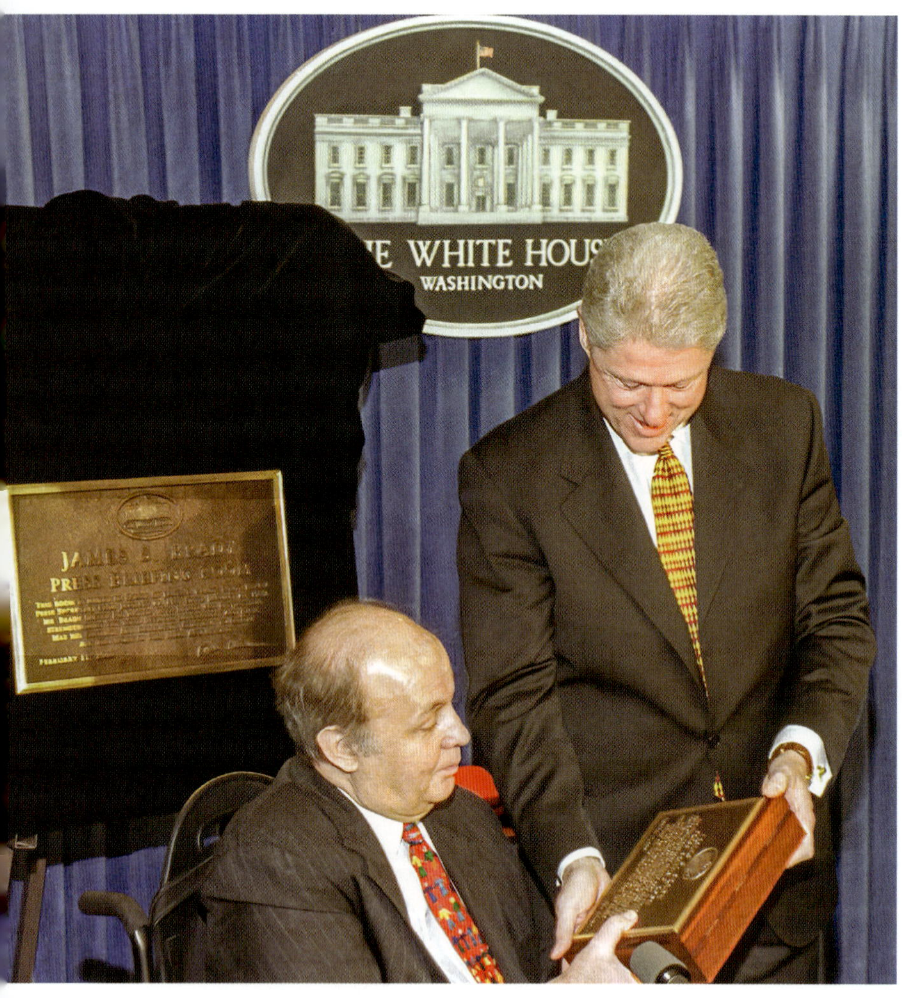

President Clinton dedicates the White House briefing room to former press secretary James Brady, February 2000.

I remember being deeply moved by President Clinton's touching remarks as he renamed the White House Briefing Room the James S. Brady Briefing Room in February of 2000. It was an honor to have been present as James Brady, the former Reagan White House Press Secretary, accepted the replica of the plaque that hangs in the room today. During the 1981 assassination attempt of President Reagan at the Washington Hilton, Brady was shot in the head and came perilously close to death. Although he was coherent, the bullet left him brain-damaged, causing partial paralysis, short-term memory impairment, slurred speech, and constant pain. After that attack, Brady and his wife Sarah went on a personal crusade for gun control, and Clinton signed the Brady Law into effect on November 30, 1993.

When I was working with Sarah McClendon, who was then in a wheelchair, we crossed paths with Brady several times, who was also in a wheelchair at that point. On two different occasions, Sarah, Brady, and I had impromptu wheelchair races down the hallways of the National Press Club. I am proud to say Sarah M. and I won the first time, but the next one was a tie.

The Clinton legacy, however, was defined not just by the president but also by his remarkable spouse, Hillary. Her presence was significant both during and after Bill Clinton's second term, as she was sworn in as a US senator representing the people of New York on January 3, 2001. The strong Clinton presence returned to the White House when, in 2009, President Obama appointed Senator Hillary Clinton to a position in his cabinet as the new secretary of state.

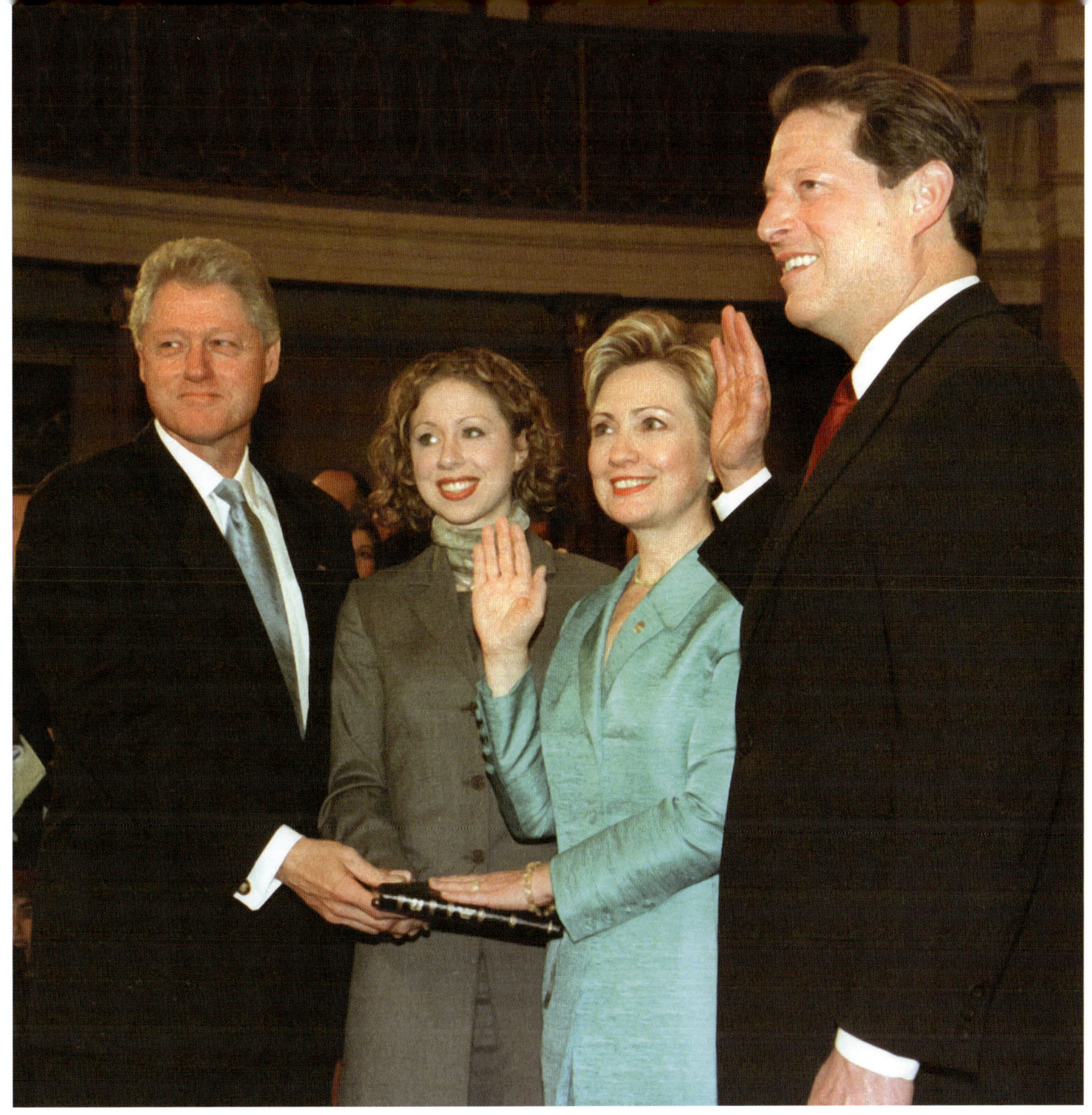

First Lady Hillary Clinton is sworn in as the US senator of New York by Vice President Al Gore.
US Capitol, Washington, DC, January 2001.

Later in the Obama administration, Hillary underwent a blistering eleven-hour interrogation by a special committee investigating the cause of an attack on a US diplomatic facility and adjoining annex in Libya where Americans were killed. Some people on the panel were members of Congress with whom Hillary had worked side by side for years.

In April 2015, Hillary Clinton announced that she would make her second bid for the presidency. The nation was collectively shocked when, contrary to predictions from most of the polls, she lost to Donald Trump in the long, close race. All along, the Clinton family remained united in support for Hillary. This support was visible to the end of Hillary's presidential run, where audience members at the 2016 Democratic Convention could witness Bill, along with daughter Chelsea, applauding for his wife with pride on the sidelines as she ran for the position her husband once held.

Whenever Clinton returns to the White House to attend an event or meet with the sitting president, he is always very friendly and outgoing with us photographers and reporters. Those years in the Clinton White House were turbulent at times, but it was nice to know that the president and the media still respected one another for doing their jobs.

Over the years, I have found that presidents and the media continue to keep an ever-watchful eye on each other as history unfurls before us.

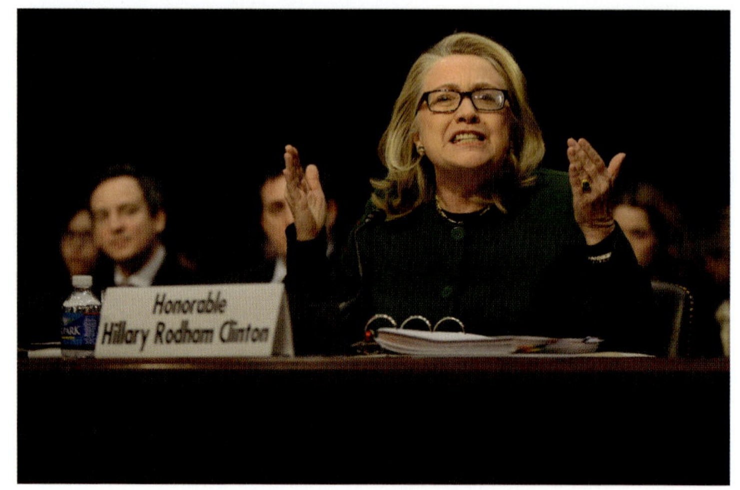

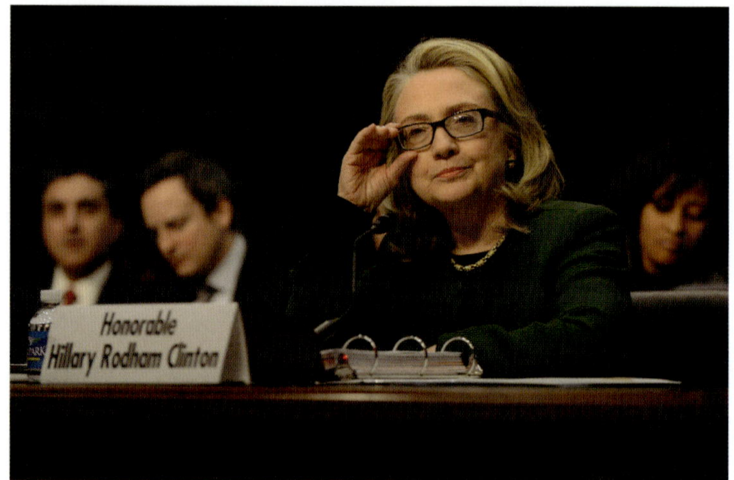

Secretary of State Hillary Clinton testifies before the Senate Foreign Relations Committee about the Benghazi attacks. The Hart Senate Building, Washington, DC, January 2013.

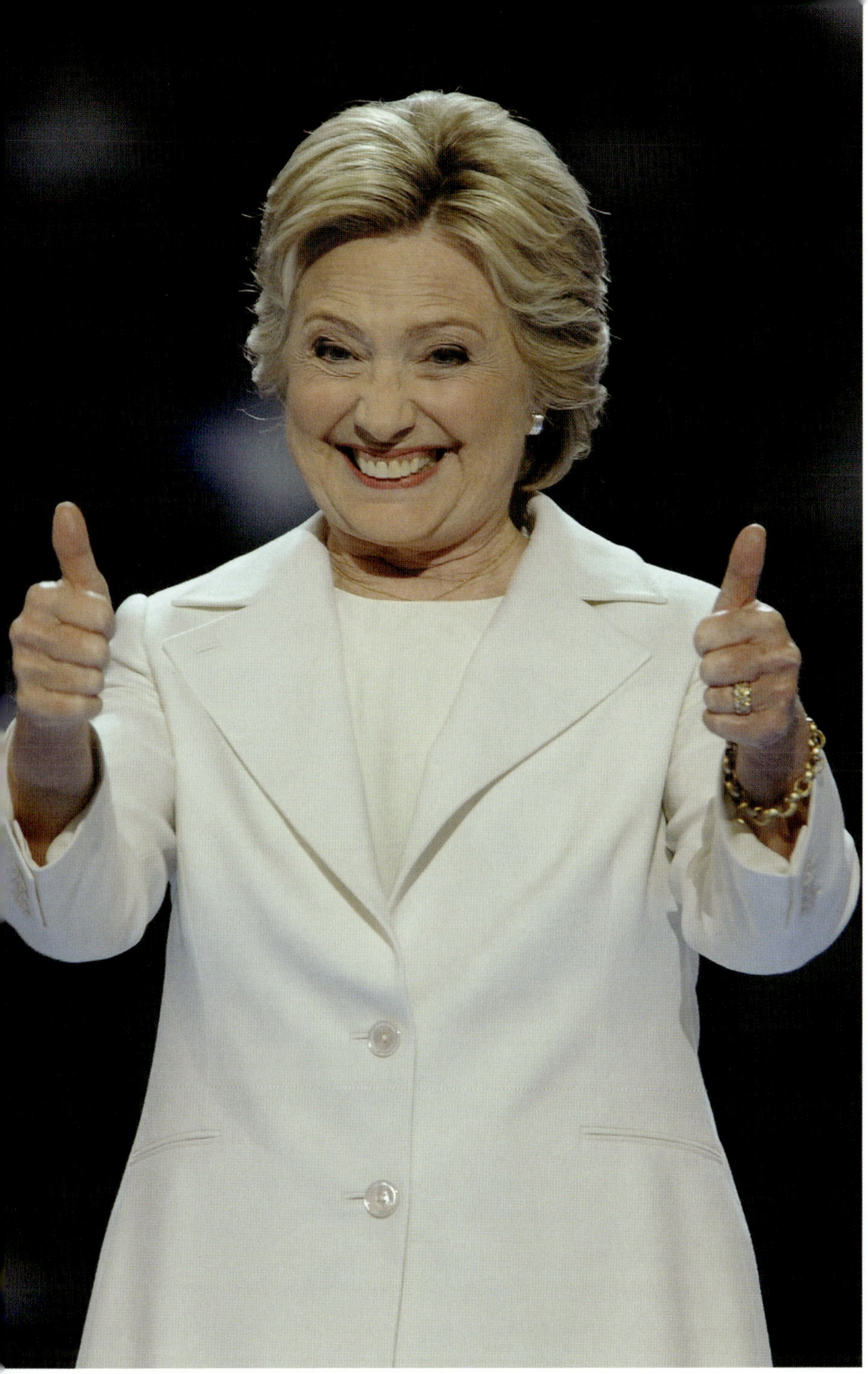

*Hillary Rodham Clinton accepts her nomination
for president of the United States from the Democratic
Party during the 2016 Democratic Convention.
Wells Fargo Stadium, Philadelphia, PA.*

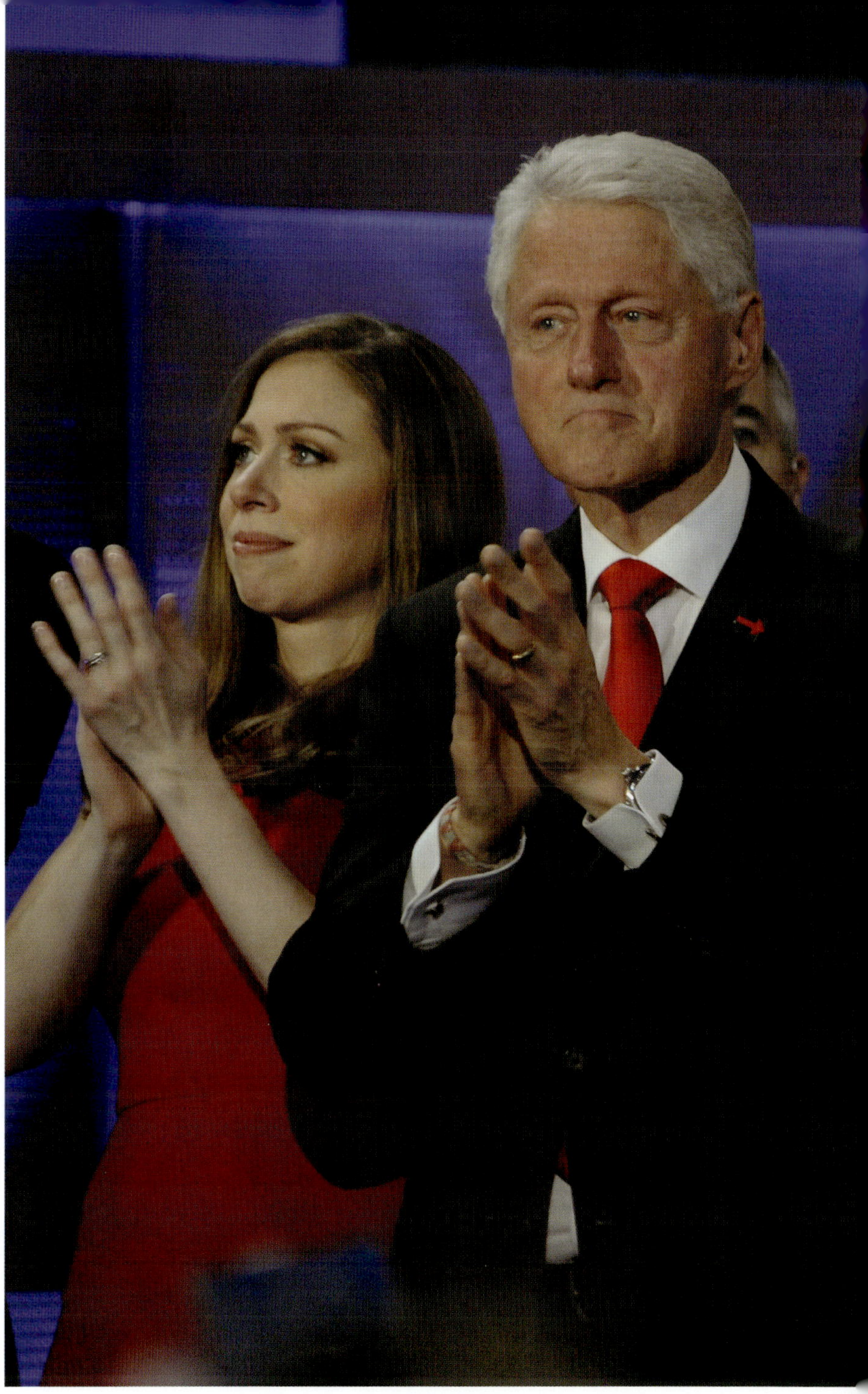

*Bill Clinton and daughter Chelsea
applaud Hillary Clinton at the
2016 Democratic Convention.*

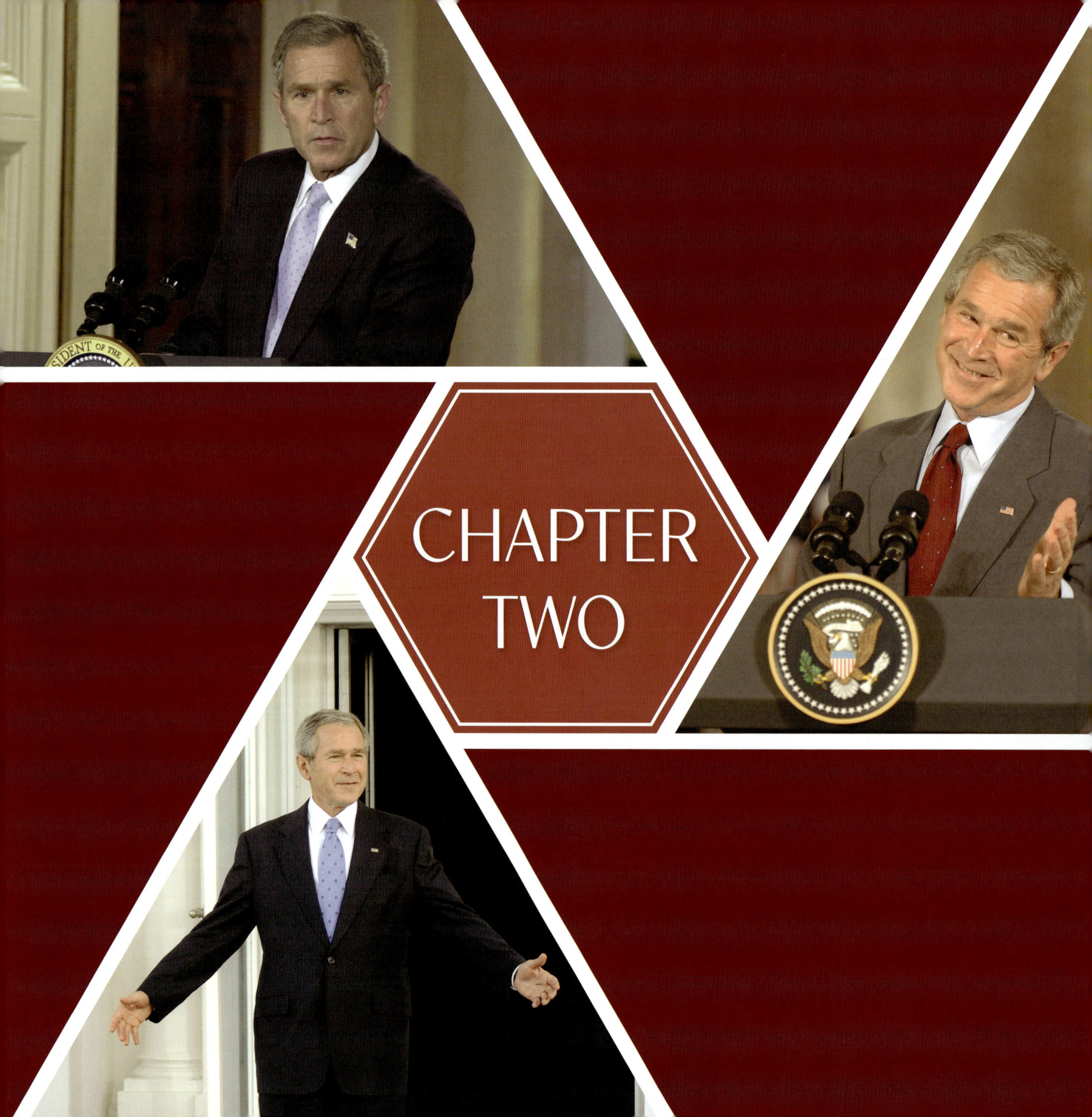

CHAPTER TWO

GEORGE W. BUSH

I have come to learn that people very often do not realize how much is involved in photographing high-profile historic events. A few of my more challenging days as a news photographer took place during the Bush '43 administration.

I first began covering George W. Bush during the Gore vs. Bush controversy. I stood with the media outside of the US Supreme Court, where hundreds of people had come to express their opinions on the potential miscount of votes for the 2000 US presidential election. As with all protests, there was plenty of signage, chanting, and police presence that continued well into the actual Bush inauguration.

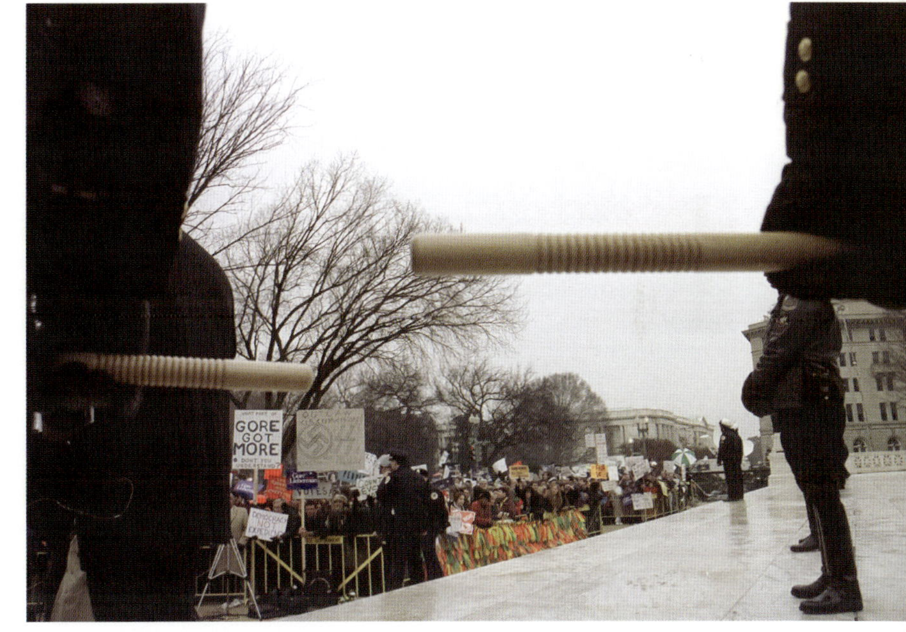

Police stand guard at the Supreme Court as Al Gore supporters protest the election results from the presidential election, December 2000.

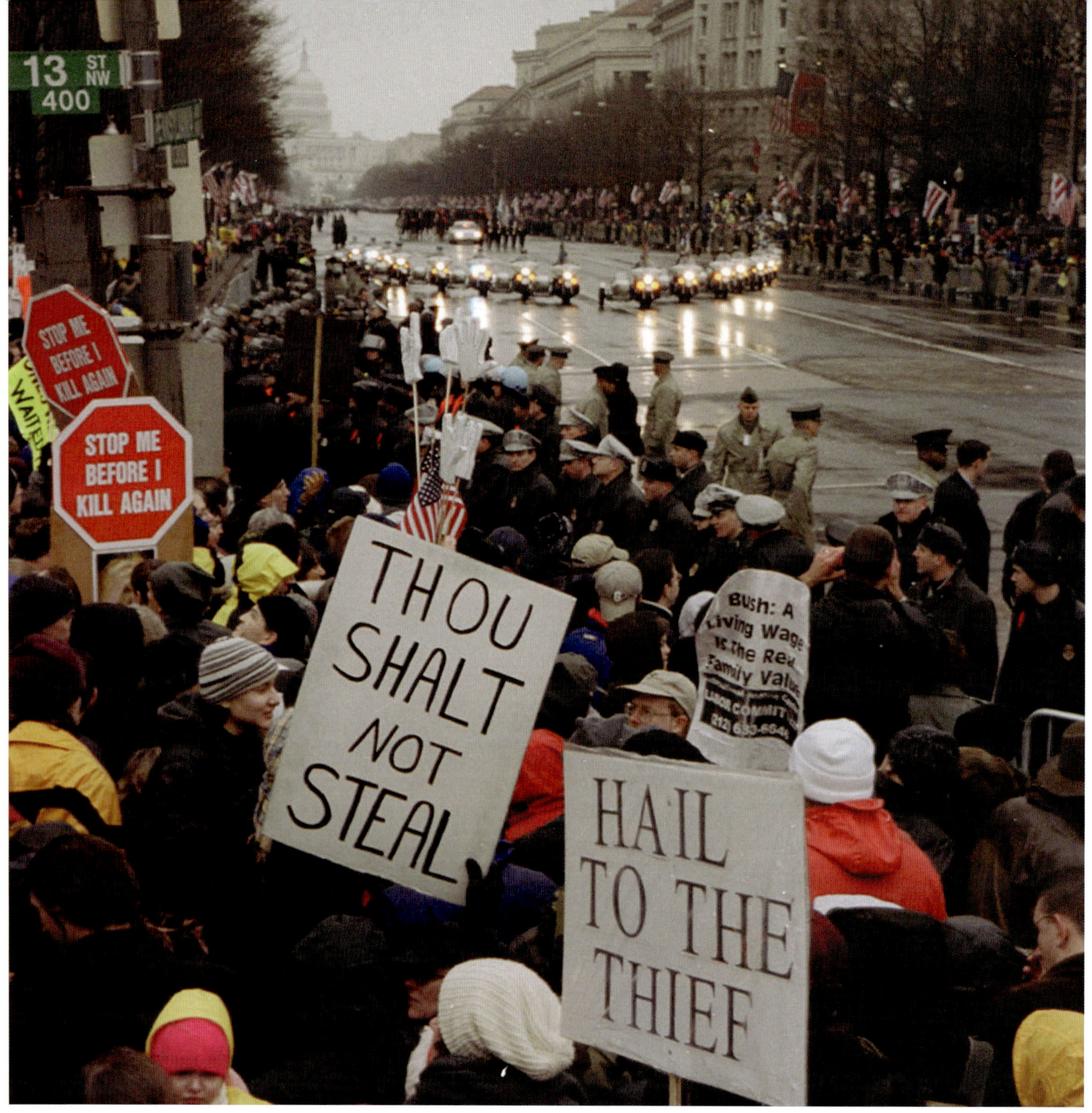

The presidential motorcade approaches Freedom Plaza where protesters
await George W. Bush during the inaugural parade, January 2001.

I photographed both of the George W. Bush swearing-in ceremonies in 2001 and 2005. Each time, the weather was the coldest of the year, with some freezing rain added into the mix.

President George W. Bush's first inauguration came with an additional layer of stress. I had agreed to photograph the lead motorcycles in the presidential motorcade for my client, Harley–Davidson. Since the United States Park Police upgrade their motorcycles every four years just prior to the presidential inauguration, my job was to showcase the new Harley motorcycles being transformed into police vehicles at a nearby Harley dealership. I then accompanied a caravan of these motorcycles to police headquarters back in Washington, DC, where I would later photograph them escorting the president in the inaugural parade.

During the parade, the signature police motorcycles would be positioned in a "V" formation to escort both the presidential and vice-presidential vehicles. The folks at Harley–Davidson wanted my image to include a DC landmark. Looking down Pennsylvania Avenue from Freedom Plaza was a direct line to the US Capitol and seemed to offer the perfect vantage point.

On that day, all pre-credentialed photographers were instructed to be on the Capitol grounds before dawn. Each presidential inauguration requires an intense, weeks-long credentialing process from both the Presidential Inaugural Committee and the US Capitol Galleries. There are typically requests for these cherished credentials from media outlets around the world. That year we were also required to have a $1 million liability policy for the day, I assumed in case we were injured and sued the DC Government. So, on January 20, 2001, I was worth $1 million . . . me! A million-dollar photographer! Sweet.

Covering the first Bush inauguration with a close-up position that didn't have any obstructions was very exciting. As the president took the oath of office, I held onto my camera with freezing-cold hands and hoped I could press the shutter fast enough with my numb fingers. I was thankful for the unique opportunity to be both witnessing and documenting the son of a former president being sworn in as the forty-third president of the United States.

I was a bit stressed about how fast I could get to my next position for the inaugural parade, even though I had formed a plan the week earlier. Immediately following the swearing-in ceremony, I jumped into action, implementing my chess-like strategy. I knew I needed to work my way down to Freedom Plaza, where tens of thousands of people had been standing for up to twelve hours, shoulder to shoulder.

A normal twenty-minute walk became a four-hour obstacle course due to the congested crowds, tight security, and street closings. After trekking through the over-trodden, soggy patches of grass that had been reduced to mud, I approached my position covered in muck. I was exhausted, soaking wet, hungry, thirsty, and in desperate need of a restroom without a long line. I trudged along with my camera gear and small ladder for hours, looking for a point in the road where the public (including the media) was allowed to cross the street, eventually having to go past Freedom Plaza for many blocks then doubling back on the opposite side of the street. The security was ratcheted up more than usual for an inauguration because of all the protestors recently disputing the final vote count in the presidential election.

I briefly panicked when I heard the marching band in the distance, which signaled that the presidential motorcade was approaching and the parade had begun. Even though I was worn out, I had to remind myself to keep pushing and find my second wind. I needed to pick up my pace, so I began to use my monopod (the pole that supports my camera and long lens) as a cattle prod, so to speak, and gently carved a path through the crowd. I remember looking ahead: I was finally about fifty yards from my goal—the press platform. Fortunately, I had been issued a parade route credential that allowed me a spot on the press platform, which meant I did not have to worry about jockeying for a position.

Hours after leaving the swearing-in ceremony, bone-weary, I pulled myself onto the press riser and stepped behind a woman newscaster. She wore a flashy crisp red suit and was perfectly made up; an assistant shielded her from the sleet by holding an umbrella over her as she waited to go "live" on the network. She stepped aside, giving me an exaggerated amount of room to pass by—I assume so that I wouldn't get her outfit dirty. My appearance that day—stringy, damp hair from twelve hours in the sleet and rain, mud-caked pants, soggy hiking boots, and a makeup-streaked face—was in stark contrast with some of the other members of the media who were reporting that day's events.

Gathering up my dignity and wiping the hair out of my face, I stepped into my waiting position and immediately began shooting as the presidential motorcade came into view just a couple of minutes later.

It was only because the parade was running late that I was able to make it to my position on time. Customarily, the inaugural parade cannot start until the previous president is "wheels up" in his plane, leaving Washington. The former presidents are allowed to have

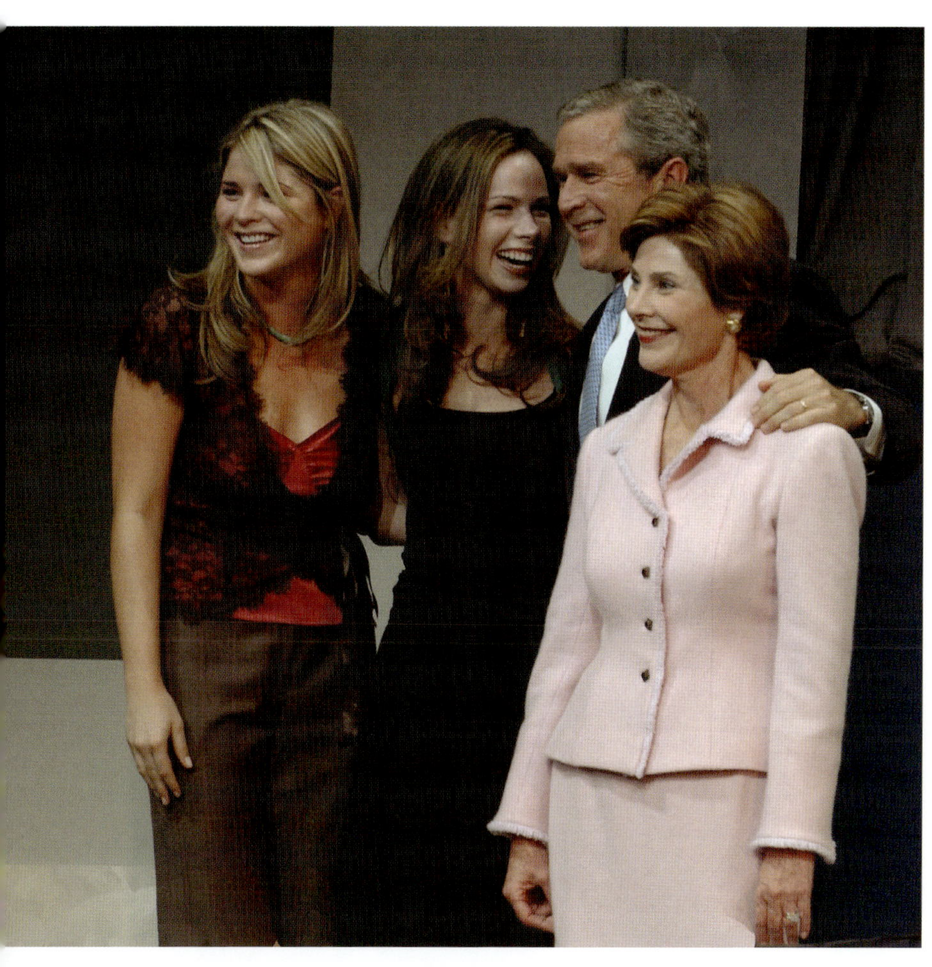

*President Bush celebrates with his family
after hearing the results of his winning his
second term in office as president of the
United States, November 2004.*

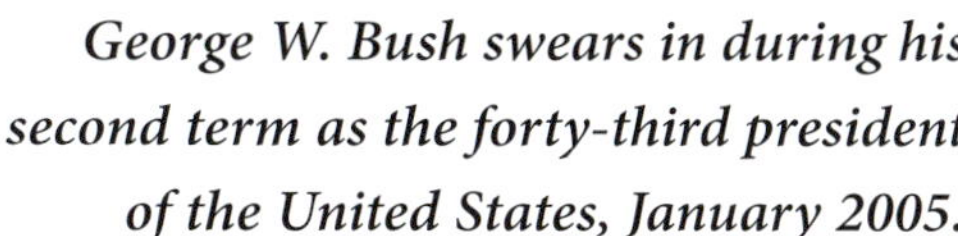

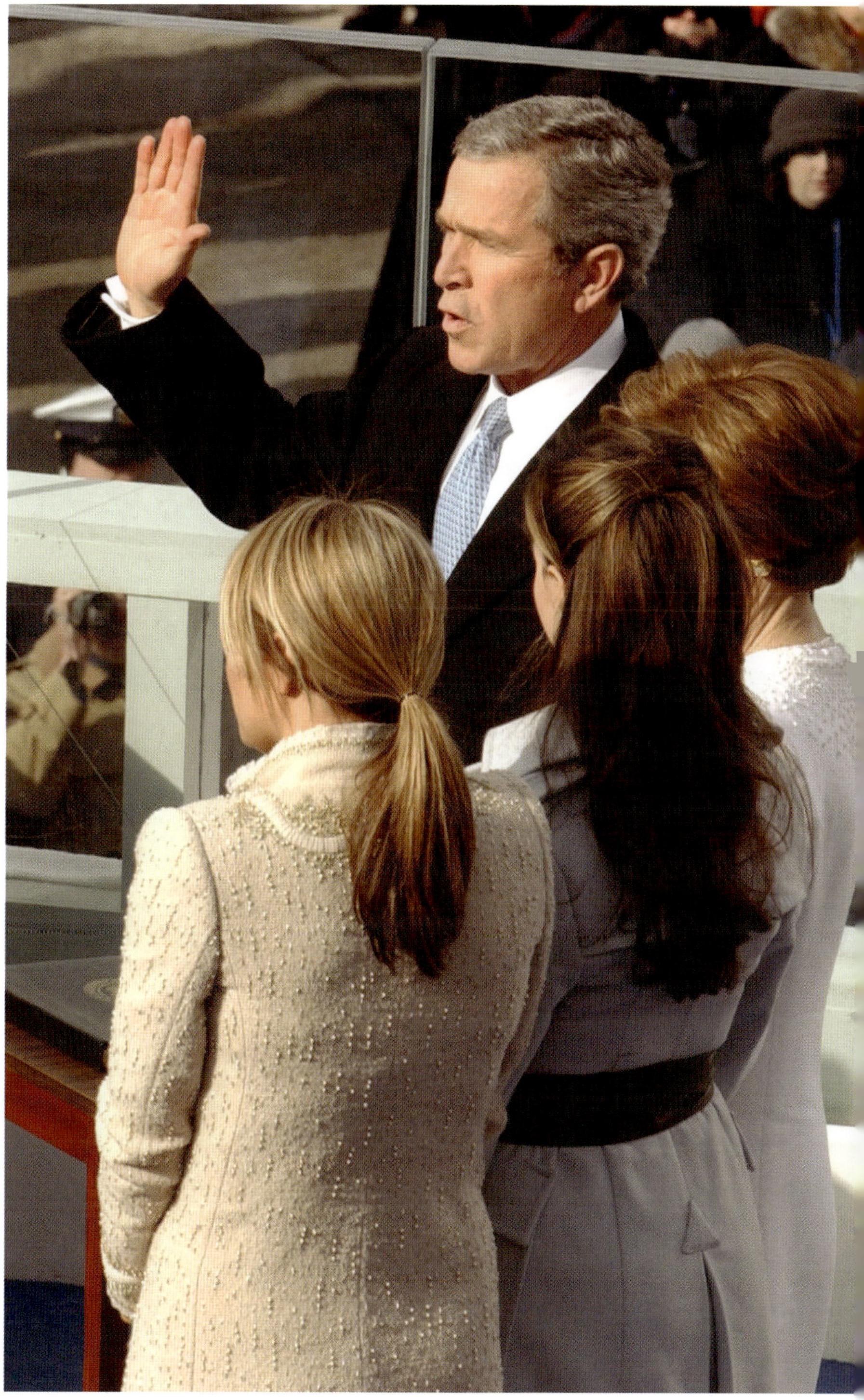

*George W. Bush swears in during his
second term as the forty-third president
of the United States, January 2005.*

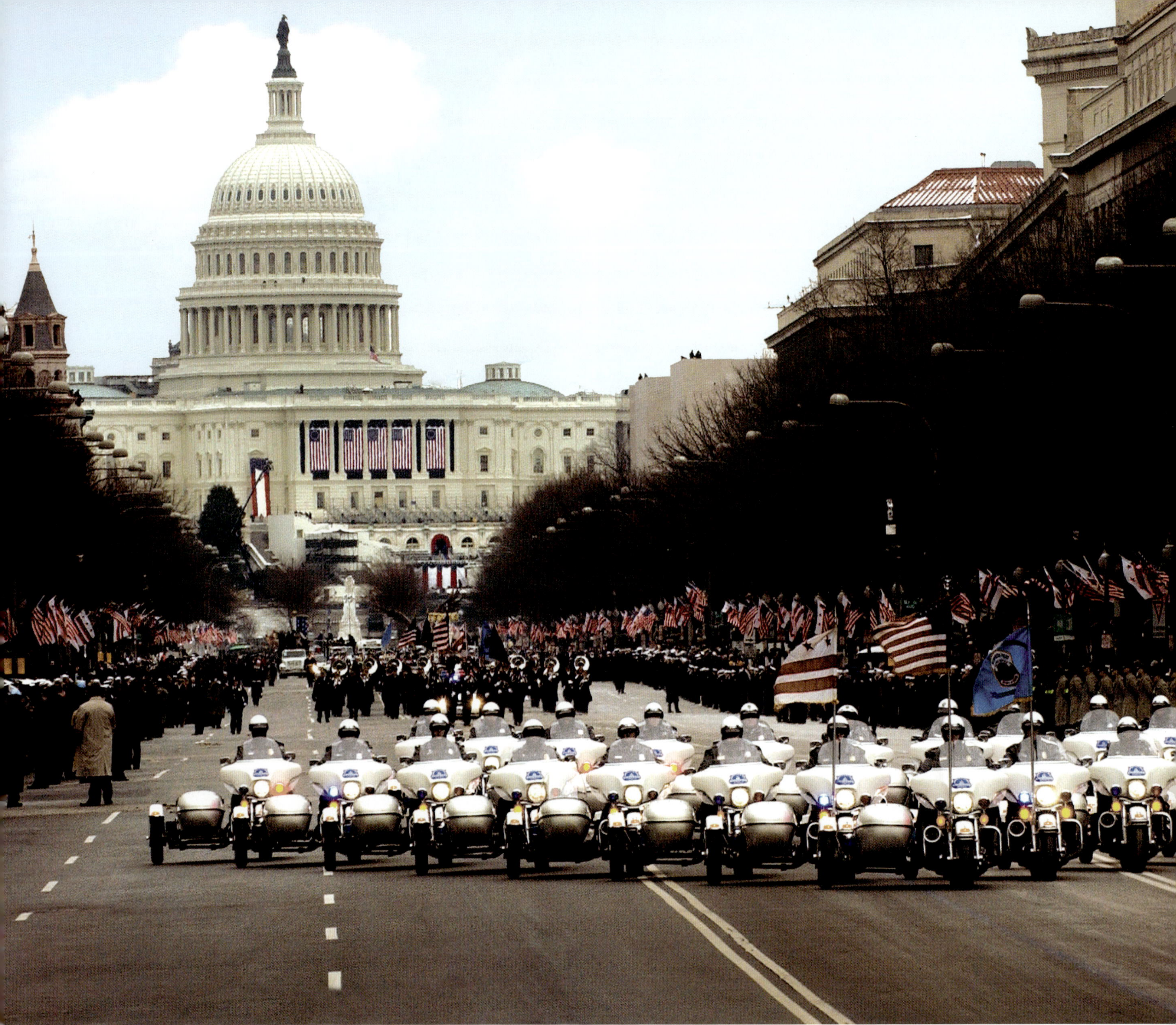

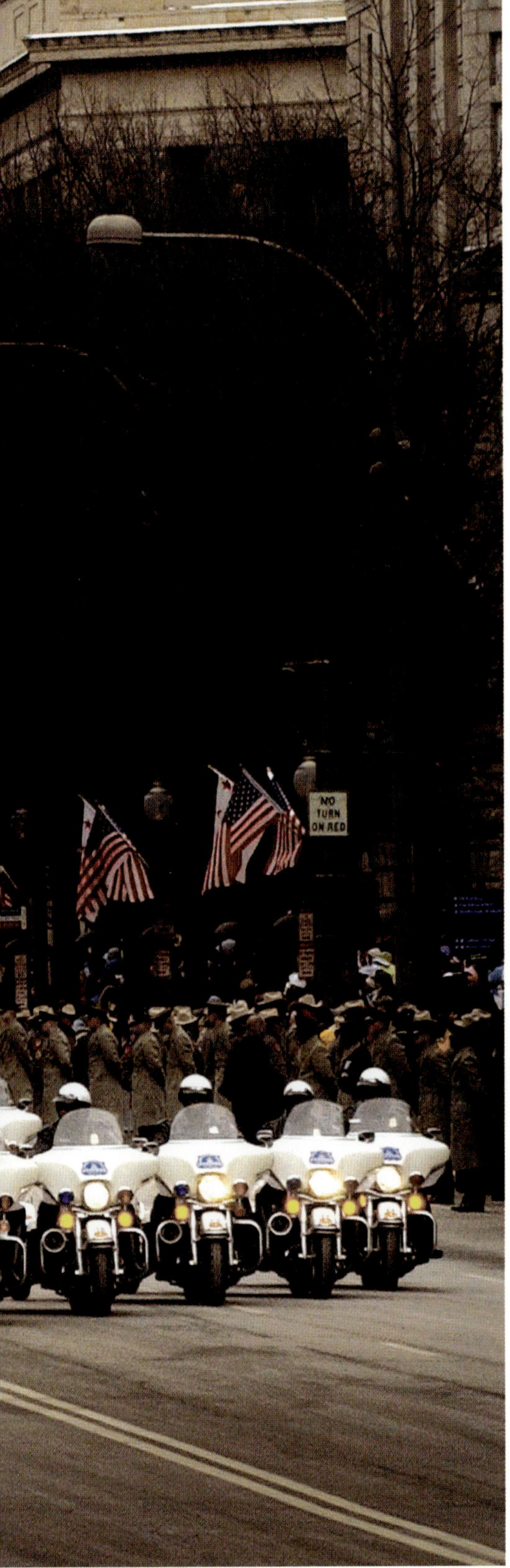

Air Force One take them on a final trip to whatever destination they choose. Former President Clinton's many good-byes and fond farewells were the reason for the holdup. (Some speculated the delay was retribution for the vote count, but who knows?)

The US Secret Service gave President Bush the code name "Trailblazer," probably because he loved to do the physical work of clearing brush on his ranch in Crawford, Texas, whenever he had a little "down time."

Because I had not previously witnessed a transition at the White House, the change had me on edge. I was apprehensive about what to expect from the new White House residents, but my fears about covering this new president were put to rest in the first week when President Bush invited all of the living Baseball Hall of Famers to the White House for lunch. As a former owner of the Texas Rangers, he expressed that he had always been a big baseball fan, and these men had been his heroes when he was growing up—some still were. As the president stood in the East Room with a riser packed with baseball champions, he admitted that he had come to realize that because he was now president of the United States, he could invite these legends of the sport to the White House and chances were good that they'd accept the invitation! He was right. Not only did they come, but they came bearing gifts: one was a baseball bat that all the living hall of famers had signed. I can't imagine what that's worth today!

I was also charmed by the close relationship the new president had with his family. Both he and his father, former President George H. W. Bush Sr., had baseball caps numbered "41" and "43," respectively, to symbolize their positions in the lineup as presidents of the United States.

The Capitol Park Police ride their new Harley–Davidson motorcycles as they escort newly sworn in President George W. Bush during his second inauguration. Freedom Plaza, Washington, DC, January 2005.

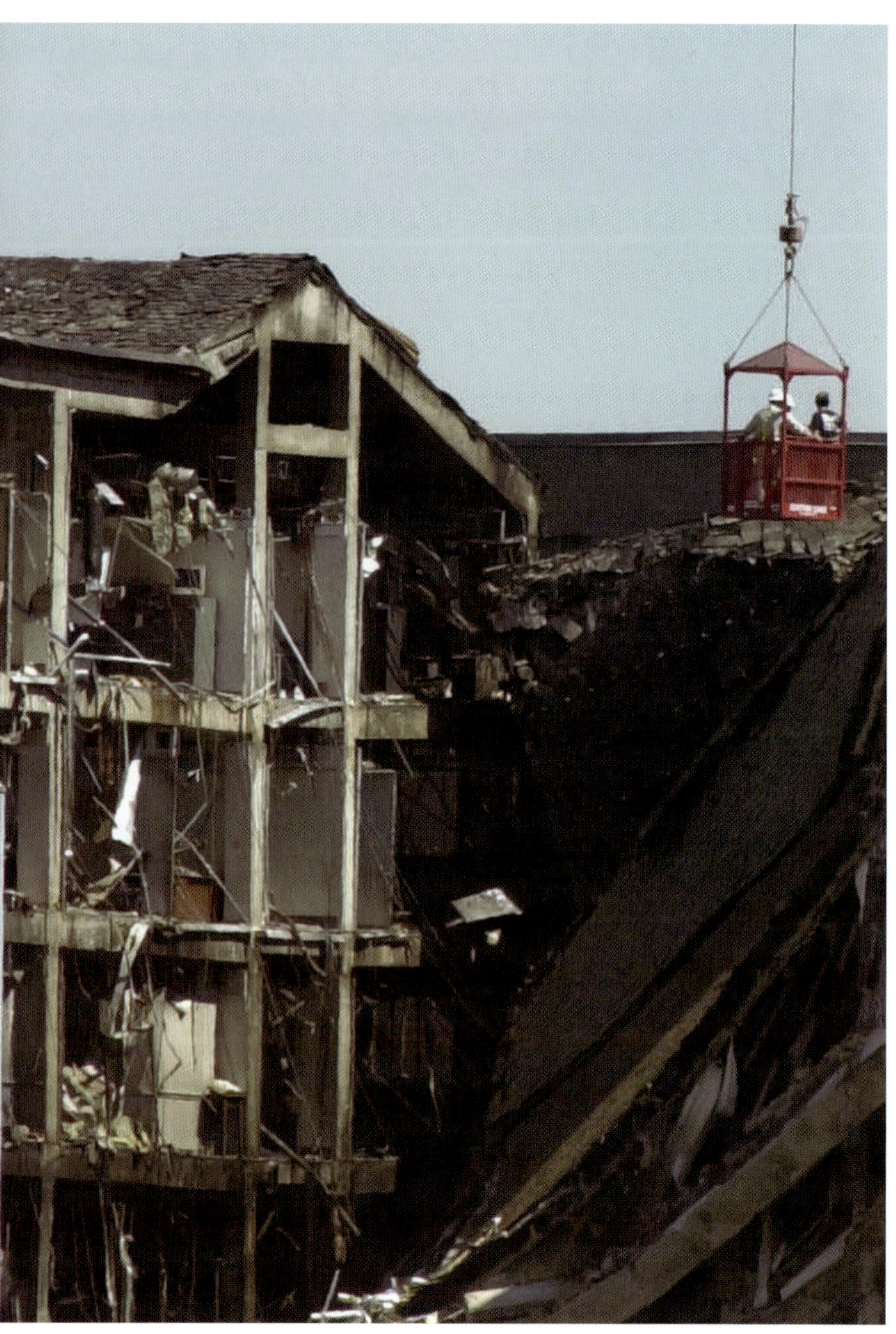

Construction workers look into the Pentagon on September 12, 2001, following the 9/11 terrorist attack.

During this Bush administration, I begrudgingly made the transition to the world of digital photography. I was so used to having physical negatives in my archives that the thought of using the new and mysterious digital memory cards that could be erased freaked me out a bit. I have since come to love the convenience of the format. It has definitely changed the world of news photography, allowing my archive to grow to almost two million images.

My first challenging lesson in the digital photography world came on the morning of September 11, 2001, when terrorists suddenly attacked our country. I found that all my camera batteries were dead that day, so I had to wait for them to charge before going downtown. I can say that has never happened since.

As I made my way downtown I learned that the Twin Towers had been hit first, and then the Pentagon, followed by a fourth aircraft that had crashed in Shanksville, Pennsylvania. The Pentagon was sealed off within minutes to anyone who didn't have a Pentagon pass. I did. In the panic of the moment, several broadcasters incorrectly announced that the Eisenhower Executive Office Building had been hit and that the White House was the next target.

Fortunately the subway trains were still running, so I headed downtown, as did many members of the

    History in the Making

media and first responders, despite the potential risks and dangers of covering this breaking news. As I got off at the Metro station nearest the White House, I saw Roland Mesnier, the White House pastry chef, standing in the middle of Farragut Park with other members of the kitchen staff. They were still in their white chef uniforms, all of them having been evacuated from the White House. Everyone was rushing to get out of downtown as police kept pushing the barricades further and further back. First responders and news people were doing just the opposite: we were rushing *toward* the danger.

Some of the same officers I routinely saw were now wearing riot gear and holding submachine guns as I photographed all the chaos around me. The officers continued to push us further away from the White House one block at a time. As a crowd, we stood united, searching frantically to make cell phone contact with our loved ones and our editors as overwhelmed cell signals failed. The cars surrounding us were all being checked for bombs, and others were towed away from their parking spaces; all routine behaviors were now suspect.

The next morning I made my way to the Pentagon, where the media area had been set up for reporters to relay the nightmare that had taken place the day before.

The devastation was sobering as I focused my lens on the exterior walls that had been blown off the building, exposing a desk, a chair, and a file cabinet that appeared relatively untouched, possibly where a worker had been sitting during the moment of impact. We all attempted to find meaning in the images we captured during those difficult moments. We struggled to maintain our professional composure; I know that I concentrated more on my shutter speeds, lighting, and composition.

> Everyone was rushing to get out of downtown as police kept pushing the barricades further and further back. First responders and newspeople were doing just the opposite: we were rushing *toward* the danger.

Two months later, I photographed one of my favorite images of President Bush: he stood outside the South Portico at sunrise, awaiting the arrival of the Olympic torch that was carried by a family member of someone killed at the Pentagon. To me, this image reveals that of a true Texas cowboy looking out on his "herd." When the torch was handed off that morning, it proved to be a very powerful and emotional moment.

Several years later while photographing the elder Bush, also known as "Papa Bush," I gave him that very picture of his son wearing his cowboy hat at sunrise. I was pleasantly surprised when the former president sent me a nice, handwritten thank-you note signed "George Bush #41." It impressed me deeply that someone of his stature would make such a thoughtful gesture. I keep that memento proudly displayed in my office today.

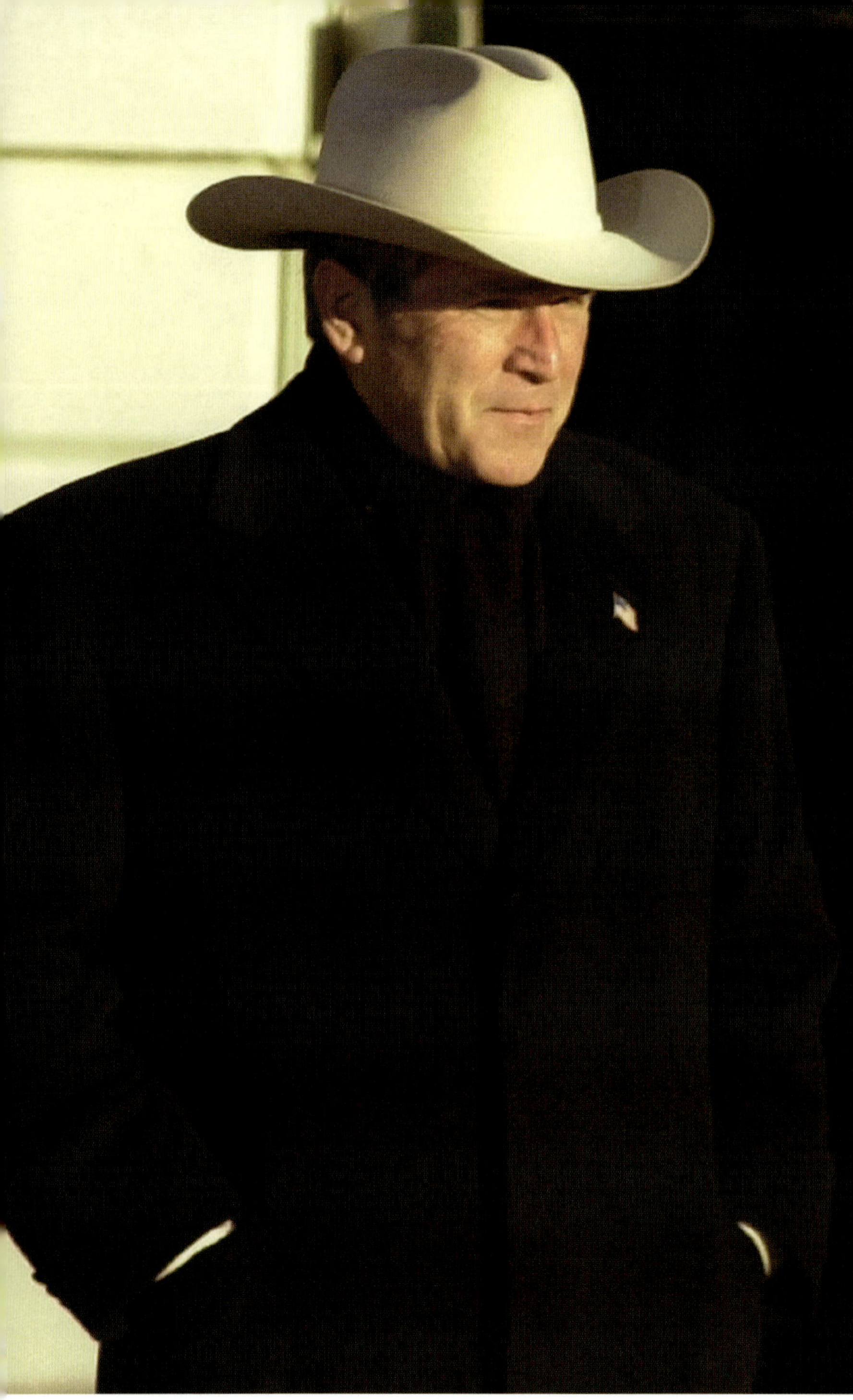

President George W. Bush watches as the Olympic
Torch is carried up the driveway of the White House.
It was carried by a surviving relative who was killed
on 9/11 at the Pentagon. December, 2001.

3-4-04
GEORGE BUSH

Dear Christy,
  I just got back to Houston. The picture of our President is here on my desk. It is a wonderful photo; and I am very grateful to you for giving it to me there at the press club yesterday.
  Many, my thanks,
  G. Bush #41

President George H. W. Bush, known as
"Papa Bush," sent me this wonderful handwritten
note after I gave him an 8 ×10 print of his son that
I had taken following 9/11. March 2004.

In the years following 9/11, there have been many memorial services and prayerful moments of silence in remembrance of that day; the most significant and meaningful one—to me, anyway—took place on September 11, 2003. The Bushes and Cheneys emerged from the White House surrounded by all the White House staff, from the administrative employees, housekeepers and chefs, to the groundskeepers. A small group of us photographers stood still for that solemn moment as a couple of hundred White House staffers from both the West Wing and private residence stood in quiet tribute; the only sound that could be heard was that of our camera shutters firing.

By the time the second Bush inauguration rolled around, using my experience gained from four years earlier, I formulated a better plan for getting around. The folks at Harley–Davidson wanted me to photograph the parade again, since this time there would be clear skies. I did not have a preset location this time around, so things could get dicey. Thanks to the motorcycle police officers I worked with four years earlier, I was driven in a police cruiser down the soon-to-be parade route following the swearing-in ceremony. I had an assistant this time, too, who was standing in place to hold my new position along the parade route. Richard and I had gone down a week earlier, and I'd shown him the exact spot that I needed him to hold for me along the parade route. Although I had warned him of what holding my precious place would entail, I do not think it fully sank in that he would need to stand in icy conditions from dawn until dusk. He did a great job though, and four years later asked to assist me again!

There were many other celebrated events during the Bush years; one of the most momentous was a visit from Her Majesty, Queen Elizabeth II, the Queen of England. The state arrival ceremony was very carefully planned, and protocol reigned. Several hours before the dinner arrival, the press corps waited on the North Lawn at the end of a long sidewalk as the crowd of photographers swelled. I was concerned about the commotion that would ensue once we were given the go-ahead to move forward and claim our spots for the Queen's arrival at the white-tie dinner. When we were greenlit, we first began walking fast but then soon broke into a child-like run in the 100-yard dash up the long sidewalk to the North Portico, trying to pass each other and racing at top speed with cameras and stepladders as all our bodies competed for a good spot to view the royal couple's arrival. This was one of those rare, aggressive press corps situations that we became famous for over the years. George W. Bush and First Lady Laura emerged at the precise moment the schedule called for as the black SUV rolled up the north driveway, the president looking handsome in his white-tie tux and the first lady fabulous in her blue designer gown.

Earlier in the day as we photographers waited for our escort, a few of us started talking about what the queen's life must be like. I spoke with another photographer who was Papa Bush's personal photographer years earlier. She had accompanied him on his state arrival at Buckingham Palace, when lo and behold, the queen appeared and greeted the president, purse in hand. There were some rumors that she used her purse to signal her handlers by moving it a certain way to communicate her wishes, such as "leave us alone" or "get this person away from me."

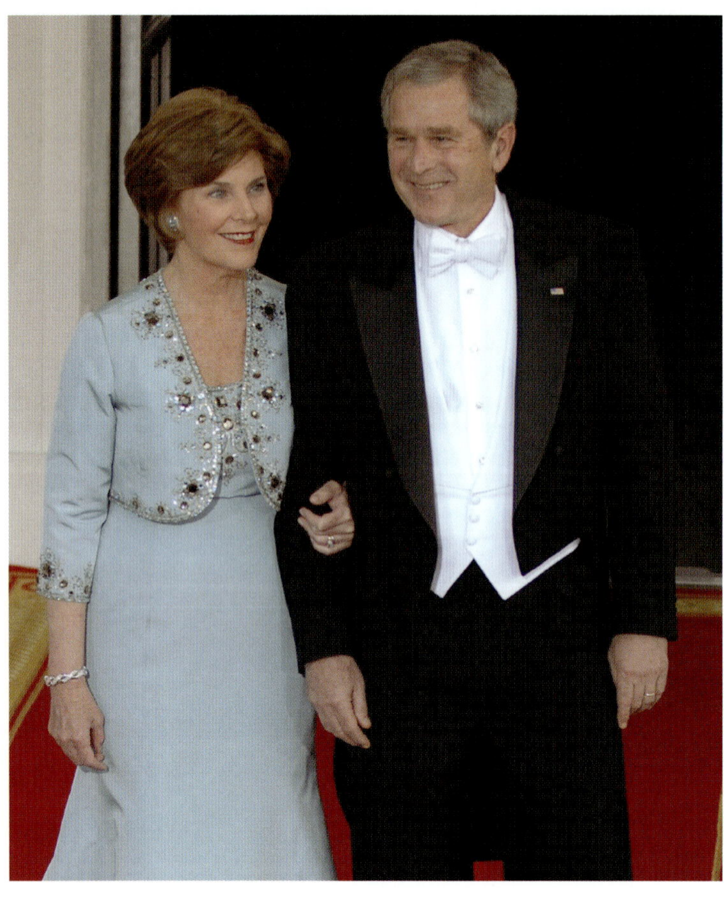

President George W. Bush and First Lady Laura Bush wait at the North Portico of the White House for Queen Elizabeth II to arrive for her white-tie state dinner, May 2007.

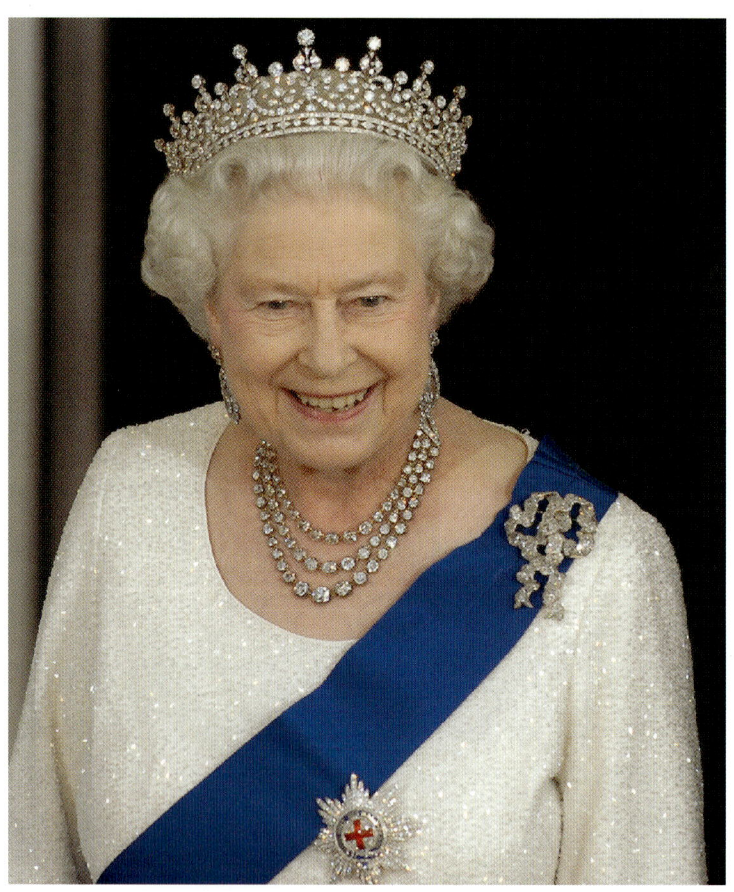

Queen Elizabeth II stops to pose for the press after arriving at the white-tie State Dinner in her honor. The White House, May 2007.

I, for one, was fascinated that she carried a purse everywhere. But what was *in* that purse? More diamonds? A tiny tiara? An embroidered hanky? Breath mints? As we photographers stood on the risers on the South Lawn during the arrival ceremony, she actually *opened* her purse just prior to making remarks, and I got my answer. Let me tell you that when she reached into her purse, we all eagerly zoomed in with our telephoto lenses to catch a peek inside! After all that hype, she pulled out her reading glasses . . . At least I finally knew one of the items that was stashed in there.

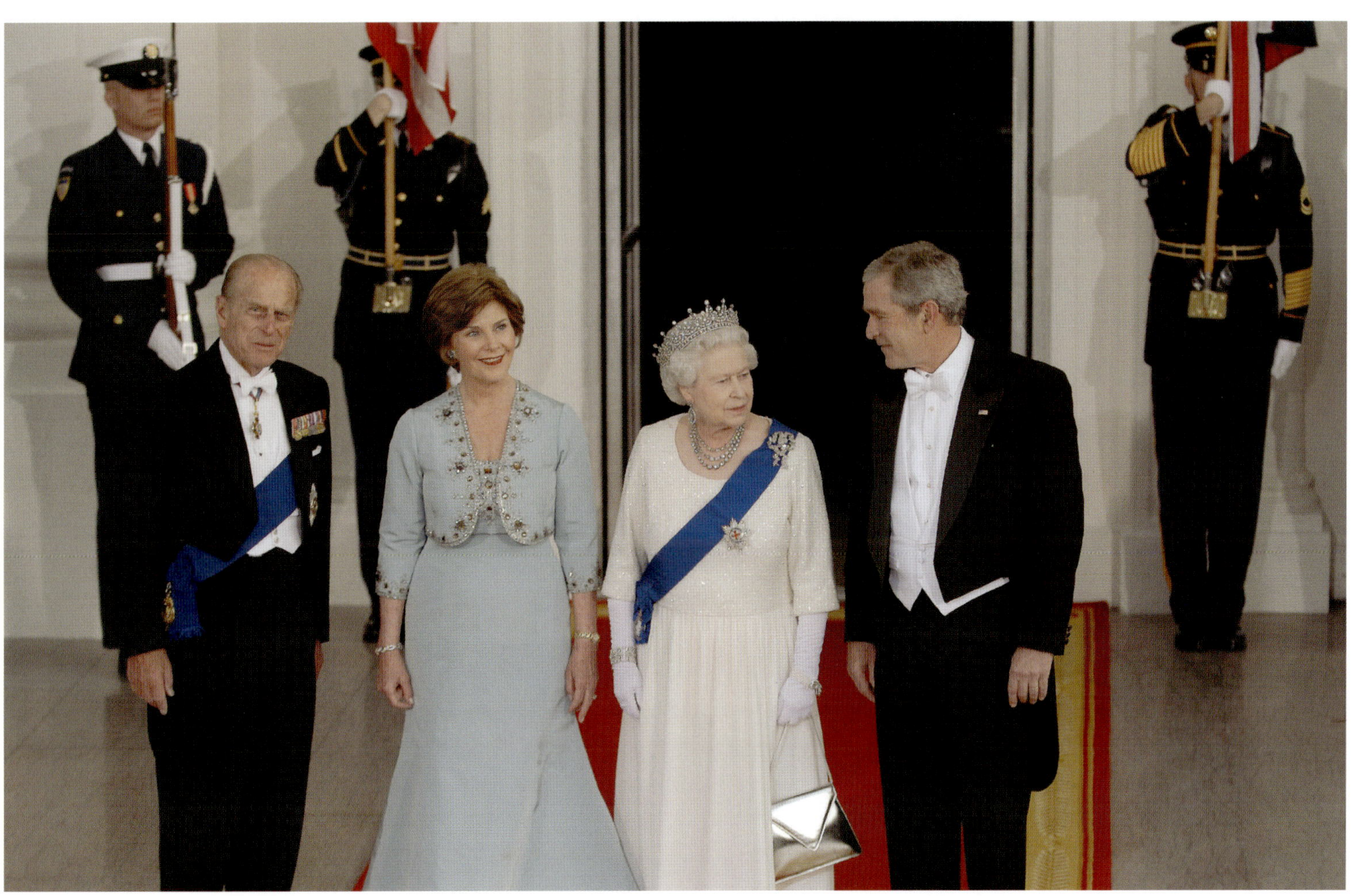

President Bush welcomes Queen Elizabeth II and his Royal Highness Prince Philip Duke of Edinburgh to the White House for the white-tie state dinner held in their honor.

On April 16, 2008, the Bush White House welcomed Pope Benedict XVI to the White House for an official arrival ceremony, complete with a twenty-one-gun salute. Following the welcoming remarks from both President Bush and Pope Benedict, we were advised, at the last minute, that both men would be walking along the Colonnade to the Oval Office. If we were to get a photo opportunity, we knew we had to move *in that very moment*. Grabbing my heavy gear and stepladder, I rushed down the stairs of the riser and quickly staked out my spot in the Rose Garden, seconds before my two subjects emerged from the Palm Room doors. The president and pope walked along, side by side, chatting casually as they drifted from shadows to bright sunlight. The pope, dressed in bright white, strolling alongside the equally bright white of the White House itself, challenged the photographic skills of the most seasoned of professional photographers. So much light! Our meter readings soared up and down, struggling with this difficult lighting situation.

Once the two leaders entered the Oval Office, we photographers moved from behind the red velvet ropes and into the holding area, waiting for the White House press wranglers to signal us to enter for a ten- to twenty-second photo op.

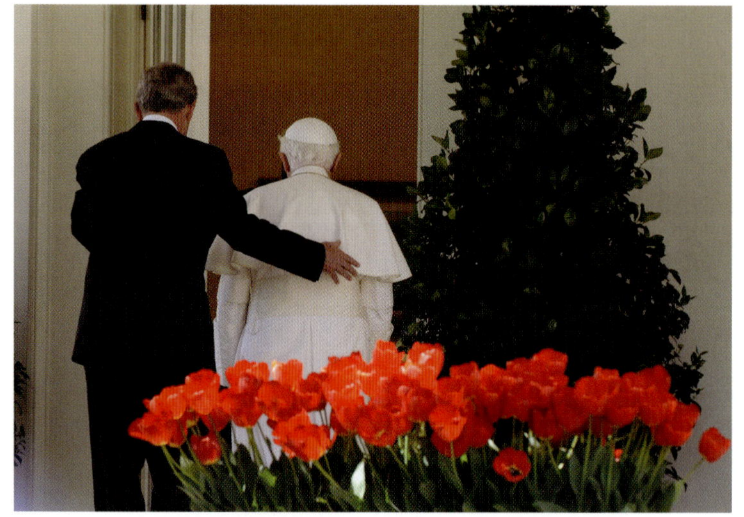

President Bush and Pope Benedict walk into the Oval Office following an arrival ceremony in the pope's honor, April 2008.

The wait can normally be anywhere from five minutes to an hour long. The press corps and visiting Italian photographers would be divided into several waves of around fifteen photographers each. I had decided that I needed to be in the first wave while both subjects were still "fresh," patient, and relatively accommodating of our presence. But if I was going to be in the first wave, I knew I needed to hustle to secure my place in line.

Walking briskly toward the Oval Office, many thoughts ran through my mind as I changed my camera settings and prepared for the photo op. I set my second camera for the proper exposure that I was accustomed to using in the Oval Office, guessing on the adjustments that would be needed to capture this rare picture of Pope Benedict at the White House. Those of us who have photographed in the Oval Office before are intimately familiar with the lighting variables, and we know ahead of time how best to preset our cameras for the correct exposure. We can't spare even one additional second to readjust once we are inside.

I was surprised that when I got to the holding position on the Colonnade, I did not even have to pause. The White House press handler immediately ushered me around the corner and into the Oval Office; the rest of the photographers were still several yards behind me. Since I was the first photographer to enter, I stood directly in front of the pope, who was seated next to President Bush in the customary armchairs in front of the fireplace. As he sat, his brilliant white robes radiated, altering all of my familiar calculations for that room. Although photographers are not supposed to speak unless spoken to first, I glanced at President Bush for a look of approval, and he smiled before I said to the pope, "Hi, Your Holiness. Welcome to Washington."

President Bush smiled at me while the pope gazed directly into my eyes. For a brief instant, he looked as if he were about to speak. But almost in that same moment, his calm gaze turned into outright astonishment as he looked over my shoulder at my fellow photographers bursting into the room. In all my years covering the White House, I can never recall being the first of the pack to enter the Oval Office for a photo. The pope silently blessed us with the sign of the cross in three directions just before we were escorted out, and I realized I came away with more than I hoped for that day.

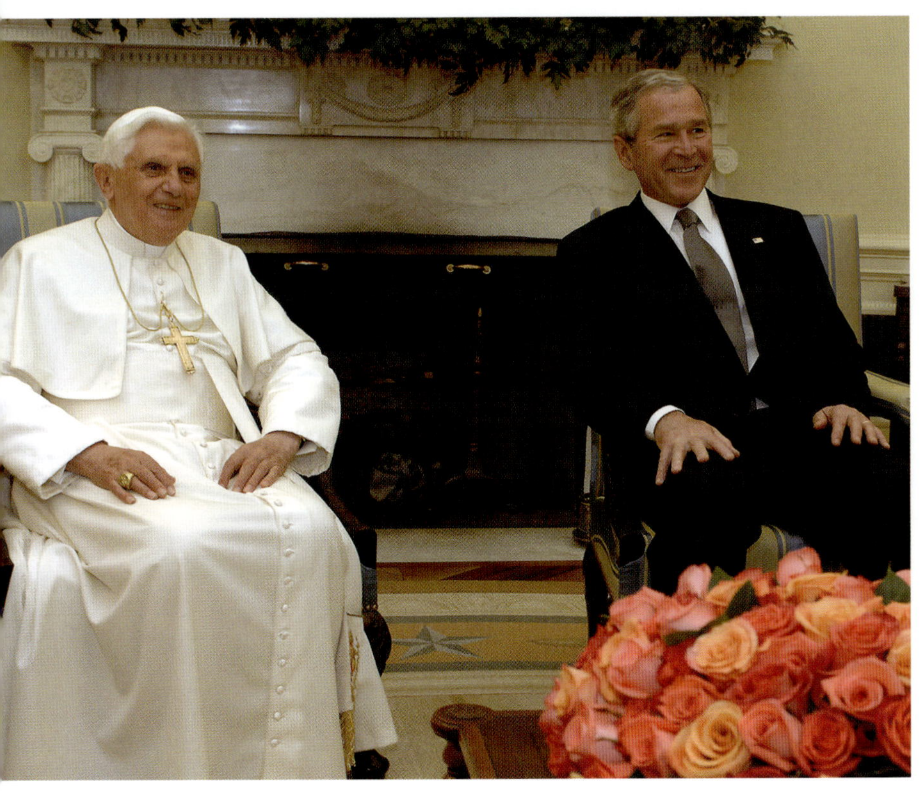

Pope Benedict meets with President Bush in the Oval Office following an arrival ceremony in the pope's honor, April 2008.

There were many memorable Oval Office photo ops with Bush and other dignitaries and world leaders. I consider myself fortunate to have witnessed—and covered—many of them.

I was deeply moved by South African President Nelson Mandela's visit to the White House on May 17, 2005. Mandela knew that he did not have much longer to live. This would be the third time I had photographed him. Although he appeared frail to me, he projected a calm demeanor as he made his way around the world, saying his good-byes to various leaders. He seemed at peace and had a certainty about him that comes from being a person who has fulfilled his destiny.

Like others before him, President Bush held a Presidential Medal of Freedom Ceremony each year of his presidency. Two of these ceremonies stick out

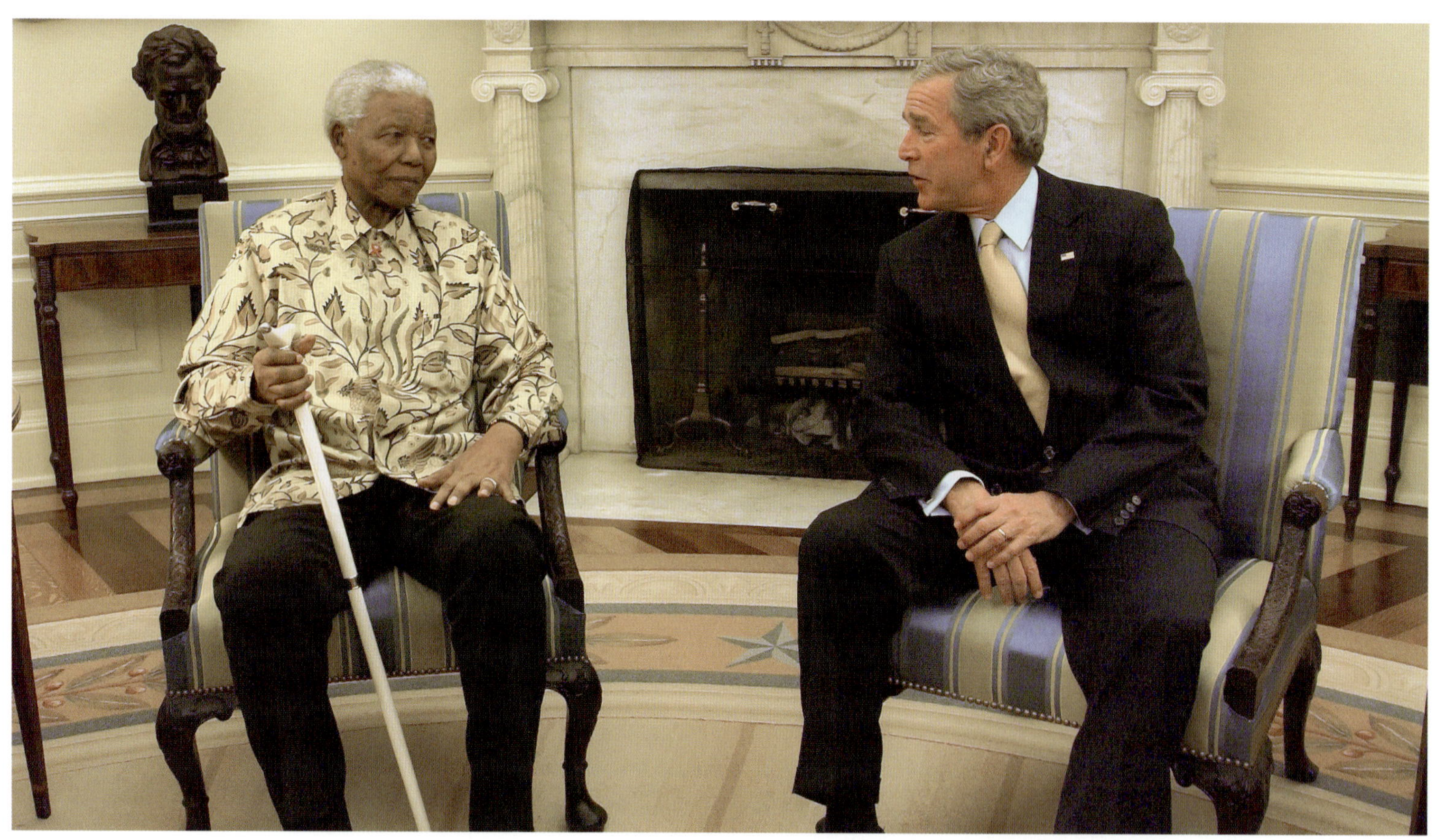

President George W. Bush welcomes former South African president Nelson Mandela to the Oval Office for his final visit to the United States, May 2005.

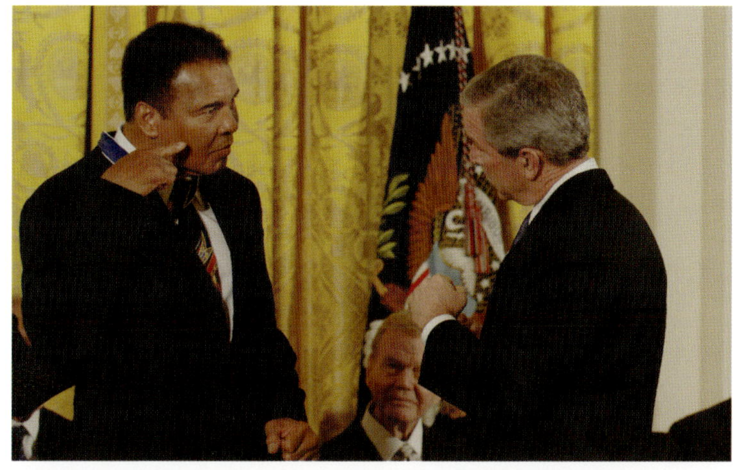

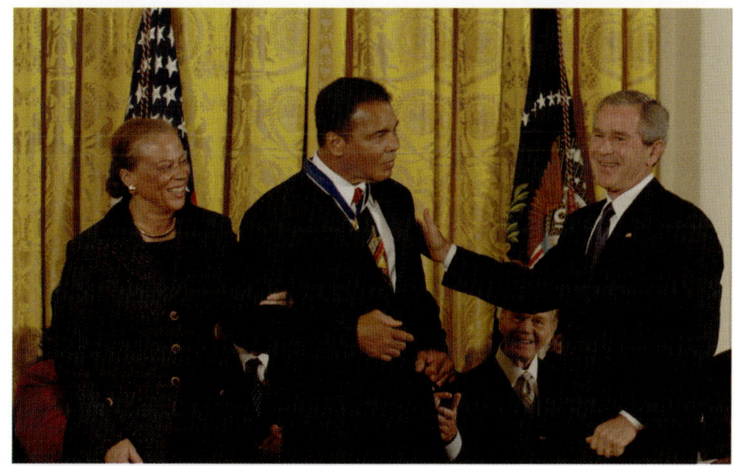

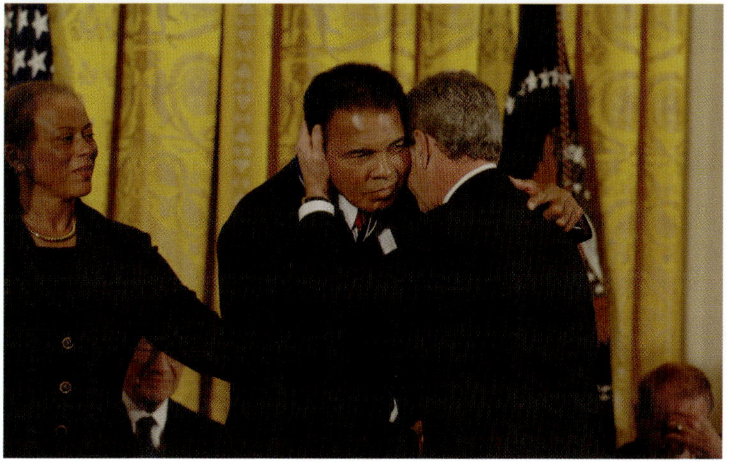

in my memory. The first was the visibly emotional "Queen of Soul" Aretha Franklin reacting as she was awarded the medal. Although she had won many awards over the course of her career, this one seemed to mean a lot to her.

During the 2005 ceremony, I was touched by the nonverbal exchange between President Bush and former heavy weight champion of the world Muhammed Ali. I had photographed Ali three different times, and he was quite the talker. This final time at the White House he was frail and no longer able to speak because of his advancing Parkinson's diagnosis. He still was able to communicate in his own way, however.

Bush respectfully connected with the former champion and then playfully made a boxing gesture to imply, "Are you ready to fight me?" Ali seemed to respond, "You're crazy to take me on," twirling his finger beside his temple. Ali appeared touched by the honor, and as Bush turned away, I could see that he too had been moved by the interaction.

President George W. Bush greets former heavyweight champion of the world Muhammed Ali during the Presidential Medal of Honor Ceremony, November 2005.

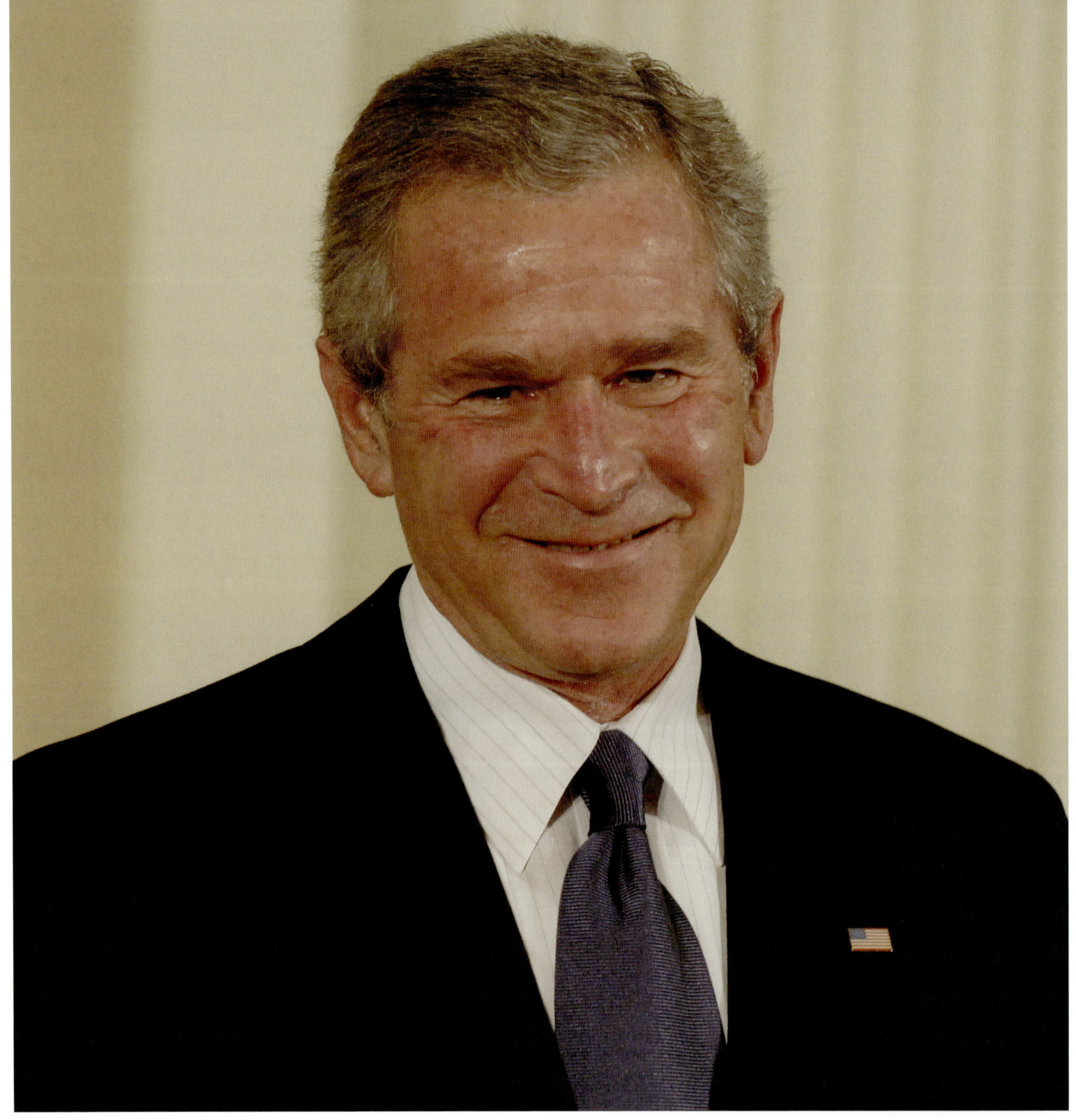

President W. Bush gets emotional after presenting a frail Muhammed Ali with the presidential Medal of Freedom.

While covering the White House during the '43 Bush administration, I had the most memorable personal exchanges with any US president to date. Even though these were just casual remarks, they were made special by the fact that I was having them with the president of the United States. When covering the Oval Office, those of us who are not in the White House pool (select photographers assigned to cover specific presidential events each day) normally have anywhere from ten to twenty seconds to take a picture of the president, who is usually sitting to the right of the visiting head of state in front of the fireplace. We traditionally receive a verbal directive from our press office handlers, "Thank you very much, ladies and gentlemen," as our queue to leave the room.

One time when I was covering a photo op in the Oval Office, I was the only woman present in the press corps for the event that day, which was unusual. (There are always more men than women though.) To signal that our time had come to an end, the standard announcement was made: "Thank you, gentlemen."

Hearing those words, the president commented, "There are not only men here, you know," to which I gratefully replied, "Thanks for noticing, Mr. President." With a wink, he responded, "I *always* notice." Maybe it was the tone he set with the spontaneous banter that showed me, in a small way, the sense of humanity within the office of the presidency. President Bush never made me feel like there was a big difference between the most powerful man in the world and the smallest photo news bureau at the White House. The way he spoke made it feel like we were on equal footing. He gave the small folks a break with some special attention. I respected that. A lot.

Shortly after his reelection in an Oval Office photo op with then–British Prime Minister Tony Blair, President Bush gazed at the dozen or so photographers, then looked directly at me and asked, "Hey, did you all vote for me?"

I was taken aback, but answered, "Why, yes I did, Mr. President."

He replied incredulously, "Really? You did?"

It looked to me as if Tony Blair disapproved of that interaction, but I thought it was such a wonderful, unscripted moment.

Sometime later, on a very hot, humid summer morning, the White House hosted a state arrival ceremony for Indian Prime Minister Manmohan Singh on the South Lawn. Following the ceremony, Bush met with Singh in the Oval Office. As I was photographing him, the president commented to me, "I saw you sweating out there."

I responded, "Yes, but I sure was glad I did not have to wear a suit and tie in all that heat like you did."

He smiled, and it was time for the photographers to leave.

Bush warmed himself to us press photographers in even more expressive ways at times.

In 2008 President Bush invited Senator John McCain to the White House to announce that he would be endorsing him for the office of the president. The presidents do not normally greet a guest at the front door of the White House during a daytime visit, yet President Bush did this time.

Somehow McCain was a few minutes late. When President Bush stepped out onto the North Portico, about twenty of us media were there waiting for McCain's arrival. The president stood there for a few seconds and then joked that he guessed he needed to entertain us while we waited—and then he broke into a tap dance. It was a fun, impromptu moment that we all appreciated. McCain soon arrived and one of my pictures of the two friends was used in the presidential campaign.

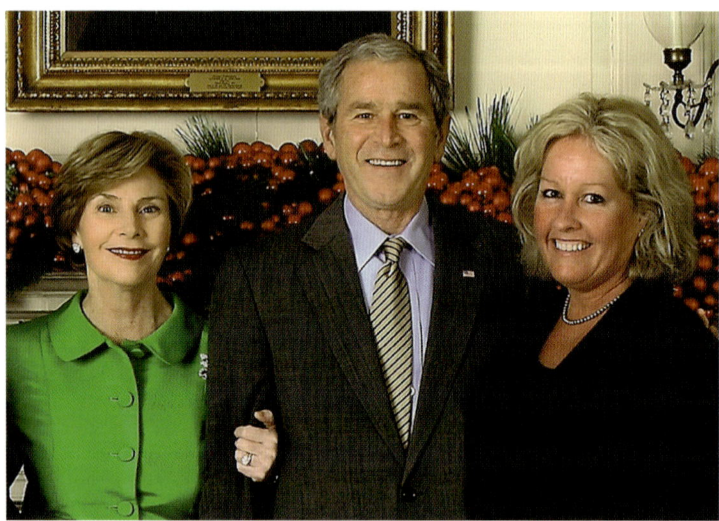

President Bush and First Lady Laura pose with me at the 2008 White House Christmas Party.

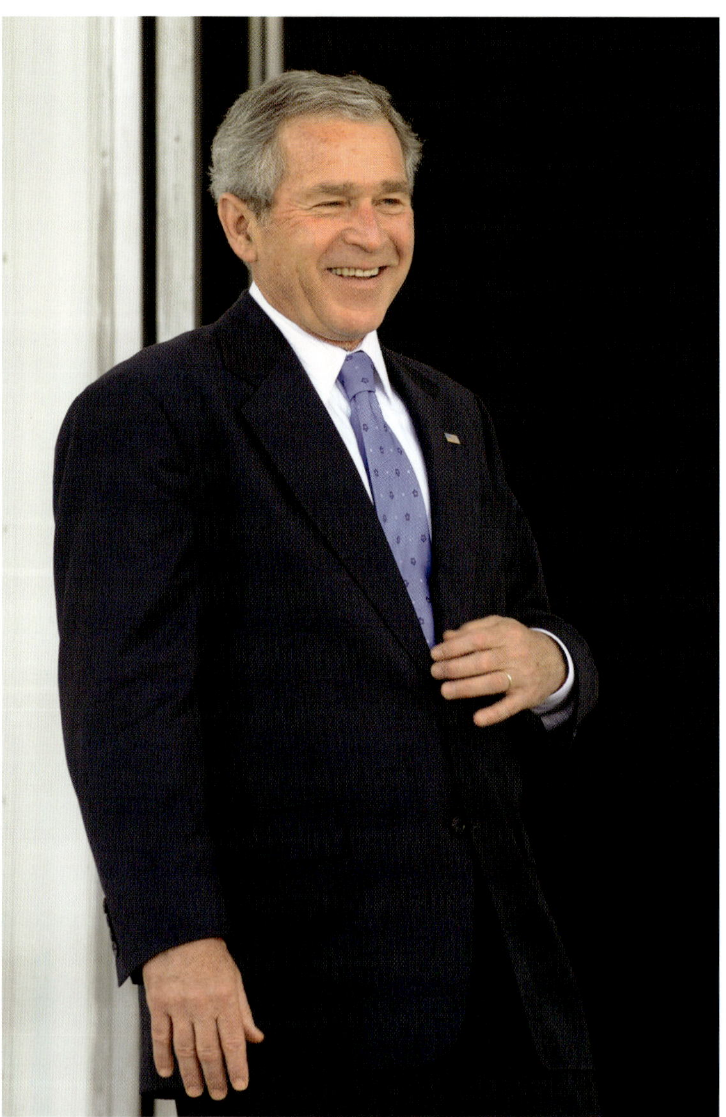

Despite the easygoing camaraderie Bush kept with the press, he installed a rule to maintain a level of professionality: no sandals or open-toed shoes in the Oval Office.

I was pulled out of the group of photographers for wearing sandals on a hot summer day and denied access for that reason. That never happened again; lesson learned.

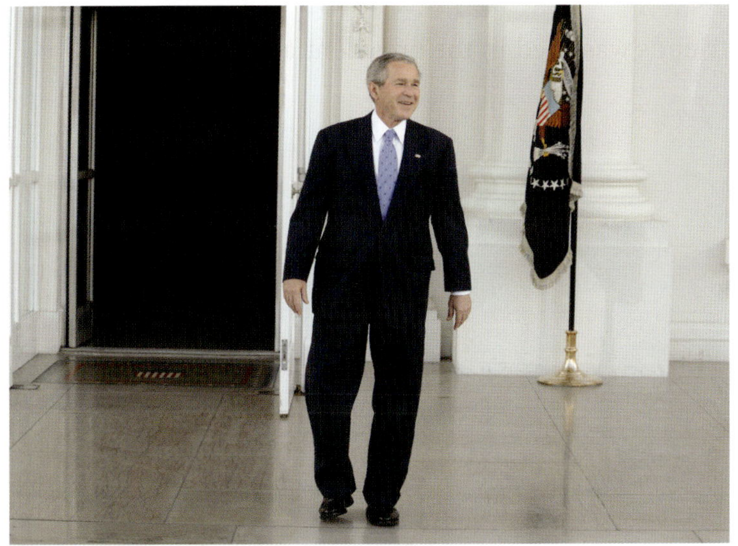

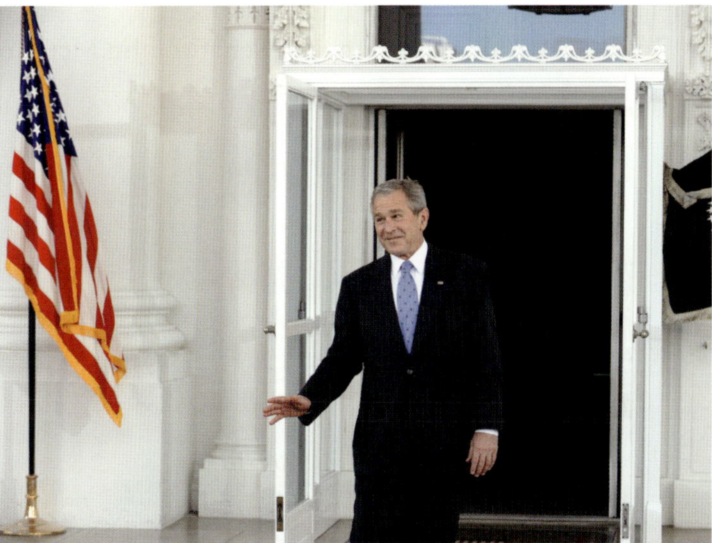

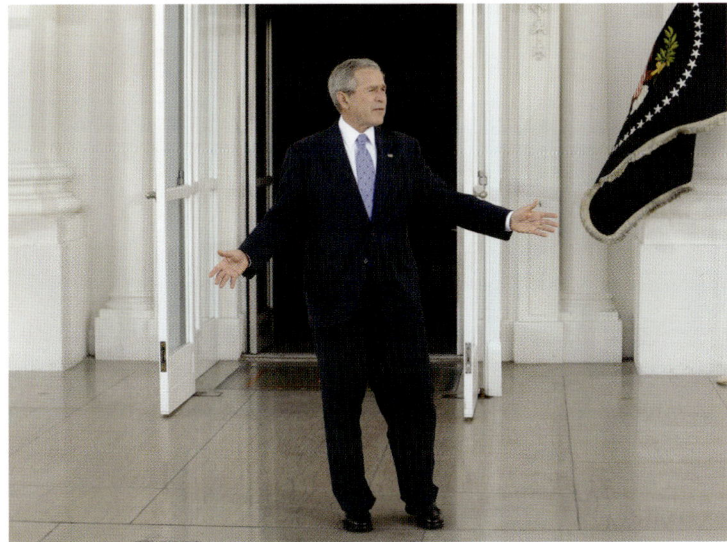

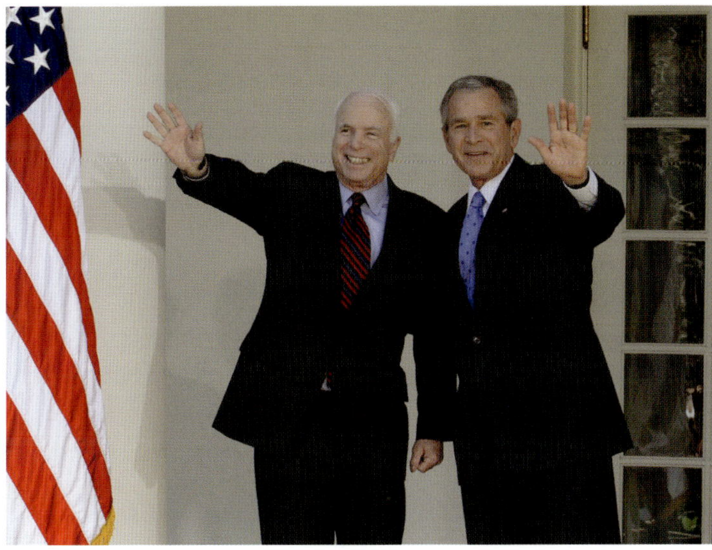

President George W. Bush playfully dances for the press corps on the North Portico steps of the White House as he awaits the arrival of presidential nominee Senator John McCain, March 2008.

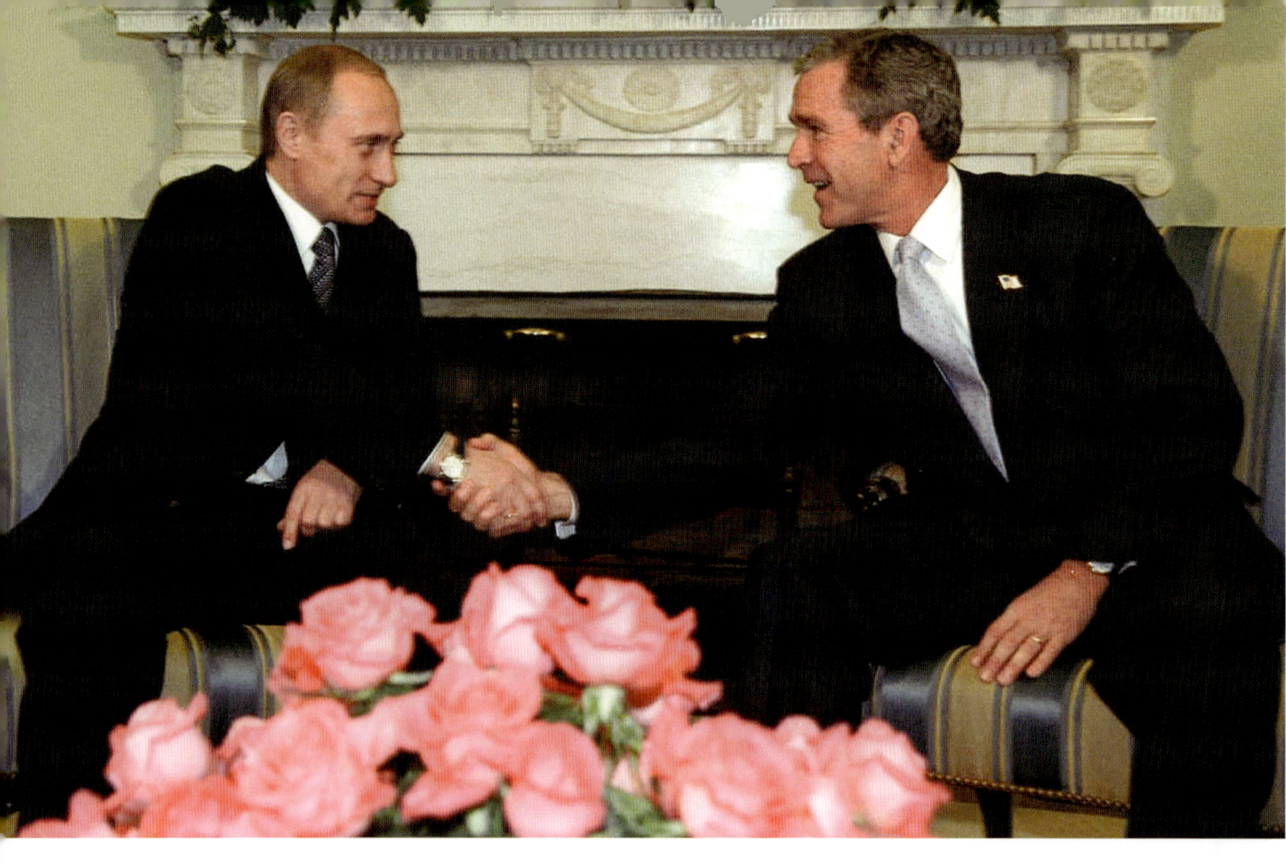

President George W. Bush and President Vladmir Putin of Russia shake hands during a meeting in the Oval Office, September 2005.

Sometimes when photographing in the Oval Office there was more a serious tone, such as on September 16, 2005, when Russia's President Vladimir Putin came for a working visit to the White House. I was allowed to photograph the two leaders talking in the Oval Office before and then as they strolled along the Colonnade on their way to the East Room, where they held a lengthy press conference. Although Putin smiled a couple of times, I found him to be intense and highly observant of everything going on around him. I would have loved an opportunity to have been present during the more casual moments between the two leaders, but I was grateful for what I got.

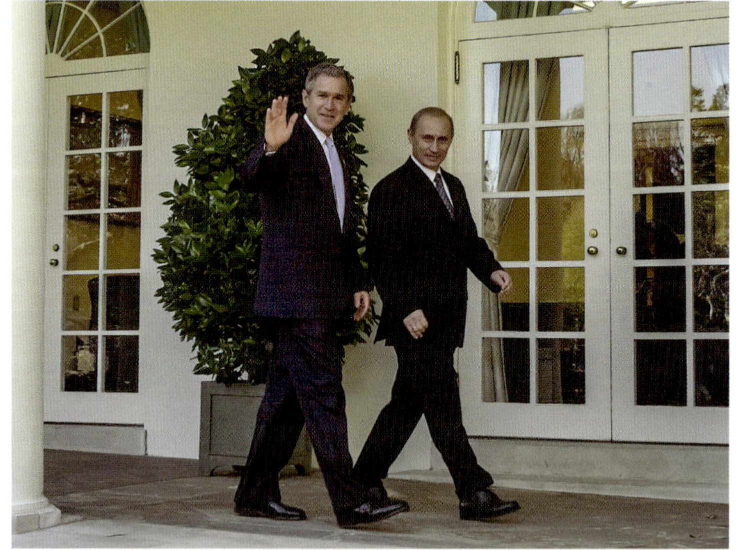

President George W. Bush and President Vladmir Putin of Russia leave the Oval Office and walk along the Colonnade by the Rose Garden on their way to a press conference in the East Room, September 2005.

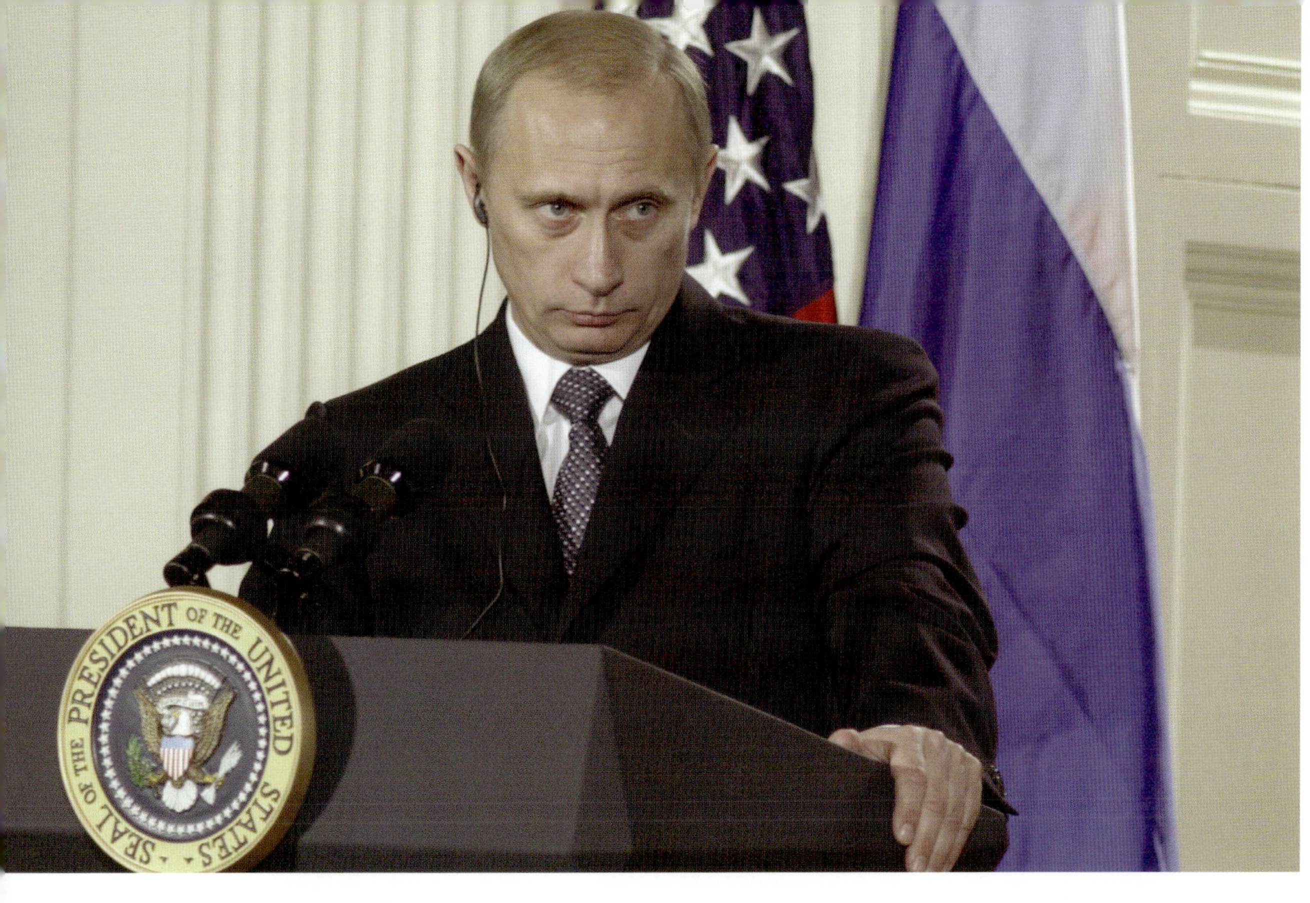

Following their remarks, President George W. Bush and President Vladimir Putin hold a lengthy press conference in the East Room. Media were allowed much closer to the president in those days.

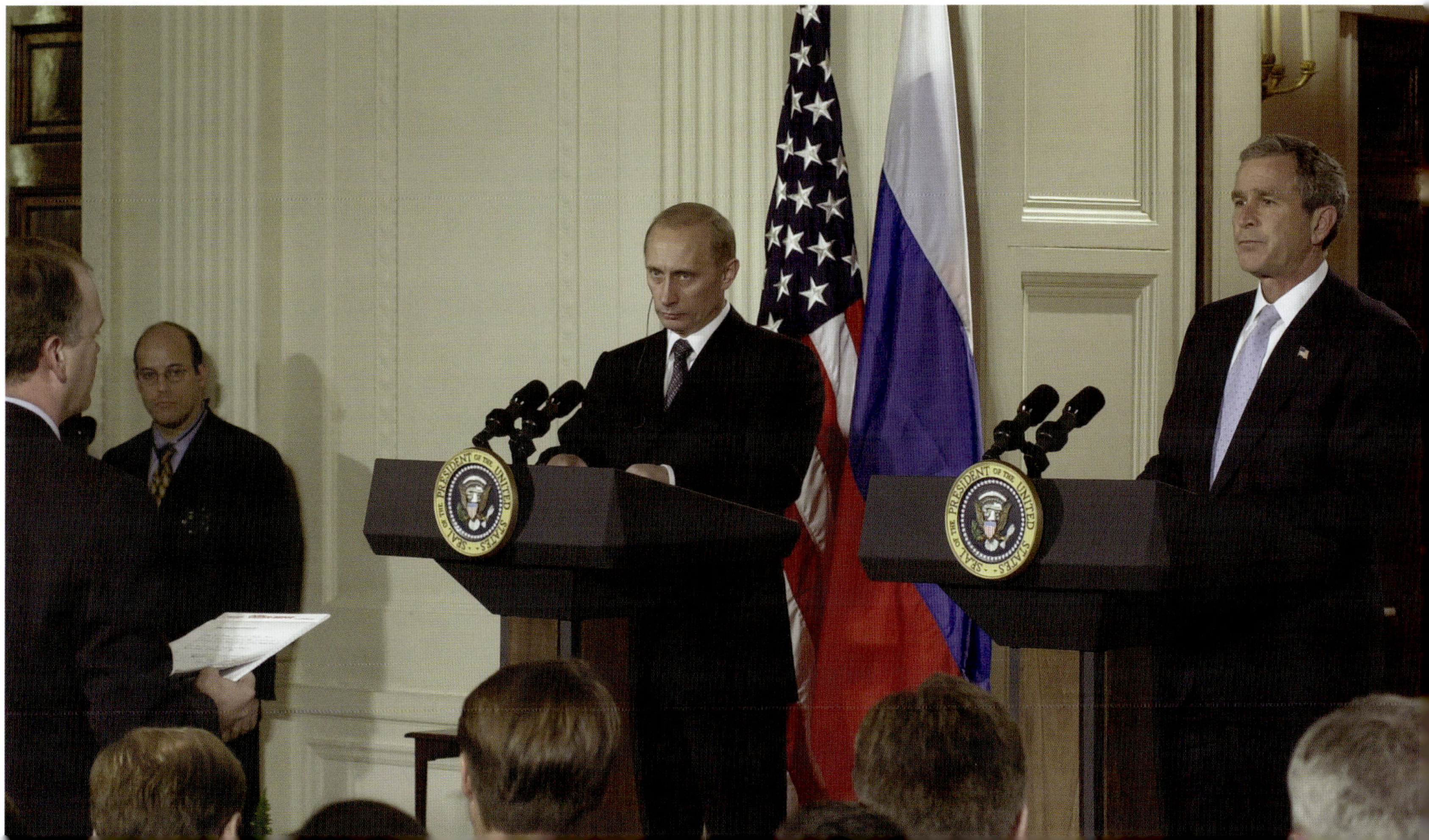

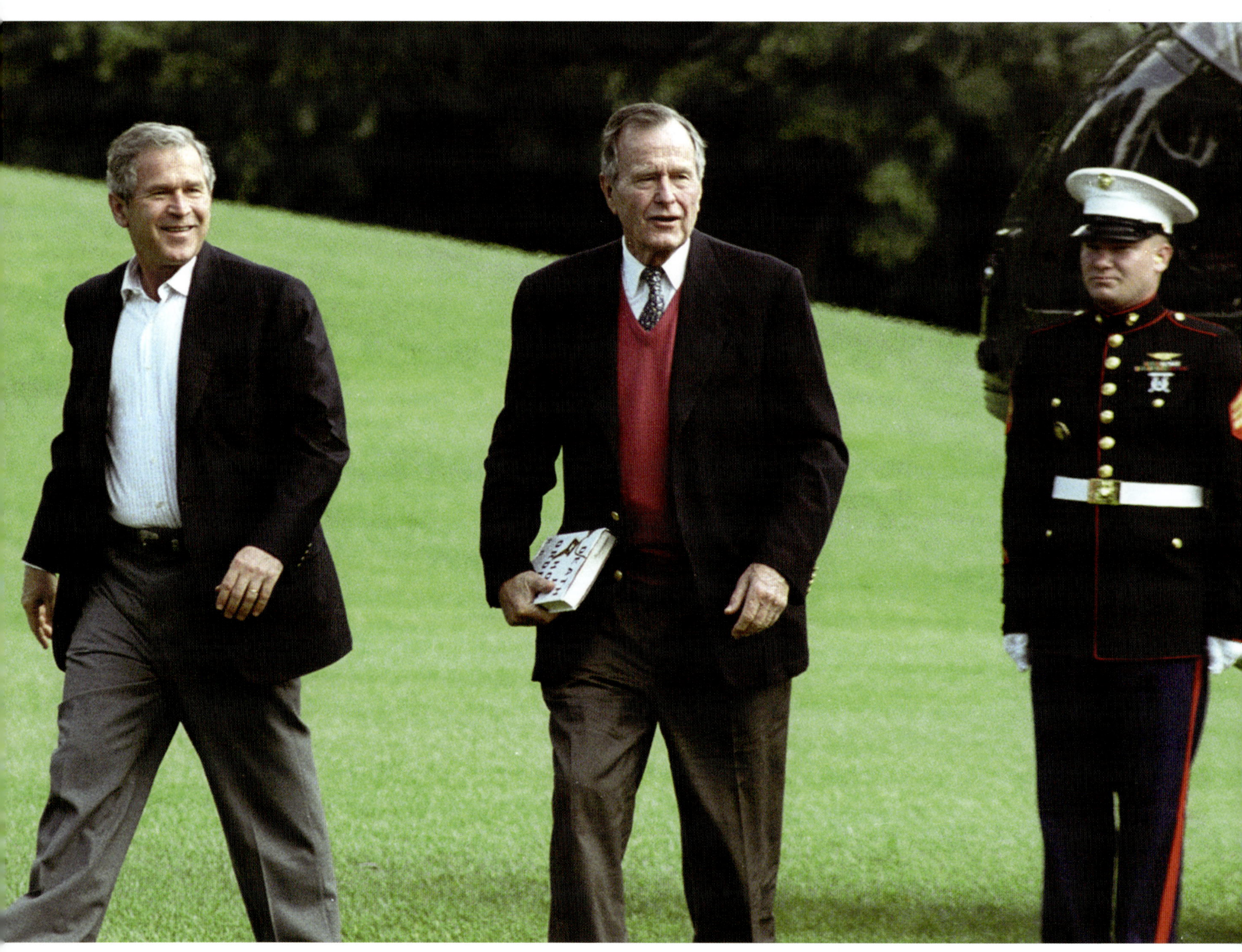

Father and son, Presidents Bush #43 and #41, exit Marine One on the South Lawn of the White House, October 2004.

    History in the Making

On a lighter note, Christmas parties for the press have always been a treat at the White House. During these parties, we are always offered a wonderful array of food and drink and allowed to mix and mingle freely on the State and Ground Floor levels of the mansion. If invited, each of us was allowed to bring a guest. Part of the fun of the evening is meeting the president and first lady, and having our picture taken with them by the White House photographer. There is always a long line of guests that snakes down the hallway and turns a corner into the Diplomatic Reception Room. As I came around the corner the last year of Bush's presidency, the traditional marine stood in dress uniform and asked for the correct pronunciation of mine and my guest's name so we could be properly introduced to the president. A moment later, I was standing face-to-face with the president and first lady.

During this brief interchange, we only have about 30 seconds to speak to the president, and at that time of year, those precious seconds are often spent wishing each other merry Christmas.

Since this was their final holiday party, I spoke from my heart and told both the president and the first lady that I would miss seeing them around the White House. President Bush then turned to me with a big smile, gave me a bear hug, and while rocking me back and forth in a paternal embrace for a couple of seconds, planted a playful kiss on my cheek and my forehead. As the moment unfolded, I remember thinking to myself, *Where is a good photographer when you need one?*

> President Bush then turned to me with a big smile, gave me a bear hug, and while rocking me back and forth in a paternal embrace for a couple of seconds, planted a playful kiss on my cheek and my forehead. As the moment unfolded, I remember thinking to myself, *Where is a good photographer when you need one?*

I always appreciated President Bush's warm, witty sense of humor. Once while speaking at a graduation ceremony, he joked to the students, "To those of you who received honors, awards, and distinctions, I say well done. And to the C students, I say you, too, can be president of the United States." He was not afraid to make fun of himself.

Each president is under intense criticism and constant scrutiny for the entire time they hold the job. President

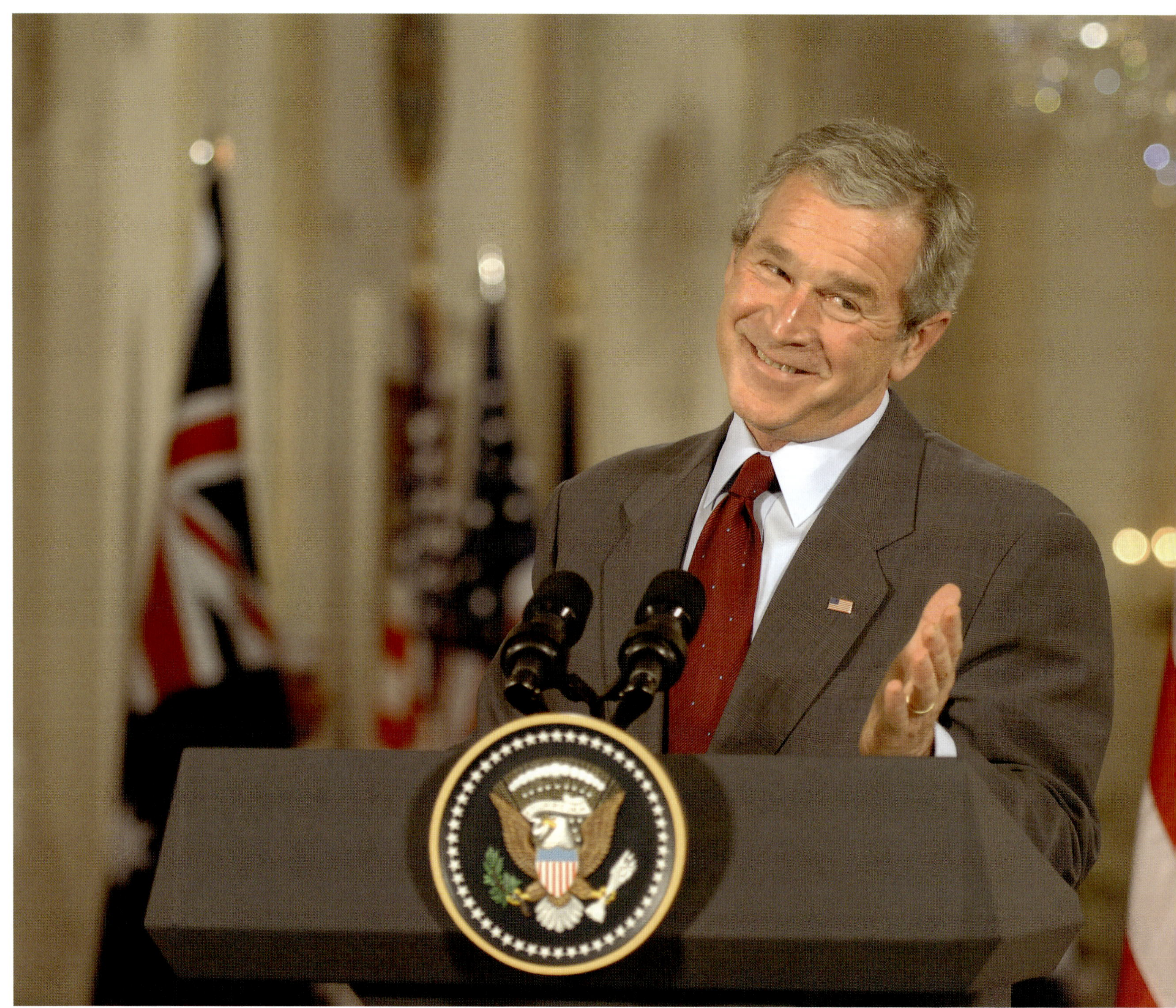

    History in the Making

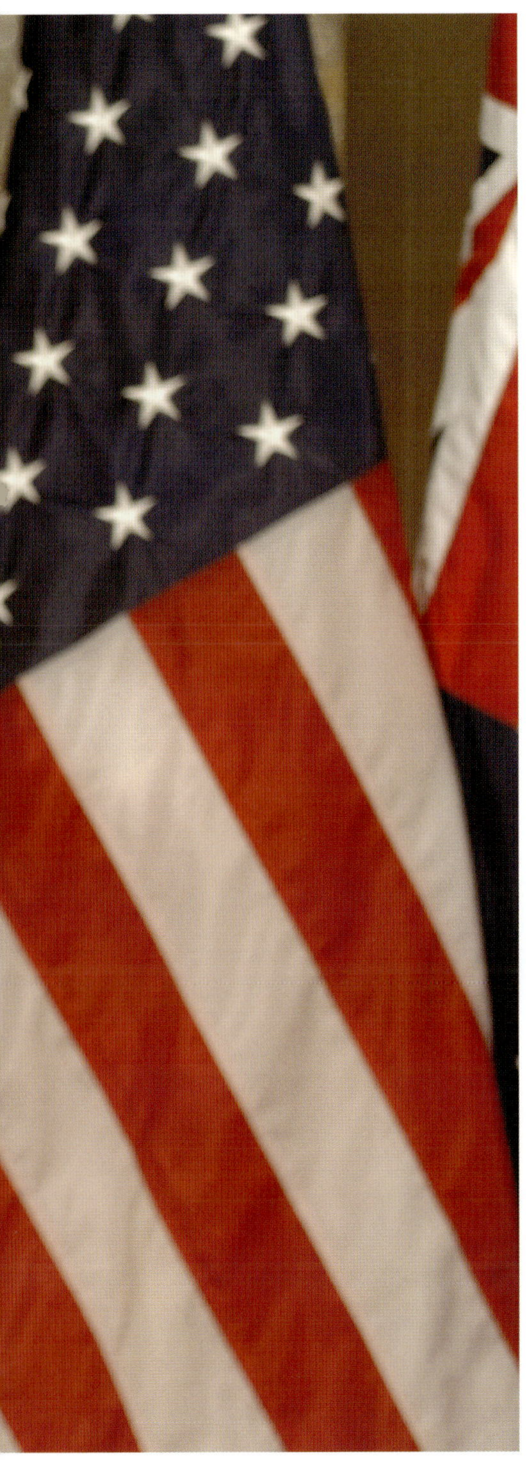

Bush's critics accused him of not being intelligent and of tripping on his words. But I want to set the record straight: of the five presidents I have covered throughout my career as a photojournalist, President George W. Bush used the teleprompter less than any of the others.

I greatly respect President Bush for refusing, for the most part, to place blame or lodge criticism against his successors. That was yet another mark, I believe, of the humanity and civility that existed in his White House.

I feel privileged to have had these special glimpses of our forty-third president inside the White House up close. It's important to remember that these presidents are *people*, with feelings, emotions, and moments of spontaneity that make them human just like anyone else. Those of us who have covered several presidents sometimes critique their character while we're waiting around for our next event. President George W. Bush's character was almost always rated among us in the press corps as being the most genuine. With him, what you saw was what you got.

President George W. Bush shares
a candid moment with the media
during a press conference in the
East Room of the White House,
July 2005.

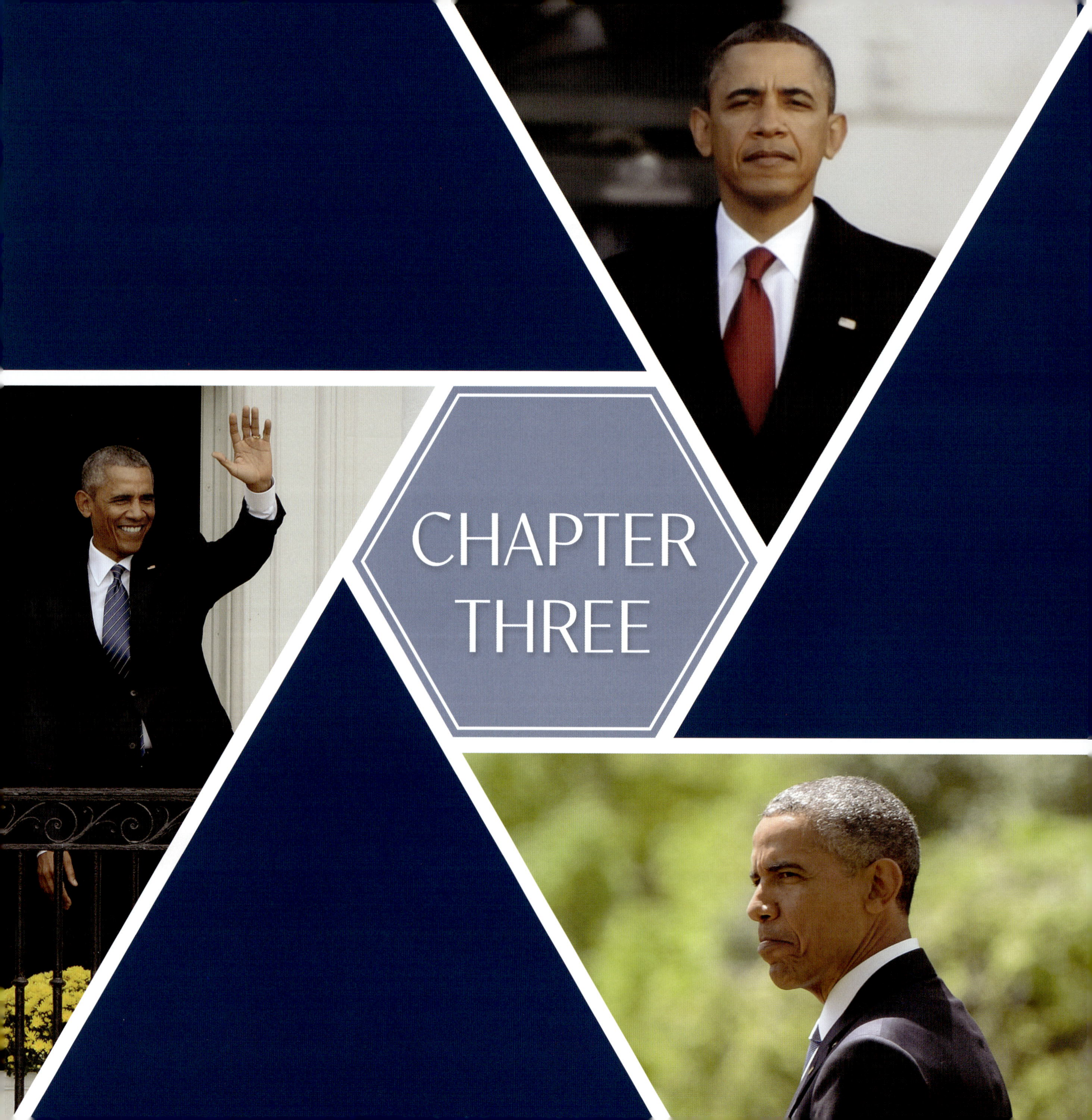
CHAPTER
THREE

Barack H. Obama

On January 3, 2005, a young, relatively unknown Barack Obama was voted into office as the freshman Democratic Senator from Illinois. Three years later, he became our nation's forty-fourth president. Of the five US presidents I have witnessed taking the oath of office, this inauguration was the most exciting and historic to date. The atmosphere was one of pride and eloquence, a declaration of the future and an acknowledgment of the past, so from my vantage point more than just history was in the air.

Once again, I applied for my special Capitol Hill credentials, which would allow me to—hopefully—be up close. Originally, I was turned down with a formal letter that my application for an inaugural press pass was denied. Credentials were being sought from around the world, so positions were limited. After several conversations with God, the late Sarah McClendon (my Patron Saint of News Emergencies), and the Senate Press Photographers' Gallery, I decided to let destiny take its course.

> After several conversations with God, the late Sarah McClendon (my Patron Saint of News Emergencies), and the Senate Press Photographers' Gallery, I decided to let destiny take its course.

But just a few days before the ceremony, I was informed that I *had* secured a position for the inauguration. I will

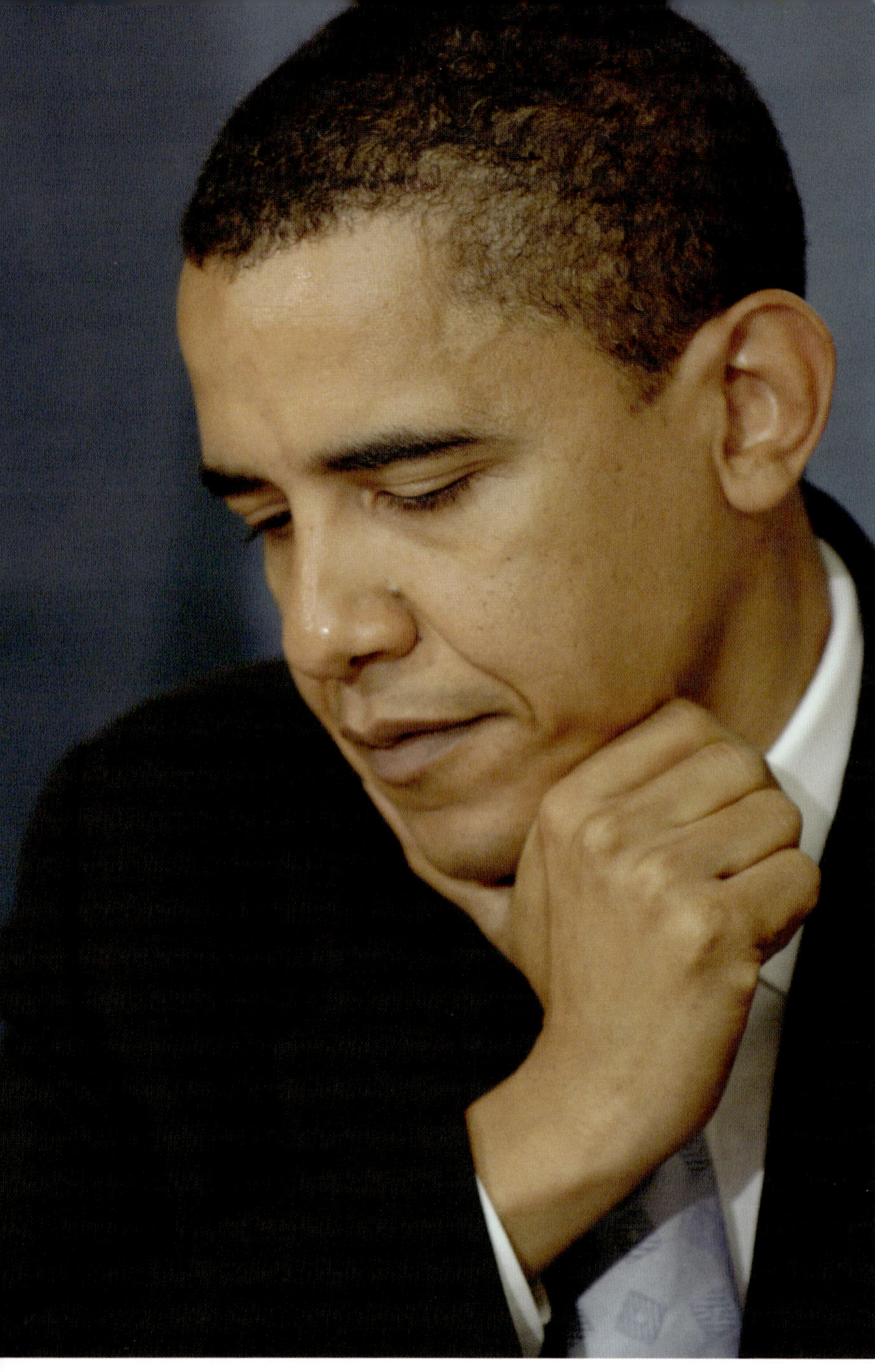

*A young Senator Barack Obama goes over his
notes while sitting on a Senate Committee in
the Hart Senate Hearing Room, April 2006.*

be forever grateful for the opportunity to capture that moment in history. When I went to pick up my coveted inaugural credentials and saw the superb position that I was assigned, I was thrilled.

As in the past, I was told that security clearance onto the Capitol grounds would be between 4:00 and 6:00 a.m. Once again the question came up: How would I get there? Taxis were not willing to go downtown because so many streets were closed around the Capitol with the increase in security. The metro trains opened at 5:00 a.m. that day, but in my neighborhood the first train to arrive was full. I made up my mind that there was *no way* that train was leaving without me. I squeezed on. Standing in the packed car, I knew, before the sun had even risen, that the day was boding well for the country and maybe even for me.

As I arrived at the Capitol, it was difficult to recognize my fellow members of the media; almost everyone was bundled up to combat the (once again) brutally cold weather. Finally, I was inside the temporary trailer that housed the metal detectors that scan each of us and our equipment, taking comfort in the warmth there for as long as I could.

After locating my spot on the press riser and introducing myself to my neighbors on the platform, we chatted about where we were from and engaged in other small talk since we had a lot of time to kill. I expressed my concern that President Obama may be blocked from our close-up view if Chief Justice John Roberts, who was performing the swearing-in, was as tall as I remembered when previously photographing him. My photographer neighbor from Chicago laughed and told me I worried too much, but my instincts told me otherwise, so I scoped out another place about ten yards down the platform. I introduced myself to a network cameraman there and asked if I could shoot over his shoulder in the event that my view was obstructed. Then, after I promised not to cause any shaking of the platform, he agreed. My plan B was in place.

As the sun came up, the landscape transformed into a backdrop with over a million inaugural attendees from all parts of the world. It was fascinating to watch. Everyone was as thrilled as I was to witness history as it unfolded before our eyes.

At last, it was time for us photographers to get into our final position for the administration of Vice President Biden's oath of office. As he was sworn in by Justice John Paul Stevens, I realized that Stevens was much shorter than Chief Justice Roberts, so I still had reason for concern. A short time later, when Roberts and Obama stood in place for the swearing-in of our new president, Obama was completely blocked—with the exception of his right ear— from where I stood.

In several seconds, this historic moment would be gone forever, with or without me. Only thirty-five words needed to be recited. Moving faster than I ever realized was possible, I gently catapulted to my plan B position, careful not to shake the riser for the sake of the TV networks.

Praying that the battery in my camera would not freeze up again as it had earlier, I opened fire with my trusty Nikon. All that could be heard besides the chief justice and the president elect's voices was the sound of camera shutters firing in unison as we captured history in our pictures.

Somewhere in the back of my mind as I photographed, I remember looking through my lens and realizing that something was wrong. Obama's expression had changed suddenly from smiling to somber. As it turned out, Chief Justice Roberts had spoken a couple of the words of the Constitutional Oath out of order, making the oath of office invalid. Obama recognized it immediately. He calmly proceeded with the oath and his inaugural address to avoid embarrassing Justice Roberts (at least, that was my impression).

Moving back to my assigned position, I found that my fellow photographer from Chicago was inconsolable. "I was completely blocked! I have nothing!" My heart went out to him. It is always a disappointment for any of us when we walk away from a big photographic moment without getting what we came for. This experience proved to me, once again, that it is always a good idea to have a backup plan; just as I had learned in my skydiving training, you

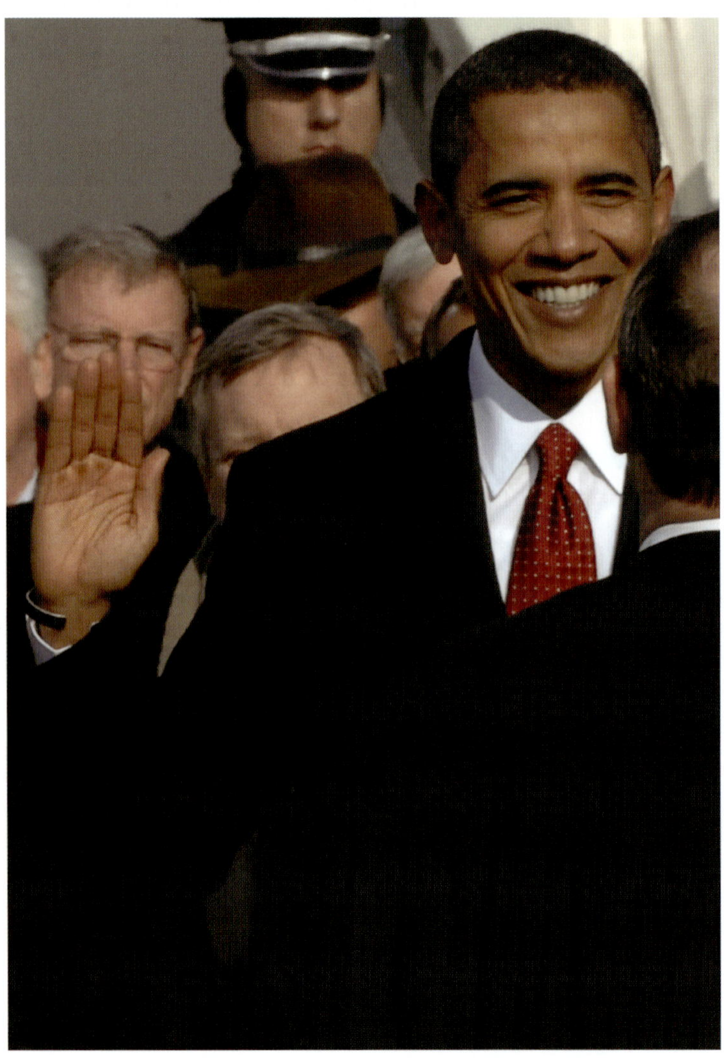

President Barack Obama smiles as he swears in as the forty-forth president of the United States, January 2009.

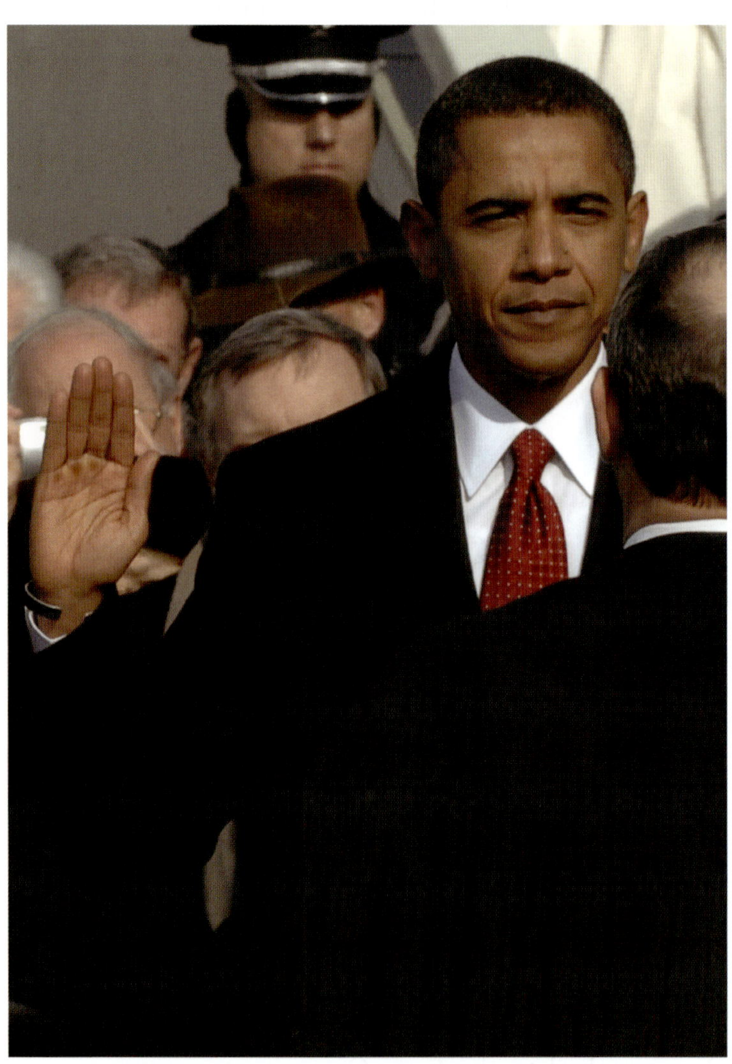

President Barack Obama gets serious as he hears a mistake being made during his swearing in as the forty-forth president of the United States.

never know when you may need to use that emergency ripcord, and you just don't get a second chance.

The next day, President Barack Obama was administered the oath of office a second time by Chief Justice Roberts in the Oval Office. Pete Souza, the president's chief official photographer, was the only one allowed to photograph the moment. Obama was now officially president and was now known as code name "Renegade" by the Secret Service.

Shortly after the inauguration, we members of the press corps eagerly waited to see what changes this new administration would bring. Sadly, one of the very first changes was that presidential access became more limited. Two waves of photographers in the Oval Office were reduced to one by order of the president himself, and a policy of responding to events via RSVP became the new normal. Both of those changes continue to this day.

Eight months later, I received a breaking news bulletin that newly elected President Barack Obama had just won the Nobel Peace Prize "for his extraordinary efforts to strengthen international diplomacy and cooperation between peoples."[1] Members of the White House Press Corps rushed to the Rose Garden to scramble for the best positions. After a long delay, President Obama emerged from the Oval Office with what I considered to be a "Who, me?" kind of demeanor. He humbly stated, "To be honest, I do not feel that I deserve to be in the company of so many of the transformative figures who have been honored by this prize, men and women who've inspired me and inspired the entire world through their courageous pursuit of peace."[2]

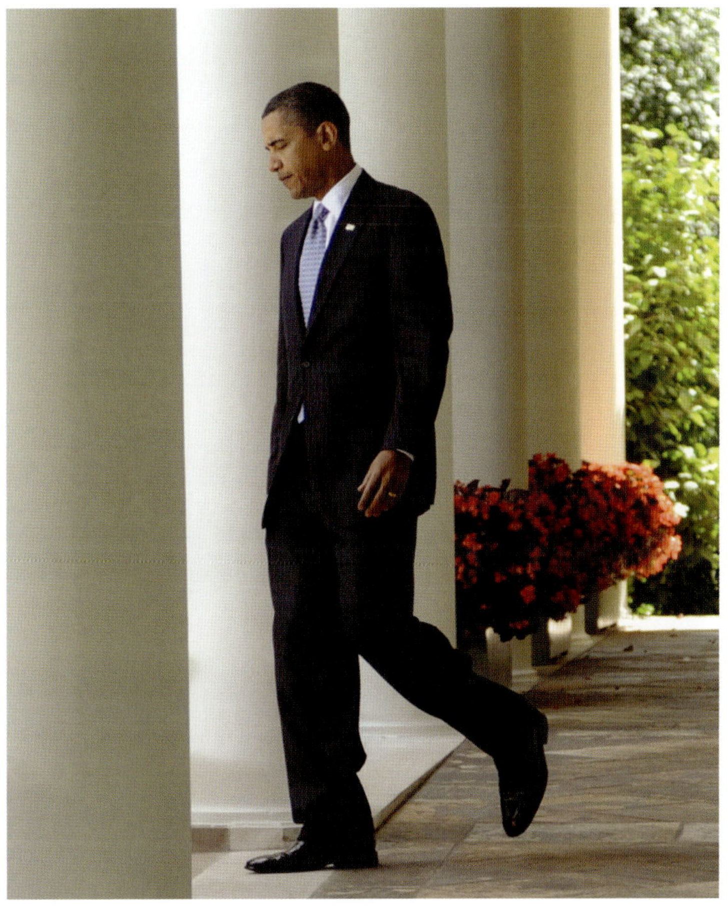

President Barack Obama walks out of the Oval Office to speak to the awaiting press corps after learning he had just won the Nobel Peace Prize, September 2009.

President Obama became the third sitting president ever to receive the prestigious award, allowing him to join the distinguished company of Mikhail Gorbachev and Nelson Mandela. Obama donated the $1.4 million prize money and split the winnings between the Clinton-Bush Haiti Fund (set up by former Presidents Bill Clinton and George W. Bush at Obama's request to help survivors of Haiti's 2010 earthquake) wounded veterans, and educational efforts for minorities.[3]

Even with the diminished access that the press corps felt, there was also a feeling of change that Barack Obama brought into the White House as he began the first part of his presidency in a flurry of excitement. As the months stretched into years, he achieved several of his goals, including signing the health care bill, which would later become known as "Obamacare," as well as settling the score with Osama bin Laden.

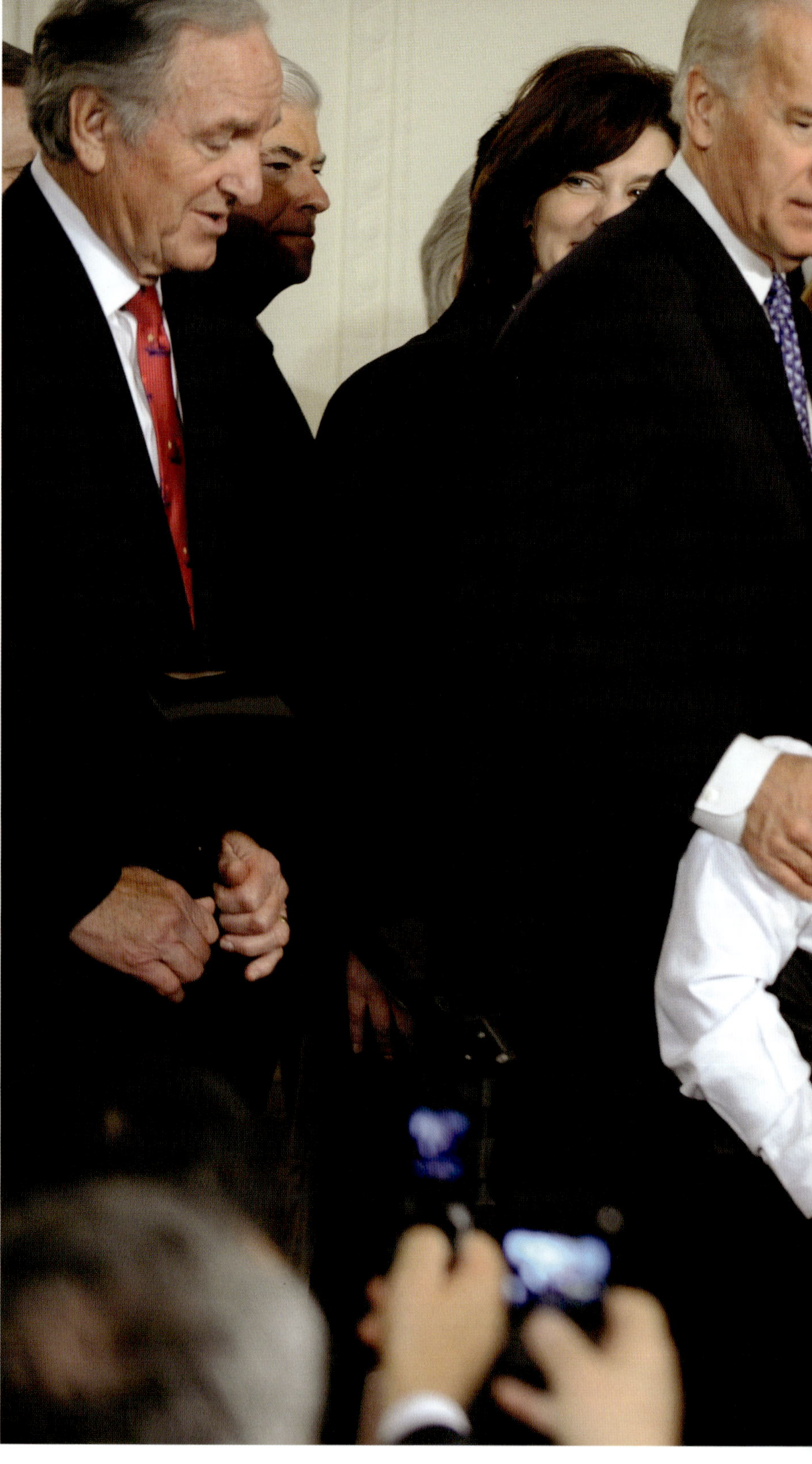

President Barack Obama signs the historic health insurance reform bill known as Obamacare in the East Room of the White House, March 2010.

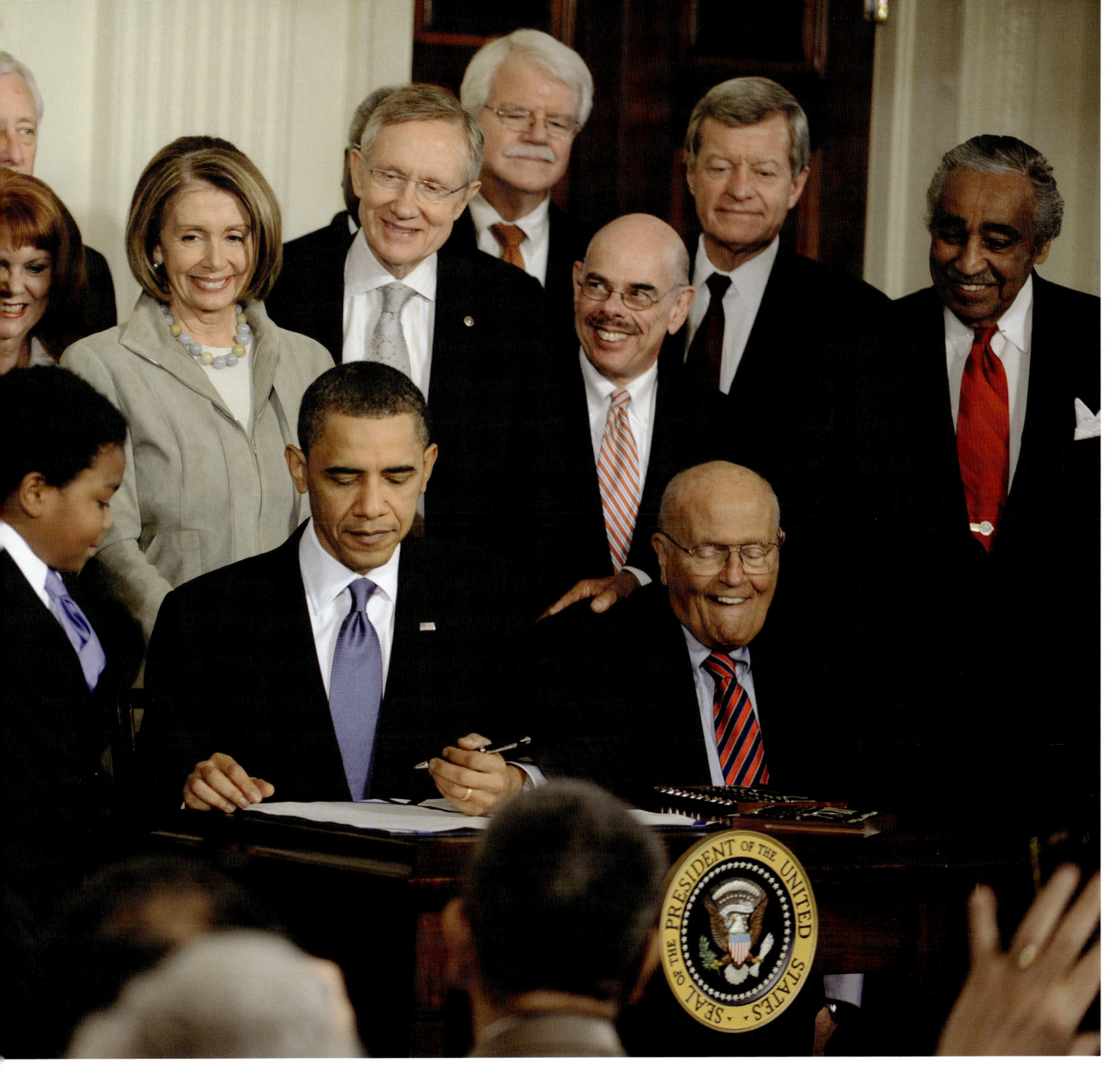

Four years later, President Obama was reelected. This time around, as I stood on the north media riser, I looked across the huge crowd. Fond memories of my former spectacular location hit me as I took in my current position: a view of the president's back for his swearing-in. As disappointed as I was, I could not do a thing about it. Panning across the VIP section, I realized I could turn this position into an opportunity. I had a great view of all the Supreme Court justices, a photographic opportunity I had sought for years.

Following the swearing-in, President Obama turned to kiss the first lady, and as his daughters, Malia and Sasha, looked on, I realized I was in just the right spot to capture that moment. In each presidential swearing-in ceremony since Obama's first in 2005, I have noticed that Justice Roberts has the oath of office written down and does not go from memory: a lesson learned four years before. After all, we are all human and make mistakes, but I am sure he will not want to take a chance like that again.

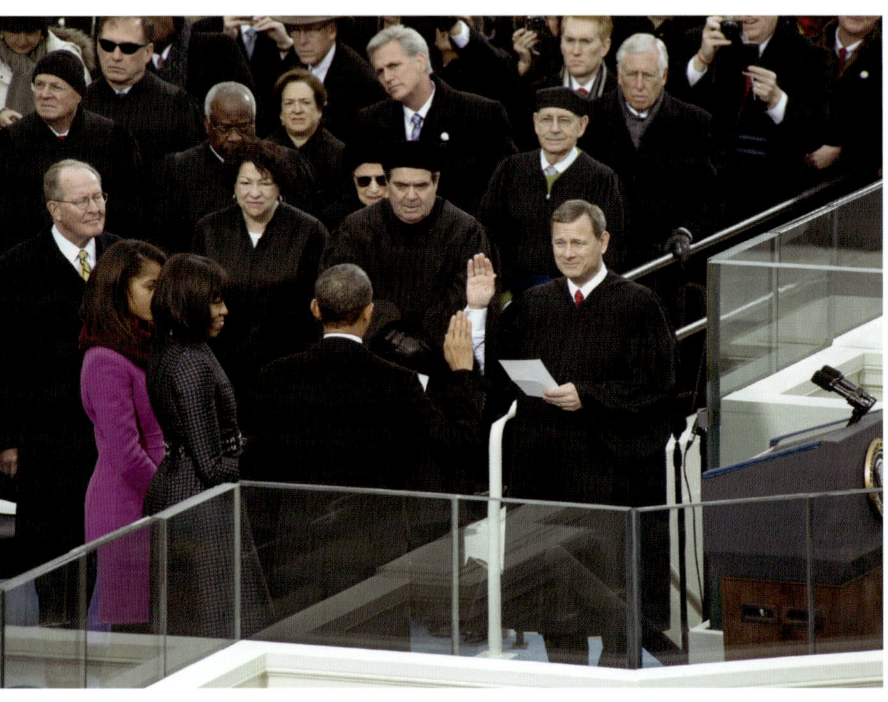

President Barack Obama is sworn in by
Chief Justice John Roberts for his second term as
president of the United States, January 2013.

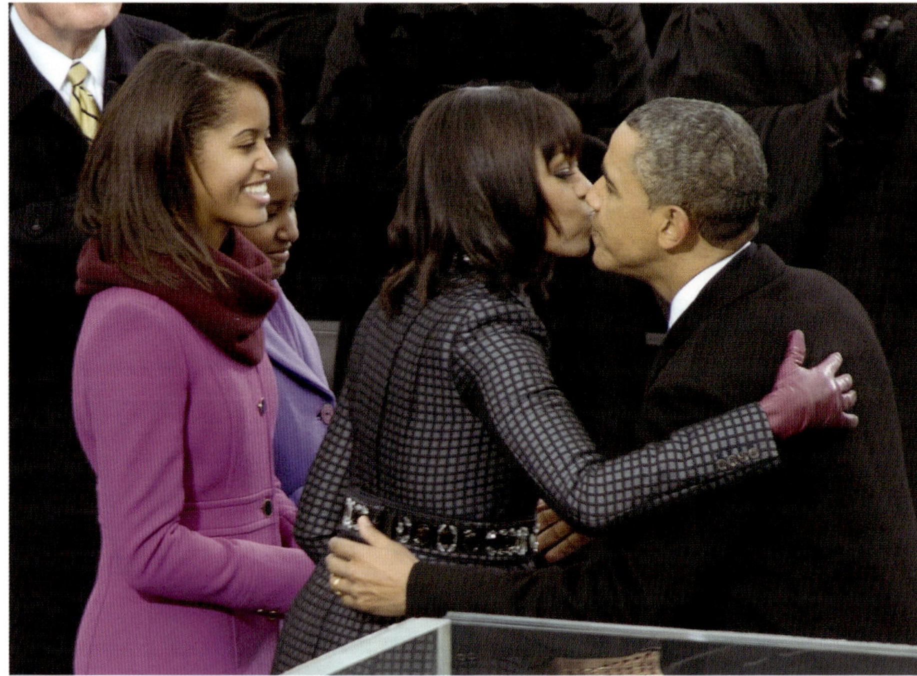

President Obama kisses First Lady
Michelle Obama following his second
swearing-in ceremony.

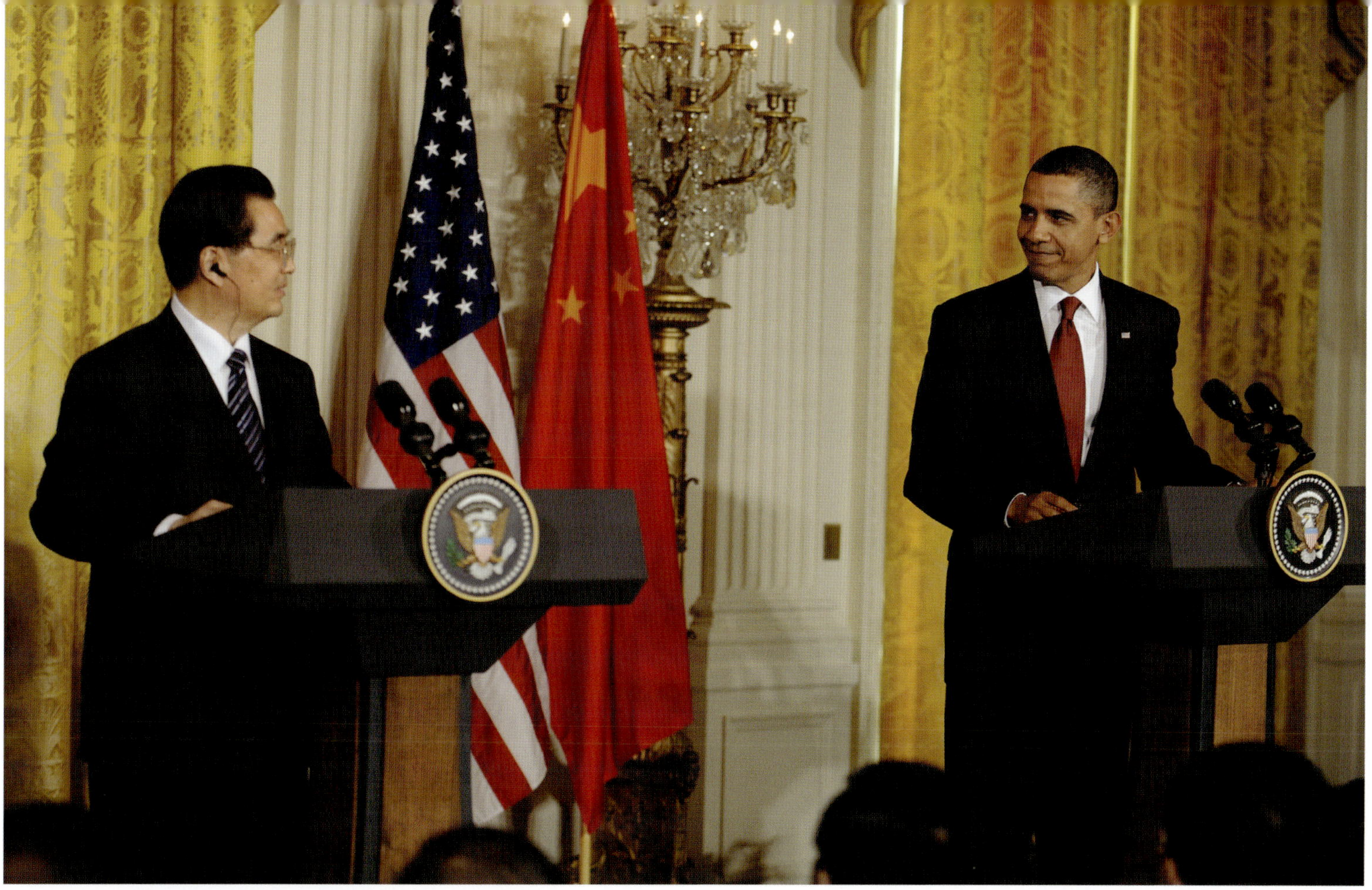

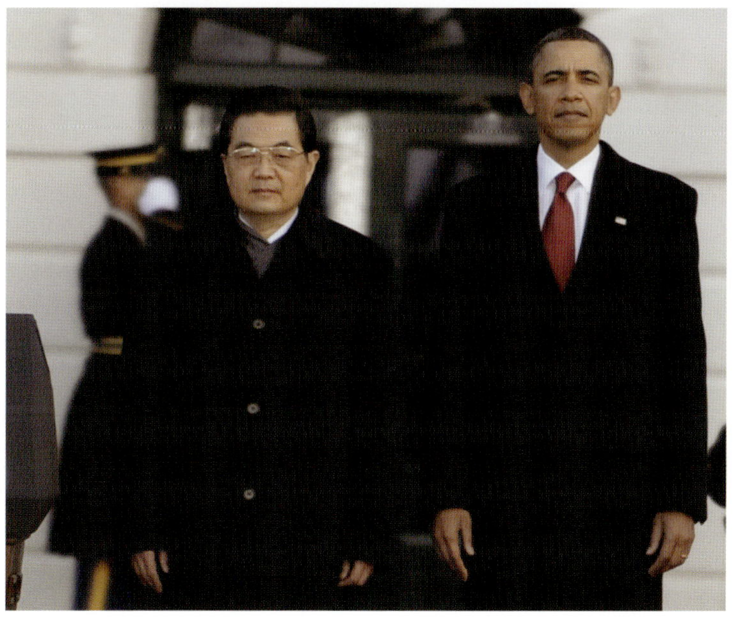

President Obama hosted two state arrival ceremonies for the People's Republic of China, first for President Hu Jintao in 2011, followed by President Xi Jinping in 2015. Obama would go on to host many world leaders during his time in office.

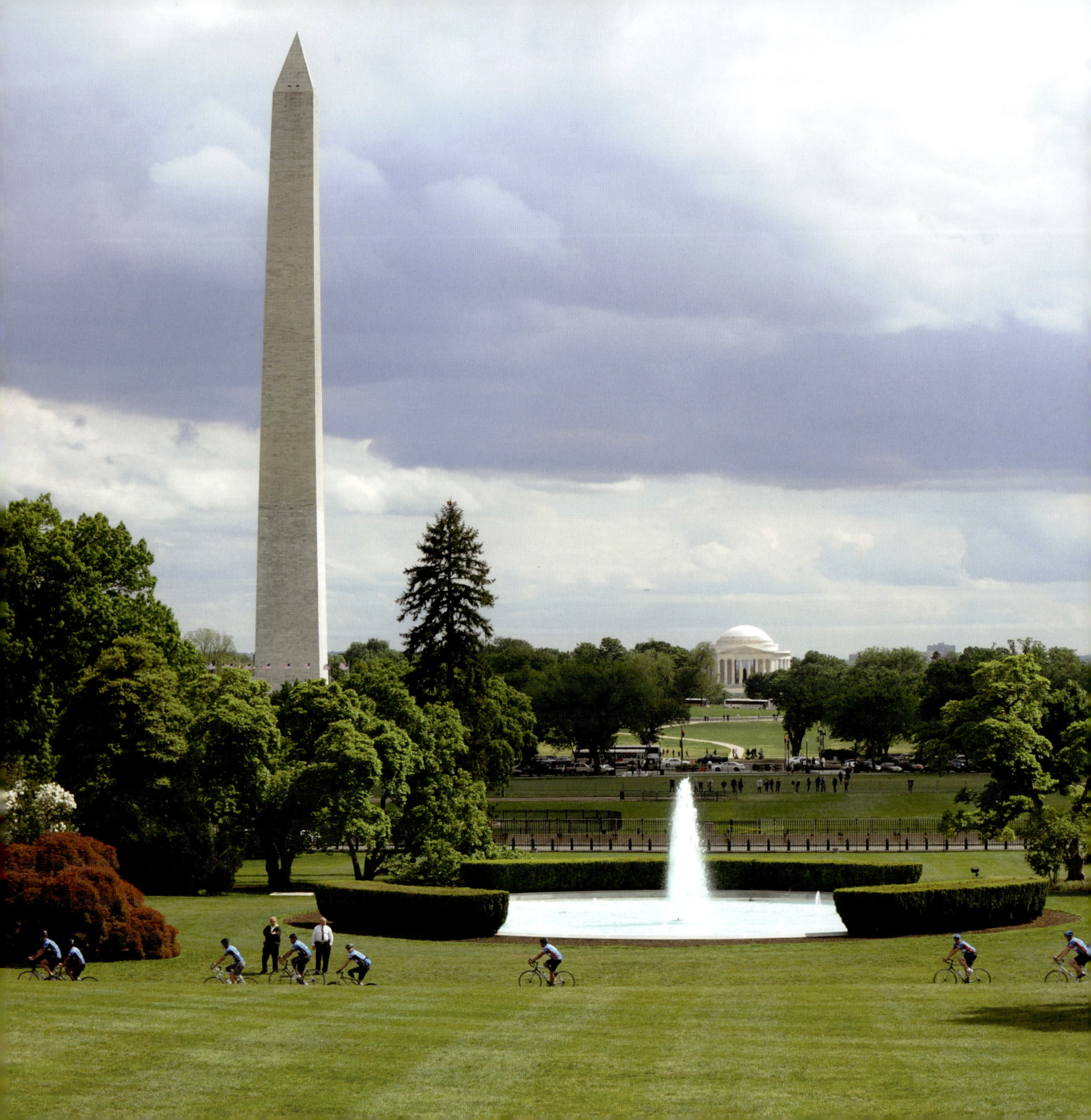

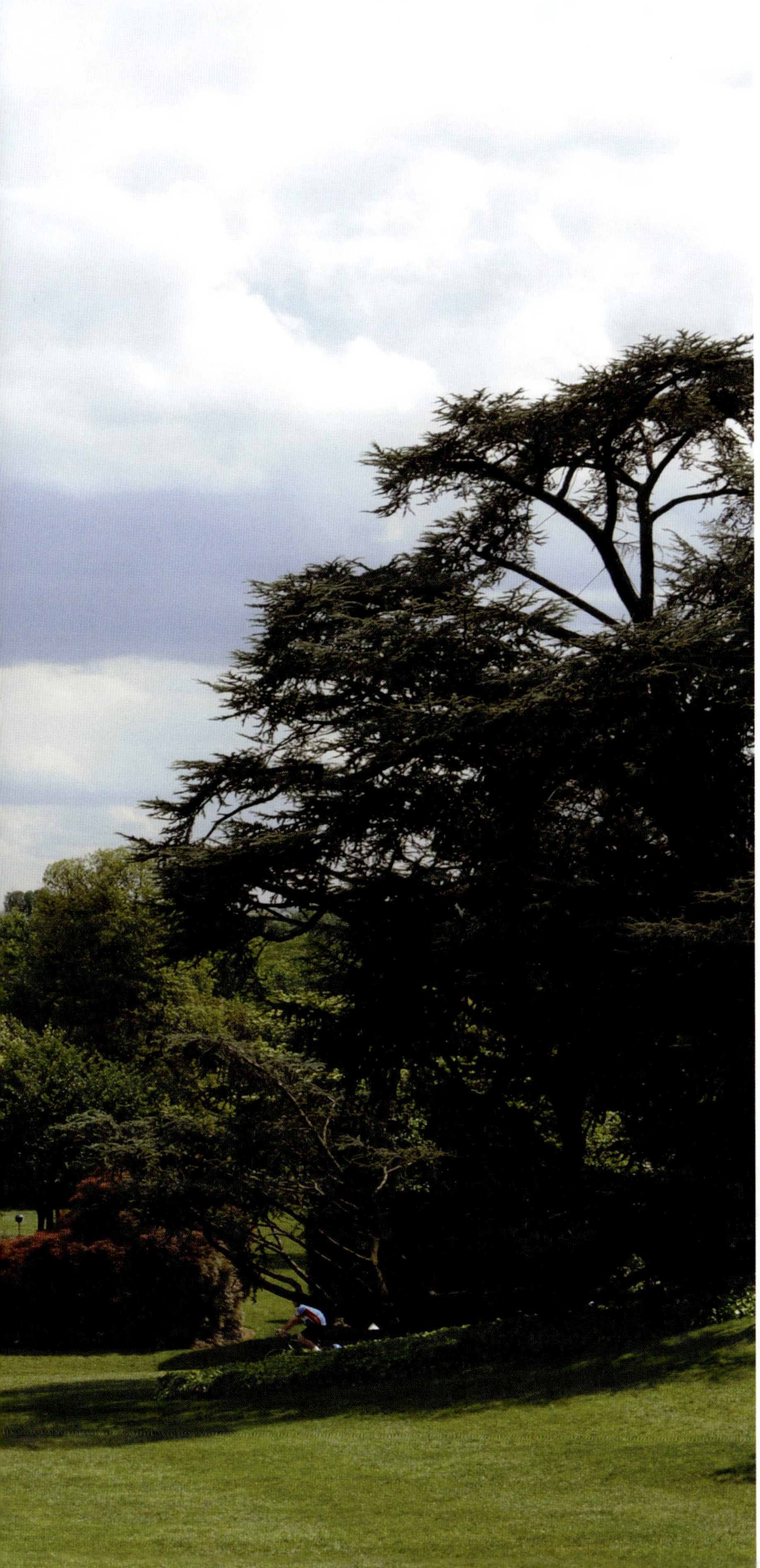

Sometimes the press corps would have days when we needed to pivot our attention as the president hosted diverse back-to-back events at the White House. For instance, on May 4, 2011, President Obama went from greeting a group of bikers to meeting with a member of royalty within a couple of hours.

That morning, President Obama welcomed the Wounded Warriors to the White House. These veterans, who were mostly amputees, rode their bicycles from the White House all the way to Annapolis, Maryland, as part of the Wounded Warrior Project Soldier Ride. The Soldier Ride is a nationally recognized cycling program which, as the program proudly attests, helps build "confidence and strength through shared physical challenges and bonds of service in a supportive environment."[4] President Obama officiated the start of their journey. I was moved as I watched the warriors ride across the South Lawn.

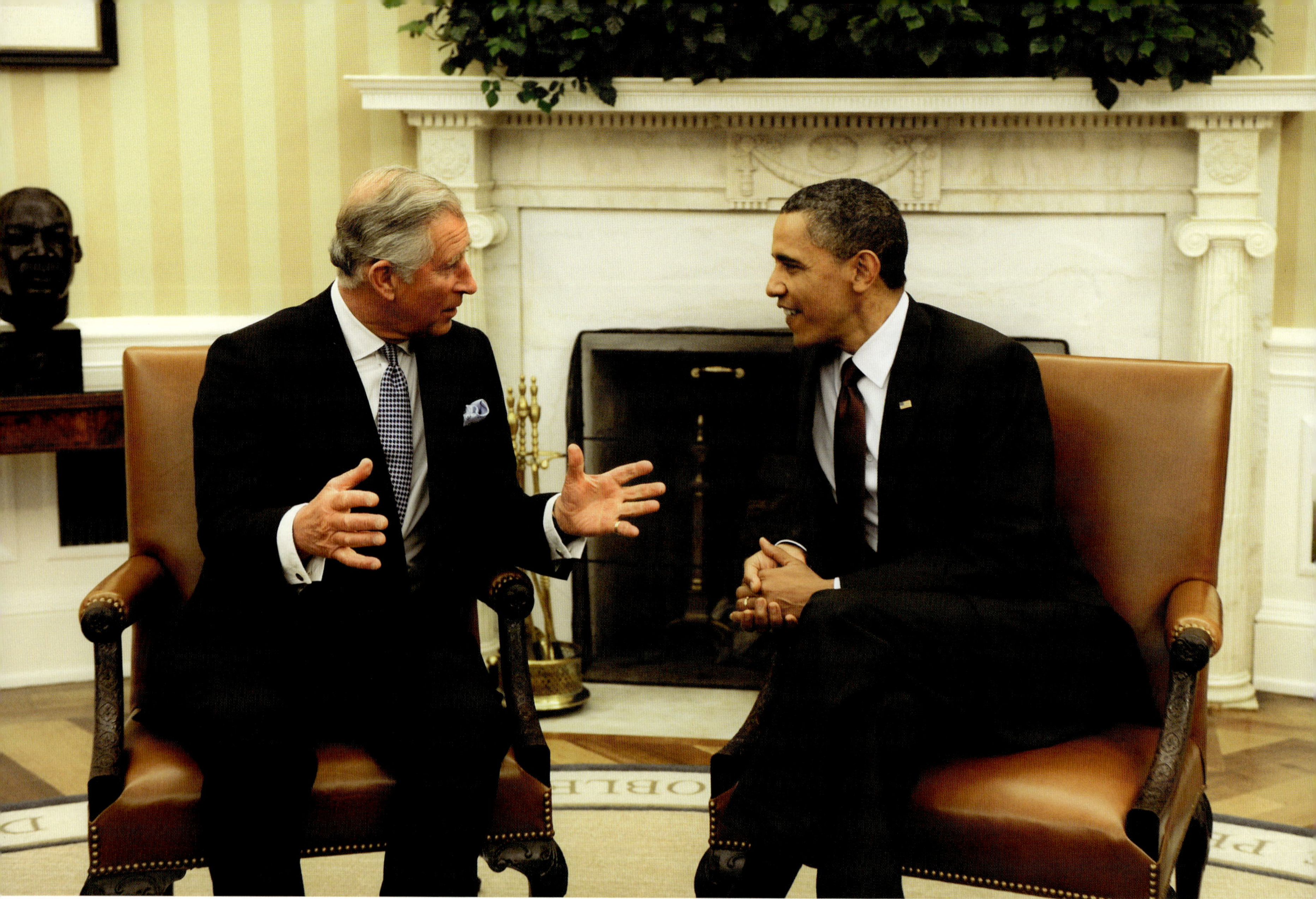

President Obama welcomes Prince Charles to the
Oval Office to discuss various topics, May 2011.

Shortly after the bikers' departure, the press corps hustled into the Oval Office for a photo op with Prince Charles, now King Charles of England. The president and prince chatted amicably as we photographers who were in the expanded pool that day swooped in for a brief photo op at the beginning of the meeting.

Aside from the everyday business in the Obama White House, I saw some touching moments as well,

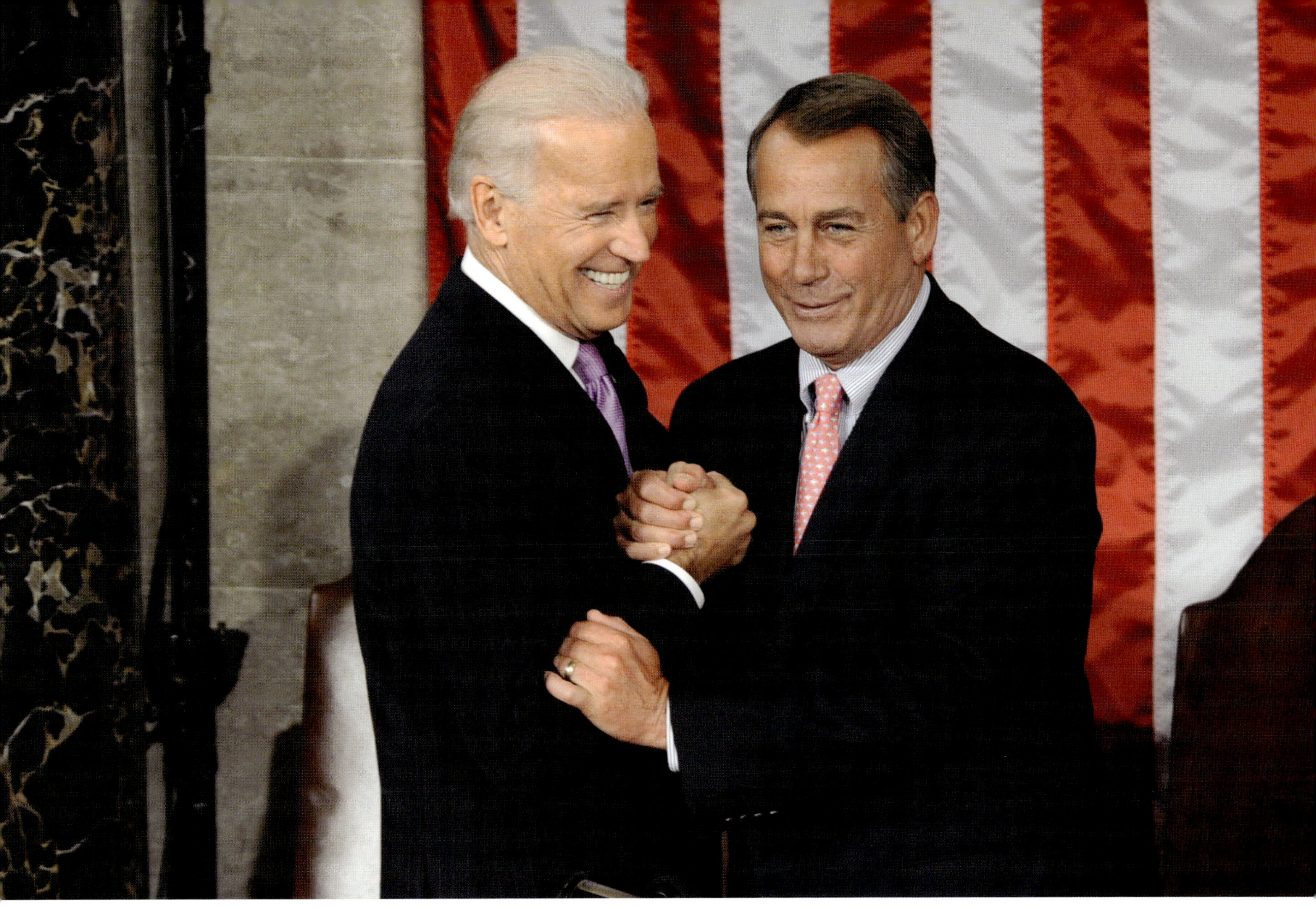

*Vice President Joe Biden and Speaker of the House John Boehner share a moment
prior to the State of the Union Address in the US Capitol, February 2013.*

like witnessing Vice President Biden and Speaker of the House John Boehner cross the aisles of their own parties for a candid moment while waiting for President Obama to arrive at the US Capitol for the State of the Union address. I always enjoy capturing the candid moments that often unfold while waiting for the big event to begin.

I also always enjoyed covering the Presidential Medal of Freedom Ceremonies. The ceremony was created by President John F. Kennedy as the highest honor a sitting president could bestow to a civilian for their contribution to making America a better place.

Although I have photographed dozens of these ceremonies, it is always so amazing to see those at the top of their field receive this honor. Twenty-five or more honorees each year come from all walks of life: Supreme Court justices, writers, inventors, musicians, sports legends, business tycoons, actors, entertainers, and more. A few of my favorites during the Obama era were Diana Ross,

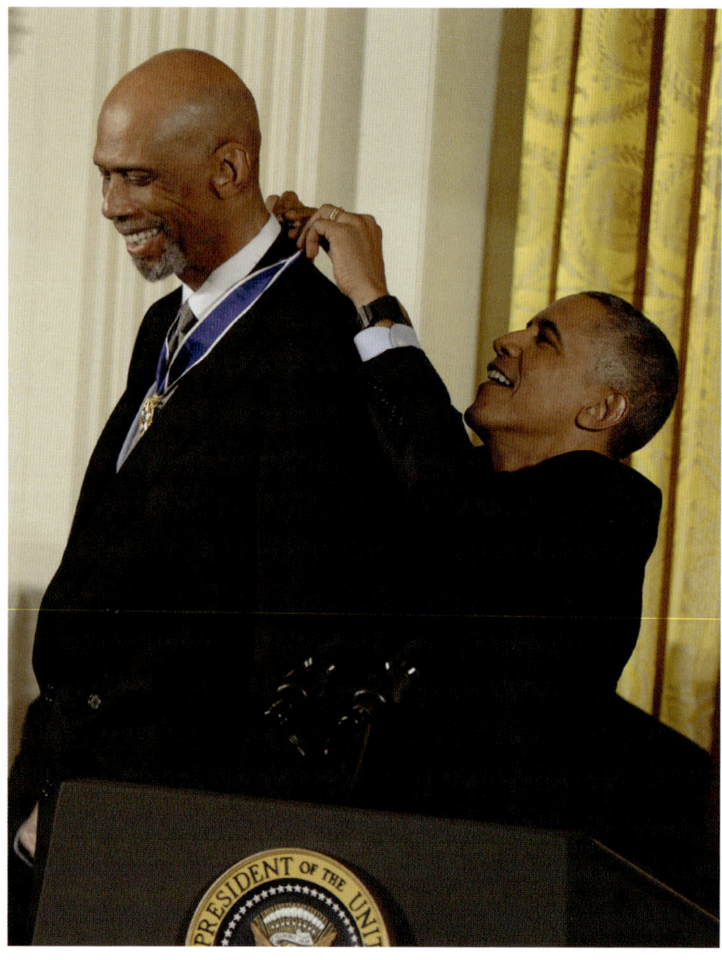

President Barack Obama awards the Presidential Medal of Freedom to Kareem Abdul-Jabbar in a ceremony in the East Room, November 2016.

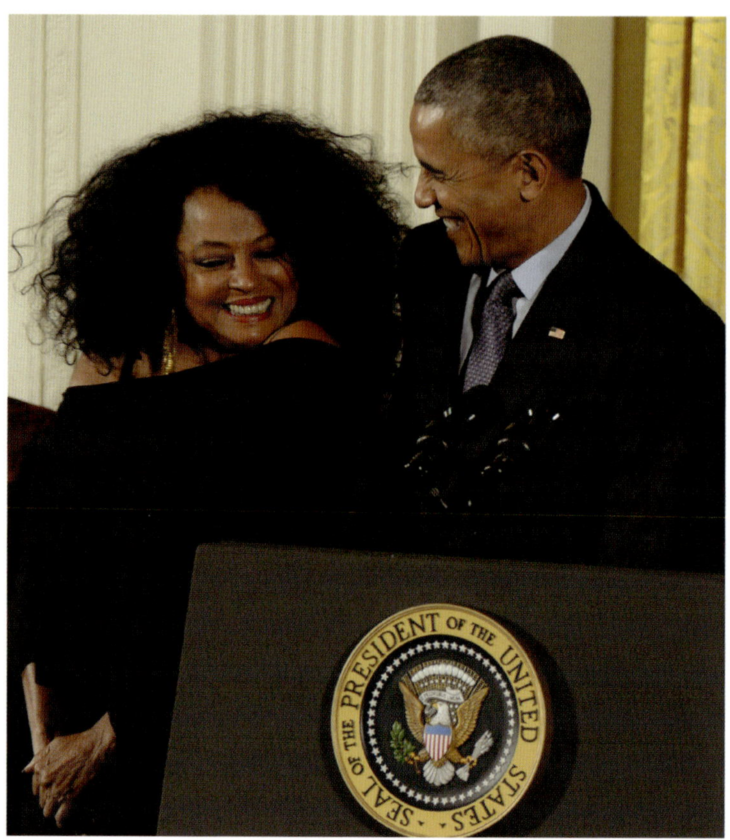

President Barack Obama and singer Diana Ross admire each other as the president awards Ross the Presidential Medal of Freedom in a ceremony in the East Room, November 2016.

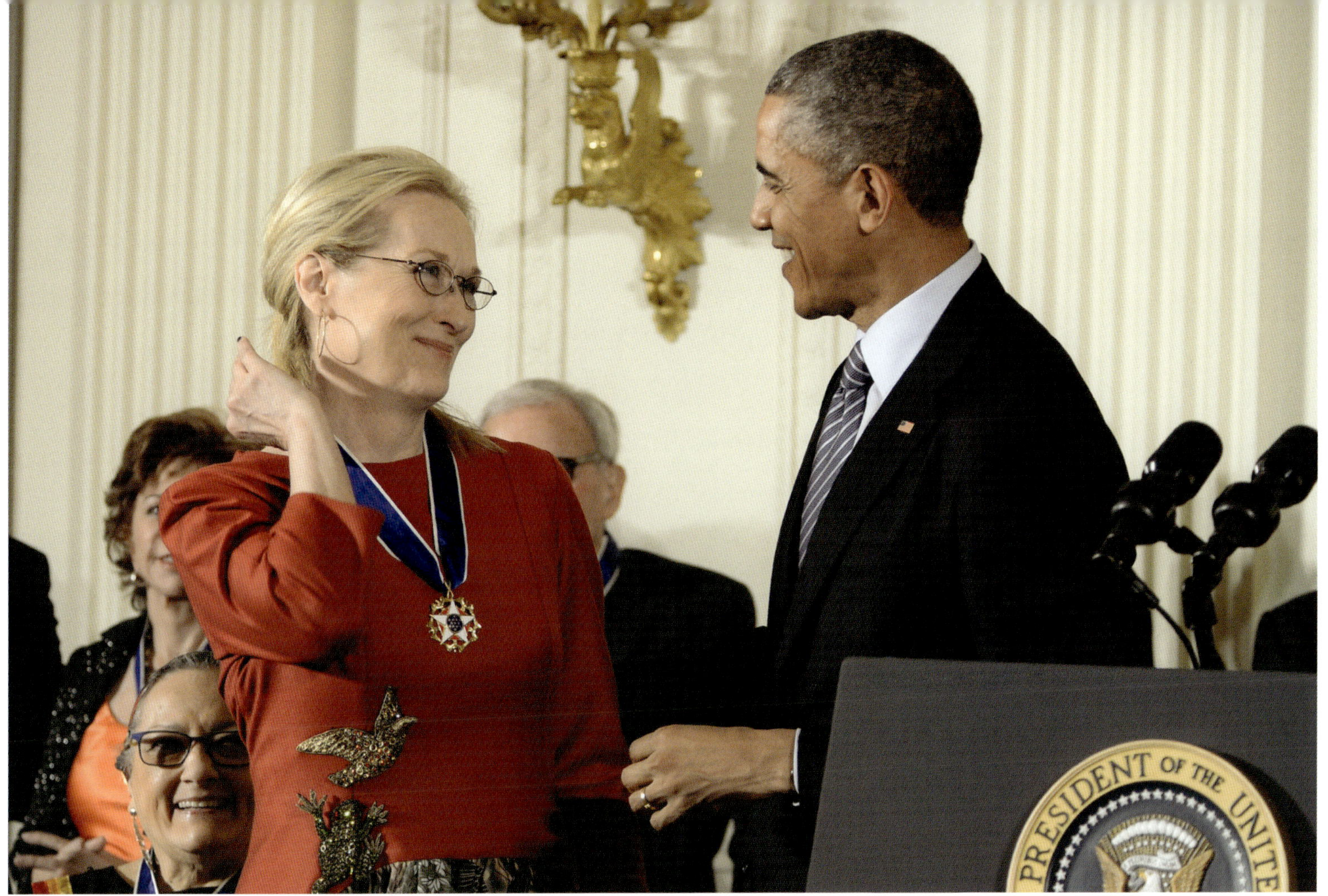

Compliments abound as President Barack Obama presents the 2015 Presidential Medal of Freedom to Meryl Streep in a ceremony in the East Room, November 2014.

Kareem Abdul-Jabar, and Meryl Streep. Diana Ross and President Obama seemed infatuated with each other, and I could feel how much they admired each other's accomplishments. When actress Meryl Streep received the honor in 2014, President Obama confessed aloud that he'd always had a crush on her, and that there was nothing he could do about it. He even said the first lady was aware of his crush. Michelle, sitting in the front row, nodded and laughed. And in 2016, President Obama got no help from awardee Kareem Abdul-Jabar as he jokingly remained standing at his full height (one foot taller than Obama), the president struggling to reach his neck. President Obama honored many other talented people from all walks of life, including Presidents George H. W. Bush Sr. and Bill Clinton, who were each awarded the Presidential Medal of Freedom.

President Obama also made an effort to honor historical figures of science. In 2009 he invited the famous Apollo 11 Space Mission crew to the Oval Office. He seemed thrilled to be meeting the first astronauts to have walked on the moon.

In contrast, there are some emotionally difficult times for all of us at the White House. On the day President Obama delivered a speech on gun control, he invited the family members of shooting victims to the White House, including some parents of the children killed in the Sandy Hook massacre. The grief was so palpable in the room that day that even some of the media were emotional.

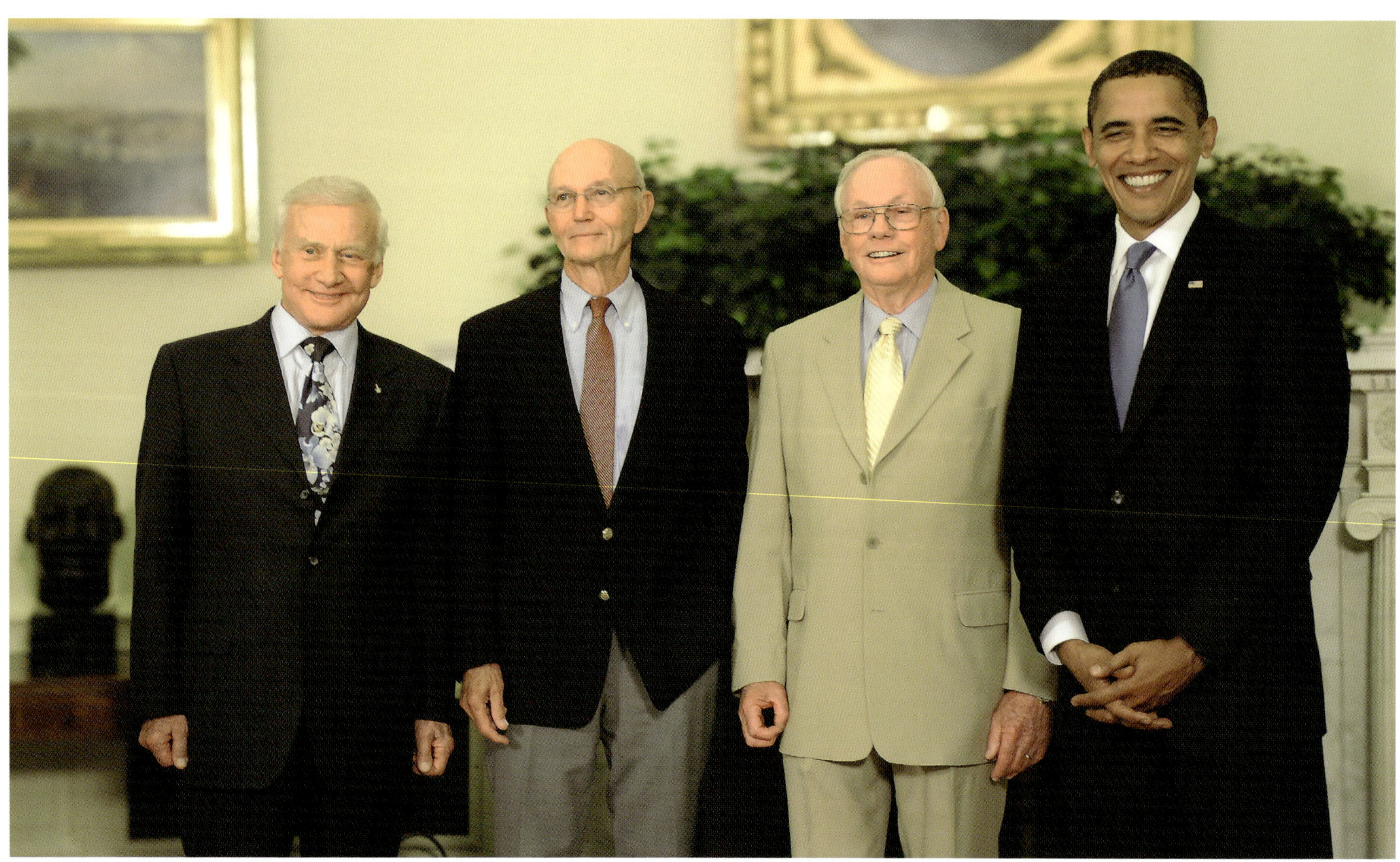

President Obama meets with Apollo 11 astronauts to commemorate them at the arrival of their mission's fortieth anniversary. **Left to right:** *Edwin "Buzz" Aldrin, Michael Collins, and Neil Armstrong. The Oval Office, July 2009.*

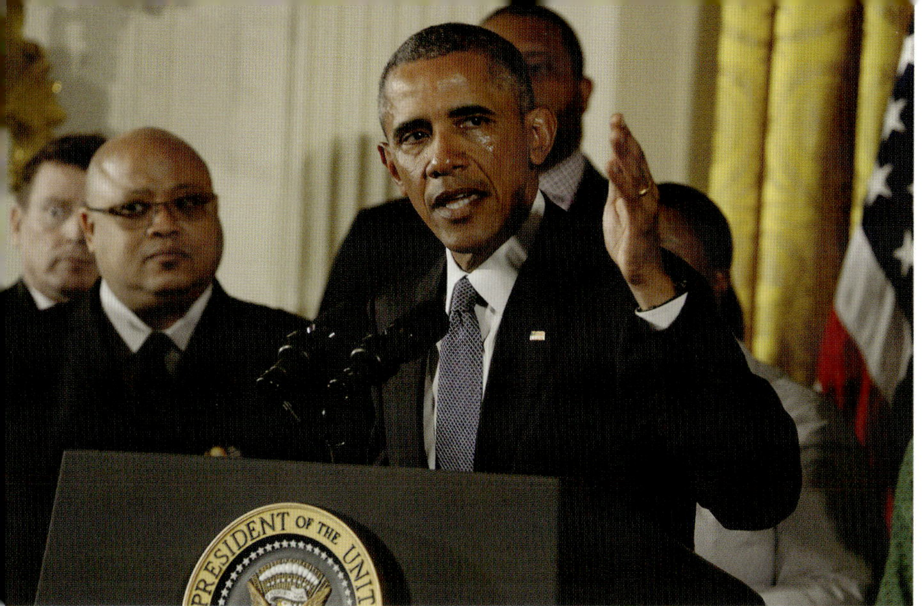

President Obama becomes emotional as he speaks to the families of the children killed at Sandy Hook Elementary School, January 2016.

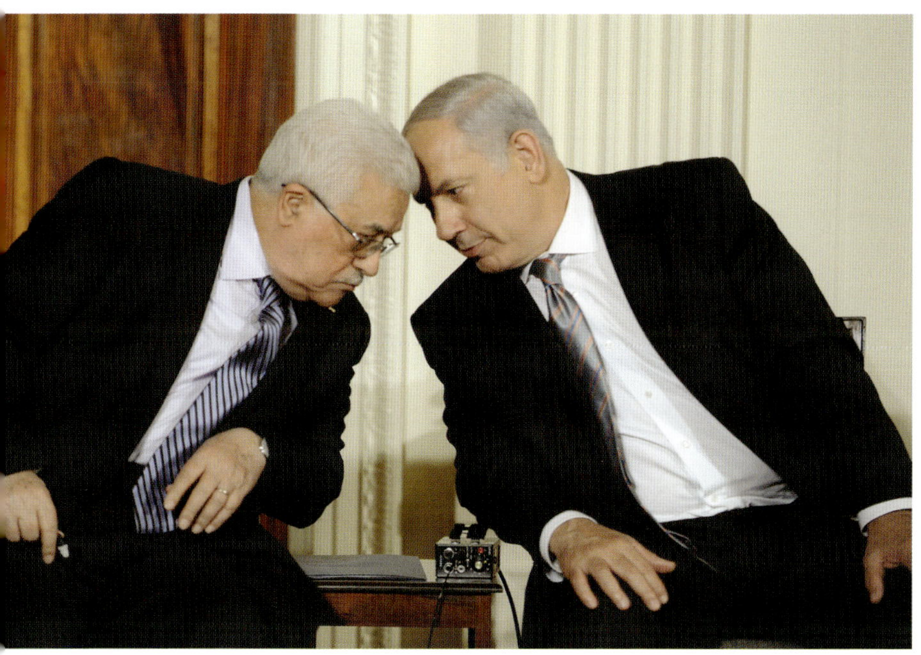

President Mahmoud Abbas of the Palestinian Authority and Prime Minister Benjamin Netanyahu of Israel share a moment before each gives a speech at the White House, September 2010.

President Obama made an effort to foster peaceful relationships among Middle East leaders. He hosted a summit that was attended by President Mahmoud Abbas of Palestine and Prime Minister Benjamin Netanyahu of Israel, among others. I was fortunate to have an up-close view of these two conflicted leaders sharing a friendly moment. Sadly, this friendly moment between the two countries did not last; as of this writing, Hamas and Israel are at war.

First Lady Michelle Obama played an important role in the Obama White House as well. She initiated a great program called "Let's Move!" that educated children on healthy eating and exercise. She even started a garden at the White House, inviting grade-school children to participate in both planting and harvesting the vegetables, and then showing the kids how to prepare dishes with that same food.

First Lady Obama also engaged with high-school students. She brought icons in the fields of fashion, music, and poetry to the White House to talk with aspiring students in those fields. The accomplished guests shared their struggles and how they forged ahead to achieve their success.

The Obamas, to me, were a loving, tight-knit family—dogs and all. Grandmother Marion lived upstairs and helped with the kids, and the entire family had dinner together regularly. It was interesting to see how, after all those years in office, the family still enjoyed spontaneous moments together, even with their Secret Service protective detail and the crowds of people continually surrounding them. For instance, elder daughter Malia shared a tender moment with her mom at the 2014 Easter Egg Roll; meanwhile, her presidential dad greeted and mingled with his young, exuberant constituents.

First Lady Michelle Obama works with children in the White House Garden harvesting its vegetables, October 2011.

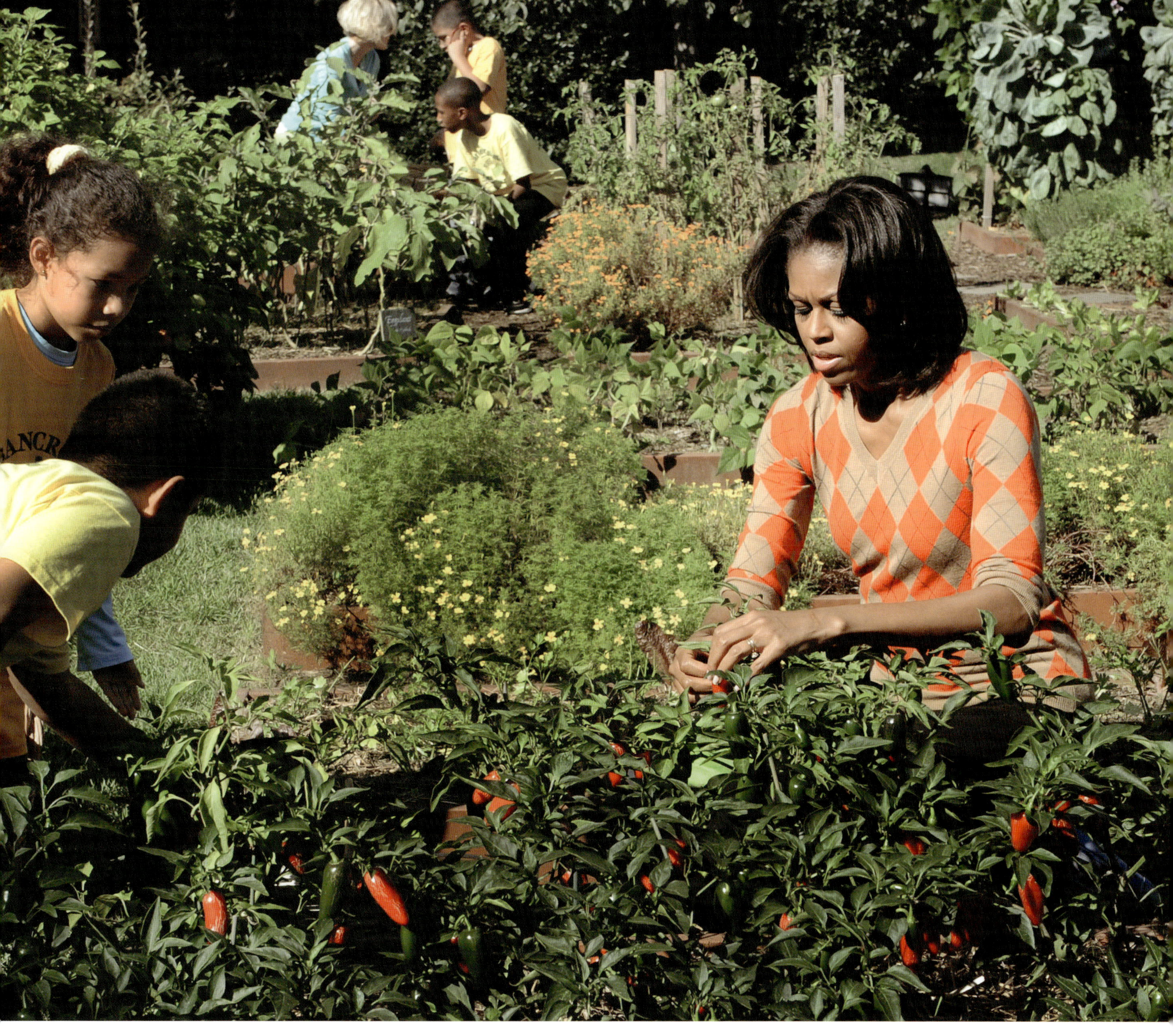

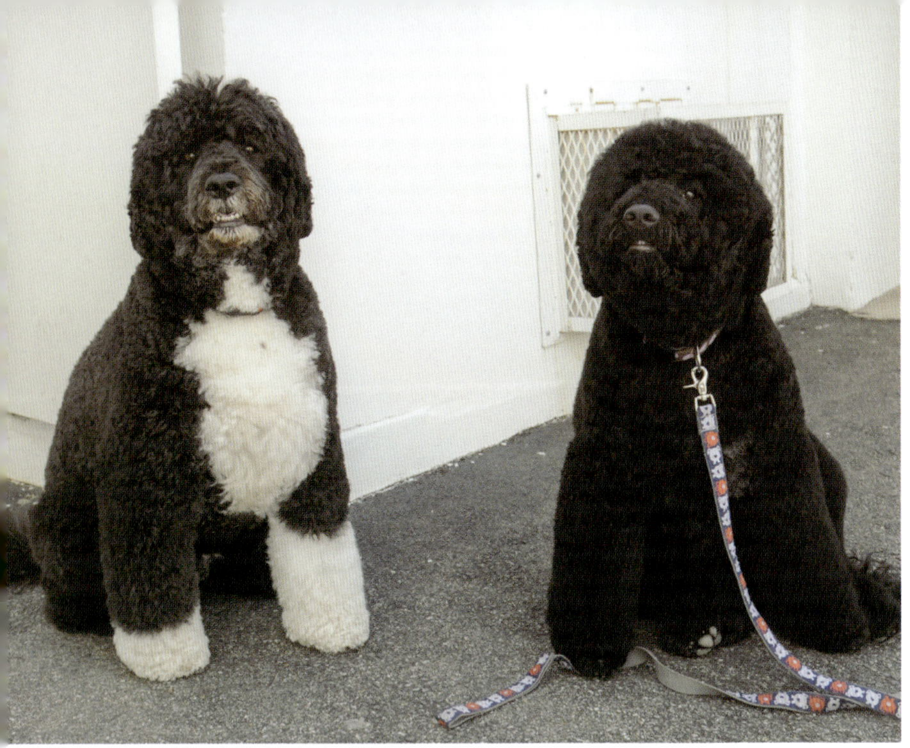

*The Obama White House's first dogs—Bo, known
as BoBama (left), and Sunny—take a break outside
the Secret Service guard shack after their walk.
Photo taken April 2014.*

*First Lady Michelle Obama talks
with children on the South Lawn
as she introduces the Obama
family dog, Bo. May 2011.*

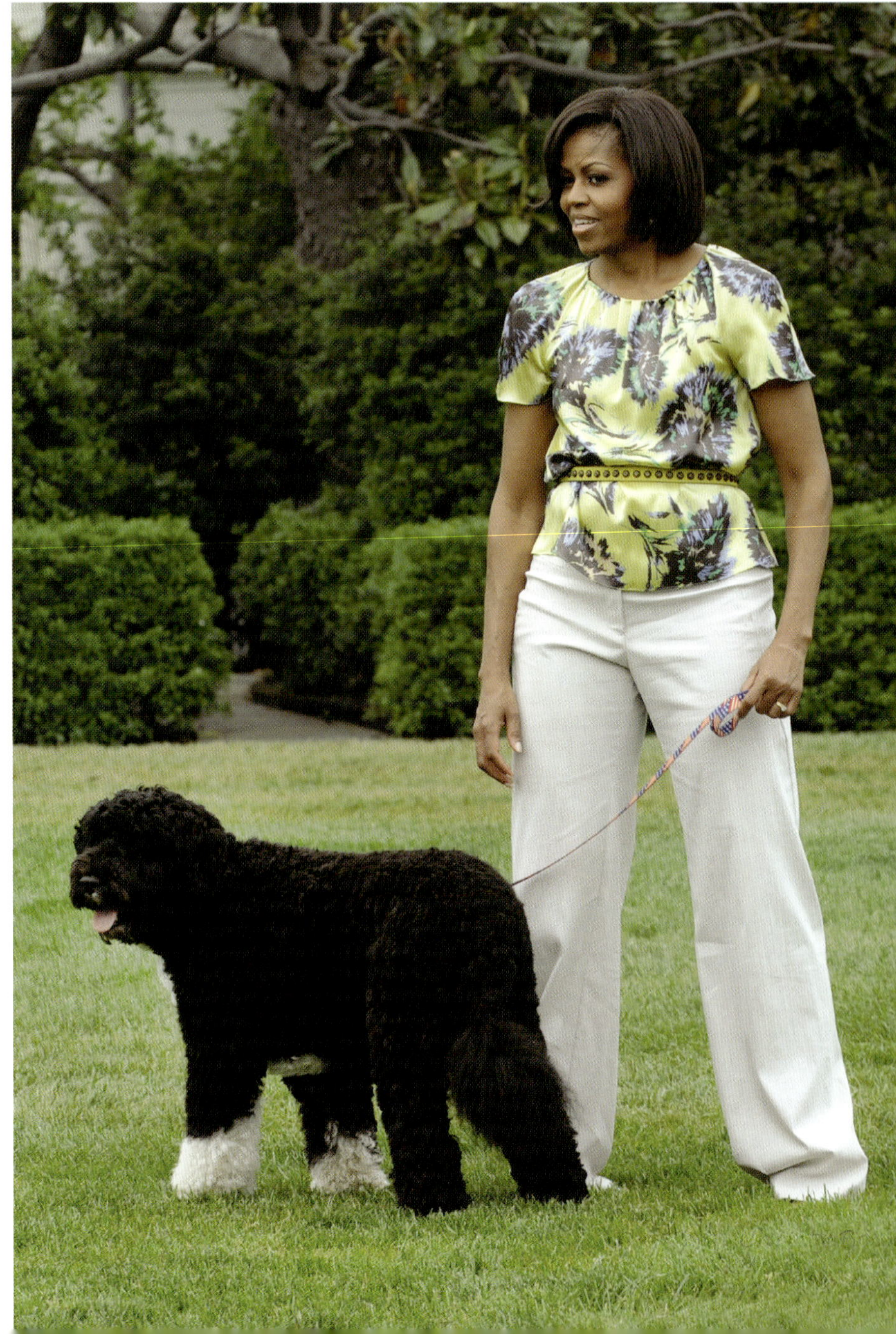

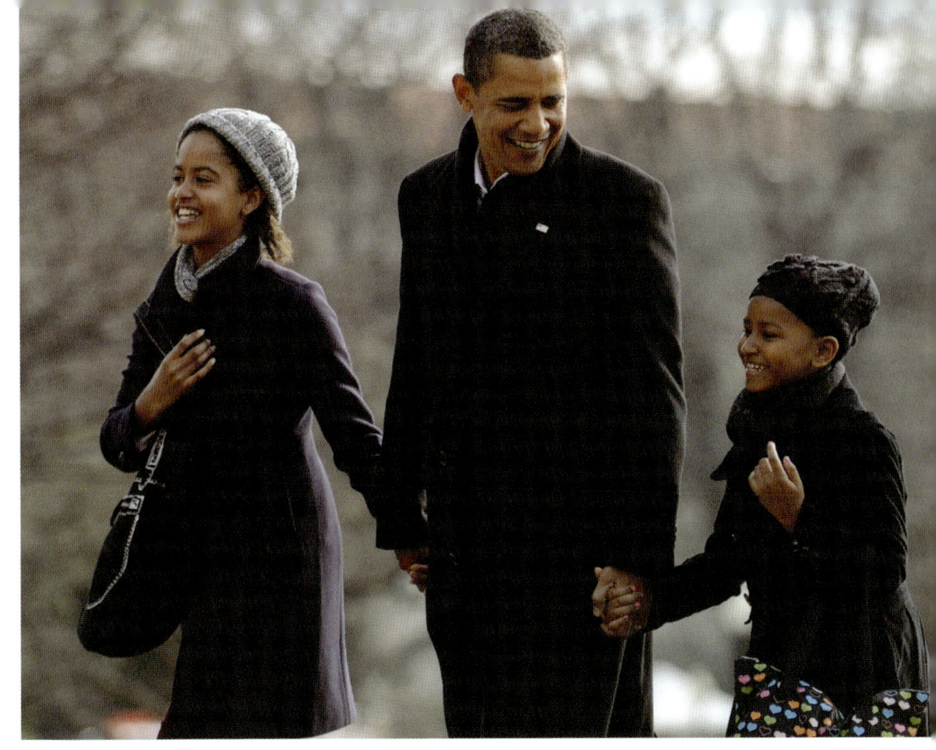

The Obama family return to the White House after spending Christmas vacation in Hawaii. The president walks with his daughters Sasha and Malia to the private residence. January 2010.

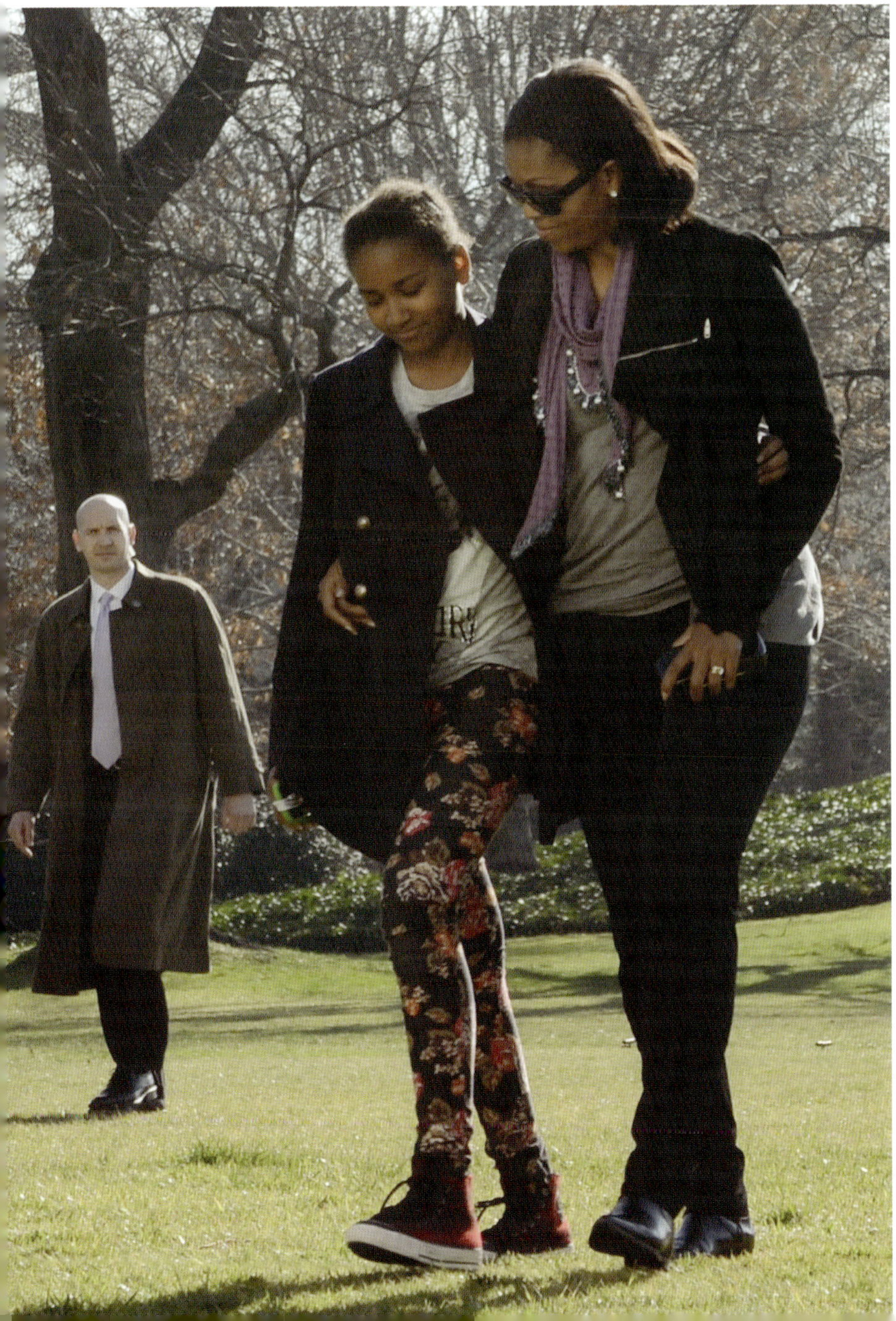

First Lady Michelle and daughter Sasha walk to the residence as a Secret Service agent looks on, January 2013.

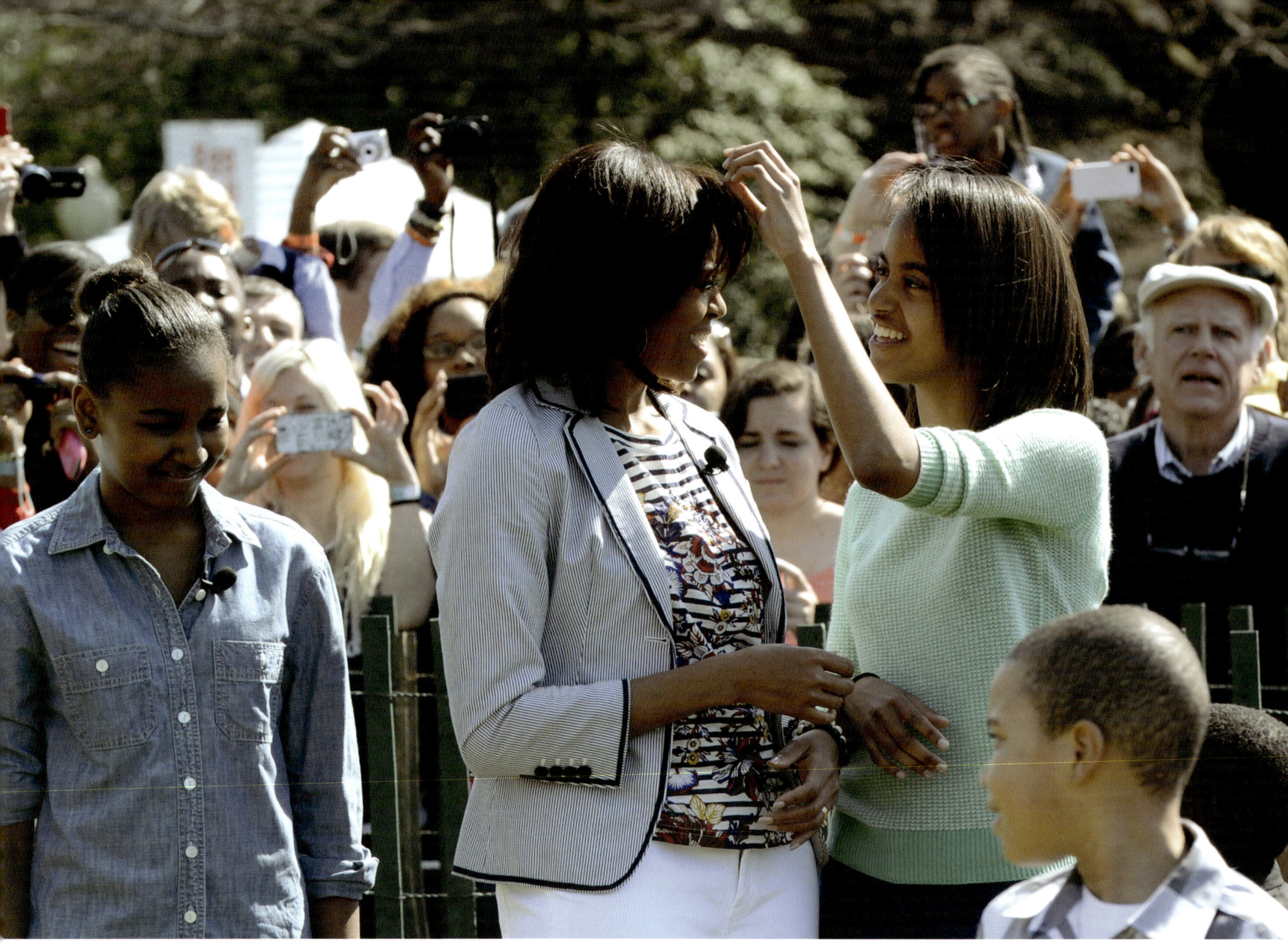

First Daughter Malia Obama fixes her mom's new bangs during the annual Easter Egg Roll at the White House, April 2014.

Most presidential appearances are photographed and therefore belong to the public and to history. Representing an independent news bureau, I am grateful to have both witnessed and captured this history in a way that embraces my own photographic style

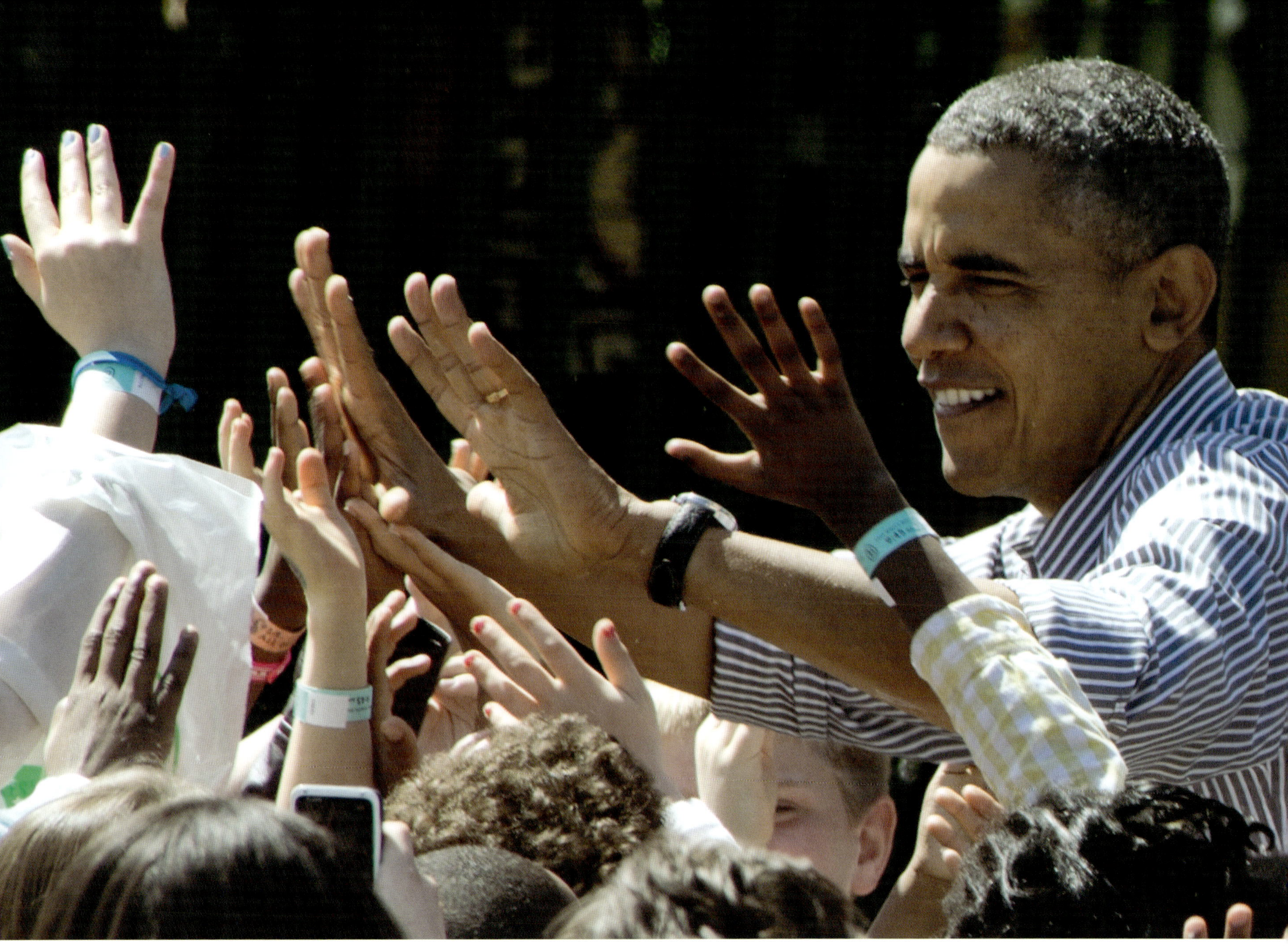

President Barack Obama high-fives kids during the 2014 Easter Egg Roll at the White House, April 2014.

while allowing me to document the emotions that take place at the White House. As this book aims to show, in a democracy, it is the role of the press to chronicle an objective, truthful record.

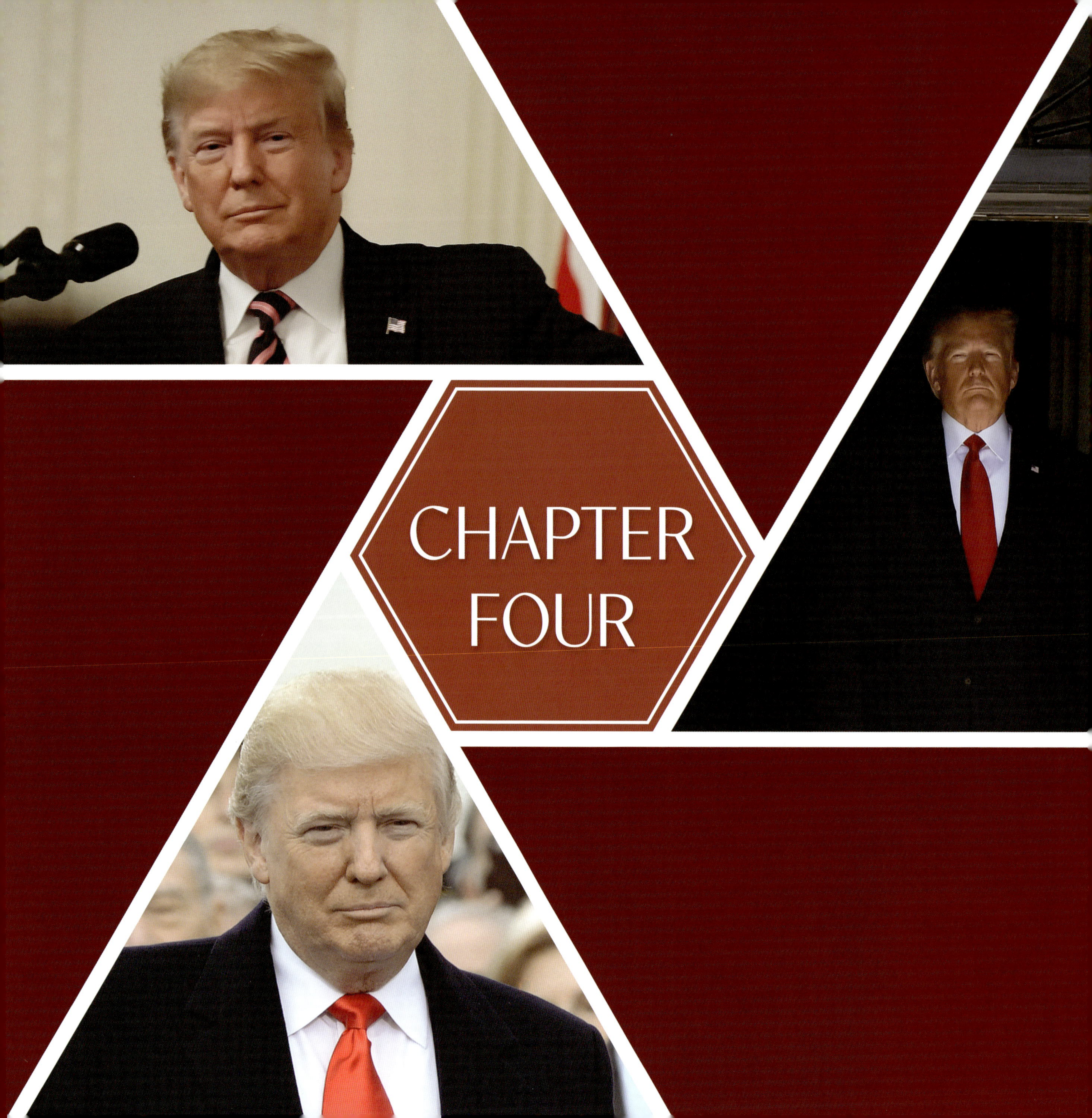
CHAPTER
FOUR

DONALD J. TRUMP

Much to my surprise, the day of Donald Trump's inauguration was not bitterly cold! Everything actually went smoothly for me, despite the chaos of previous presidential swearing-in ceremonies.

Having had some medical issues from carrying my heavy gear for all this time, a couple of surgeries later I was now the proud owner of a disabled-parking pass. After many years in this profession, carrying all the heavy camera gear takes its toll on the body. Yet my injury came with some benefits; on inauguration day especially, it permitted me to pass through many of the barricades on my way to the coveted parking space just outside my destination at the US Capitol. Avoiding the struggle of the Metro subway and hauling my gear for hours made such a difference.

After going through security and arriving at my position, I looked out over the assembly of people in front of the Capitol as the sun came up; it seemed the crowd had gotten a slow start, but the inauguration *was* well attended.

From that day on, the Trump White House never had a shortage of ongoing news stories. There were many challenging assignments during those four years and beyond.

Right out of the gate, on day one after the inauguration, women from all over the country spoke out against Trump's election by holding a "Pink Revolution"

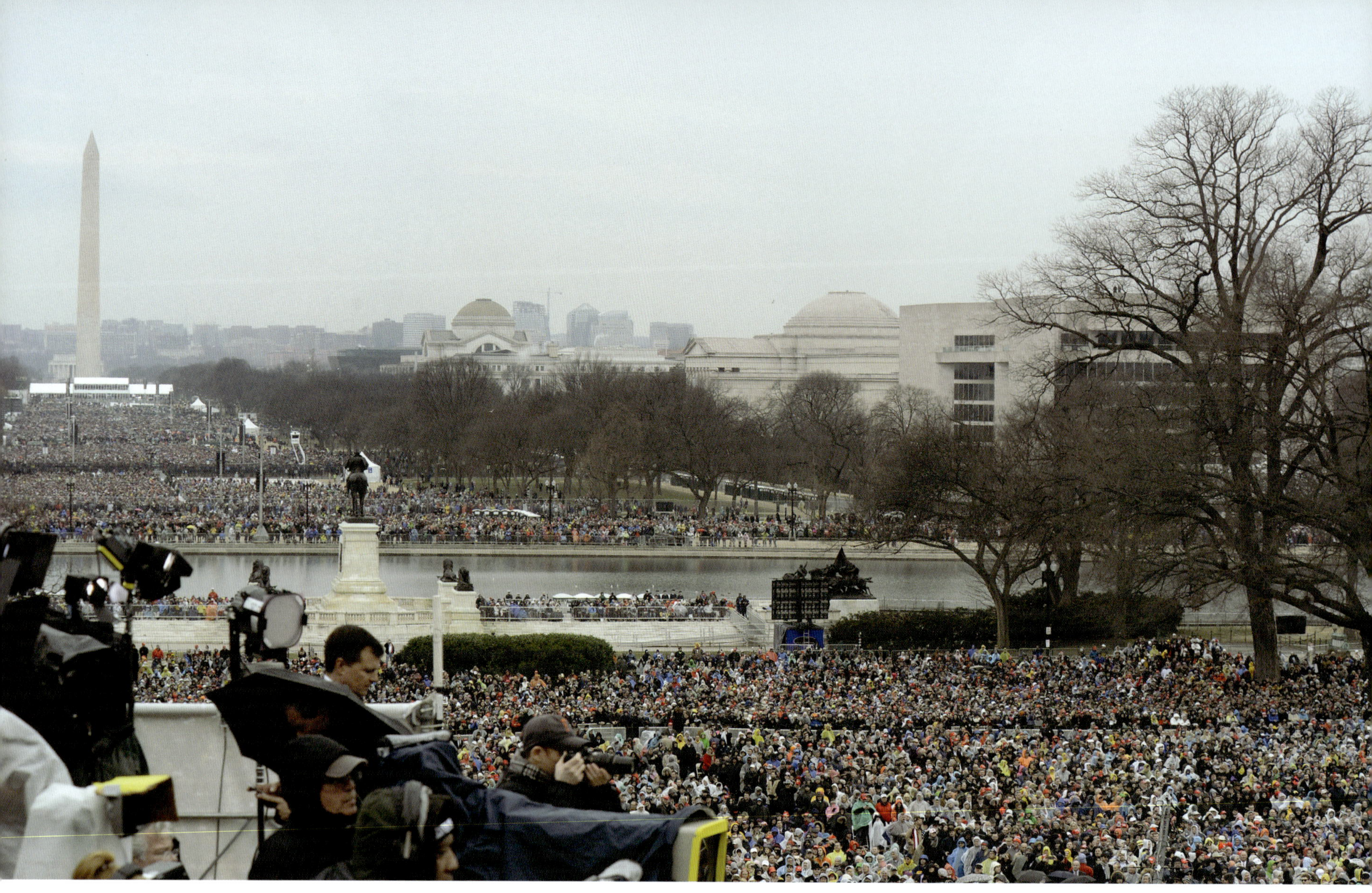

*The crowd is in place as President Elect Donald Trump is about to be sworn in as
the forty-fifth president of the United States at the US Capitol, January 2017.*

protest. A huge rally was held in Washington, DC, and thousands of women marched simultaneously in many cities—both here and abroad—wearing pink hats in solidarity. Weeks before the election, Trump had been accused of sexually violating more than sixteen women. This was quickly followed by public outrage stemming from an audio clip of a conversation where he had admittedly bragged about grabbing women by their private parts and getting away with it because of his fame.

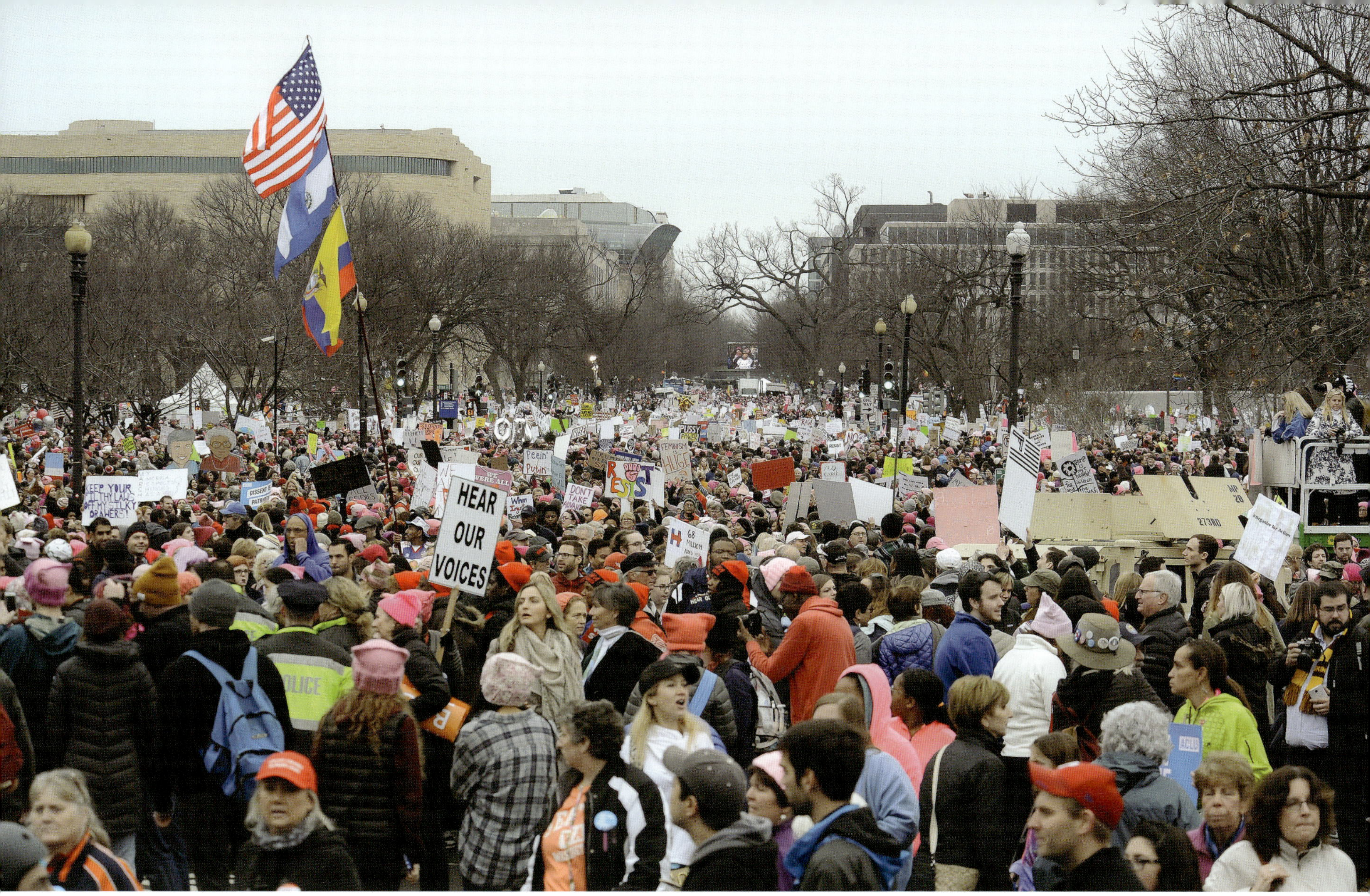

*Protesters swarm the streets of Washington, DC, to protest the inauguration
of President Donald Trump the day before. January 2017.*

As we transitioned to the Trump administration, there continued to be a lot of chaos both inside and outside the White House. In fact, the entire way that news was reported continued to change, and not all because of the president. The twenty-four-hour news cycle in place was fueled by social media posts from everyone, even the president himself. Through tweeting, President Trump (Code Name "Mogul") seemed to be reporting on himself. I felt that he was using Twitter to bypass others' interpretative reporting of his opinions and comments. President

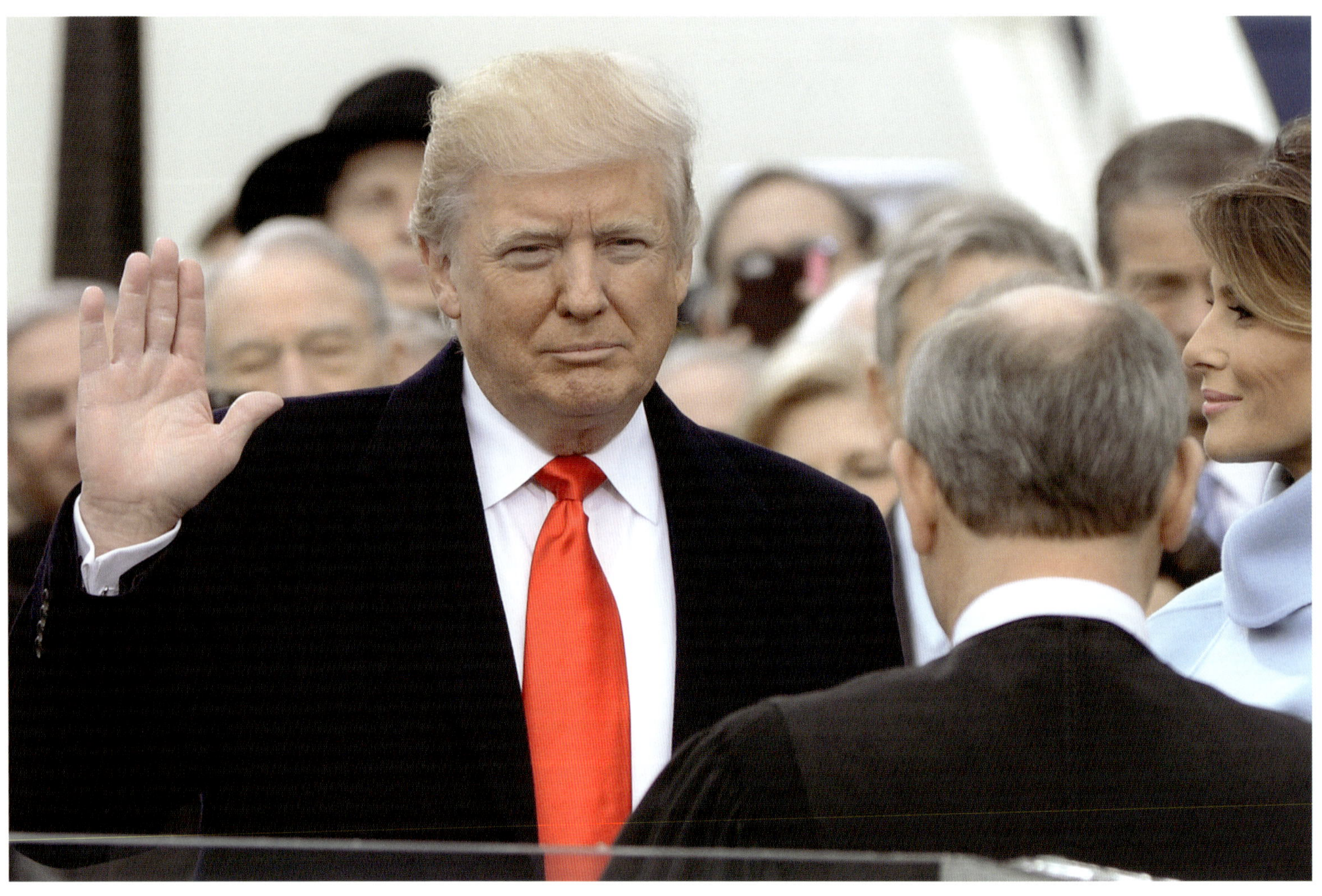

Trump was once quoted as saying, "When somebody challenges you, fight back. Be brutal, be tough."[1]

Somewhere along the way, members of the press corps had become public enemy number one to President Trump. Eventually, Trump lost his Twitter account and began a new social media platform, Truth Social, so that he could continue communicating with his followers and control his message. The face of the news had been forever changed. Several reporters covering Trump rallies were forced to hire bodyguards because the president would often point to the press risers and shout derogatory remarks about the media, which caused thousands of Trump supporters to boo and jeer at reporters, making them feel unsafe.

Somehow, over time, a significant amount of reporting has become about espousing opinions and the public needing to choose between opposing networks. The people then decide who they agree with, which media outlet is most closely aligned with their partisan views . . . and tune in for their news. Gone are the days of just straight-fact reporting.

On a personal level for President Trump, there was a lot of family involvement in the Trump White House. First Daughter Ivanka held the title of Assistant to the President, and her husband, Jared Kushner, was a senior advisor. Both became vital members of the president's team and gained access to the Oval Office and the entire West Wing. We even occasionally saw their small children when the family traveled on Marine One. After a significant period of time it came out that Kushner did not have appropriate security clearance, but that was quickly resolved.

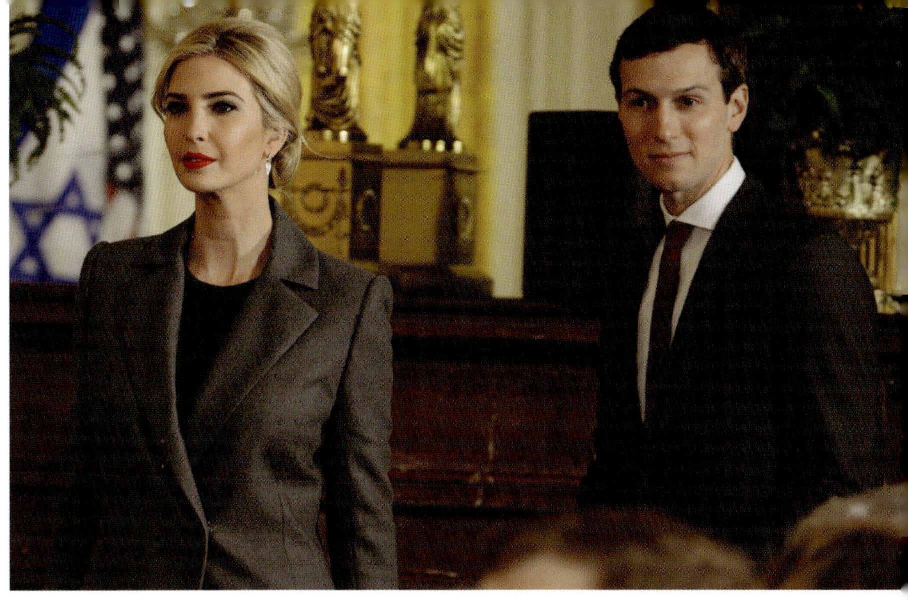

First daughter Ivanka Trump and husband Jared Kushner enter the East Room for a joint two-and-two press conference with President Trump and Prime Minister Netanyahu of Israel, February 2017.

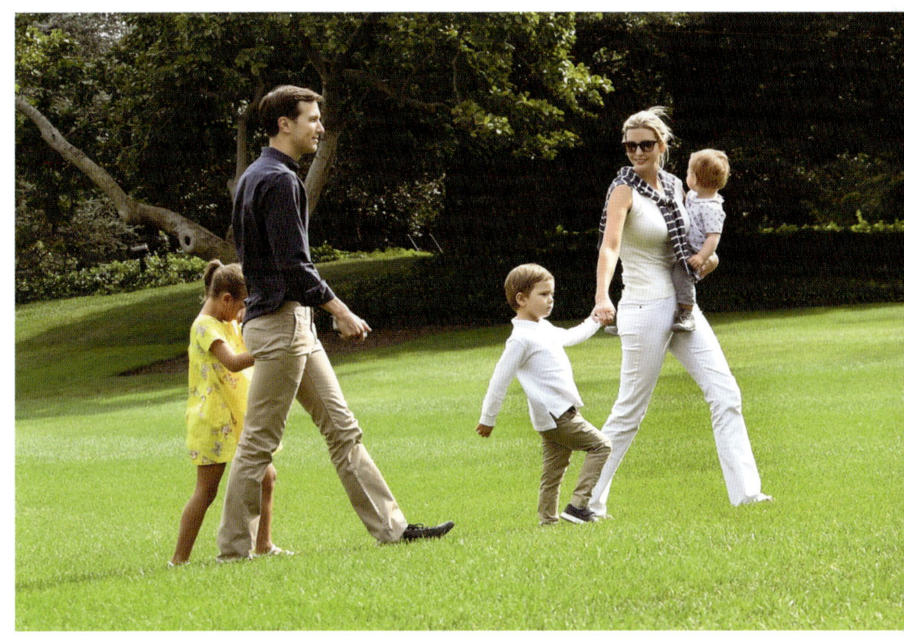

First Daughter Ivanka Trump, husband Jared Kushner, and their children Arabella, Joseph, and Theodore walk away from Marine One. August 2017.

First Lady Melania captivated everyone with her beauty and sense of fashion. Melania had taken up an initiative that encouraged positive social, emotional, and physical habits for children, called "Be Best." She did not

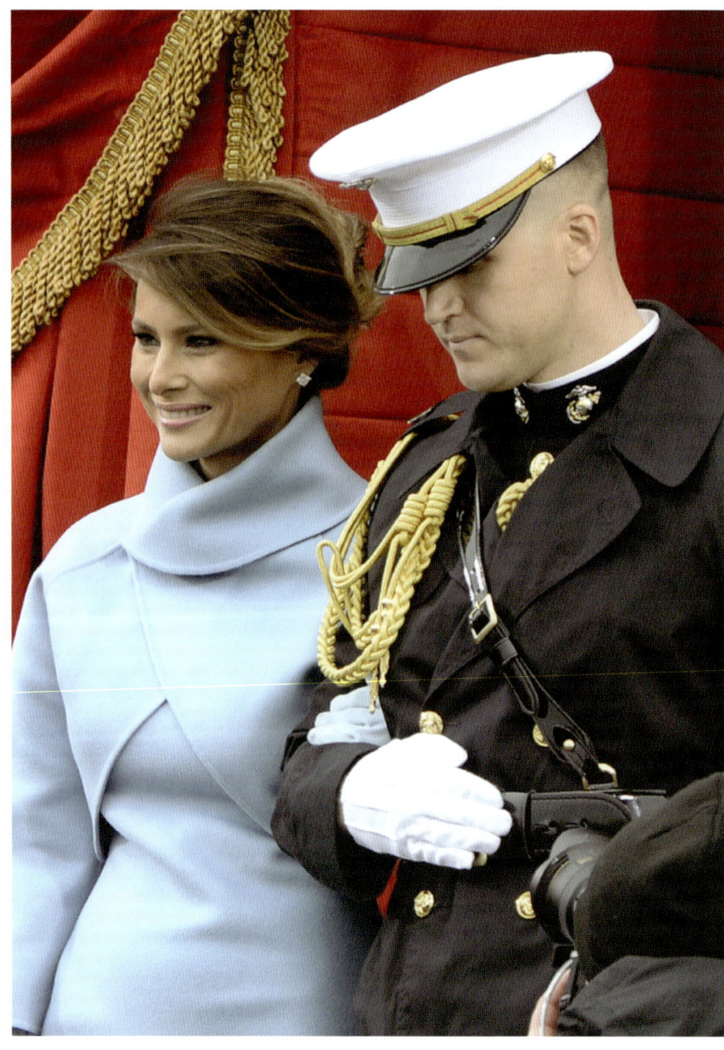

The new first lady, Melania Trump, is escorted to her seat prior to the swearing-in ceremony at her husband's presidential inauguration. January 2017.

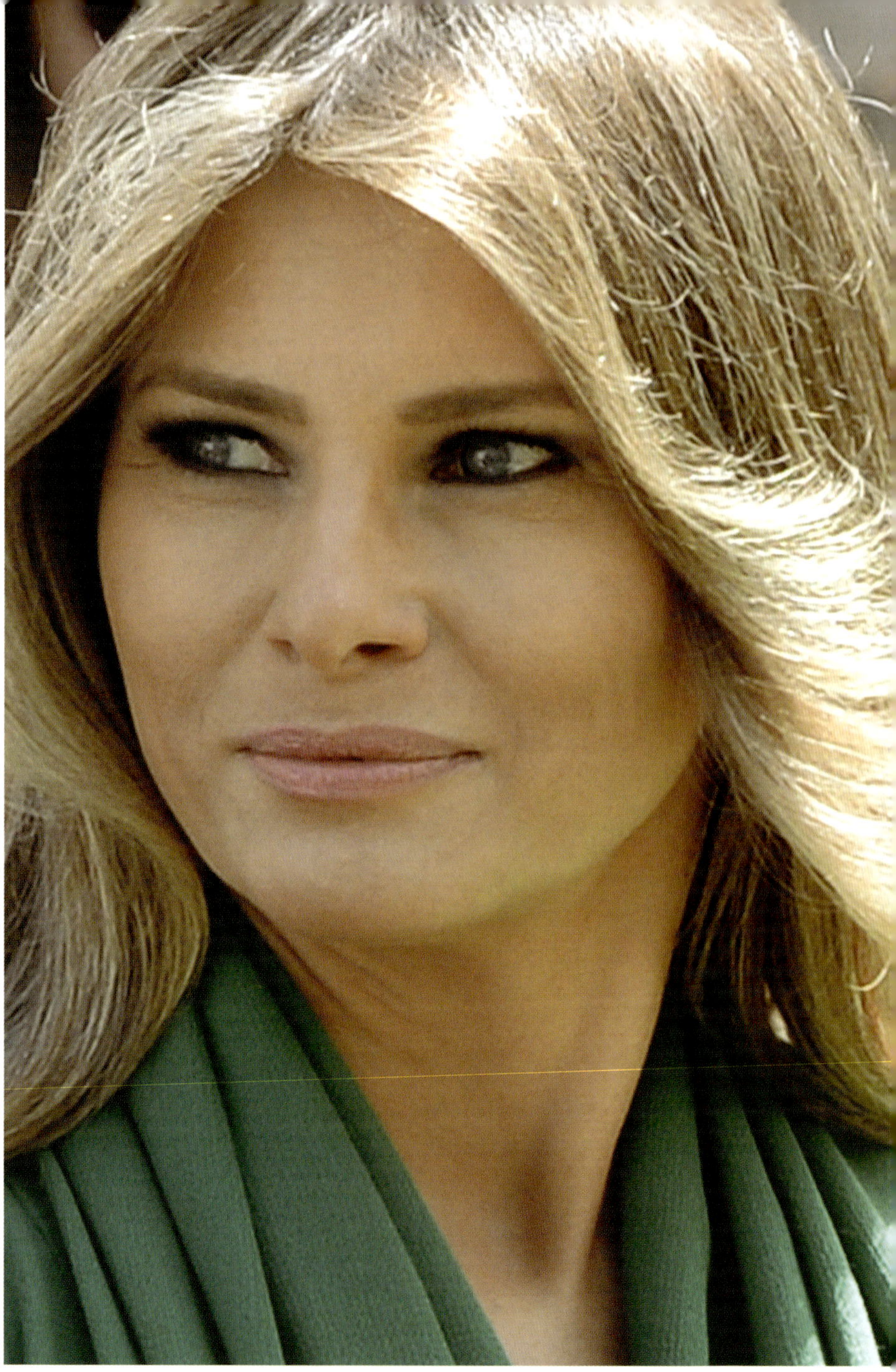

First Lady Melania Trump looks over at the media in the Rose Garden at the White House, April 2017.

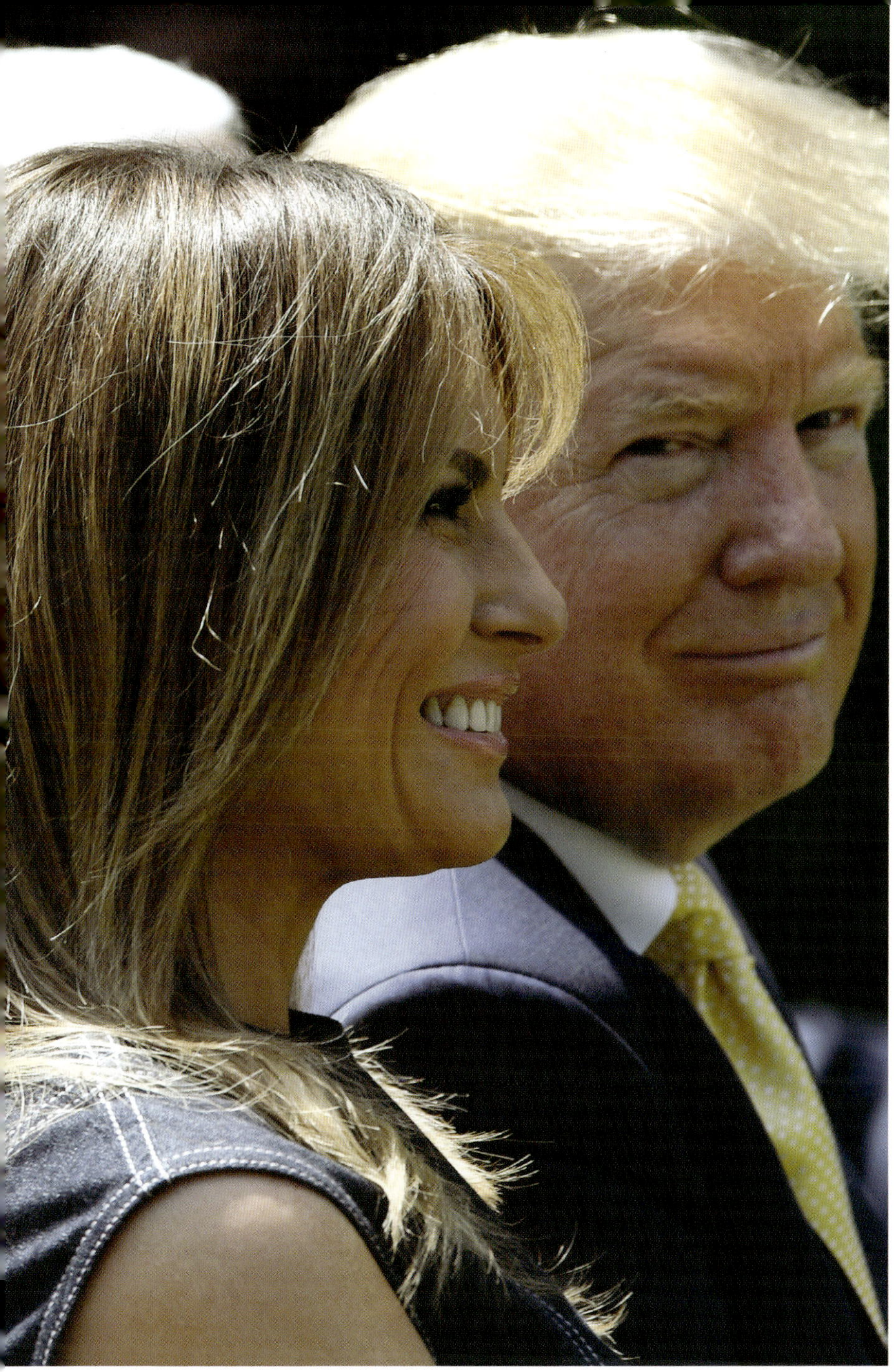

hold a lot of events while in the White House though, so I was not around her as much as I had been with Michelle Obama.

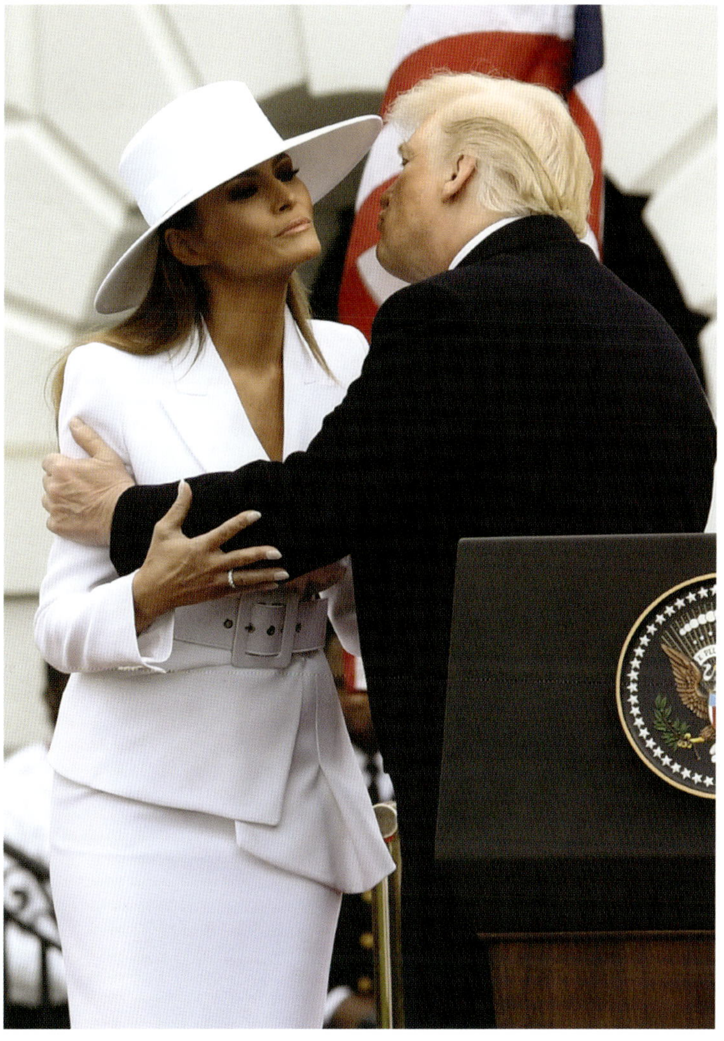

President Trump kisses First Lady Melania during the first state arrival ceremony of his administration for President Macron of France, April 2018.

First Lady Melania Trump hosts the celebration of the first anniversary of her "Be Best" initiative in the Rose Garden of the White House. The president and first lady listen to speakers. May 2019.

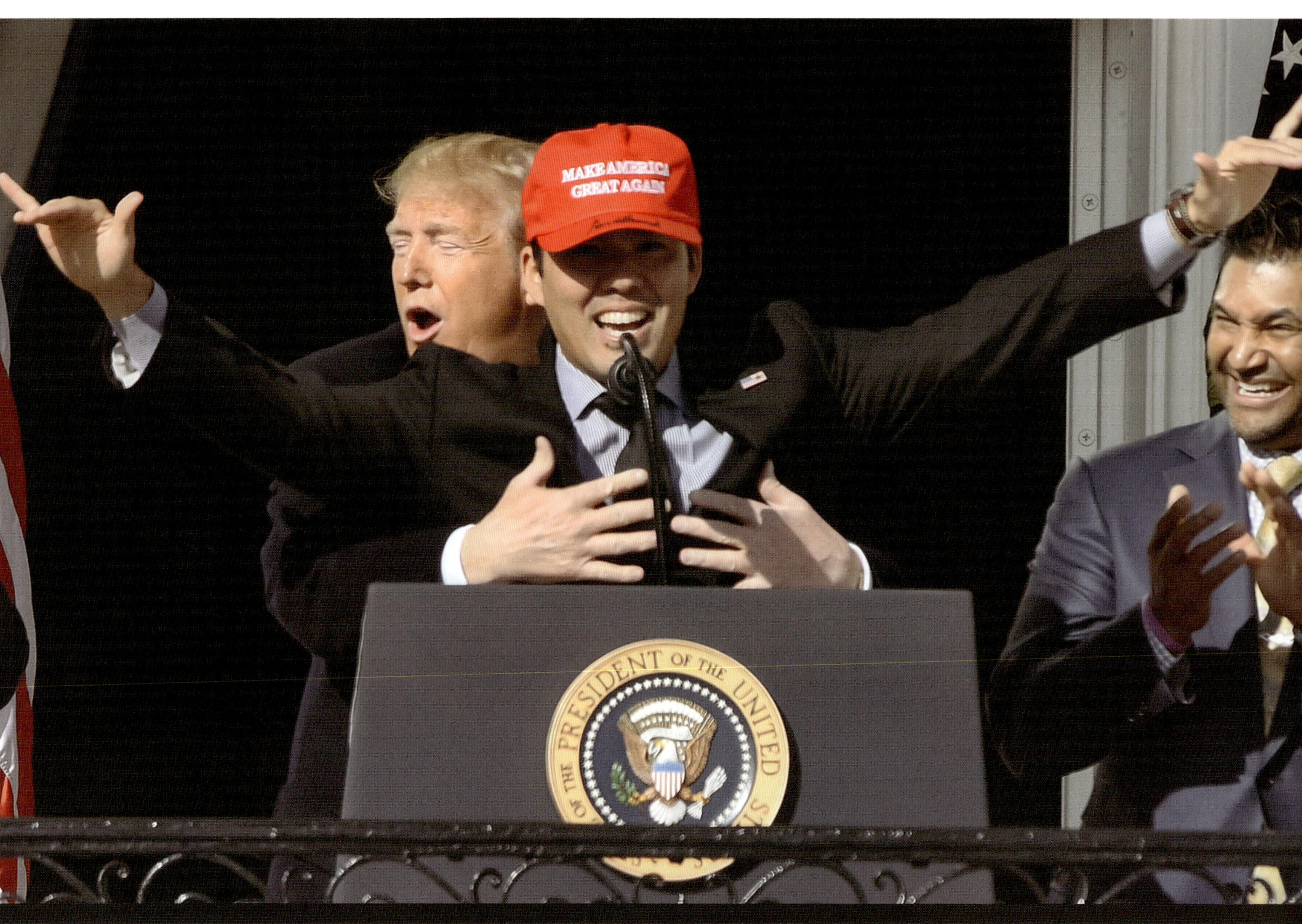

President Donald Trump welcomes the Washington Nationals, baseball's 2019 World Series Champions, to the White House to celebrate. Pitcher Kurt Suzuki wears a MAGA hat as he comes up to the podium to make short remarks while President Trump jokes with him. November 2019.

Things were never boring during Trump's administration, but there were some lighter moments. On November 4, 2019, President Trump welcomed home the Washington Nationals baseball team shortly after they won the World Series. In a joyful moment, Trump spontaneously gave pitcher Kurt Suzuki a big bear hug. I am proud to have had my picture of that moment acknowledged as one of the pictures of the week by the *Wall Street Journal*.

At the Trump White House, members of the press corps were required to be there three to four days a week in order to preserve a hard pass. Translated: we had to be on the White House grounds on days when the president was not even there. He traveled a lot—sometimes a couple of trips in one day. This stipulation caused many members of the press corps to lose their hard passes during that period.

Although there were only a couple of traditional press conferences during his time in office, President Trump did make himself accessible when he left to travel. Large crowds of media would gather each time there was a presidential arrival or departure from the South Lawn of the White House. Since there was a long period of time where daily briefings were not held at all by the press secretary, Trump created his own way of hosting press briefings. He would come over to the large gathering of media when he was on his way to Marine One and take questions from many different reporters, talking from ten to thirty minutes—totally in control of how long it would last. Meanwhile, all of us breathed in the fumes from the engine of the presidential helicopter. Trump had the option of saying he could not "hear" the question, or he could leave whenever he chose. A lot easier for him than being trapped with the media in a traditional press conference for an hour or more.

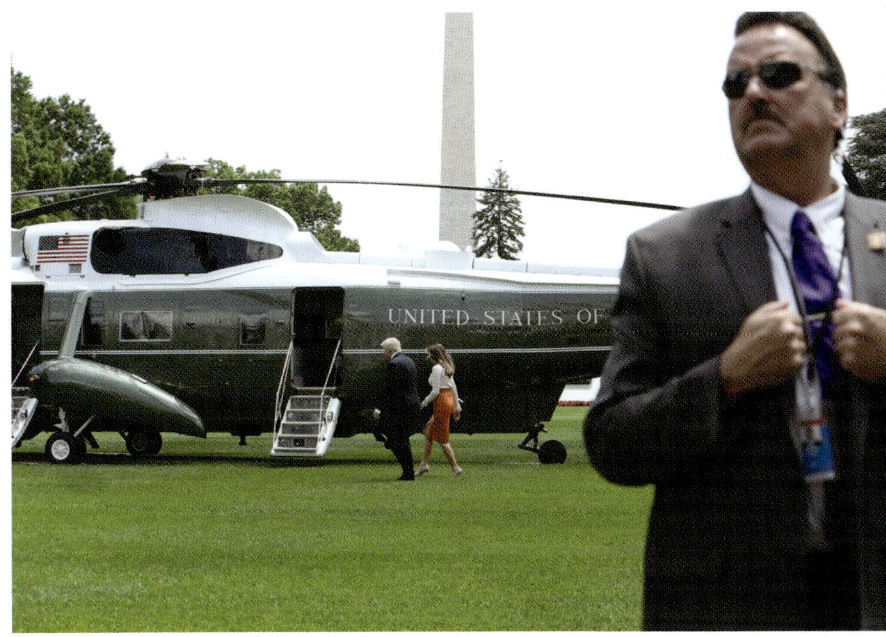

President Donald Trump and First Lady Melania Trump walk to Marine One as they leave for a nine-day overseas trip, their protective detail looking on. May 2017.

President Trump did not like the sound of camera shutters, so we all needed to set our cameras to silent mode when photographing him in the smaller venues, like the Oval Office and the Roosevelt Room. He also personally tested the lighting in the East Room to make sure he looked his best on camera. Unfortunately, he banished the usual TV lights in favor of the natural-light look, which was not always as complimentary.

The White House began to thin out the herd even more a year or so into the Trump administration, and many of us once again lived in fear of losing our passes. At one point, the press office came up with what I called a "lesser pass" to pacify those who lost their full-access passes. The new pass had a picture of the White House on it, but no picture of the passholder and no embedded computer chip like the official credential. After a short time, the Secret Service declared that the new passes were not legitimate and they would not honor them.

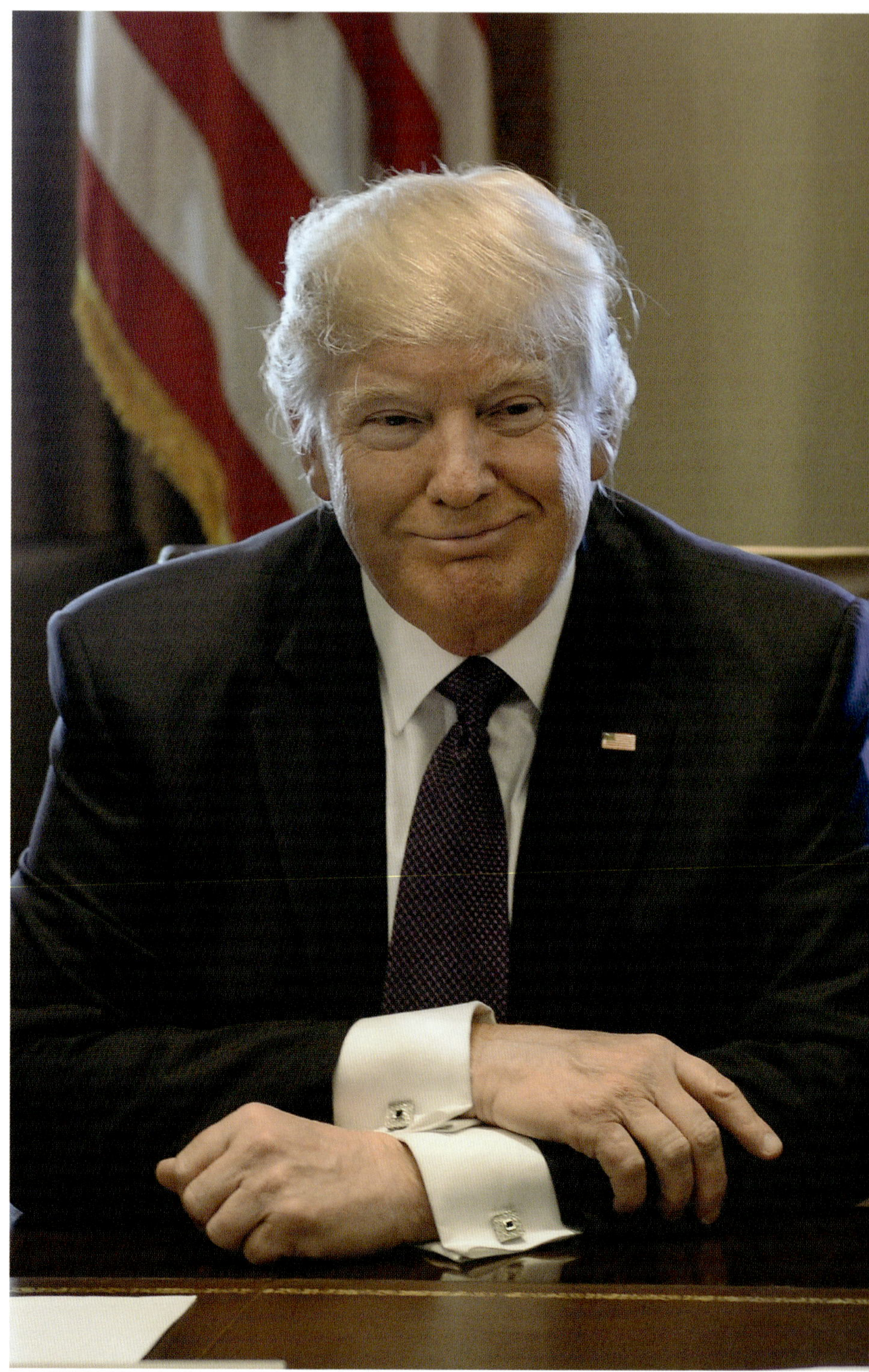

At the beginning of a meeting
President Donald Trump looks over
at photographers from his chair in the
Cabinet Room, February 2017.

    History in the Making

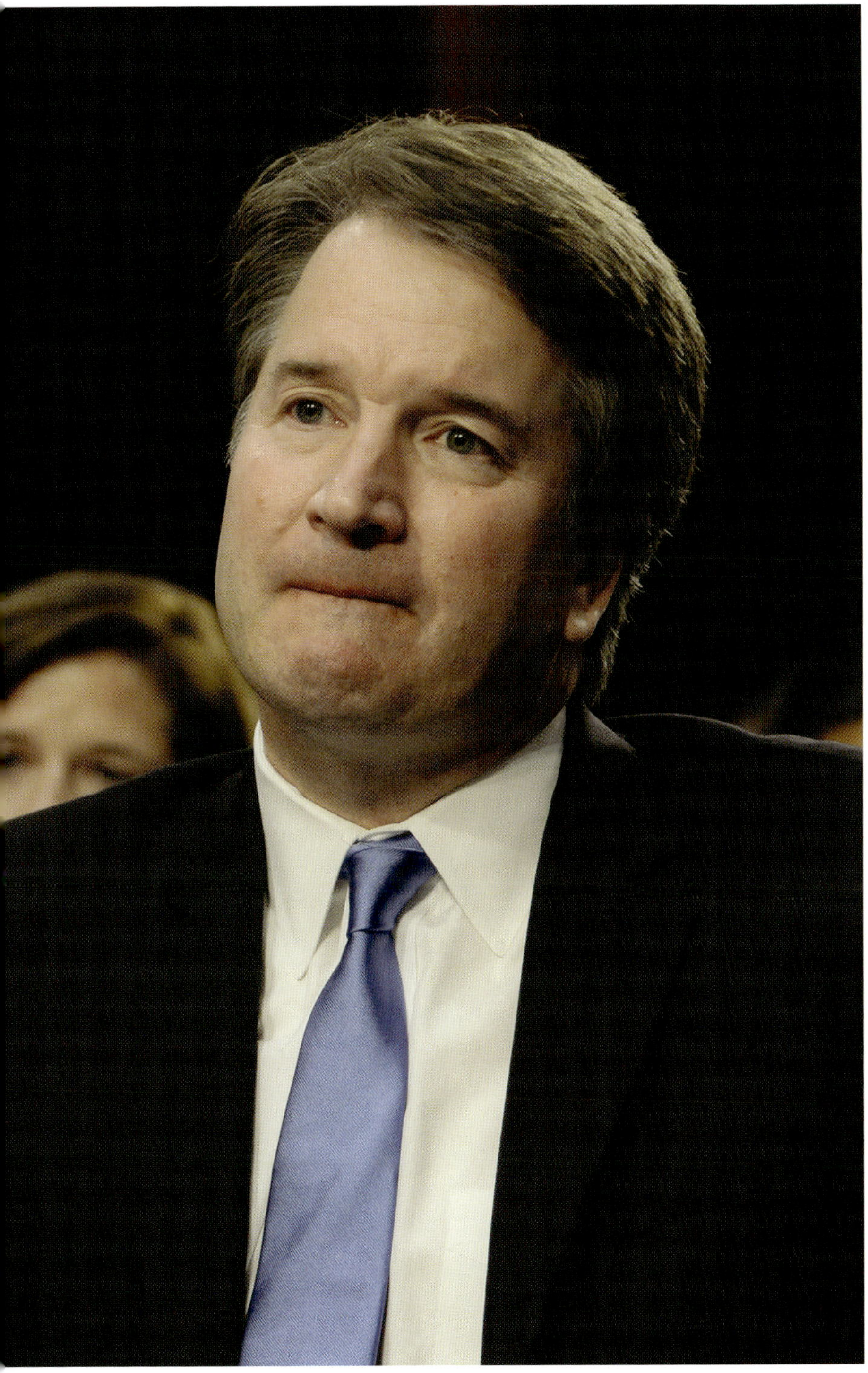

The responsibility of nominating US Supreme Court justices is one of the duties of a sitting president. Of the eight Supreme Court confirmation hearings I have witnessed, the Brett Kavanaugh hearing was, by far, the most contentious of all.

Democrats united in an attempt to postpone the hearing, having been given insufficient time to read all the documents, while more than sixty protesters inside the hearing room challenged Kavanaugh's record and his influence on the future—and that was just day one.

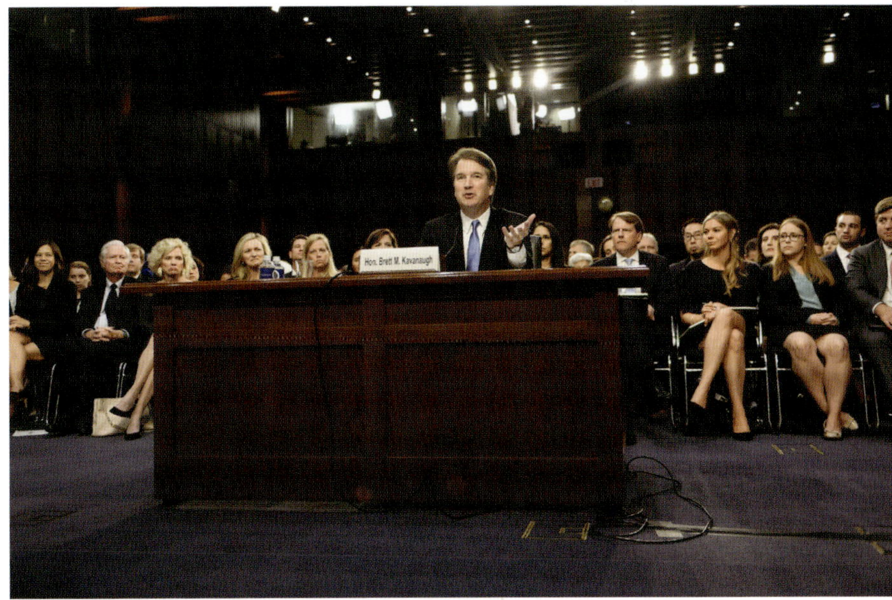

Judge Brett Kavanaugh begins the Senate Judiciary Committee process to determine if he will be the next US Supreme Court Justice, replacing Justice Anthony Kennedy. Capitol Hill, Washington, DC, September 2018.

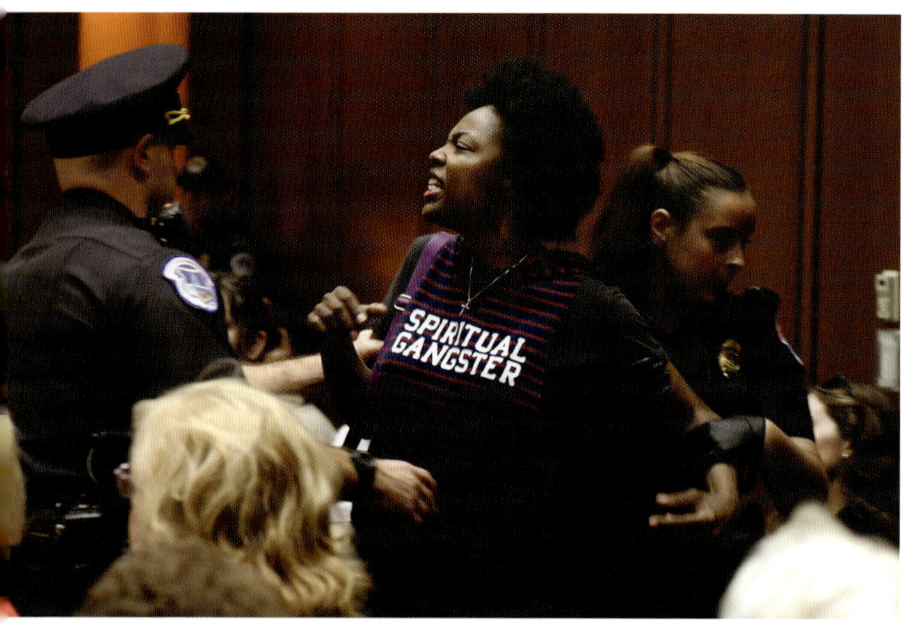

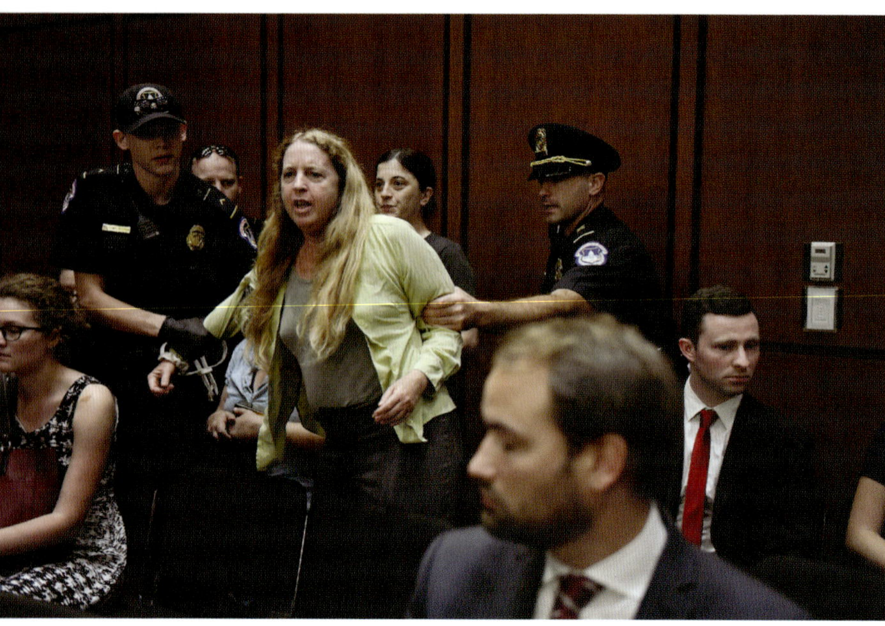

*Protestors shout out during the confirmation hearing
of Judge Brett Kavanaugh during his Senate Judiciary
Committee hearing, September 2018.*

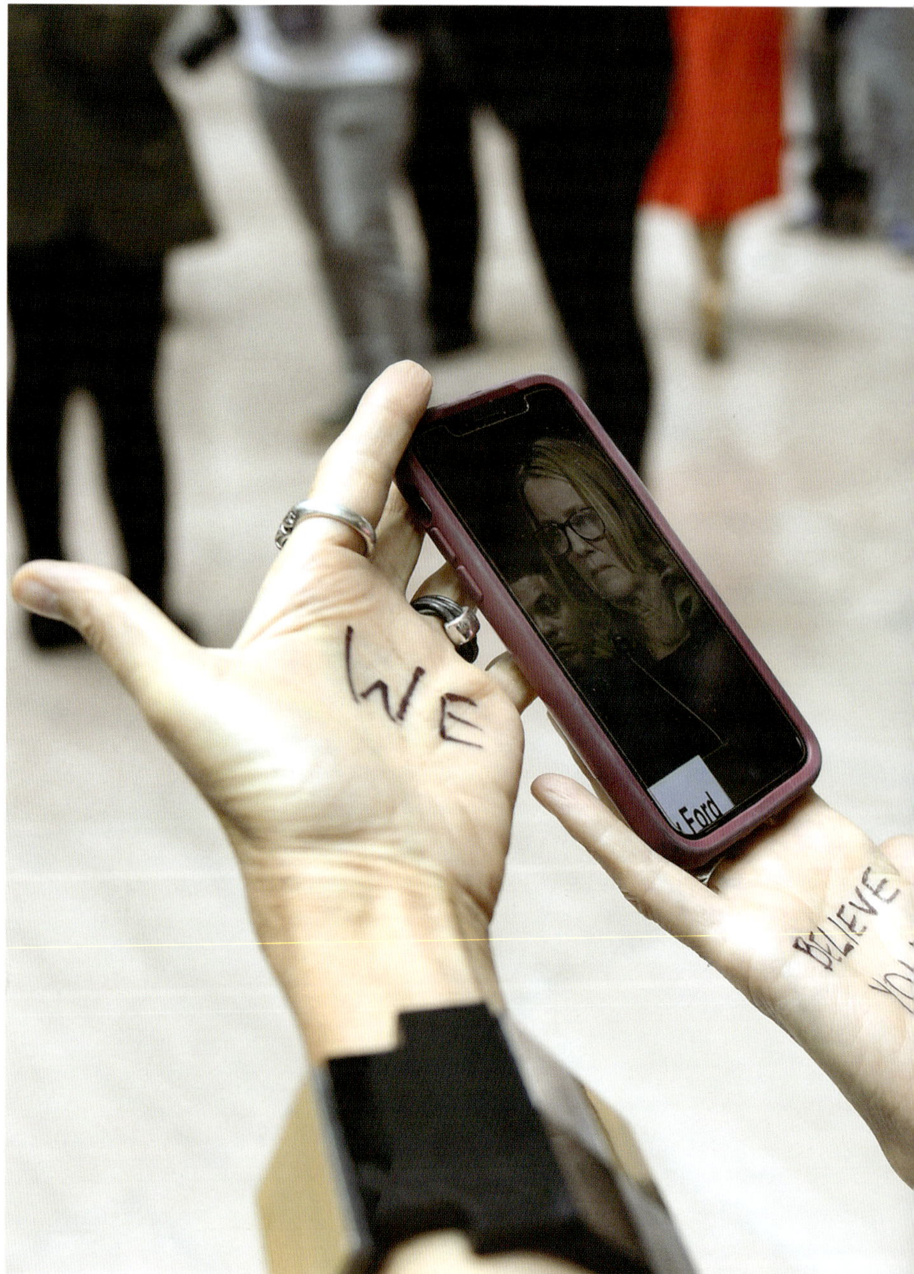

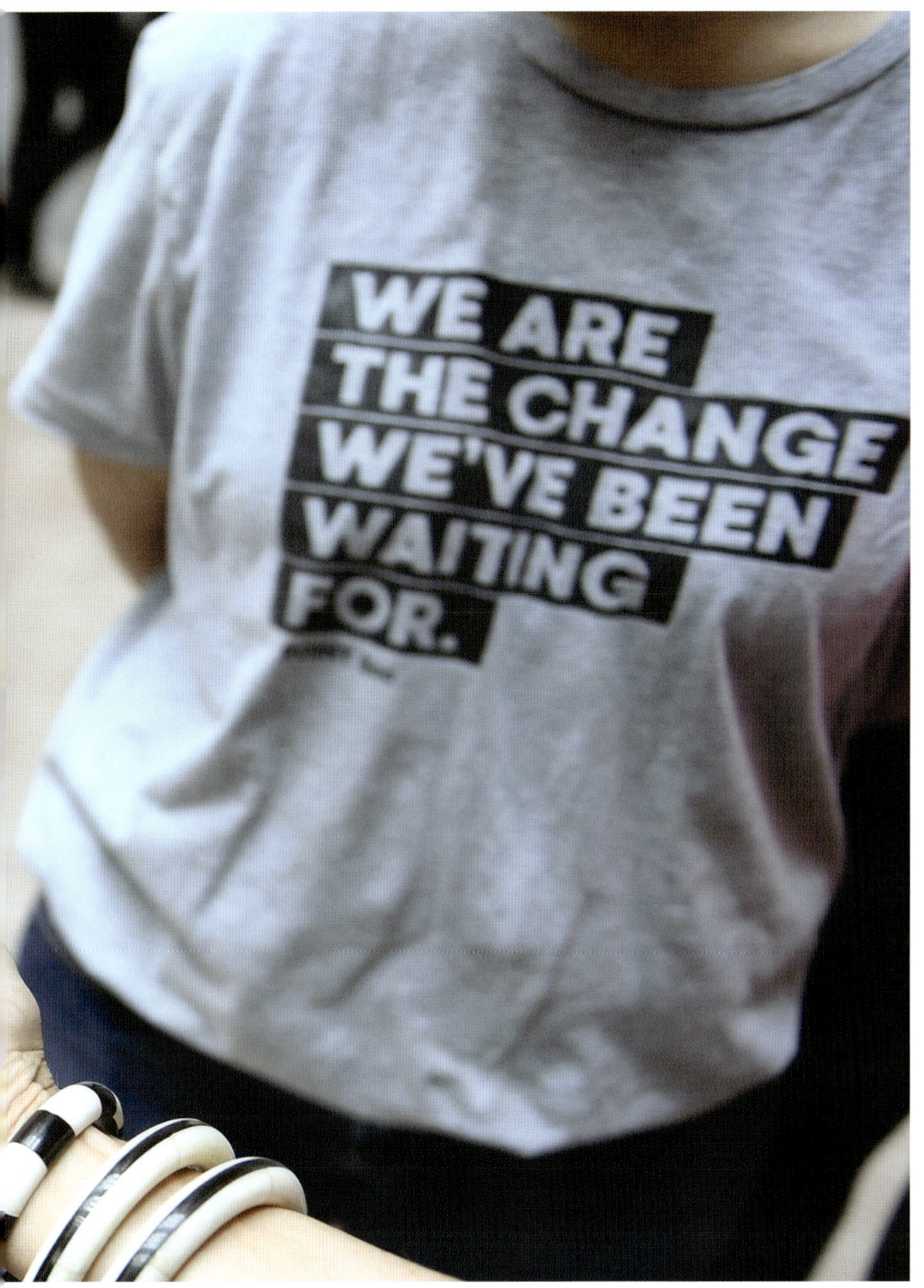

The largest hearing room in the Senate was packed with reporters, photographers, and protesters. The public, too, were waiting in line for their chance to briefly sit in the back of the hearing room and witness the hearings—hundreds were lined up in the hallways waiting to be escorted in. Also embedded in the line were protesters who, once allowed in the room, began to stand up and shout. Police developed a system of handcuffing them with plastic ties before escorting them out a side door and down the elevator to a waiting paddy wagon that would take them to the police station. After a while, I was able to spot the ones who would be arrested as soon as they arrived.

Dr. Christine Blasey Ford testifies before the Senate Judiciary Committee about her alleged attempted sexual assault by Judge Brett Kavanaugh when they were in high school. Supporters of Ford swarmed the Hart Senate Office Building voicing their opinions as they watched the hearing on their cellphones. September 2018.

Following Justice Kavanaugh's three-day hearing, just as the committee was about to vote, Dr. Christine Blasey Ford came forward and alleged that a drunken Kavanaugh had tried to sexually assault her when they were teenagers at a party.

Kavanaugh responded, defending himself: "This whole two-week effort has been a calculated and orchestrated political hit, fueled with apparent pent-up anger about President Trump and the 2016 election, fear that has been unfairly stoked about my judicial record, revenge on behalf of the Clintons, and millions of dollars in money from outside left-wing opposition groups. This is a circus. . . . This grotesque and coordinated character assassination will dissuade confident and good people of all political persuasions from serving our country."[2]

The #MeToo movement then exploded across the country; more allegations came forward and an FBI investigation was ordered. Both the Kavanaugh family and the Ford family went through intense media scrutiny as the country awaited the results of the investigation. One week later, the Senate approved Brett Kavanaugh to be the next justice of the US Supreme Court.

During Kavanaugh's swearing-in ceremony at the White House, President Trump began his remarks with, "On behalf of our nation, I want to apologize to Brett and the entire Kavanaugh family for the terrible pain and suffering you have been forced to endure."[3]

Justice Kavanaugh responded, "The Senate confirmation process was contentious and emotional. That process is over. My focus now is to be the best justice I can be. I take this office with gratitude and no bitterness."[4] He looked over at his supportive friends and former classmates in the audience and, with emotion, told them he loved them.

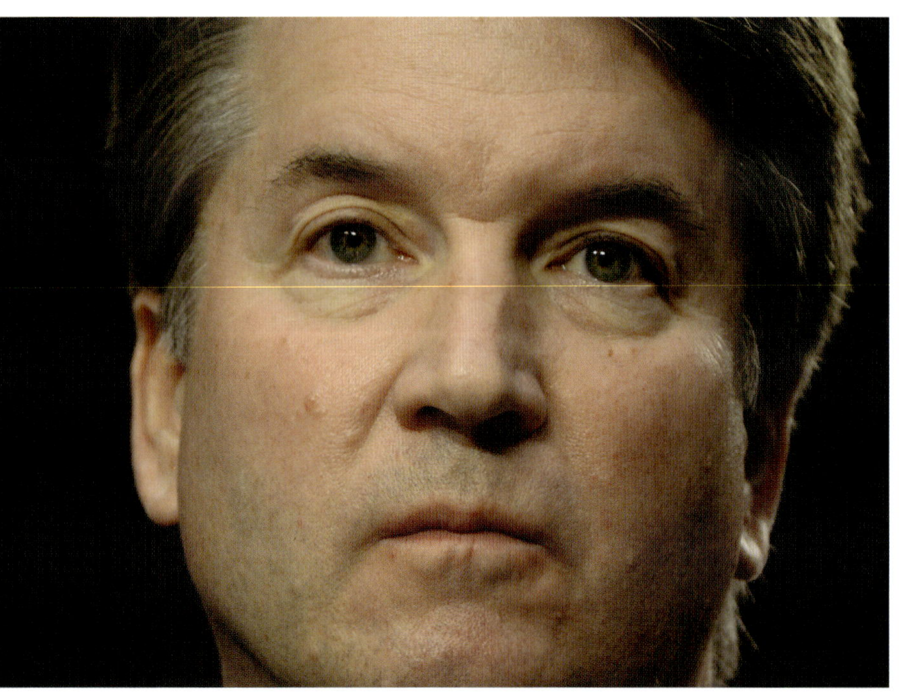

Brett Kavanaugh bristles at questions from the Senate Judiciary Committee, September 2018.

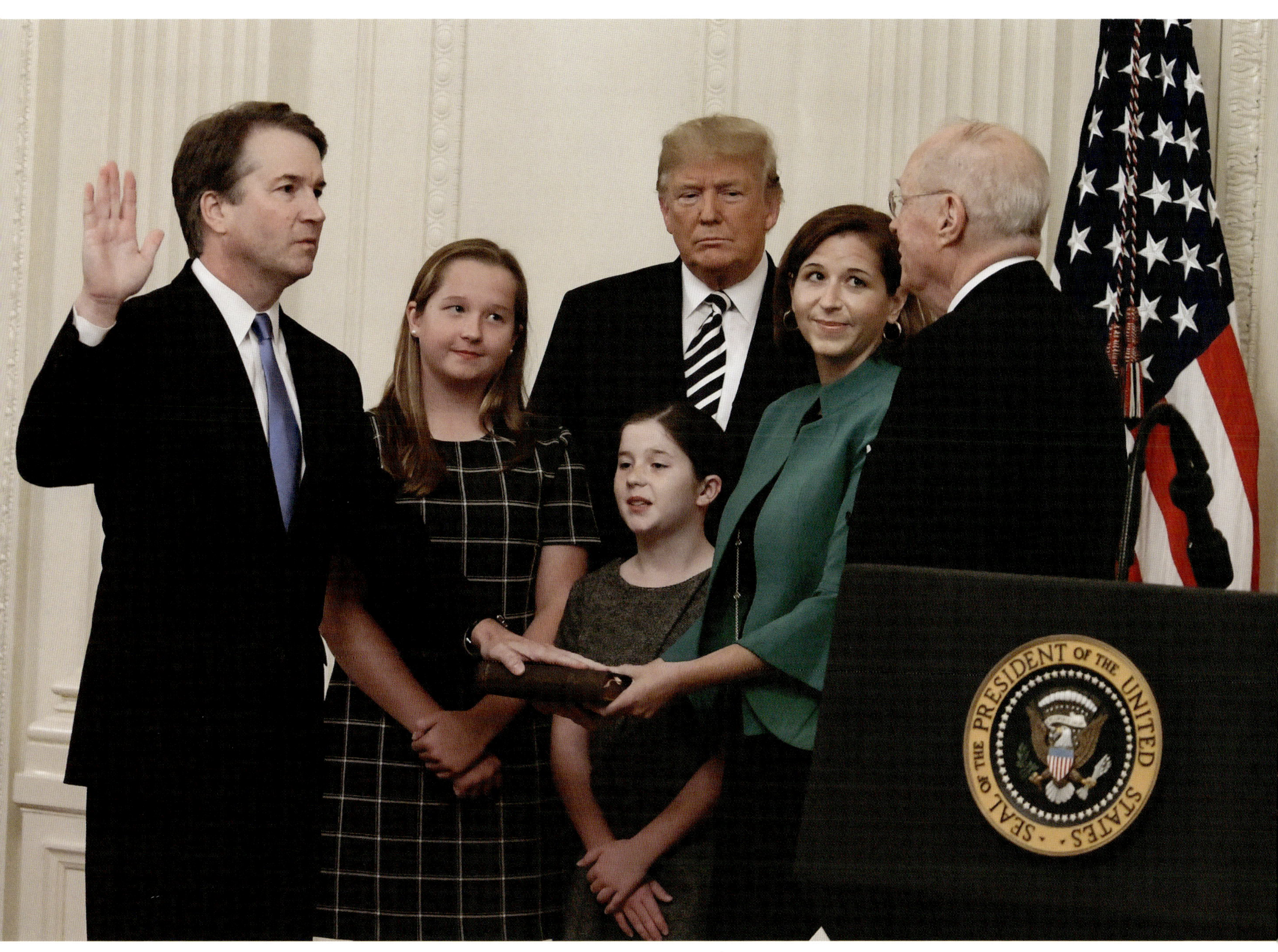

Judge Brett Kavanaugh is sworn in as an associate justice on the US Supreme Court replacing Justice Anthony Kennedy, whom he once clerked for. October 2018.

Chaos ensued again when President Trump fired FBI Director James Comey on May 9, 2017. One month later, Comey testified before the Senate Intelligence Committee on what had transpired between him and the president in at least two private meetings at the White House. Throughout my career I have covered many hearings on Capitol Hill, and usually the witness arrives loaded up with paperwork containing dates and names that are relevant; this was not so with Comey. He arrived empty-handed, all his information in his memory.

Turmoil continued to follow the president into his third year in office; Speaker of the House Nancy Pelosi stepped back into office with her boxing gloves on. Pelosi and Trump engaged in a power struggle over immigration and the border wall he was proposing to build. Things heated up so much that the State of the Union address was postponed.

We could feel the tension at the 2019 SOTU as President Trump reached out for the traditional handshake with the Speaker of the House.

Later in his speech, Trump graciously welcomed the newly elected female members of Congress. This was the largest number of women elected to Congress in history. Making a solidarity statement, the Democrats dressed in white; Nancy Pelosi was clearly in command. Nine days later, President Trump emerged from the Oval Office to announce that he was declaring a national emergency to gain funding for the border wall. The ongoing conflict between President Trump and Speaker Nancy Pelosi erupted again in a battle of strategy. Pelosi stated that President Trump was not "serious" and needed a way out of negotiations over a $2 trillion infrastructure plan that he could not pay for. She accused Trump of being involved in a "cover-up" just before she and Senator Chuck Schumer were to meet with him. Trump responded, however, by walking out of the meeting he was hosting with them at the White House and instructing his staff to summon all the media on site to *immediately* relocate to the Rose Garden. His actions preempted Pelosi and Schumer from their normal full media coverage at the stakeout position outside the West Wing.

On February 27, 2019, the president's personal attorney, Michael Cohen (known as "the Fixer") testified in a controversial hearing before Congress. He disclosed specific private details about his long, close working relationship with President Trump just before leaving to serve his prison term. Then, after almost two years in the making, Special Council Robert Mueller's report was finally released as the first big announcement from newly appointed Attorney General William Barr. The report

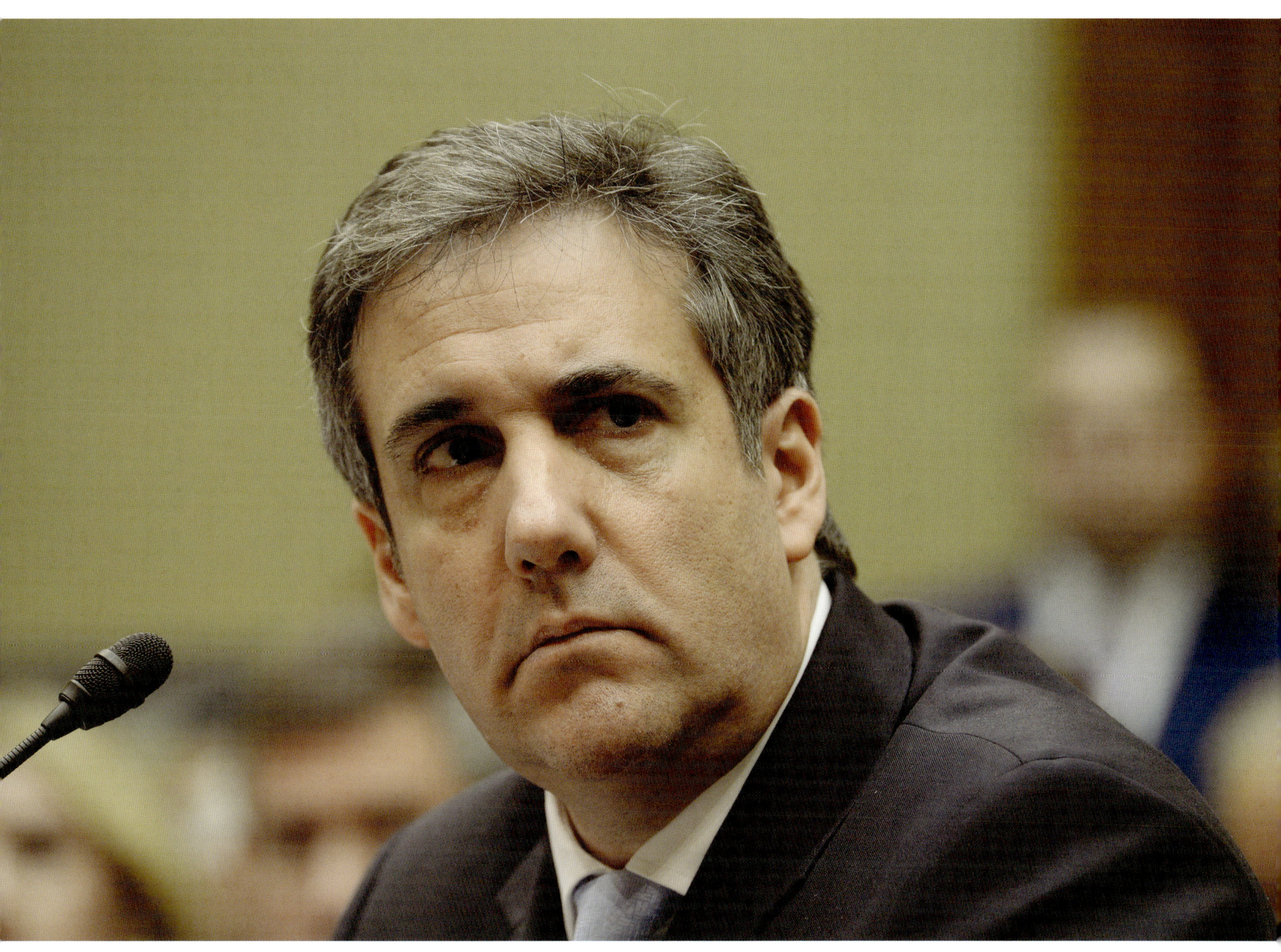

Michael Cohen, formerly President Donald Trump's attorney, testifies before the House Oversight Committee on Capitol Hill. February 2019.

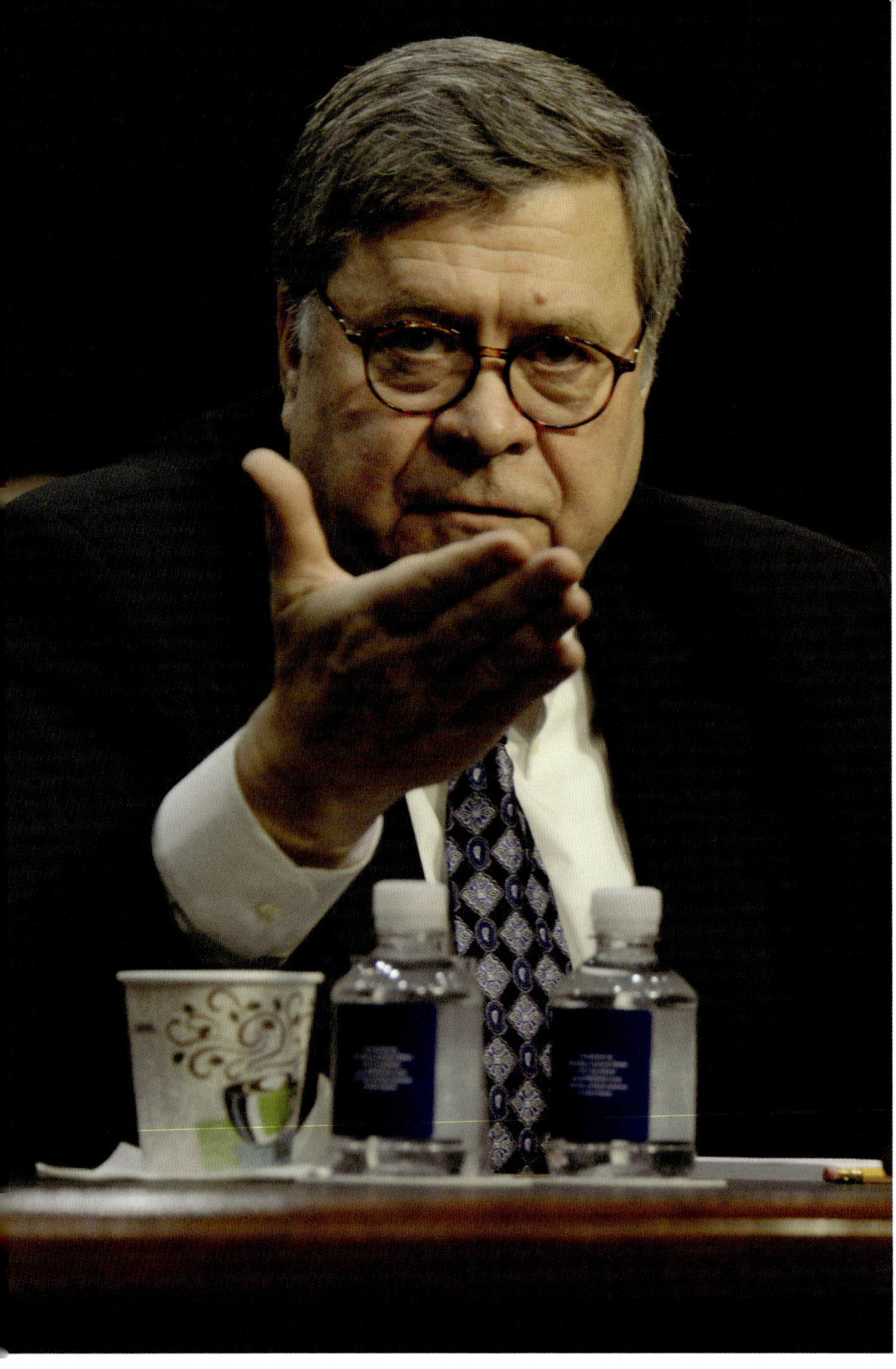

US attorney general nominee William P. Barr goes through the Senate Judiciary Committee's confirmation process on Capitol Hill, January 2019.

investigated Donald Trump for possible collusion with Russia during the 2016 election and other obstruction of justice charges.

Later that year, Mueller was subpoenaed by Congress to testify in more detail about his findings. An impeachment inquiry was initiated by Nancy Pelosi two months later, citing that Trump had a conversation with Ukrainian President Volodymyr Zelensky and had withheld funding designated for Ukraine in exchange for Ukraine investigating then–presidential candidate Joe Biden and his son Hunter. The White House pushed back and ignored the subpoenas from Congress, which called for several in the Trump administration to testify. Nevertheless, President Donald John Trump, the forty-fifth president of the United States, was impeached by the House of Representatives on Article I, abuse of power, and Article 2, obstruction of Congress.

January 20, 2020, marked the start of the Senate impeachment trial of President Donald J. Trump. There was silence in the hallways of the Capitol as the official procession of the House managers delivered the articles of impeachment to the Senate Chamber.

As tensions mounted, security was heightened as special passes were issued to allow media access into the Capitol.

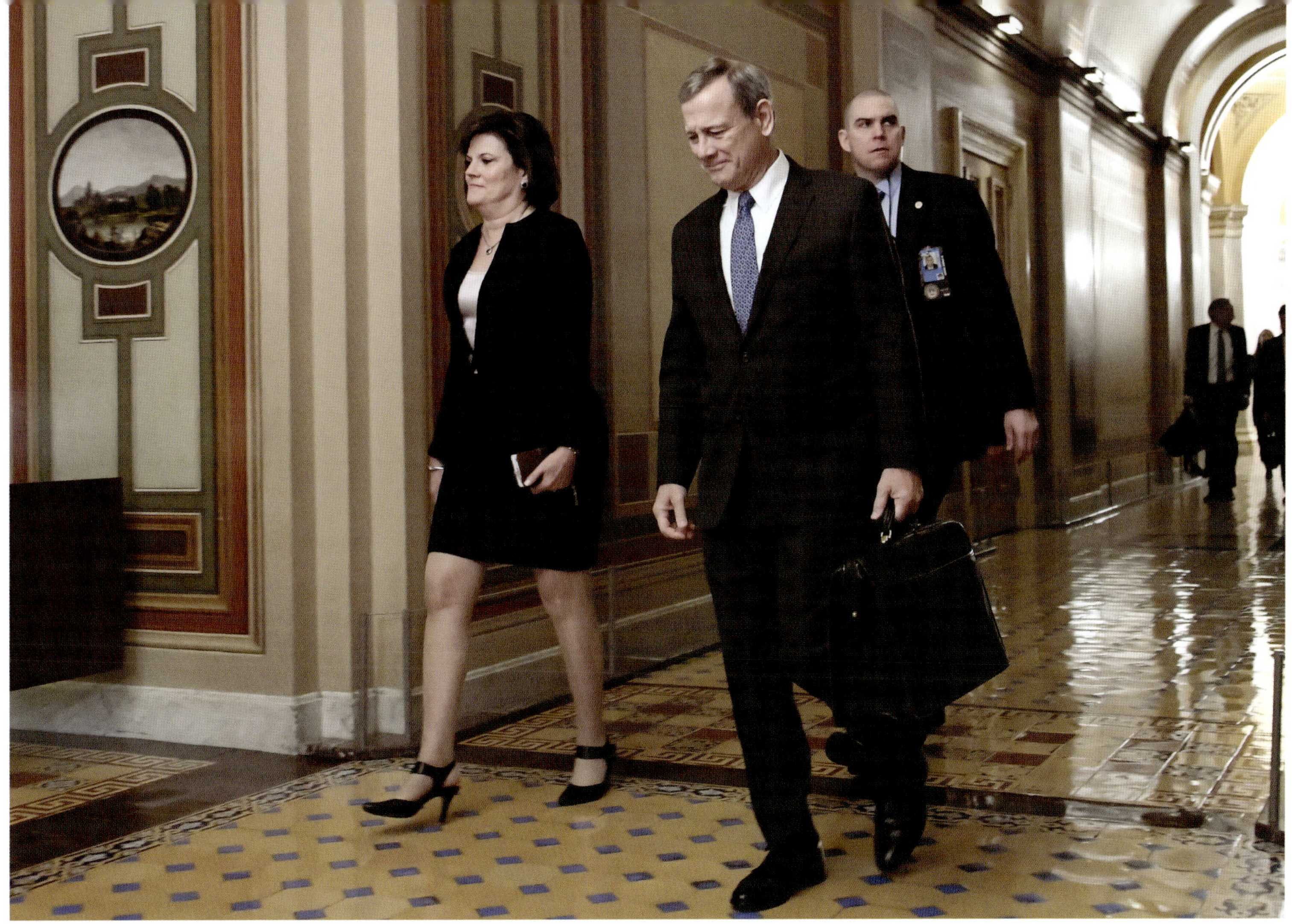

US Supreme Court Chief Justice John Roberts is escorted to the Senate Chambers where he will preside over the Senate impeachment trial of President Donald J. Trump, January 2020.

US Supreme Court Chief Justice John Roberts presided over the impeachment trial. Each day, Justice Roberts, surrounded by security, was escorted into the Capitol and through the hallways to the Senate Chamber, carrying a brown leather bag that contained his judicial robes.

Once inside the chamber, the senators were prohibited by federal law to use cell phones or bring in reading material to ensure their full attention. I think a few of them were happy to be approached by the flurry of reporters who swarmed them as they exited the chamber to take a break. Since that was also an election year, several of the senators running for presidential office were frustrated about being stuck in the hearings, listening to impeachment testimony, while their opponents were able to continue campaigning all over the country.

Once again, being a small news organization, it was very challenging to know where to go during the hearings because there were so many places to be at one time within the Capitol and, of course, the White House. Many of us photographers crossed paths while we waited outside the halls of the Senate. We exchanged information with each other on alternate stakeout locations for senators as they paraded in and out of the Senate Chamber, sometimes stopping to make a comment or take questions.

As I sat outside the Senate Chamber listening to the live radio broadcast, I was acutely aware that this was my second sitting US president to be impeached. As the world waited to see if he would be removed from office, I was grateful that I had graduated to being *inside* the Capitol this time around.

> As I sat outside the Senate Chamber listening to the live radio broadcast, I was acutely aware that this was my second sitting US president to be impeached.

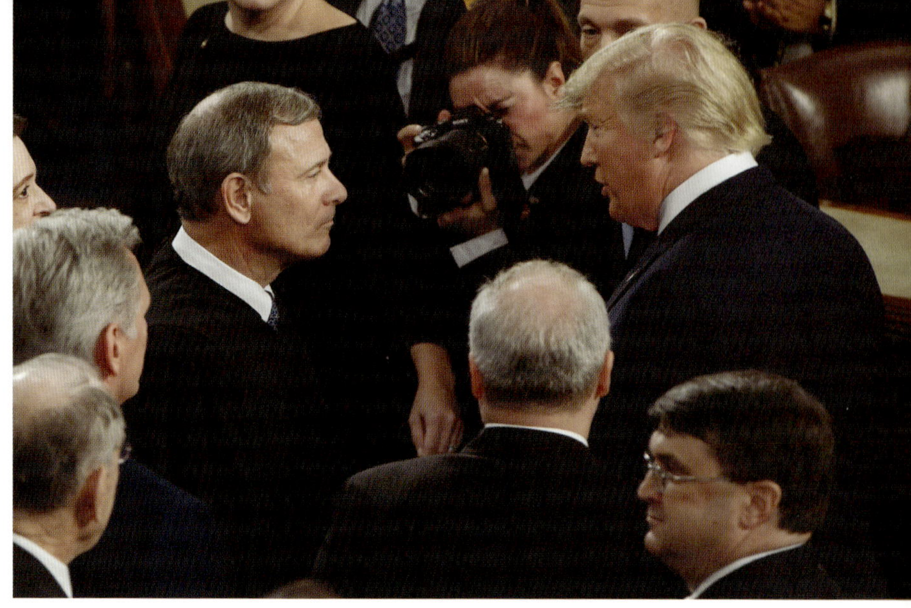

On his way up the aisle to deliver his February 2020 State of the Union Address, President Trump is greeted by US Supreme Court Justice Roberts.

The 2020 State of the Union address took place on February 4, 2020, just before the final vote from the Senate was decided. On his way up the aisle in the House Chamber, President Trump greeted Supreme Court Chief Justice Roberts, who was presiding over the impeachment hearings. The Senate was due to vote the next day on whether Trump would be removed from office. I am sure that was an awkward moment for the two, but they did not show it.

Minutes later, things got off to a rocky start. After President Trump handed Speaker Pelosi her customary copy of his State of the Union speech, he refused to shake hands with her. At the end of the evening, Speaker Pelosi tore up her copy of President Trump's remarks in

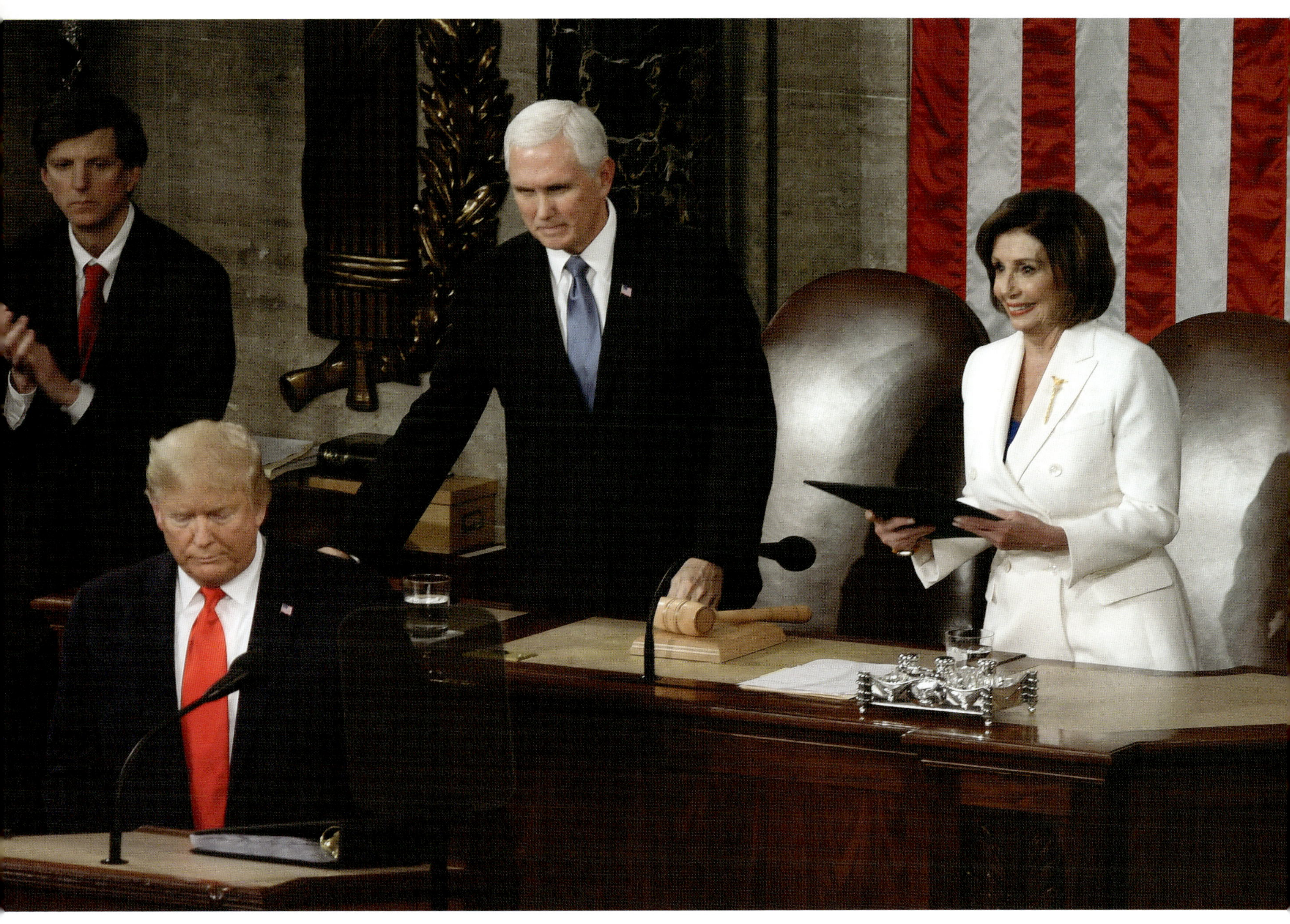

*After refusing to shake hands with Speaker of the House Nancy Pelosi,
President Donald J. Trump prepares to deliver his State of the Union
Address in the midst of his impeachment trial. February 2020.*

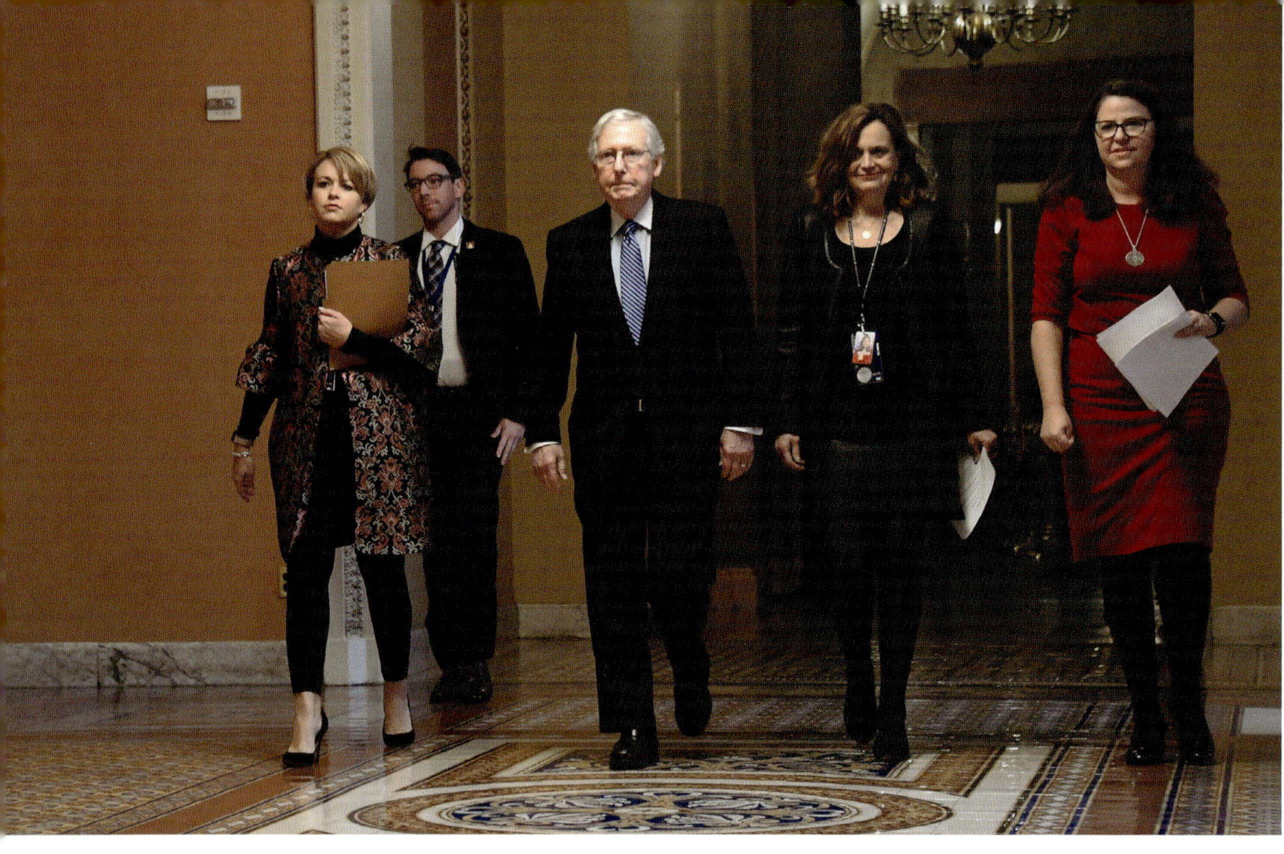

Senator Mitch McConnell walks to the Senate Chambers for the impeachment vote, February 2020.

retaliation; the gesture cemented their ongoing conflict. Unfortunately, I was not in the House Chamber at that moment and missed the famous shot.

The very next morning, Senate Majority Leader Mitch McConnell walked to the Senate Chamber for the final impeachment trial vote. A group of us stood outside the Senate Chamber doors as we listened to the votes being called out. Again, I witnessed history as we heard the crack of the gavel, signaling the trial had ended. We all lifted our lenses as we waited for the door to open, knowing the history-making moment was at hand as Supreme Court Justice John Roberts emerged from the court room. The votes were 52-48 against abuse of power and 53-47 on obstruction of Congress. President Trump was acquitted.

The next day, we rushed down to the White House to an open-press access event in the East Room, where President Trump was to make a statement about his acquittal. The room was more packed than I had ever seen, with media and many members of Congress. I was so grateful to be in the room as the president thanked his supporters and proudly held up the front page of *The Washington Post*, publicizing his acquittal. I felt I had come full circle in my career as I captured yet another sitting US president responding to the conclusion of his impeachment hearings.

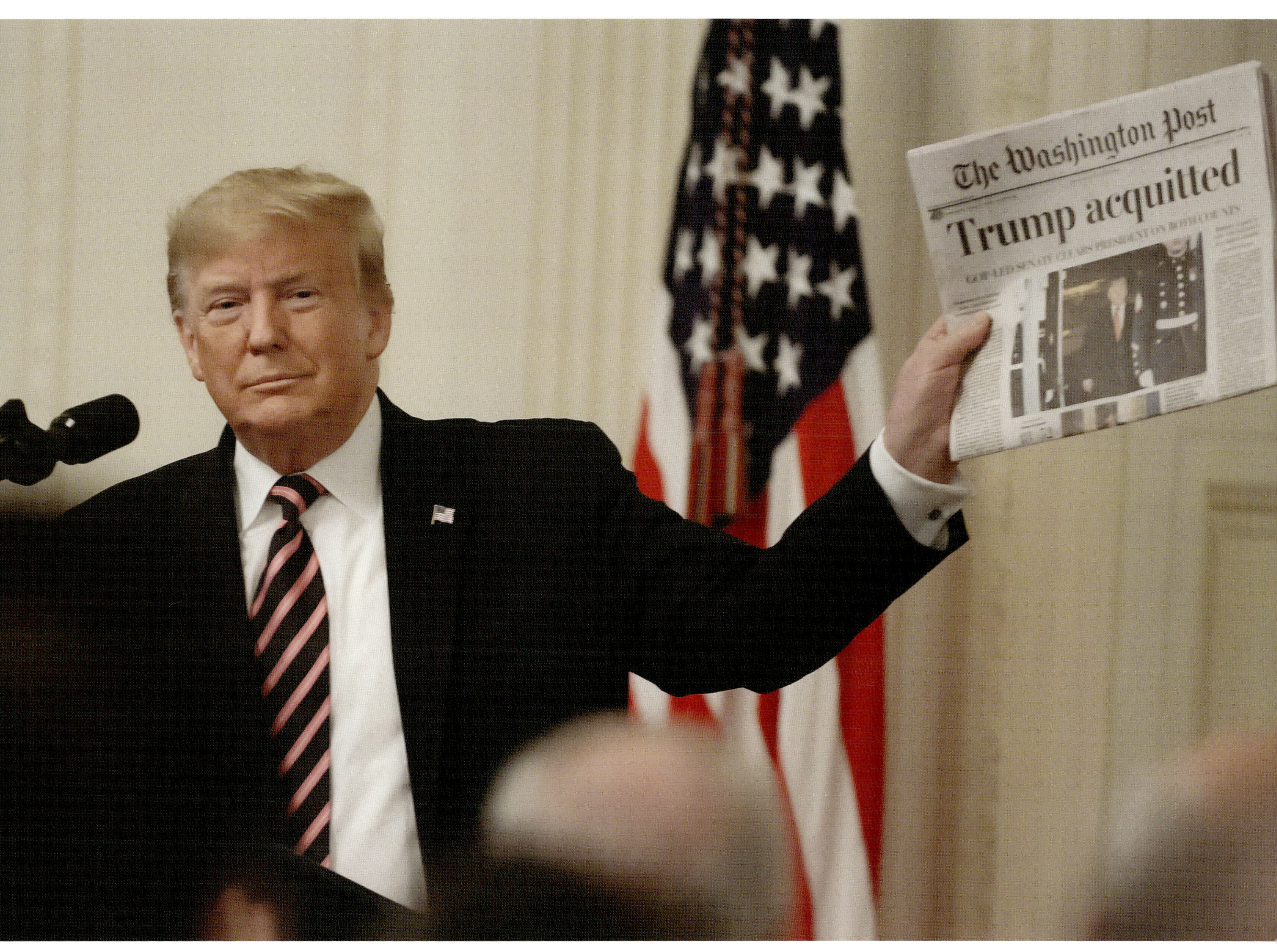

President Donald J. Trump verifies his acquittal by the Senate by holding up a copy of the front page of the Washington Post *during his remarks in the East Room.*

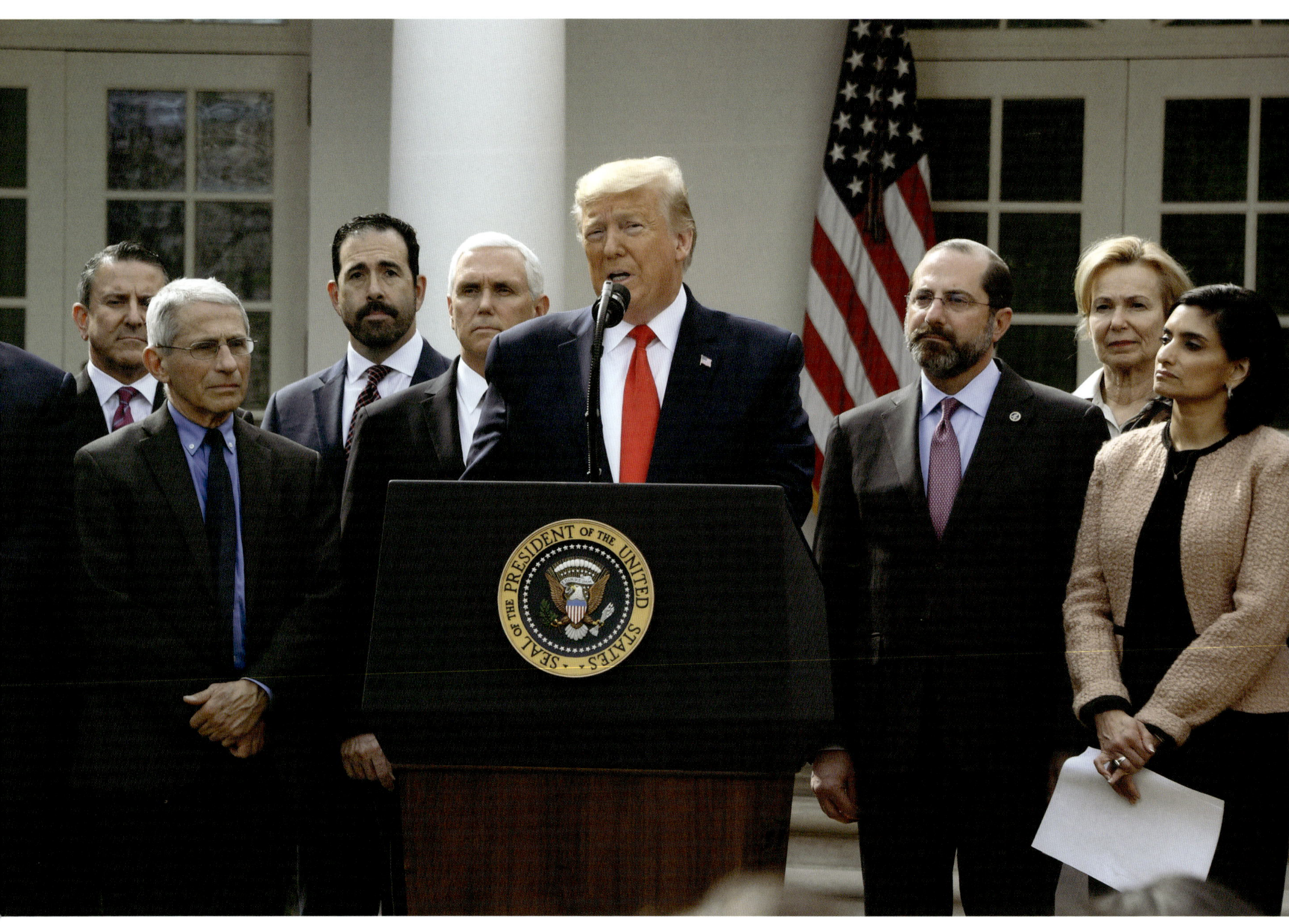

Surrounded by medical professionals and corporation representatives, President Donald Trump holds a press conference in the Rose Garden to announce he is declaring a state of emergency for the nation due to the coronavirus threat and would be ordering businesses and schools to close across the country for a period of time. March 2020.

We had all taken a big exhale from the impeachment drama when President Trump declared another national state of emergency on March 13, 2020, as the world began the battle with the COVID-19 pandemic. The president began holding almost daily briefings with his Coronavirus Task Force, headed by Vice President Mike Pence. Pence and his team of doctors alongside other health professionals updated the nation, discussing the new findings and strategies to try and deal with the deadly virus. Many in the media said that the president was taking the opportunity to campaign for reelection during those briefings while he had the nation's attention.

Then, on May 25, 2020, George Floyd, a black man, died when a white Minnesotan police officer used his knee to hold Floyd down by his neck for over eight minutes. This exploded into outrage, resulting in demonstrations and riots that rippled across the country for almost two weeks. The Black Lives Matter movement blasted its message loud and clear as protests took place around the world. Since everyone was quarantined at home, people were able to focus more closely on this tragedy as the shocking clips were constantly aired on the networks. This helped fuel the perfect storm of rage and frustration. Floyd's murder followed several other recent killings of black people by white police officers in just a few months' time.

Covering this important and painful part of history during the middle of a pandemic was tricky for those of us in the media. We risked our own personal safety, not only from potentially violent protesters but also from exposure to the COVID-19 virus as well. However, most of the protesters did wear masks.

One week later, President Trump ordered the use of tear gas and rubber bullets to forcibly remove peaceful protesters from the vicinity of St. John's Church. St. John's, also known as "the Church of the Presidents," is located across from the White House. Trump wanted to clear his path so that he could participate in a photo op with some of his staff at the church's front entrance. He did not make any remarks, but only stood silently, holding a Bible upside down (accidentally, I hope) for a couple of awkward minutes. Needless to say, this enraged many people on a lot of levels.

The Covid epidemic suddenly closed in on the White House itself when, on October 4, 2020, President Trump was hospitalized at Walter Reed Hospital for treatment of the disease. During his three days of treatment, hundreds of his supporters showed up to offer their encouragement. Acting against medical

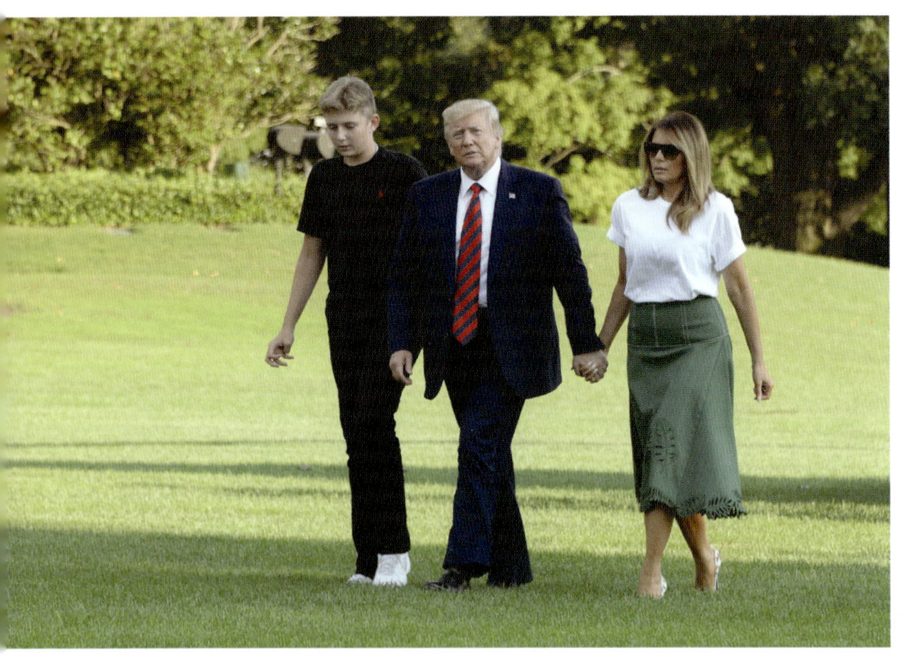

*President Donald Trump, First Lady Melania, and
son Barron walk to the White House residence from
Marine One after arriving back from their summer
vacation in Bedminster, New Jersey. August 2019.*

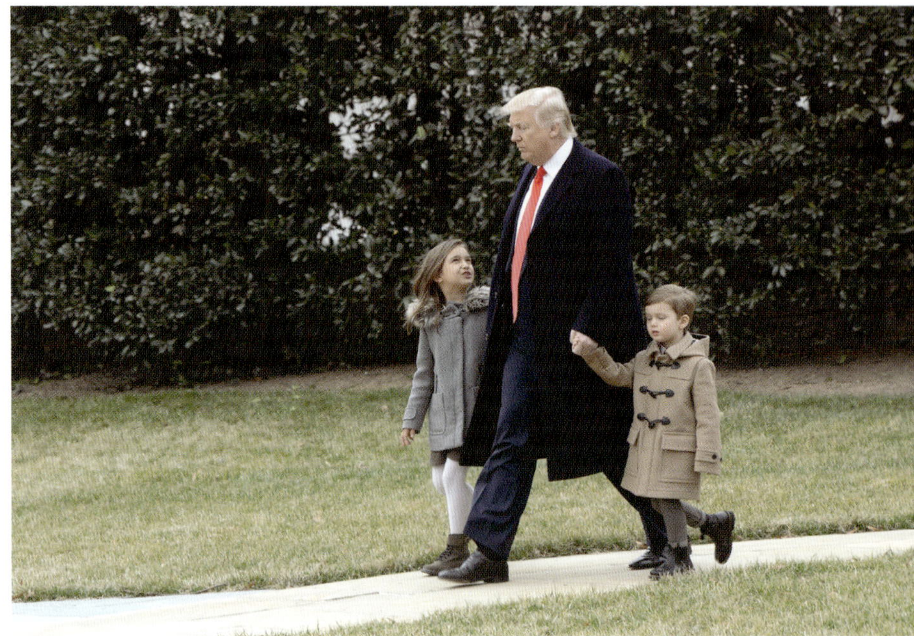

*President Trump leaves the Oval Office with
grandchildren Arabella and Joseph Kushner as
they walk to their awaiting Marine One helicopter
on the South Lawn, February 2017.*

advice, the president had his staff drive him around the block to wave at his fans. Upon being released, he hit the ground running as he continued to hold campaign rallies across the country—sometimes as many as three in one day. He held many rallies in airport hangers, using Air Force One as the backdrop, to make it easier for him.

Through all the controversies of the Trump administration, President Trump seemed to maintain a close relationship with his family and would return to see them after day trips. We news photographers would sometimes witness him with his grandchildren as he escorted them to Marine One to travel with him for a special occasion, or walking with his son Barron and Melania as they all returned from a weekend getaway.

He was happy to share the spotlight with the first lady from time to time as well, such as at his final State of the Union address when he had her award controversial radio talk show host Rush Limbaugh the Presidential Medal of Freedom from the first lady's box.

Following the 2020 presidential election, results showed Joe Biden to have won the race, making him the 46th President of the United States. Yet President Trump refused to accept the election results, citing widespread electoral fraud, and vowed to fight the results in court. Trump went on camera stating, "The only way they can take this election away from us is if this is a rigged election. . . . We're going to win this election."[5]

Trump remained mostly out of the public eye as he figured out his next move. But still, the world watched and waited. President Trump made his final public appearance as president when he took the stage on January 6, 2021, at a "Save America" rally on the Ellipse, a 52-acre park north of the National Mall.

It was rumored that he was going to encourage his supporters to march to the US Capitol in protest of the presidential election results. Congress was finishing the Electoral College process, where the votes from each state would be formally counted. All members of Congress would be in attendance, and Vice President Pence would preside.

I decided to stake out the Capitol that day because I felt that it would be a better vantage point to see where the crowd was headed.

When I arrived at the east side of the Capitol, there was a large crowd of mostly older white people, many who were veterans, attentively listening on their smartphones to President Trump's live remarks taking place just down the street. Even though COVID-19 was still in full effect, very few people wore masks. Trump's voice rang out on the hundreds of phones that were set on speaker, making it sound like his voice was everywhere. Vice President Pence arrived at the Capitol toward the end of those remarks and immediately went inside, relatively unnoticed.

That's when I looked down and saw that I had lost my new iPhone! I thought it was gone for good, but a while later a former Vietnam vet and Trump supporter managed to find me in the middle of the chaos and return my phone, refusing a reward. Such a kind soul in the middle of the growing tension.

Out on Constitution Avenue, a large group of protestors approached the Capitol, which was a few blocks away. Several Capitol Hill policemen near me appeared to be growing more anxious as the crowd, which was only getting bigger, steadily headed our way.

As I turned, I suddenly found myself face-to-face with over a dozen or so of the "Proud Boys." Several of them had walkie-talkies. They marched with an air of

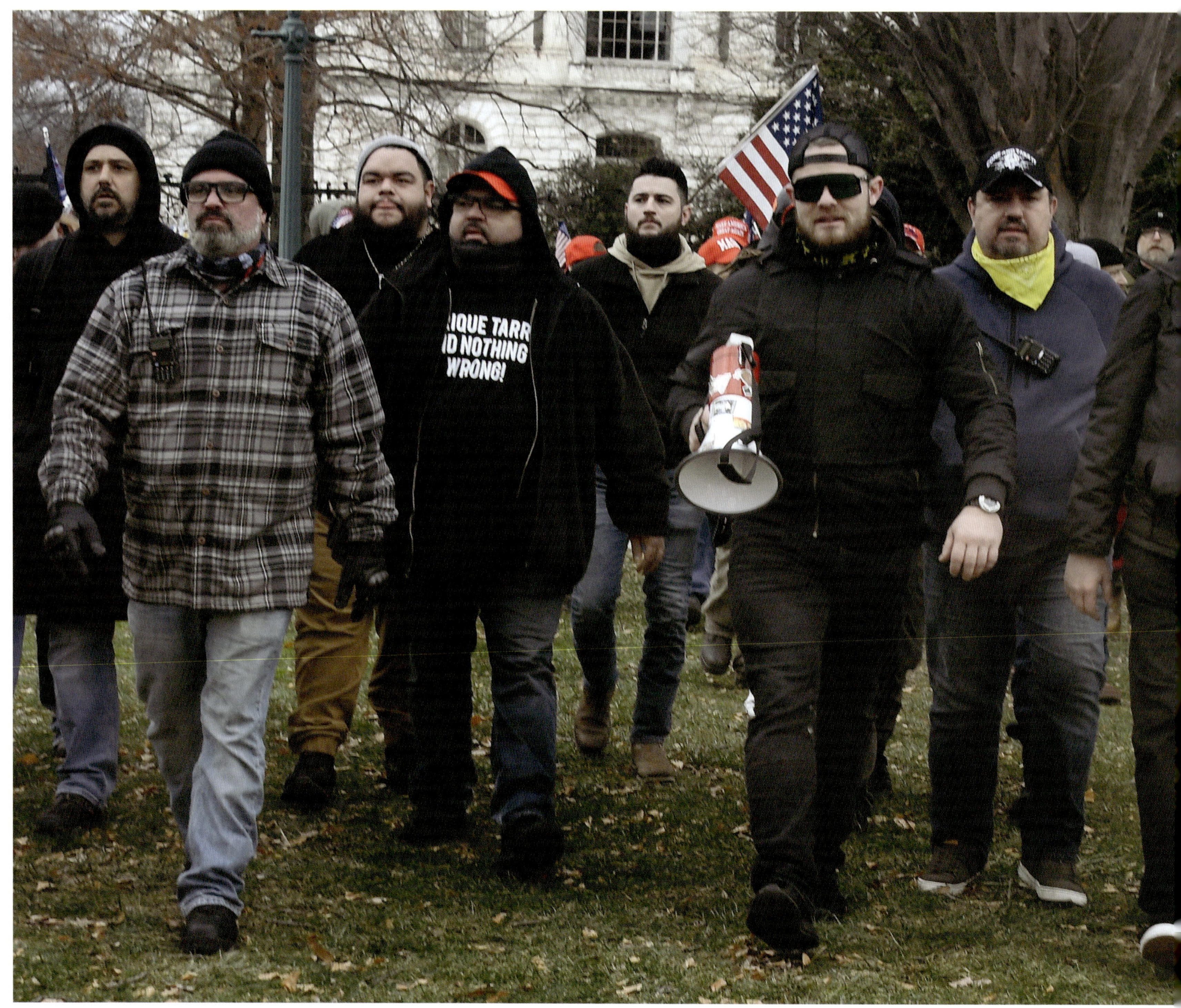

     History in the Making

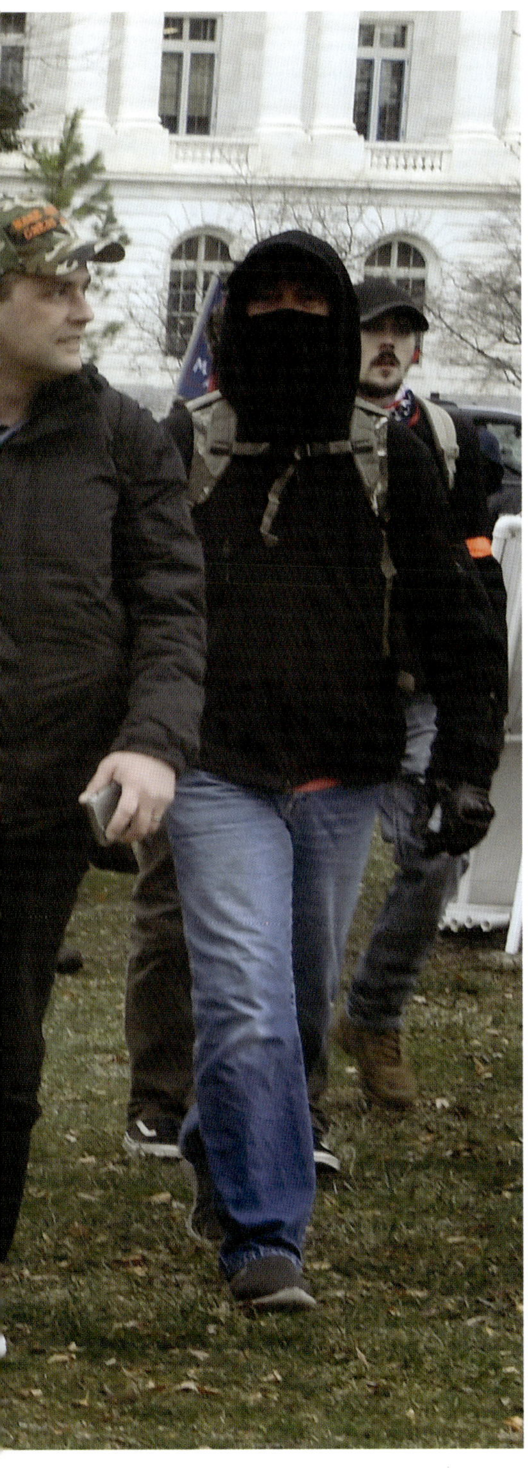

authority toward me, but I continued to fire away, focusing my camera as I walked backward. One of them began shouting "F—– the media!" as if it were a battle cry. I could hear others shouting that the media was "fake news" and could not be trusted. My instincts told me to stash my media credentials under my jacket. As I continued to walk through the crowd taking pictures, there was an undeniable shift in the atmosphere taking place. The threat of violence was growing.

A short time later, a man near me warned an older woman that his group was about to break down the security fencing near us and she should move, or she would likely be trampled. It was then that the crowd began shouting "Stop the Steal!"

The man pointed to the barrier twenty yards away, where more police in riot gear were arriving. The mass of protestors began to swell, pushing back against the Capitol Hill police officers and breaking down the protective fencing.

The crowd that had been peacefully protesting was now merged with the swarm of people that kept arriving from Trump's speech. The two herds joined together and marched to the steps of the Capitol.

The police tried to keep the crowd from advancing, but they were dramatically outnumbered and forced to retreat inside the building. Hundreds of people rushed up the stairs to the doors of the Capitol chanting, "Stop the Steal! Stop the Steal!" As they became more enraged, the chanting subtly changed to "Hang Mike Pence! Hang Mike Pence!"

Dozens of the Proud Boys arrive at the US Capitol on January 6, 2021, just before the rioting begins.

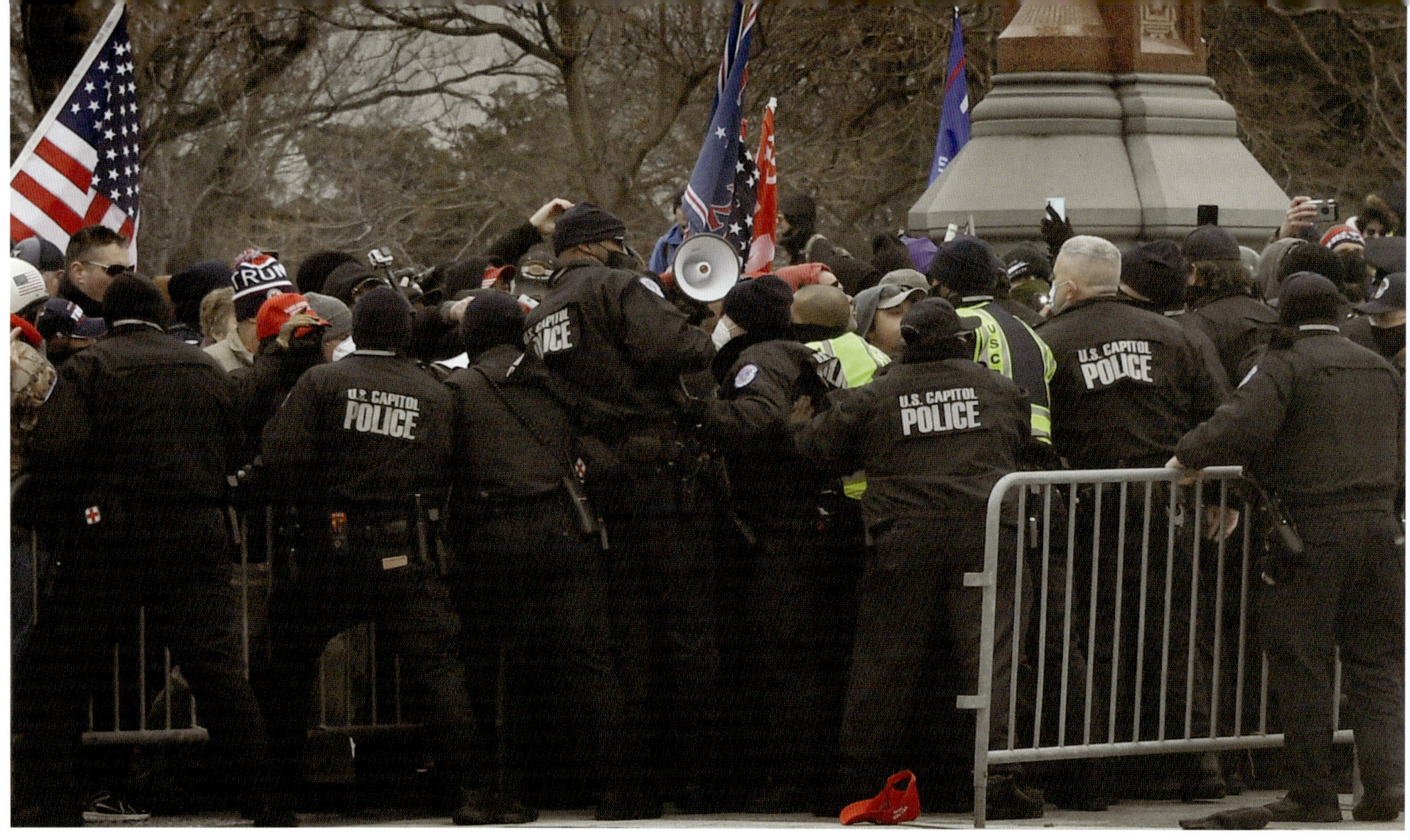

Capitol Police push back against January 6 rioters attempting to force themselves through protective fencing.

I paced myself with the crowd and moved to the steps of the Capitol. After walking up a dozen or so steps, I realized the crowd had transformed into a mob. Fortunately, I was able to change my position to the outer periphery of the mob so that I would not be pinned in; otherwise I would not have been able to take pictures of anything other than the back of the people's heads who were directly in front of me.

The now fired-up crowd reached the top of the Capitol stairs and banged on the doors and windows, eventually breaking through the glass. I heard the sound and headed over to the west side of the Capitol, where things were becoming more violent by the second. I was greeted by another photographer who was retreating, eyes watering because of the tear gas and deer spray that were being deployed by both protesters and later by the police. I had no protective gear and was forced to retreat.

Members of Congress were locked down as the rioters made their way into the building, gaining access to the House floor itself, where just a short time earlier Vice President Mike Pence had stood.

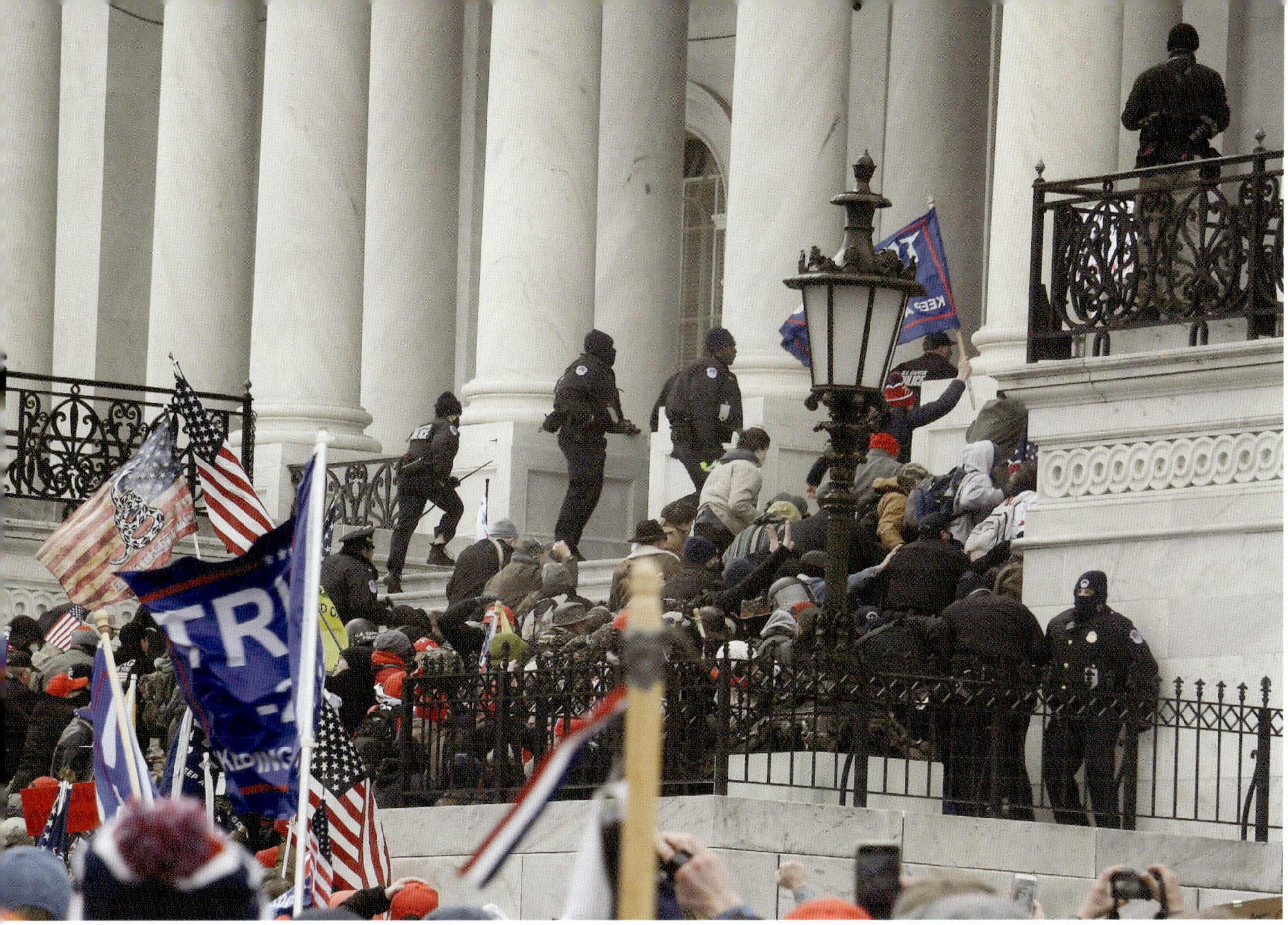

A crowd rushes up the stairs to the US Capitol Building during the January 6 riot.

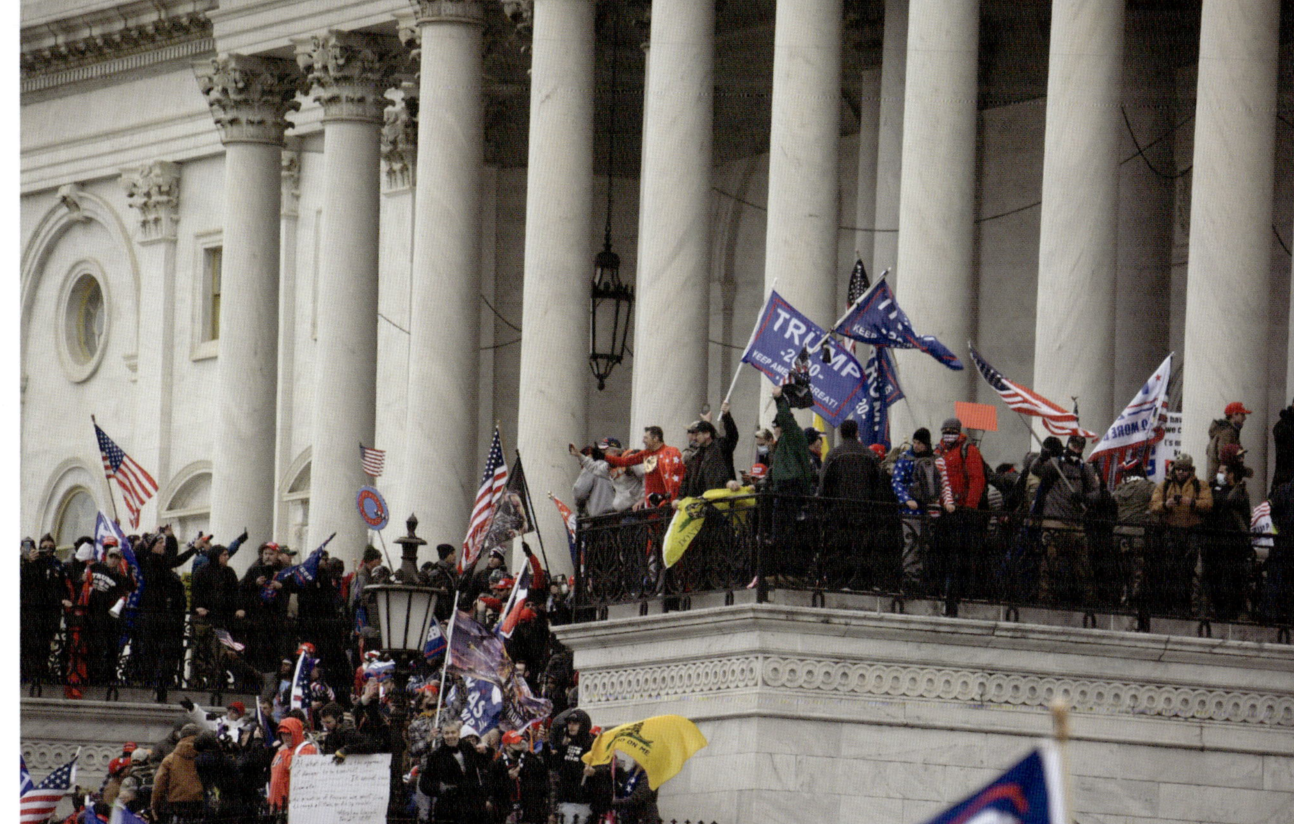

A crowd shouts from a balcony at the US Capitol Building during the January 6 riot.

Five people died and 140 police officers were injured due to this riot at the Capitol. What I had witnessed was an insurrection.

One week before the Biden inauguration, President Trump was impeached for the second time by the House of Representatives. The charge this time was incitement of insurrection against the United States, but the January 6 hearings were not scheduled to take place until after Trump had left office. President Trump chose not to attend the Biden inauguration, instead flying on Marine One for the final time over the US Capitol just hours prior to the ceremony, on the way to his own departure ceremony at Joint Base Andrews.

Shortly after the attack on the Capitol, the incident began to be trivialized. Statements from some members of Congress were being circulated that the January 6 happenings were just some unruly tourists getting rowdy; other members on the scene testified that they were fearful for their lives, crying and shaking while being interviewed. Thankfully, Biden and a number of congressional members made sure that day was recorded in history, as it was made public record when they awarded the Congressional Gold Medal to several Capitol Hill and Metropolitan Police Department officers who were injured that day.

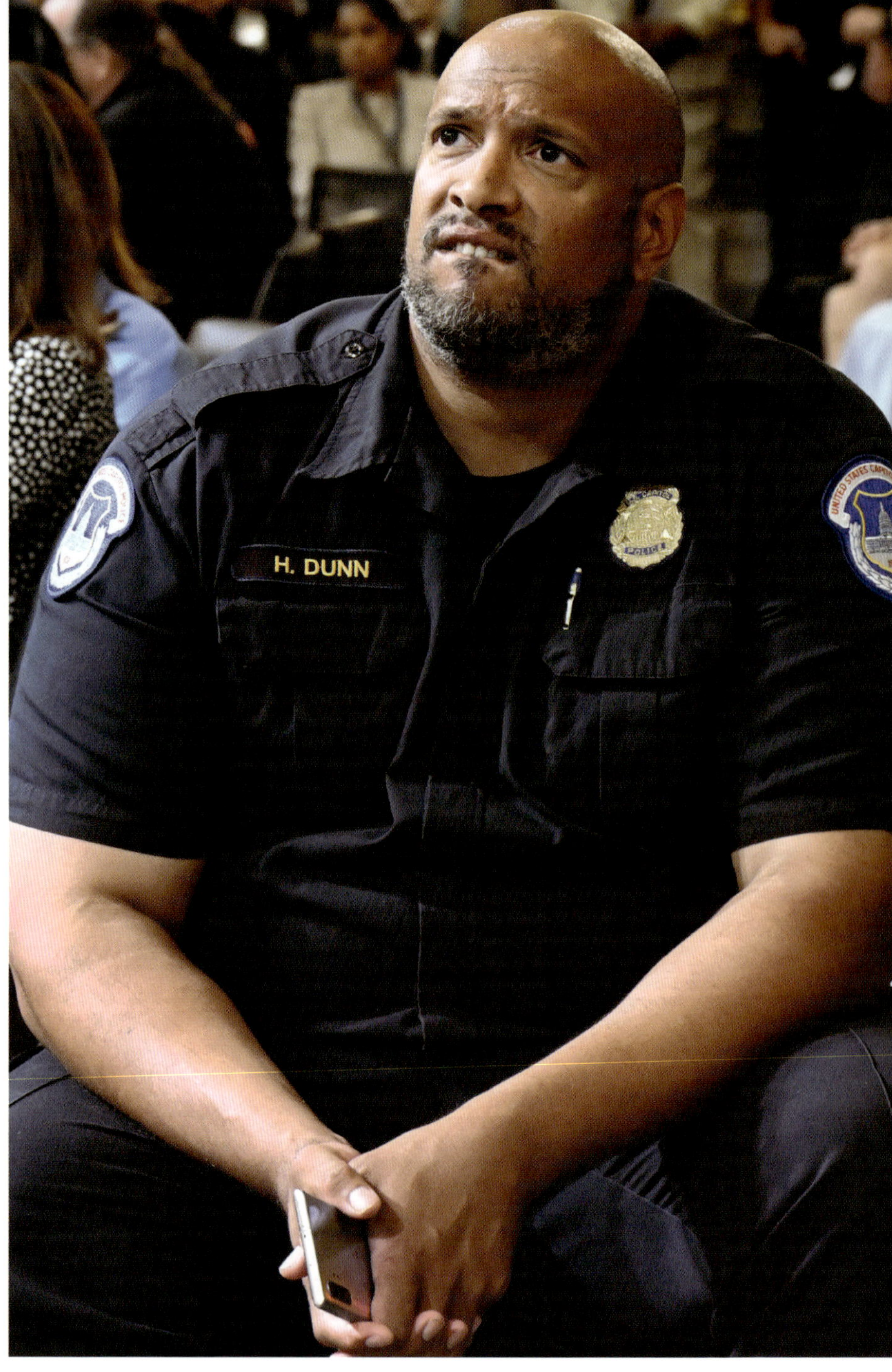

Sitting in the front row of the January 6 hearings, Capitol Hill police officer Harry Dunn, who was injured during the riot at the Capitol, observes new pictures and video evidence. July 2022.

  History in the Making

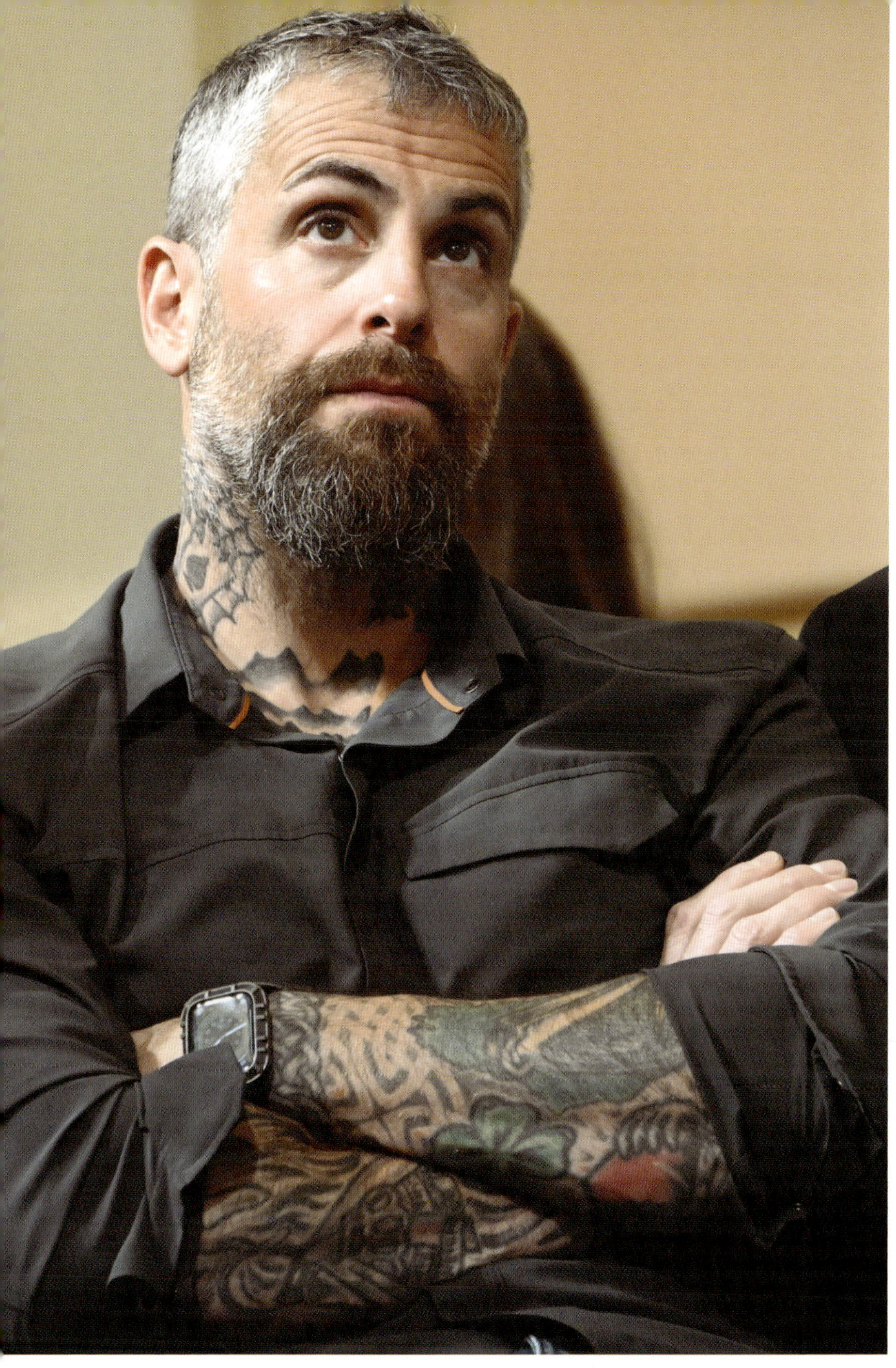

*Injured Metropolitan police officer Mike
Fanone watches video footage being shown
by the January 6 Committee as they hold the
seventh hearing investigating the events leading
up to the violence at the Capitol, July 2022.*

In June 2022, a series of hearings were held by the members of Congress who had formed the January 6 Committee, created to investigate the causes of the insurrection. I covered a few of those hearings and photographed several of the injured police officers who bravely defended the Capitol on that day. They were given honorary front-row seats in the hearing room and bravely relived their experiences as they watched the large movie screen behind the US House Select Committee. The intensity of their facial expressions revealed their genuine anguish. It was disturbing to watch the footage from the White House staffers who were called as witnesses and to hear them testify what they had seen take place from the safety of inside the White House while the riot was happening. Some of the police officers were not ever able to return to work. Many continue to suffer from PTSD and other physical injuries, cutting their careers short. No one could have ever predicated that all of those officers would be injured while defending the US Capitol against their fellow Americans.

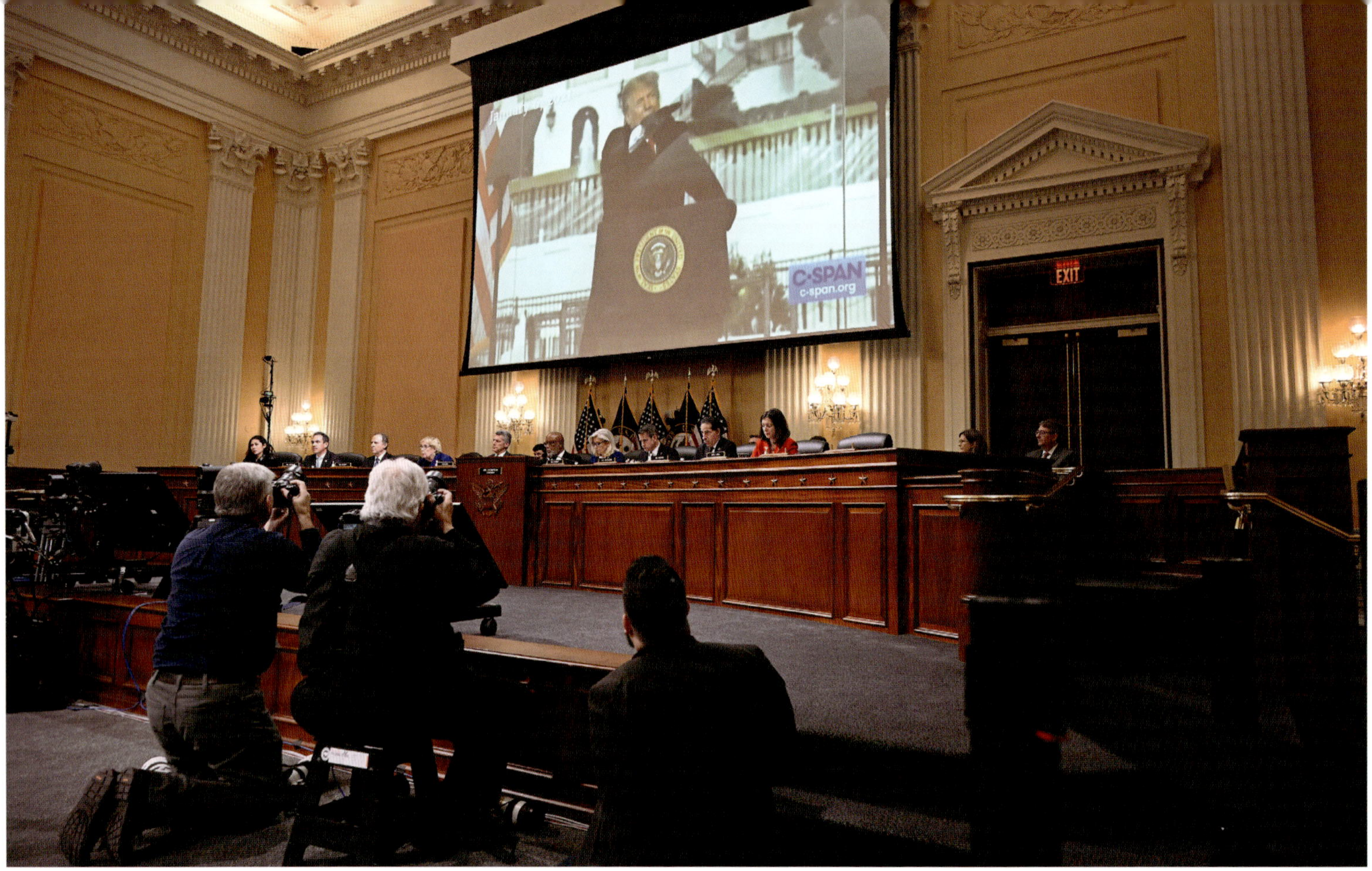

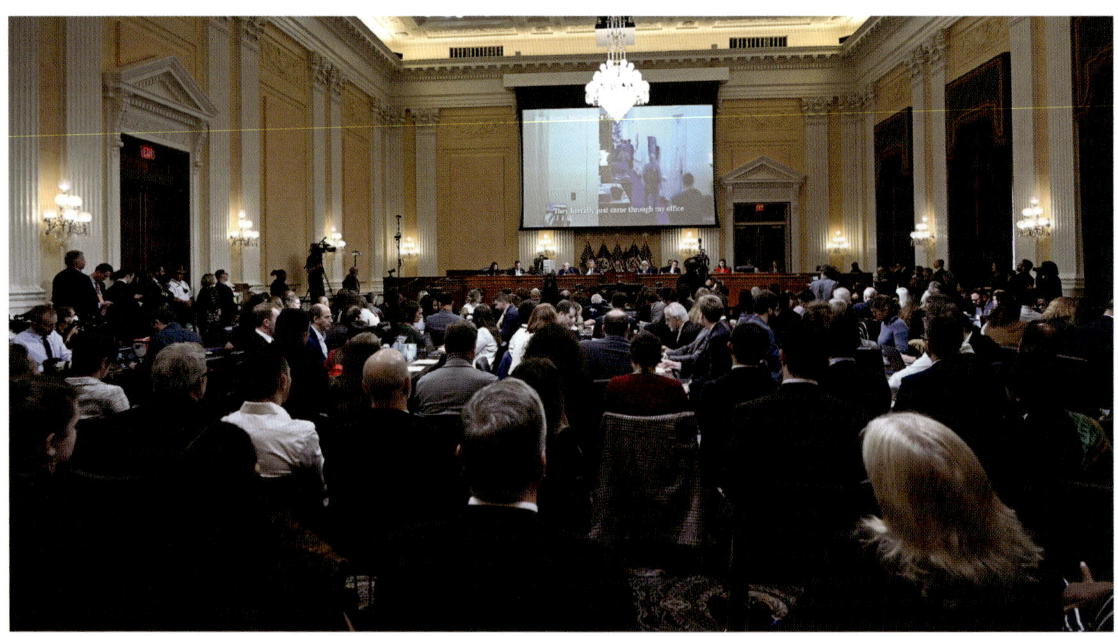

*Members of the
January 6 Committee
meet once again for a
series of hearings where
a restricted amount of
photographers were
allowed in the room,
July 2022.*

     History in the Making

On August 3, 2023, former President Trump was arraigned on federal charges for attempting to overturn the 2020 presidential election. His arrival at the E. Barrett Prettyman US Courthouse in Washington, DC, was a major media event. Trump arrived in his large motorcade and was quietly driven to the back of the courthouse in his black SUV, complete with tinted windows. He pleaded "not guilty" on all the following charges: the January 6 insurrection, the Georgia election interference case, the classified documents case, and the "hush money" case involving adult entertainer Stormy Daniels. No former or sitting US president in history has ever been criminally indicted until now, and yet Donald Trump remains highly popular among his loyal followers as he continues to run for president of the United States for a second time in the 2024 election. On May 30, 2024, former president Donald J. Trump was found guilty by a New York jury on thirty-four counts of falsifying business records in a scheme to illegally influence the 2016 election by concealing the hush-money payments. An angry Trump, now considered a felon, is planning to appeal the verdict as he continues to run for a second term as president of the United States. In America, truly anything is possible.

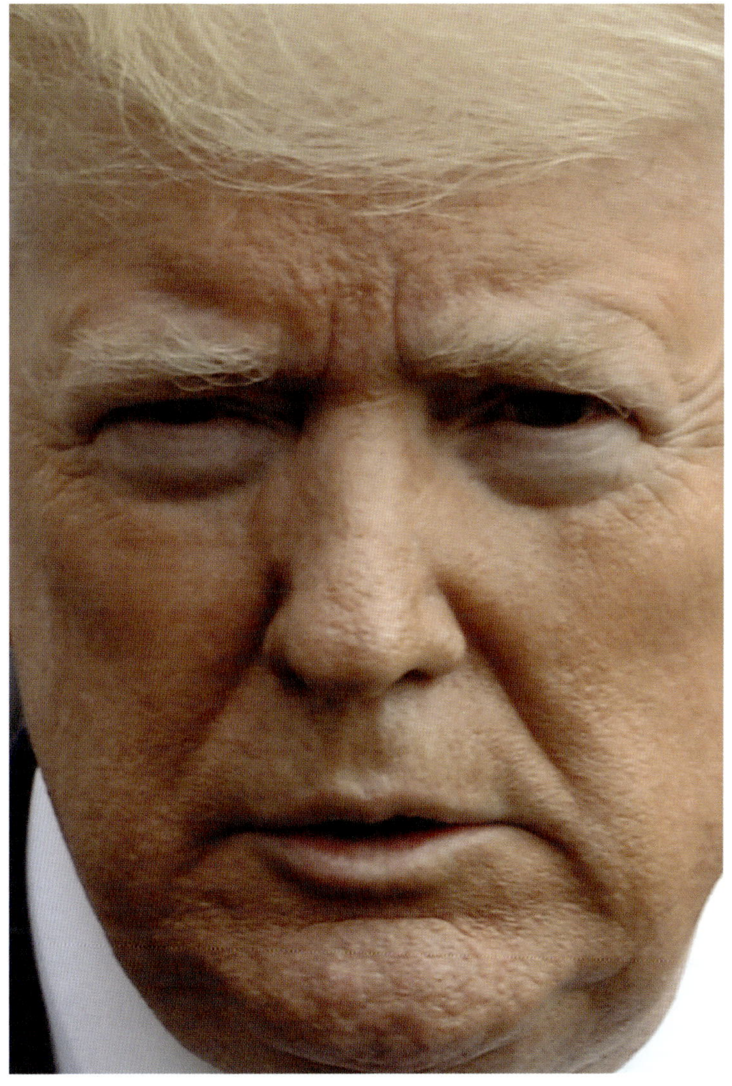

President Donald Trump stops to speak with reporters on his way to Marine One at the White House, October 2019.

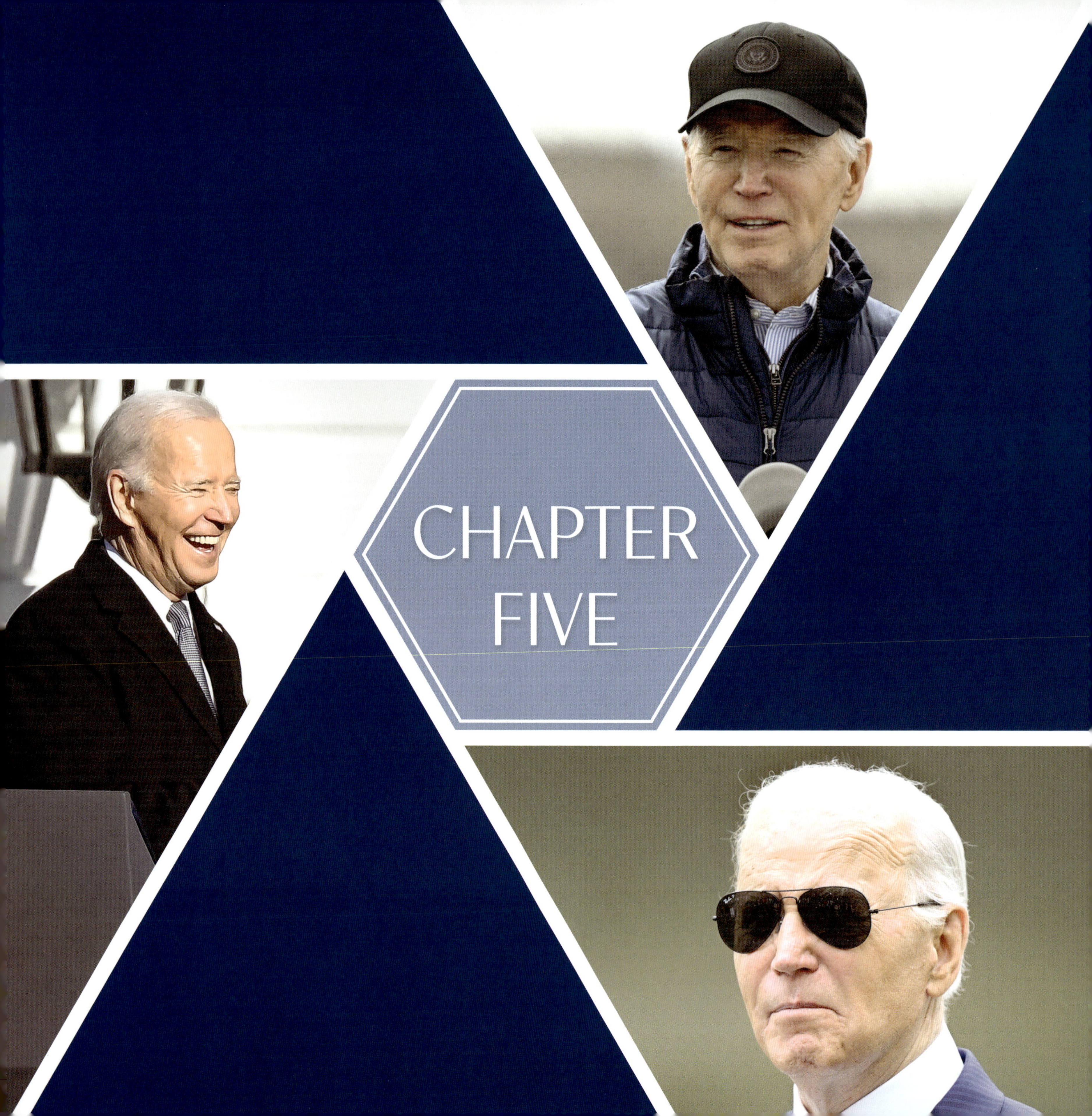

CHAPTER
FIVE

JOSEPH R. BIDEN

I first began covering Senator Joe Biden on Capitol Hill many years ago. One of my favorite memories was photographing him in 2007 with Bono, lead singer of the band U2, as he showed the rock star around Capitol Hill before meeting with other senators. I remember the excitement that day as members of Congress and their staffers lined the hallways. They were using any excuse to catch a glimpse of the "rock star in the House!"

President Joseph R. Biden (code name "Celtic") had an inauguration like no other. It was my eighth time photographing the swearing-in of a president and between COVID and the insurrection at the Capitol, there were a limited number of positions this time around; unfortunately, I was dealt a terrible spot. From

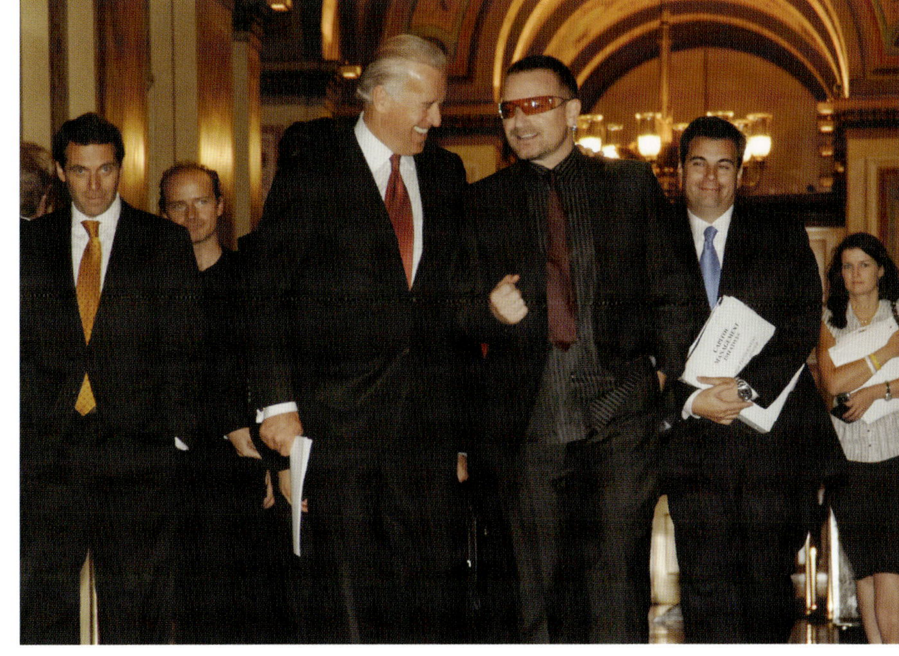

Senator Joseph Biden meets U2 singer Bono at the US Capitol to discuss global development, AIDS, and the poverty crisis. November 2012.

my vantage point, I was visually blocked by the podium and unable to capture Kamala Harris, the first African American woman to be sworn in as vice president of the United States. Once again I found myself coming full circle, disappointed but grateful to be on the grounds *at all* for this historic event. I guess I will only have those images archived in my memory. Due to the pandemic restrictions, all the festivities were televised and shown virtually, making my coverage of the day a lot shorter than normal.

Even considering the former president's refusal to attend Biden's inauguration, I felt that during this exchange of power there was a collective exhale among the press corps after all the recent havoc that took place in the Trump White House.

Things seemed surreal, however, as we members of the media recalled that only one week earlier, in the same place on the US Capitol grounds, a deadly insurrection had taken place. Those of us inside the buffer zone looked out at the nine-foot riot fencing complete with razor wire and the twenty-five thousand armed National Guards. I will always remember that haunting scene when I watched them patrolling from inside the fencing; it gave our nation's capital a tense, prisonlike vibe.

As I began covering my fifth president, I felt the words from my old friend and bureau chief Sarah McClendon hit me once again: "Keep an eye on the president." Members of the press corps switched gears into the Biden White House fairly smoothly, but there were again further limitations to presidential access. This was partially due to COVID restrictions, but things never did quite get back to normal.

President Biden did not embrace the arrival/departure presser format of his predecessor, and the traditional press conferences were curbed even more.

President Biden had one traditional press conference when he first came into office four years ago. Michael Shear of the *New York Times* wrote the following in April 2023: "More than any president in recent memory, Mr. Biden, 80, has taken steps to reduce opportunities for journalists to question him in forums where he can offer unscripted answers and they can follow up. The result, critics say, is a president who has fewer moments of public accountability for his comments, decisions and actions."[1]

President Biden participates in a two-and-two press conference in the Rose Garden during the state visit of Republic of Korea president Yook Suk Yeol, April 2023.

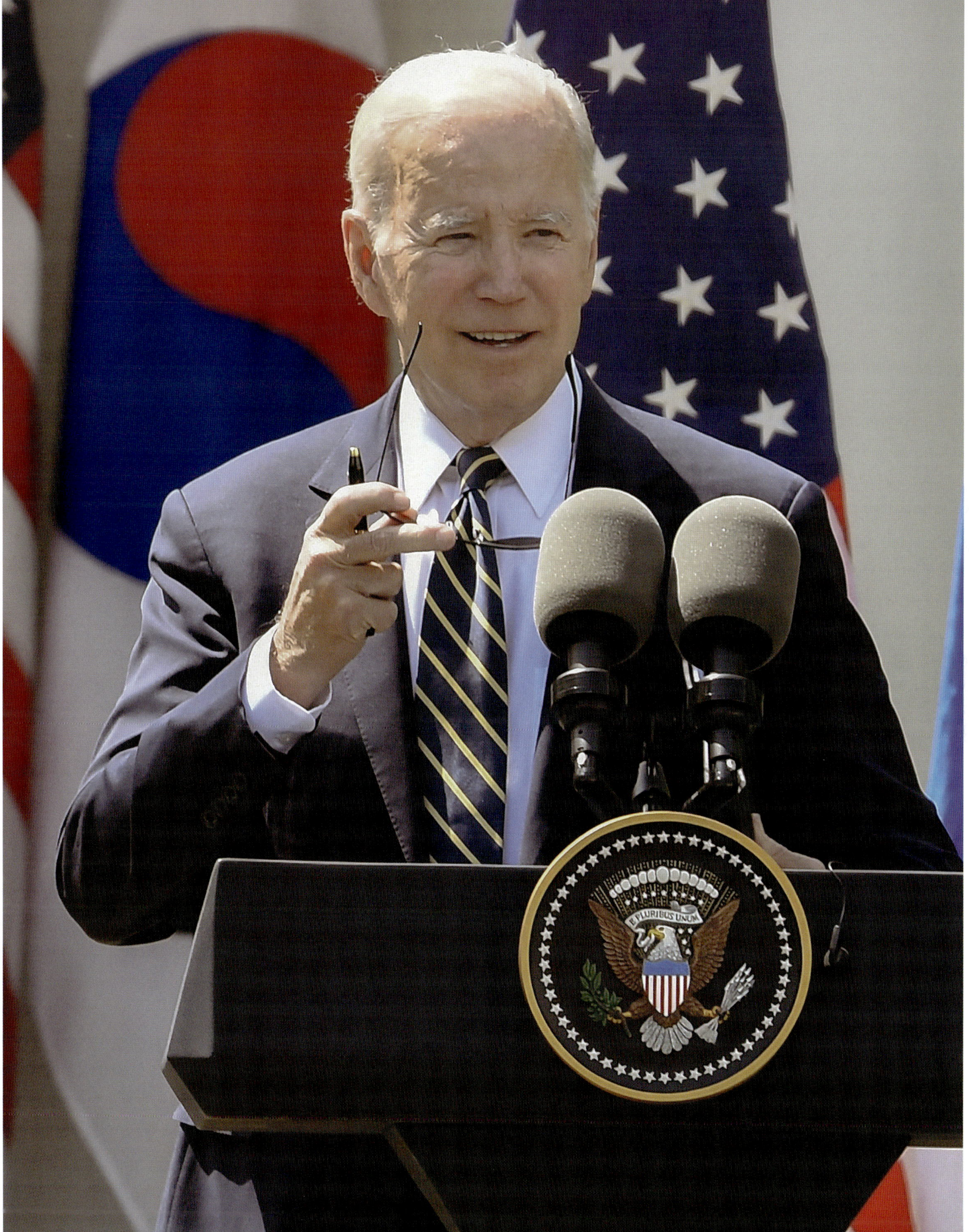

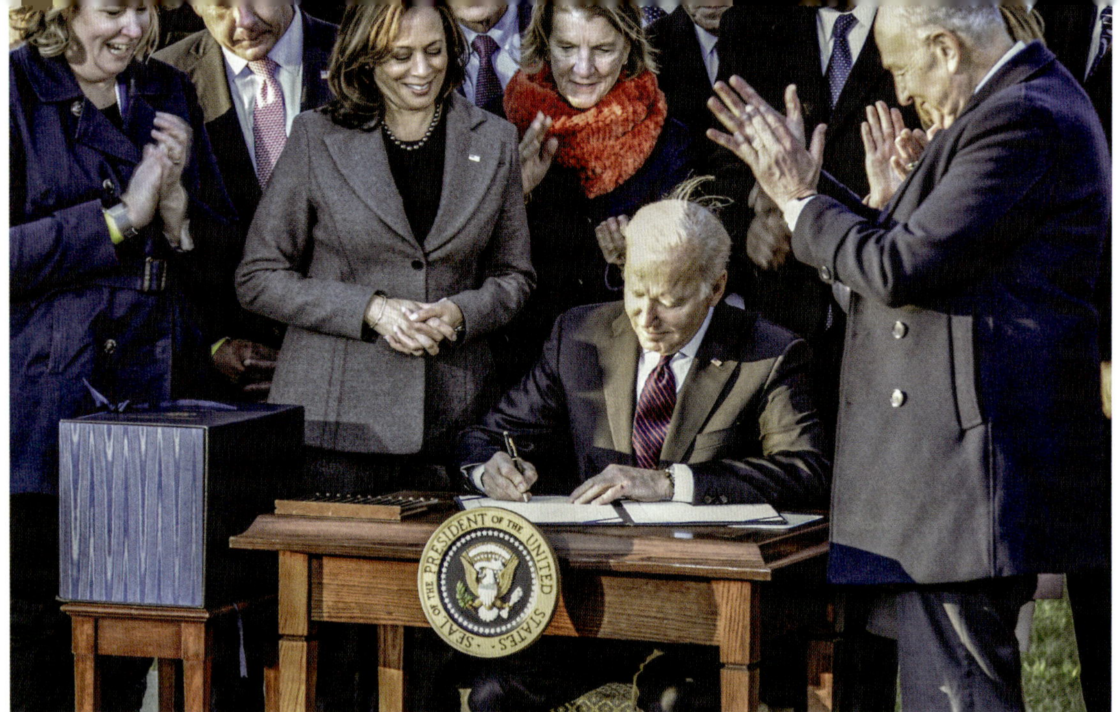

President Biden signs his bipartisan infrastructure bill on the South Lawn as Vice President Kamala Harris and Senator Chuck Schumer celebrate beside him, along with the other lawmakers who helped this happen.

My coverage of the Biden White House, as well as that of my fellow members of the media, has become quite limited. I did not photograph President Biden at any significant event until November 15, 2021, when he signed the $1.2 trillion Bipartisan Infrastructure Bill into law during a ceremony on the South Lawn. There was a feeling of celebration in the air for this legislative accomplishment. Congress and the president had come together and succeeded in providing funding for much-needed infrastructure repairs across the nation, which would also provide a boost to our country's job market. I was among a small number of photographers to cover that event.

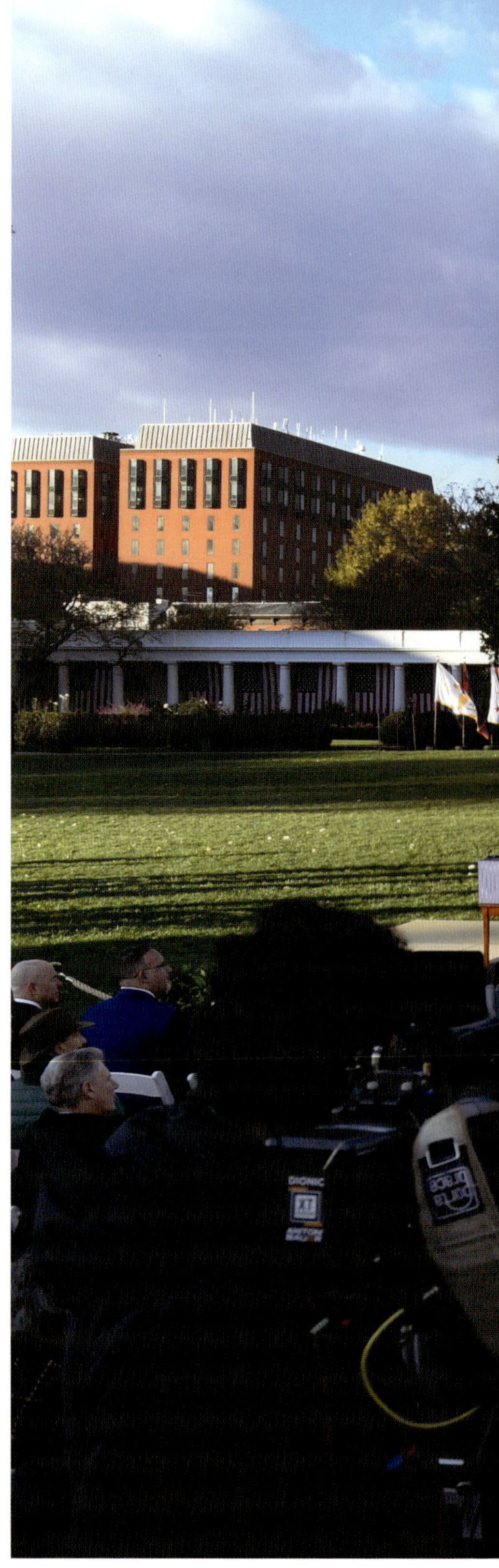

President Joe Biden speaks prior to signing the $1.2 trillion bipartisan infrastructure bill into law during a ceremony on the South Lawn of the White House, November 2021.

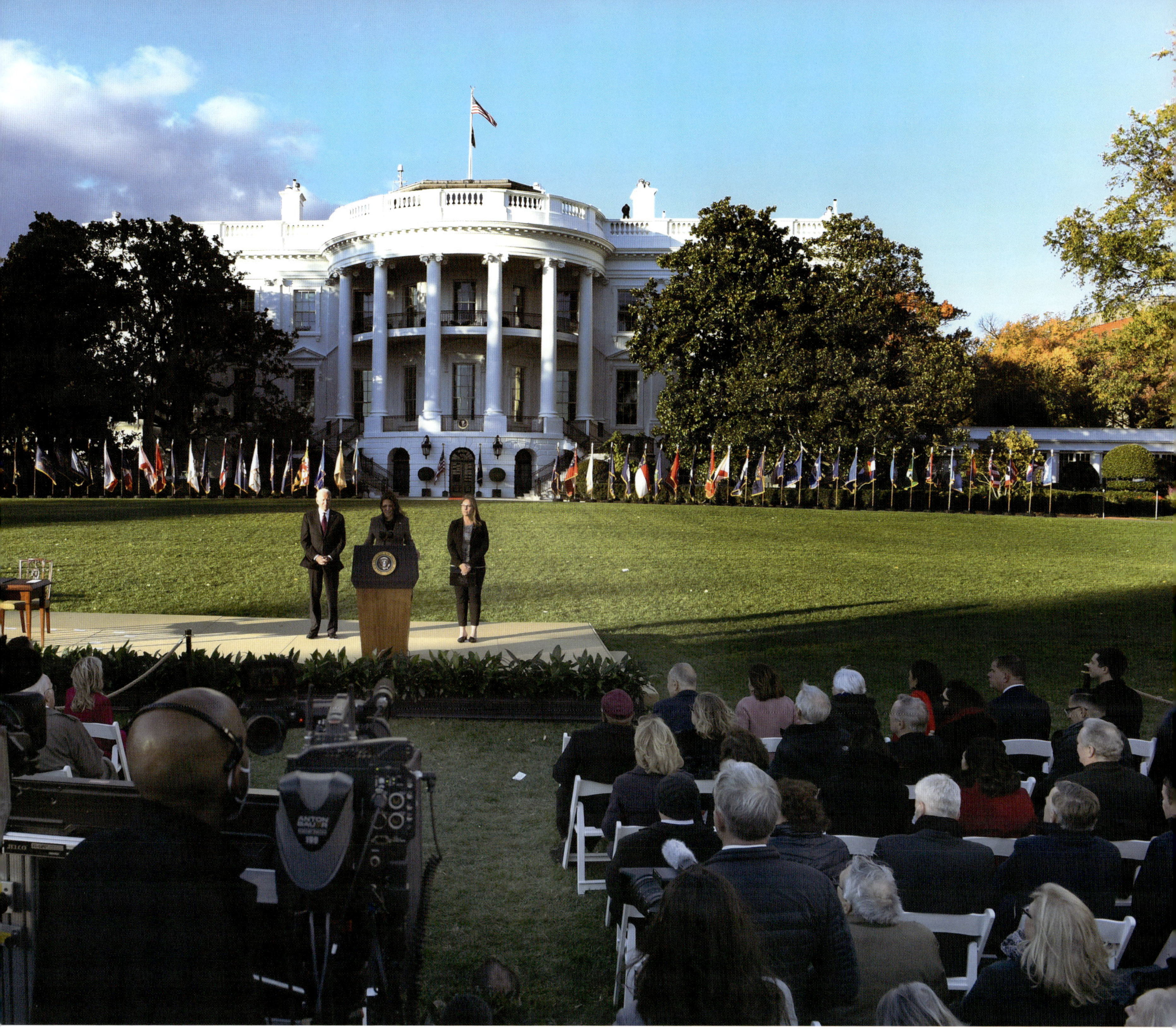

President Joseph R. Biden   135

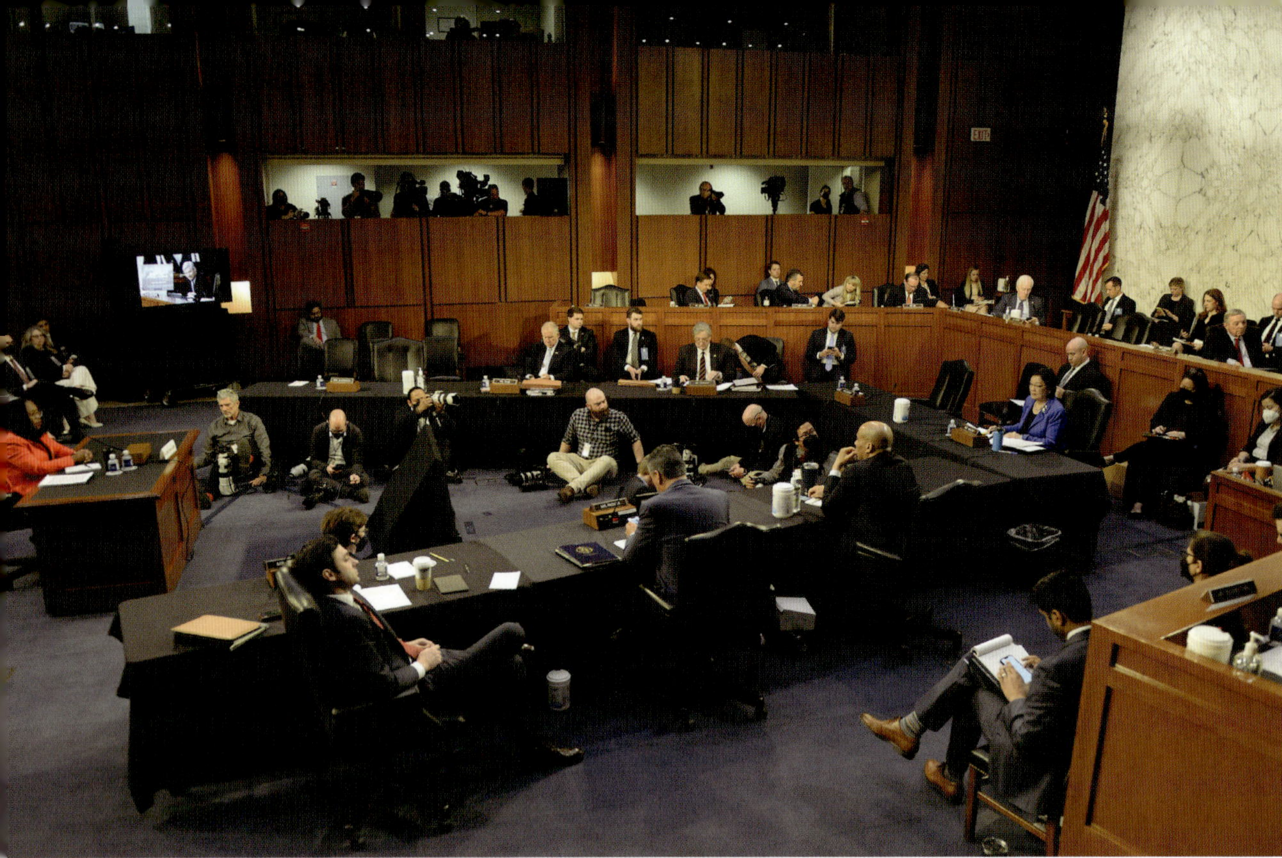

Due to COVID restrictions, a limited amount of photographers are allowed in the well of the hearing room to photograph Judge Ketanji Brown Jackson as she takes questions from the Senate Judiciary Committee.

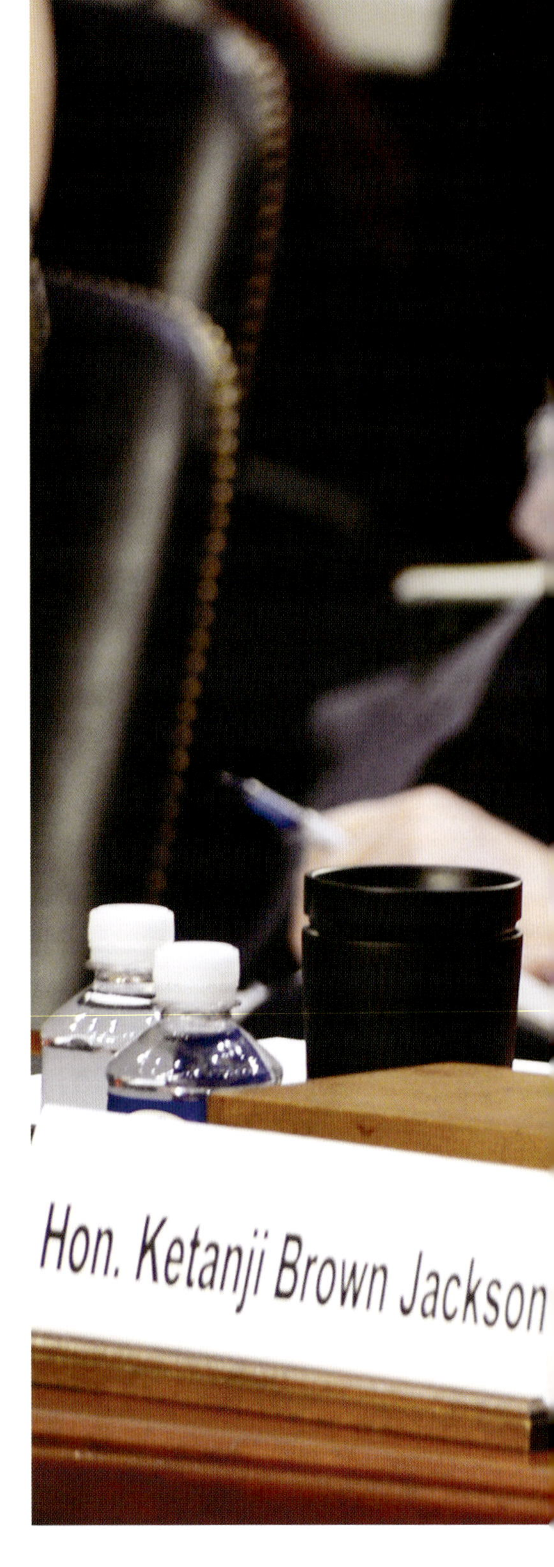

Judge Ketanji Brown Jackson sits before the Senate Judiciary Committee during her confirmation hearing that will decide if she will fill the seat on the US Supreme Court, March 2022.

Unfortunately, my luck did not last. When President Biden nominated the Honorable Judge Ketanji Brown Jackson for a seat on the US Supreme Court to replace retiring Associate Justice Stephen Breyer, the confirmation hearing was not open to the press as it would have typically been due to COVID restrictions. I was only able to briefly photograph the confirmation of our first African American female Supreme Court justice following a long wait to get into the hearing room.

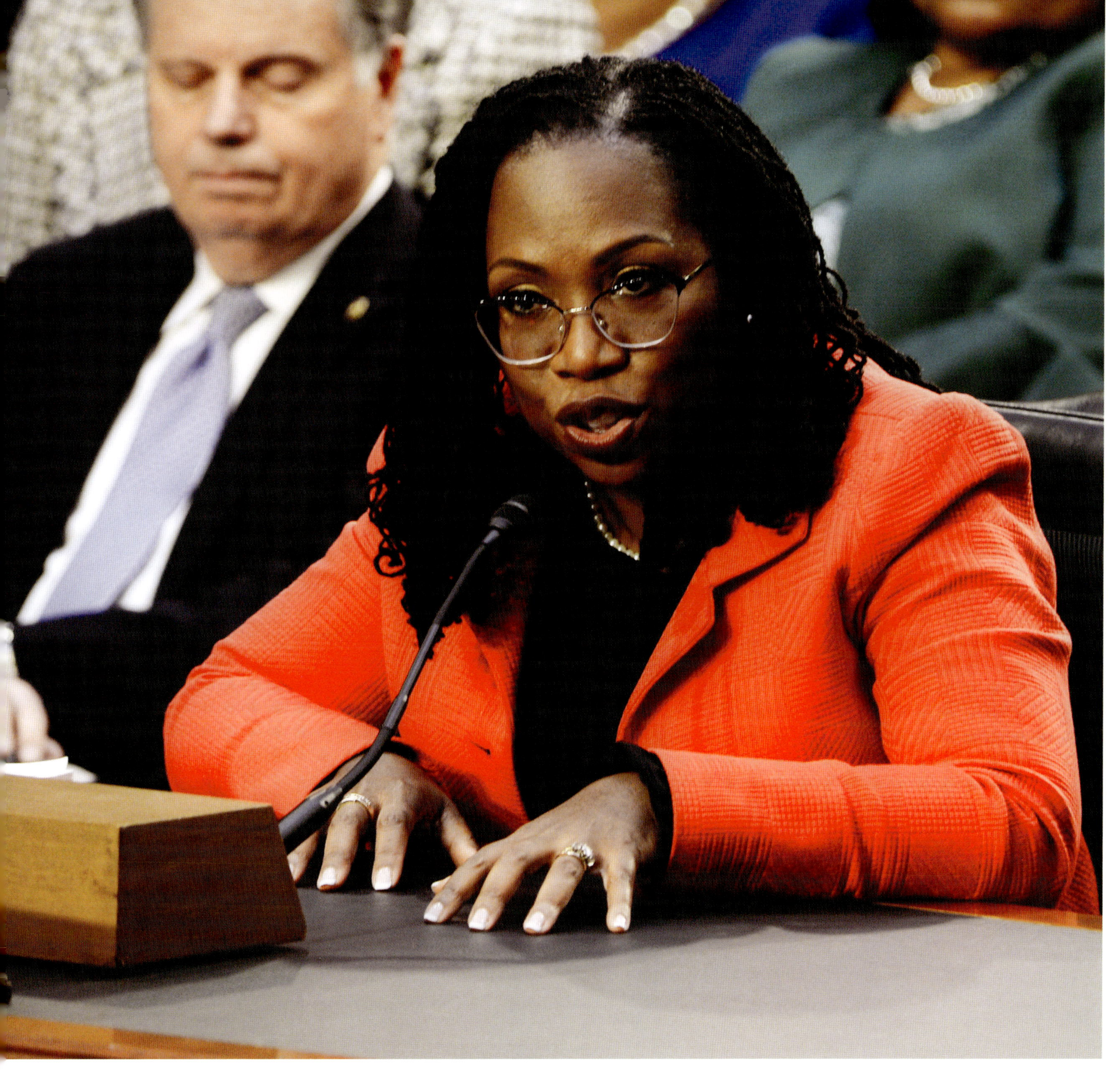

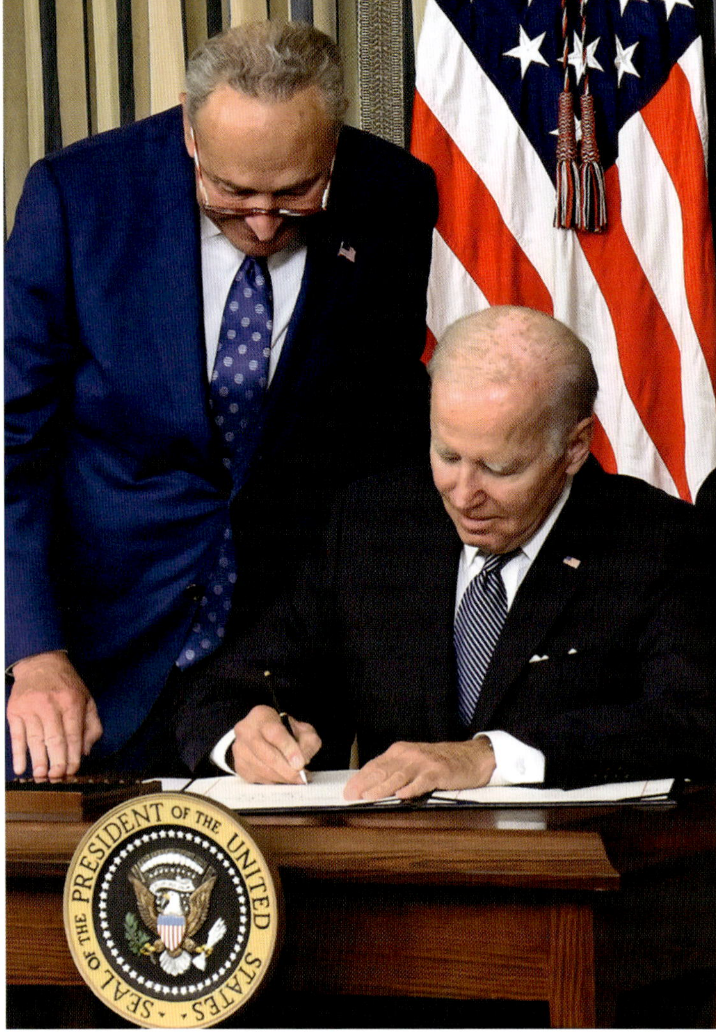

President Joe Biden signs the Inflation Reduction Act as Senator Schumer looks over his shoulder in the State Dining Room of the White House, August 2022.

The next significant accomplishment of the Biden administration that I was able to photograph occurred when the president signed the Inflation Reduction Act into law on August 16, 2022, using the State Dining Room of the White House as the backdrop. Biden has used this venue for bill signings more than most of the other presidents; perhaps the large portrait of President Lincoln that hangs over the fireplace in that room helps to inspire him.

Each of the presidents I've covered has had a different preference for the settings they like to use for press activities. President Biden also seems to enjoy using both the Rose Garden and the South Lawn when the weather is appropriate. He doesn't typically have any photo ops in the Oval Office, other than when there is a visiting head of state and coverage has been restricted to a select few news groups.

There are also lighthearted events at 1600 Pennsylvania Avenue. For example, each November the White House has a fun tradition known as the presidential turkey pardon. This little event has been happening since the time of President Lincoln, with our presidents receiving turkeys as gifts. Over the years the ritual has been streamlined a bit: Each sitting president hosts an event with two large turkeys, whose names are voted on by the public, donated by a turkey breeder chosen from varying states. The turkeys normally stay in a fancy hotel suite the night before going to the White House, and during the ceremony the president officially pardons one of the turkeys from ending up on the dinner table. Both turkeys are then sent to a farm to live out a happy, peaceful life. It was reported that, in 1989, animal rights

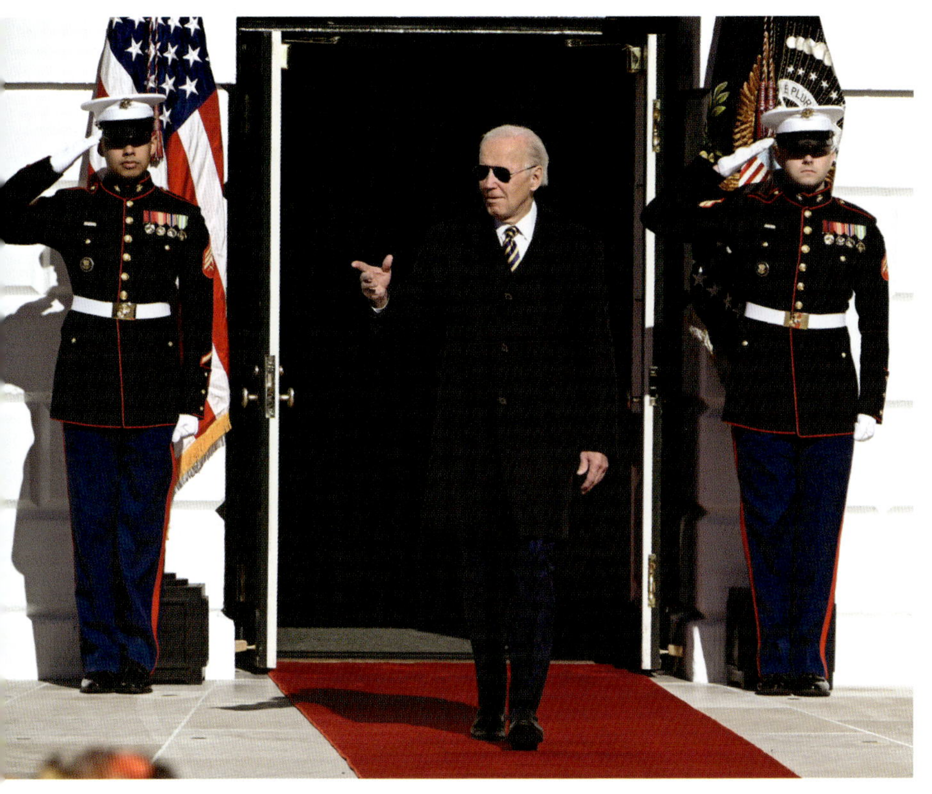

President Joe Biden walks onto the South Lawn for the turkey pardon ceremony as his Marine honor guards position themselves, November 2022.

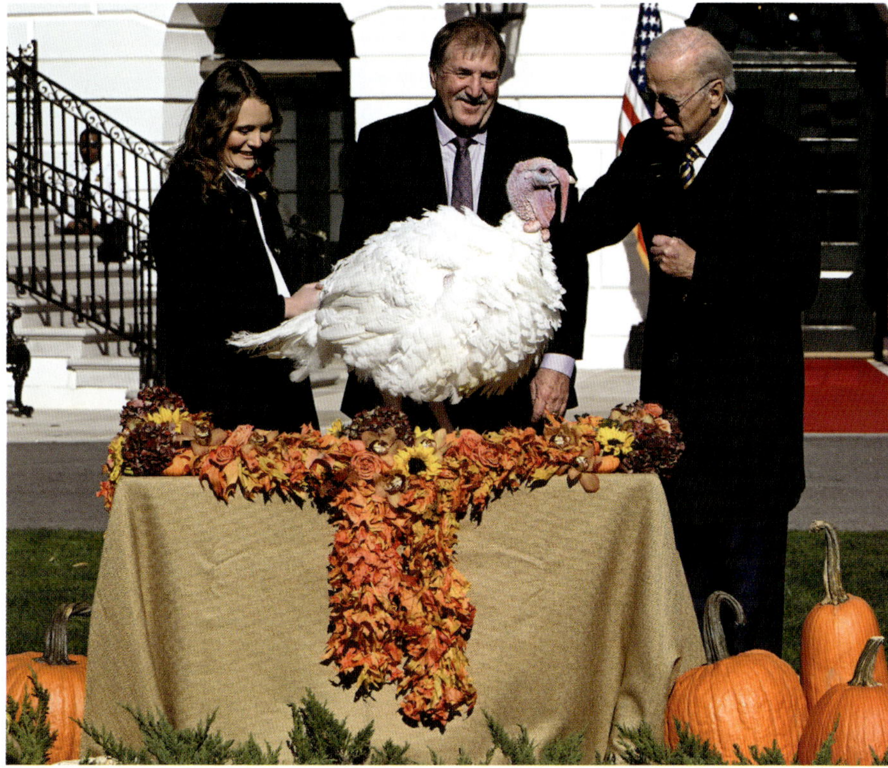

Biden pardons Chocolate, the National Thanksgiving Turkey, as he is joined by the National Turkey Federation Chairman Ronnie Parker, and Alexa Starnes, who represents Circle S Ranch, from where Chocolate traveled.

activists were protesting outside the White House when President George H. W. Bush joked, "But let me assure you, and this fine tom turkey, that he will not end up on anyone's dinner table, not this guy—he's granted a presidential pardon as of right now—and allow him to live out his days on a children's farm not far from here."[2] On November 21, 2022, President Biden hosted the traditional turkey pardon on the South Lawn. The Biden family—a loving, loyal clan—came together, like most families, for the holidays. President Biden was upstaged by son Hunter and grandson Beau when they came out onto the South Lawn where the turkeys were waiting for their "pardon." Moments later, President Biden made the typical grand presidential entrance and proceeded to the job at hand of pardoning the turkeys, named Chocolate and Chip.

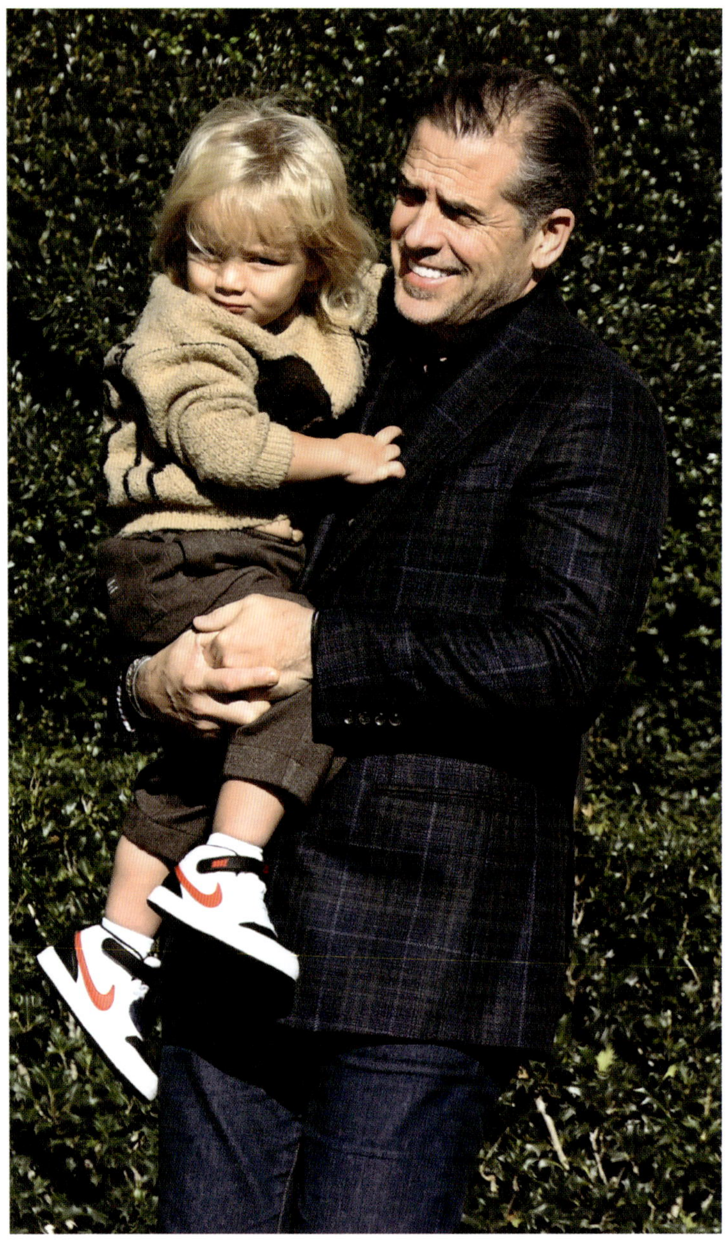

Hunter Biden carries his son Beau over to take a look at the two turkeys before the annual White House Turkey Pardon, November 2022.

So far in his presidency, Biden has held five state and official arrival ceremonies, and it is always impressive to watch how seamlessly the White House puts together these events. The schedule is usually very predictable and everything must be timed precisely, including the 19- or 21-gun salute. After the ceremony, there is always a brief press conference followed by a restricted Oval Office photo op, meetings, and state dinner. The first state arrival ceremony of Biden's administration occurred on December 1, 2022, when the president and First Lady Jill Biden welcomed President Emmanuel Macron and First Lady Brigitte Macron of France to the White House. The two leaders seemed to get along quite nicely.

Later that month, members of the White House Press Corps received notice that President Volodymyr Zelensky of Ukraine would be making a sudden visit to the White House in just a couple of hours. Security was extremely enhanced, the red carpet was rolled out, and American and Ukrainian flags were placed along the driveway. Like clockwork, the black SUV rolled up to the doors of the South Portico, and the president and First Lady greeted the jet-lagged Zelensky. He had just flown around the world nonstop and driven directly to the White House. Our photo op lasted for about twenty seconds, with no remarks made or questions answered.

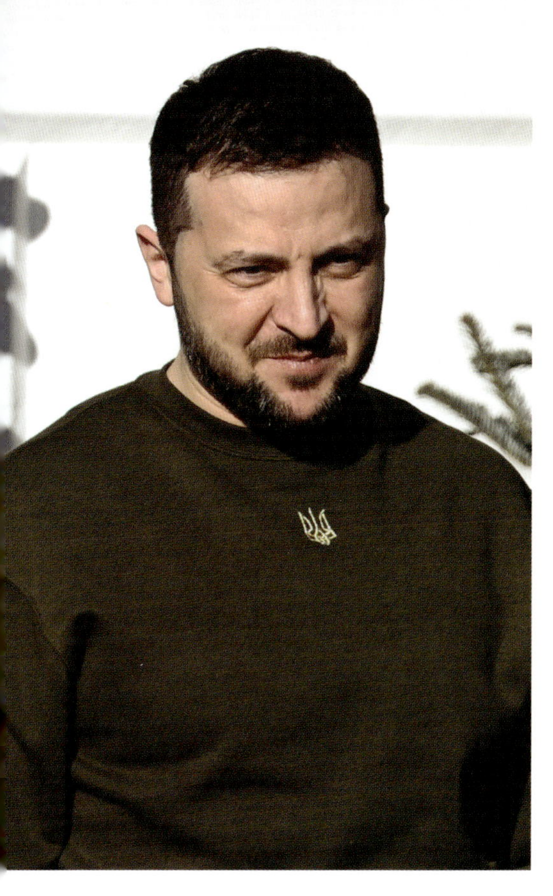

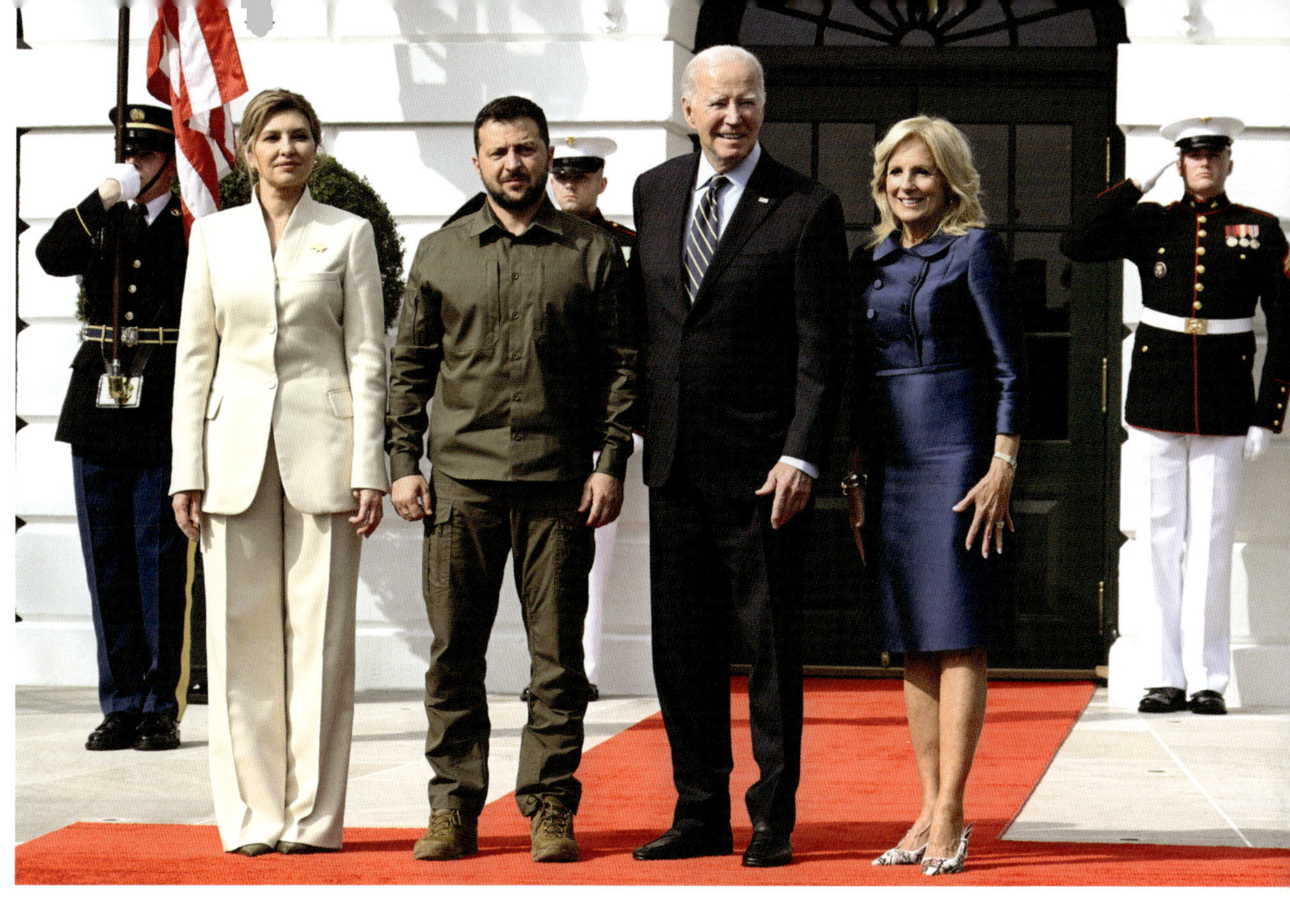

*Zelensky makes a surprise
visit to the Biden White
House, December 2022.*

*President Joe Biden and First Lady Dr. Jill Biden welcome
President Volodymyr Zelensky and Mrs. Olena Zelenska
of Ukraine to the White House, October 2023.*

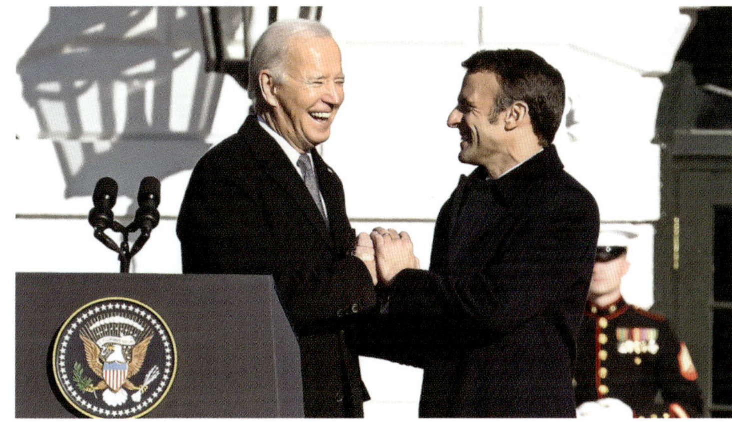

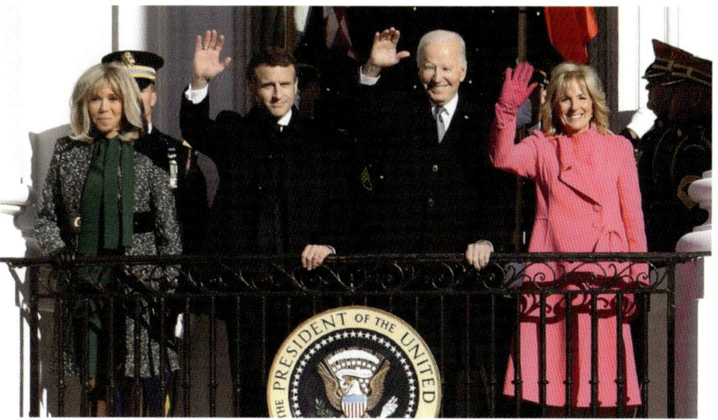

*Joe Biden and Emmanuel Macron share
a friendly moment during Emmanuel
Macron's state arrival ceremony.*

*President Joe Biden welcomes president of France
Emmanuel Macron and First Lady Brigitte Macron to
the White House on the South Lawn, December 2022.*

President Biden's initial State of the Union address on February 7, 2023, was the first I had been allowed to attend since President Trump's final one. The prior year was restricted access due to COVID precautions, so we only received the pictures taken by the few selected pool of photographers.

There was yet again no Oval Office access when President Biden hosted President Yoon Suk Yeol and First Lady Kim Keon-hee of the Republic of Korea for a state arrival ceremony on April 26, 2023. While the two leaders did hold a brief press conference in the Rose Garden following the arrival ceremony, I would have liked to get a more intimate view of their interaction.

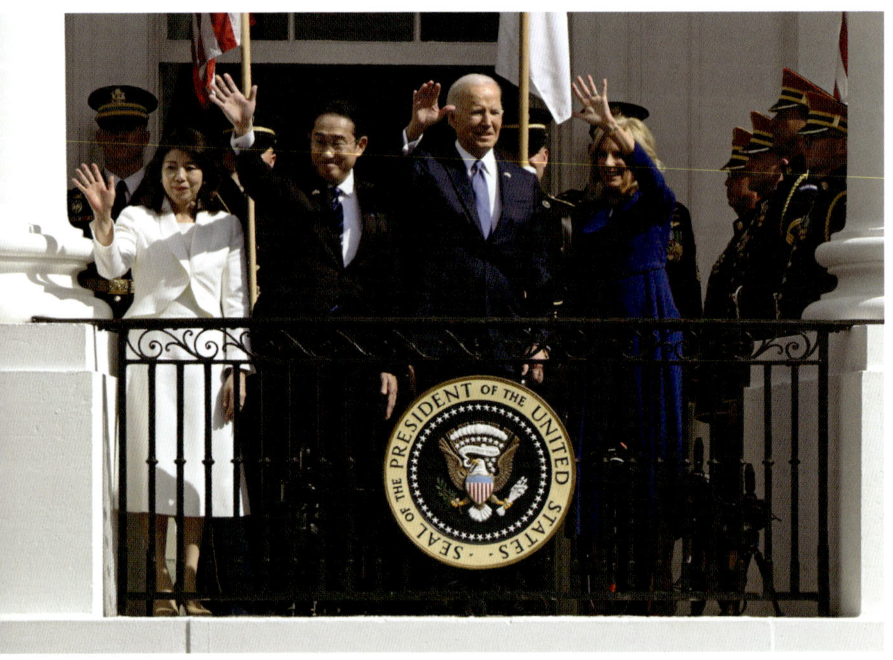

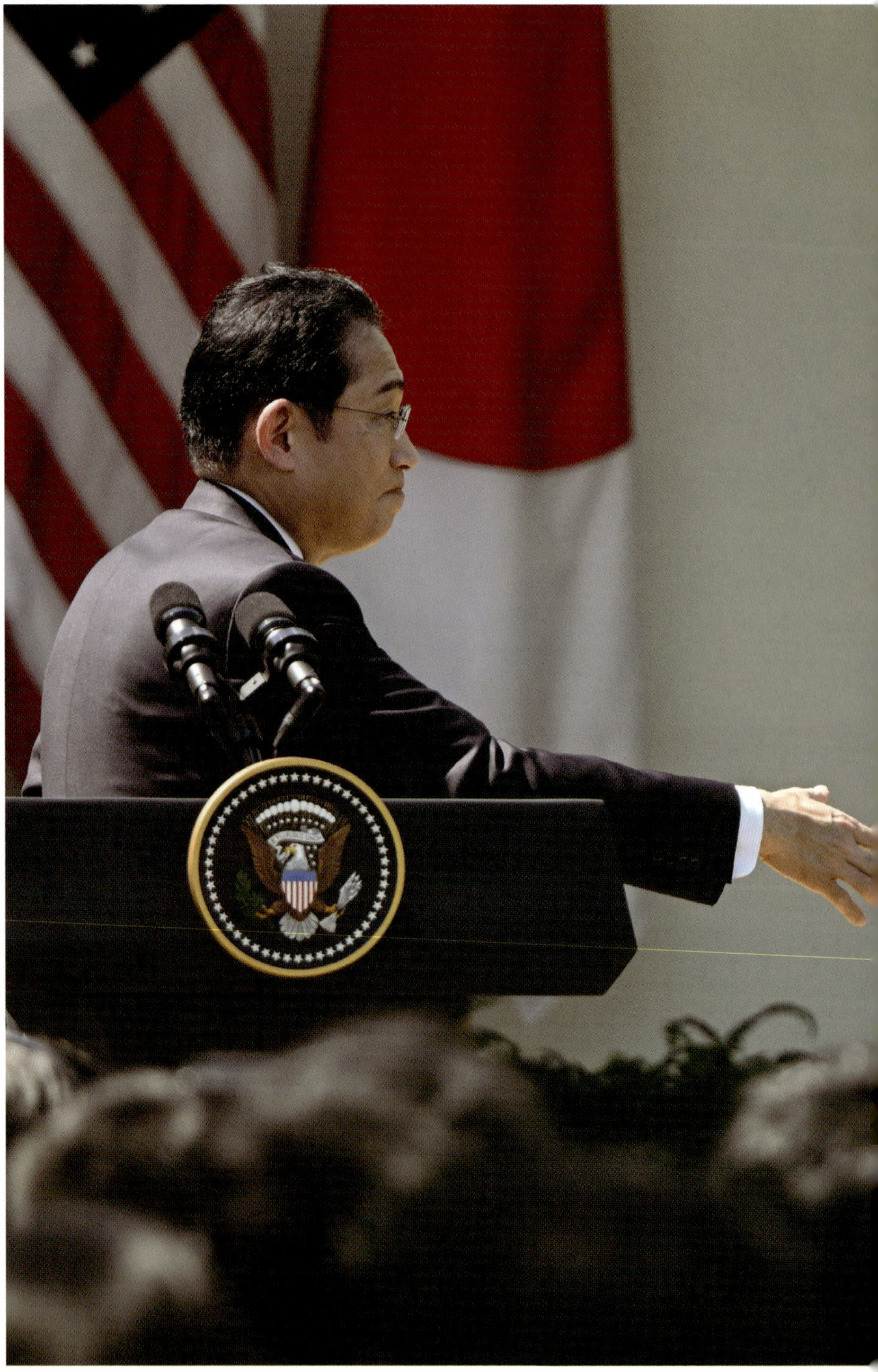

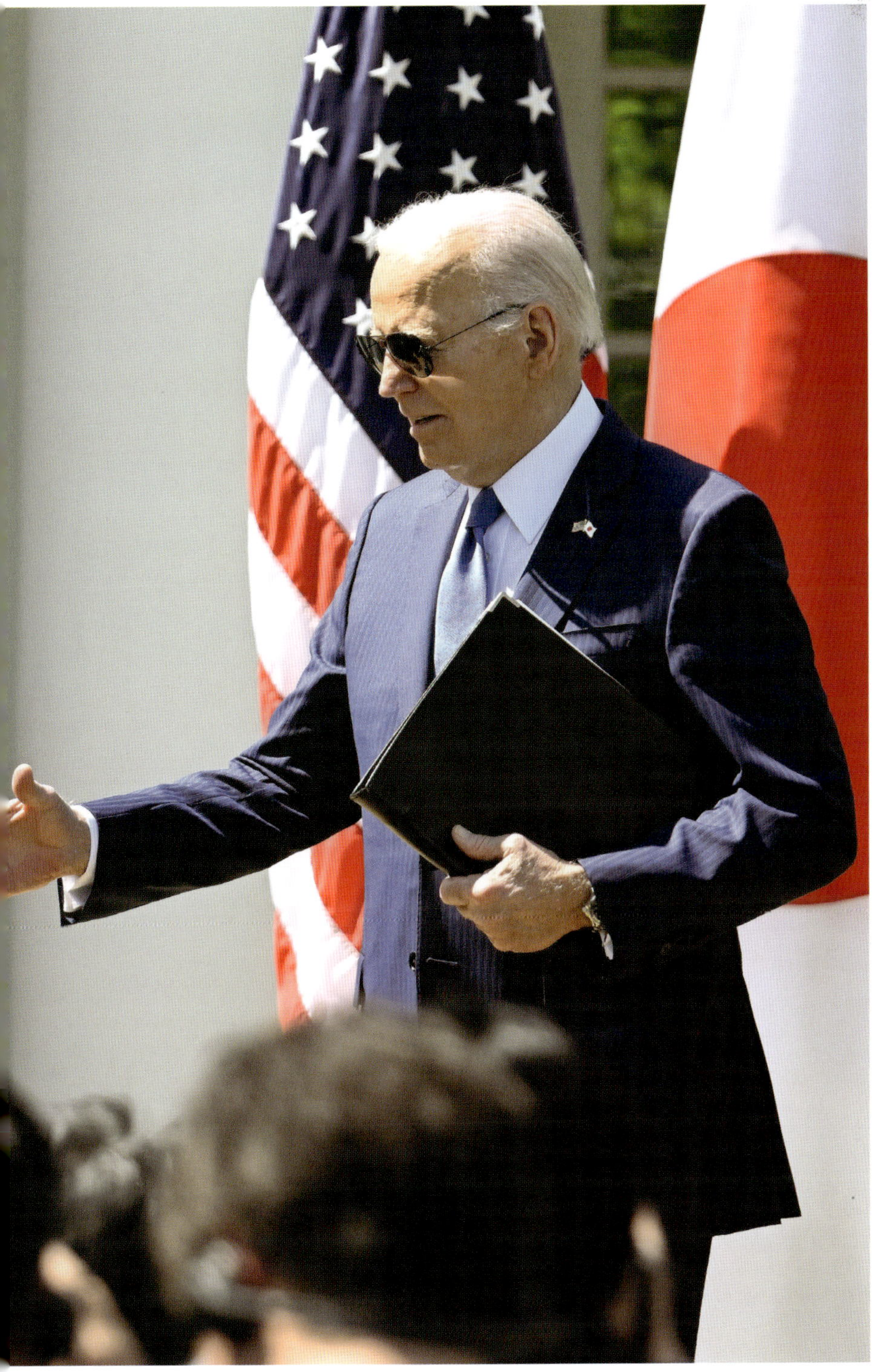

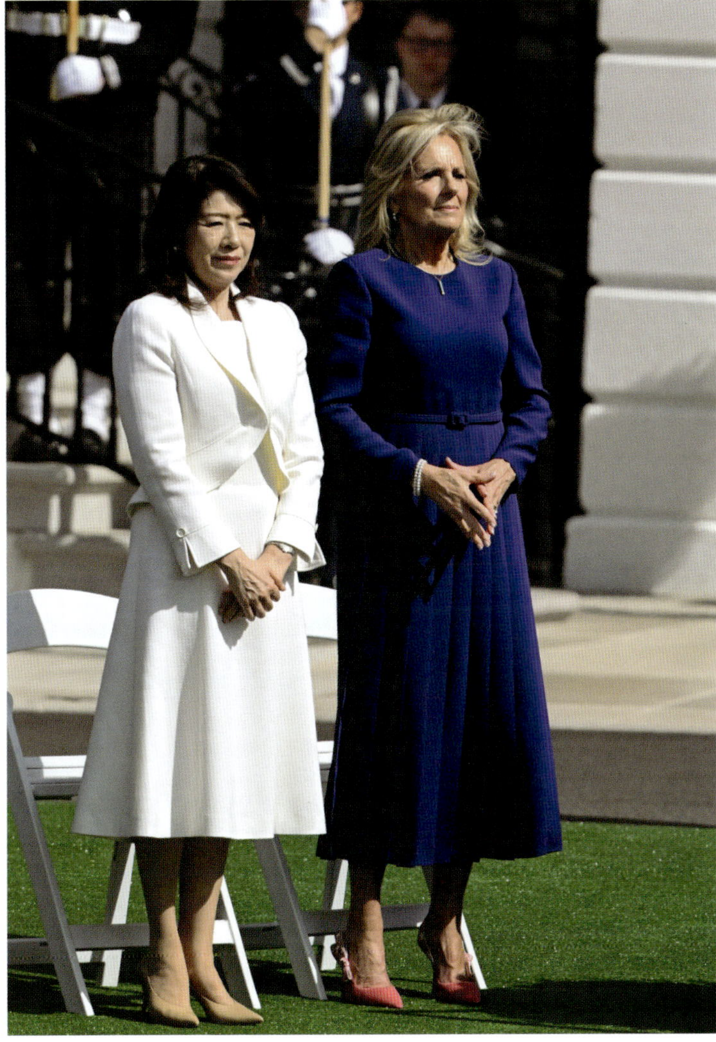

First Lady Jill Biden and First Lady of the Republic
of Korea Kim Keon-hee watch the marching bands
before moving to the Truman Balcony.

President Joe Biden welcomes President
Yoon Suk Yeol of the Republic of Korea
to the Rose Garden following the arrival
ceremony in his honor, April 2023.

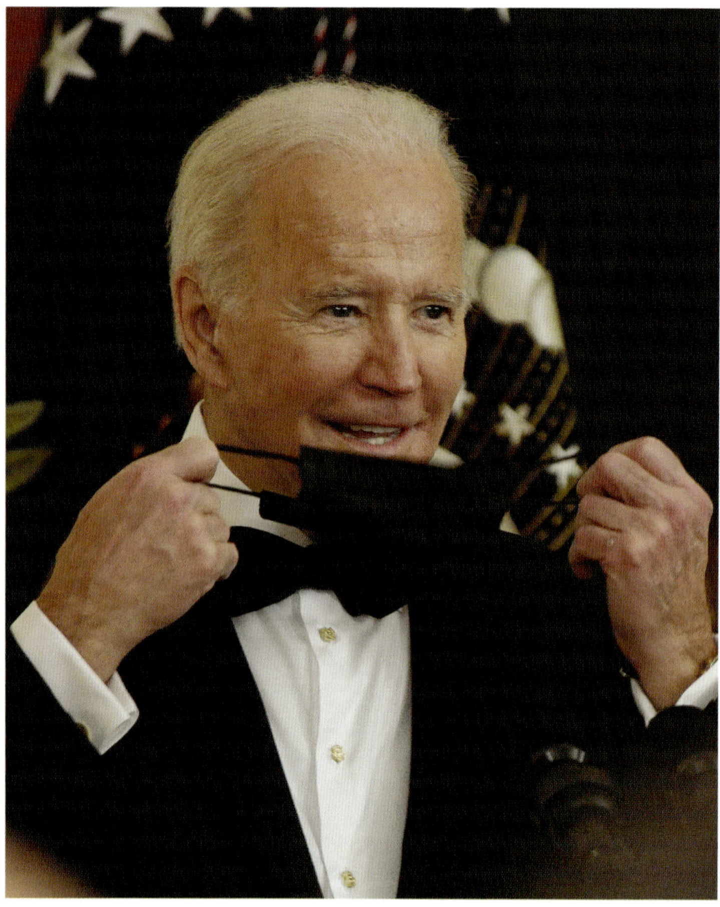

During the COVID epidemic, President Joe Biden takes off his mask as he makes remarks during the 44th Kennedy Center Honors reception for the honorees in the East Room, December 2021.

He joked with all of us in a cheerful manner, and even playfully called hundreds of us media to order with a whistle at the start of the dinner.

President Biden attended the White House Correspondents' Dinner for the second time as president on April 30, 2023 (both Biden and Vice President Harris have made an appearance at all three such dinners held during their term). He joked with all of us in a cheerful manner, and even playfully called hundreds of us media to order with a whistle at the start of the dinner.

Staying true to his passion for infrastructural improvement, President Biden has joined forces with the Quadrilateral Security Dialogue (Quad), the strategic security alliance that joins the United States, Australia, India, and Japan. This group of four countries are dedicated to improving infrastructure for the benefit of the Indo-Pacific people. In June of 2023, the Bidens invited Prime Minister Narendra Modi of the Republic of India for an official arrival ceremony at the White House. Modi and Biden appeared to have a warm relationship, and I was impressed with the large number of Modi followers who showed up to support him. The cheering could be heard for blocks as he arrived. Throughout the course of his presidency, Biden has invited leaders from several nations to the White House, both those in the Quad and others.

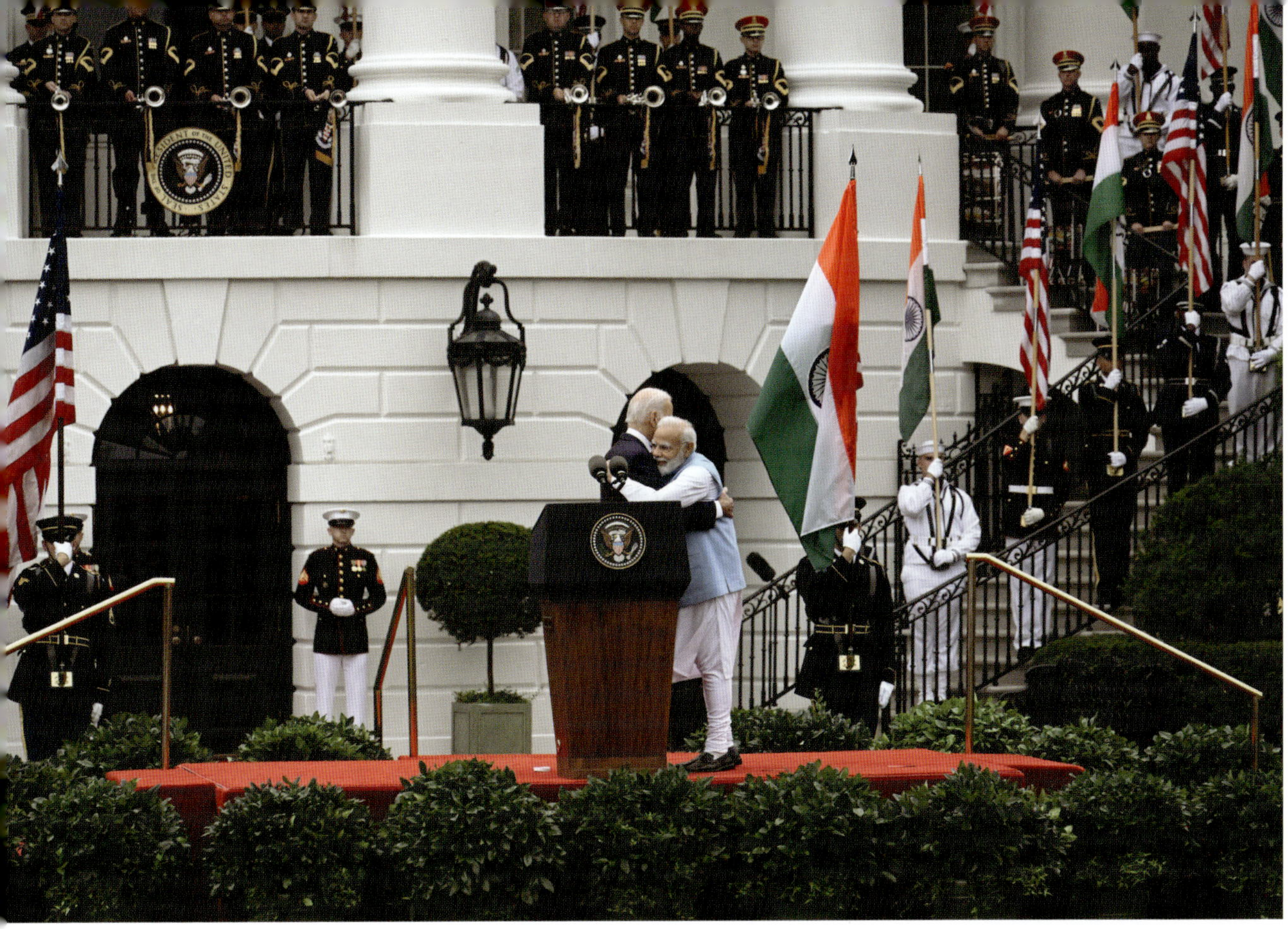

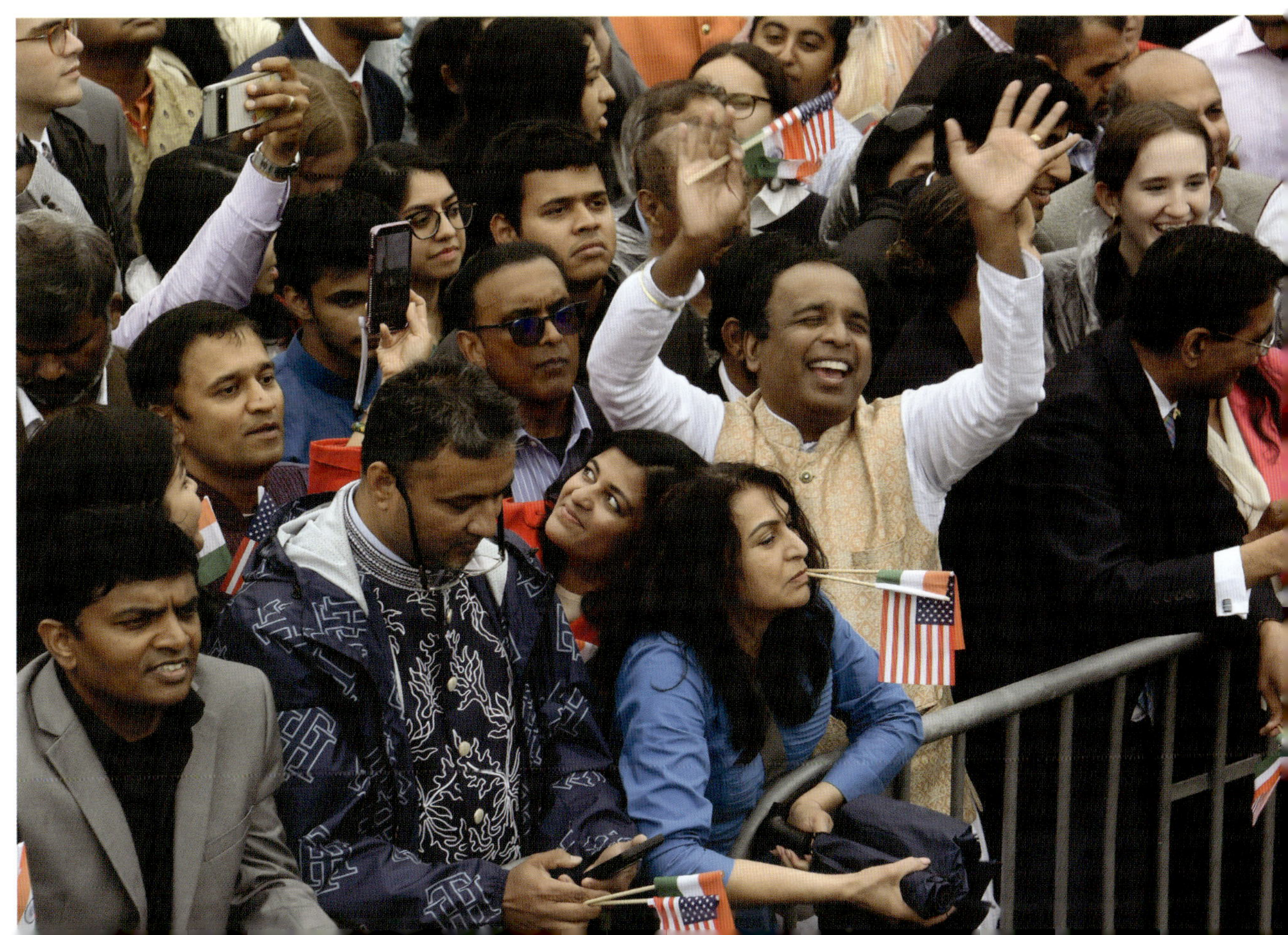

President Biden and Indian Prime Minister Narendra Modi embrace on the South Lawn during a state visit at the White House, June 2023.

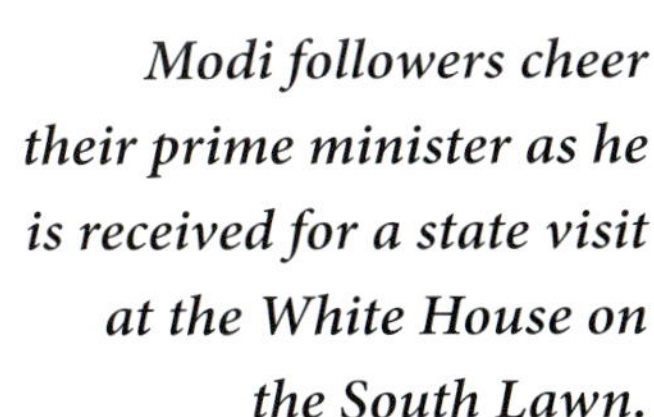

Modi followers cheer their prime minister as he is received for a state visit at the White House on the South Lawn.

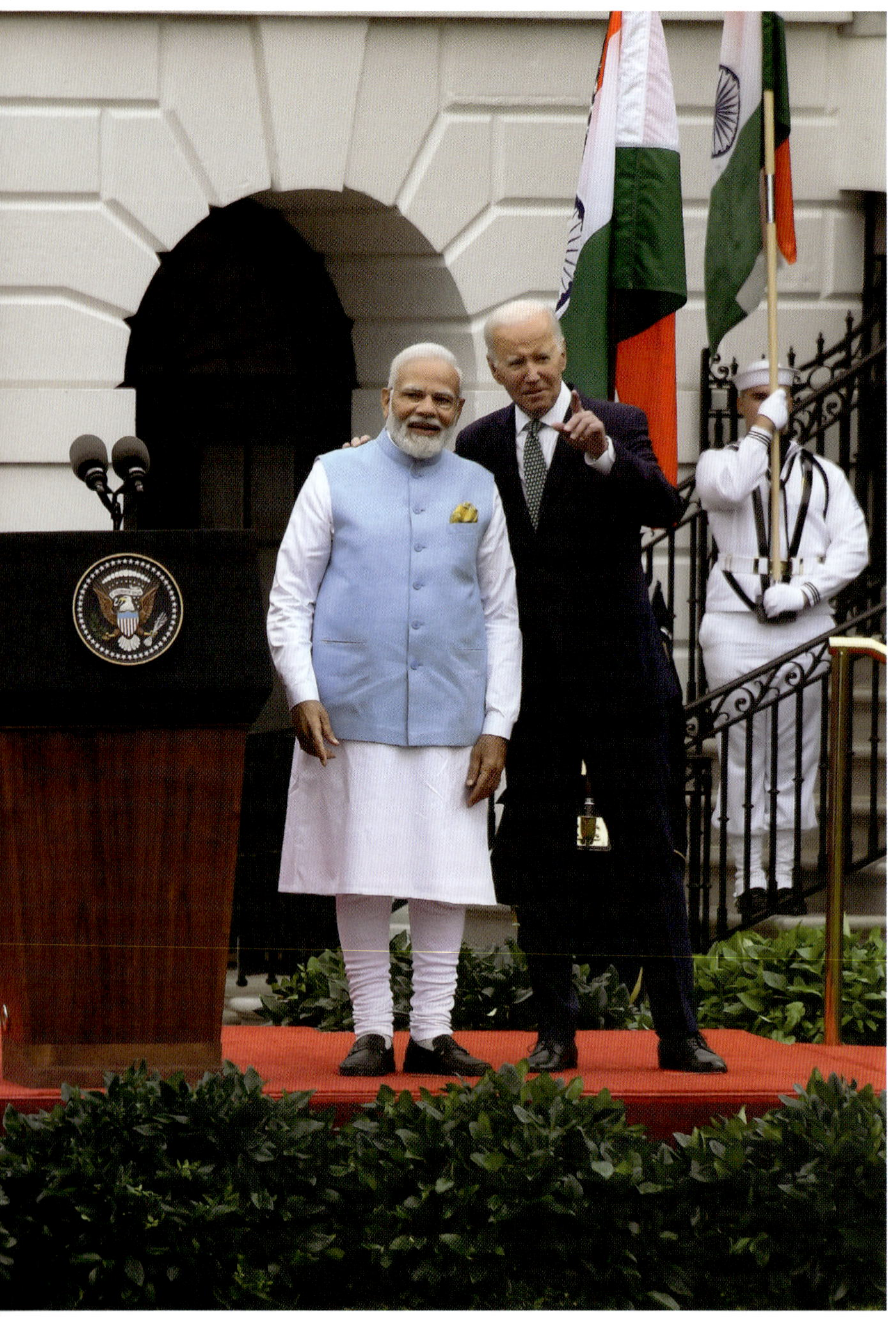

President Biden and Prime Minister Modi watch the twenty-one-gun salute during a state arrival ceremony on the South Lawn.

On September 21, 2023, the President and First Lady welcomed Ukraine President Volodymyr Zelensky again, but this time he was accompanied by his wife Mrs. Olena Zelenska. President Zelensky had already visited the White House once before, but this time, he and his wife had traveled to Washington, DC, following meetings in New York under less-rushed circumstances. Despite having less distance to travel, the Ukrainian president and first lady were a couple hours late. When they finally arrived, the press corps only had about a ten-second photo opportunity before the two couples went inside the White House—no remarks or questions taken from reporters, yet again.

Political turmoil erupted when the Palestinian Sunni Islamist group called Hamas launched an unprecedented assault on Israel on October 7, 2023. One week later, an estimated three thousand Palestinian supporters marched to the White House to protest the Israel-Hamas war. Through chanting and signs, they made it known that many innocent Palestinian people were being killed by both Israelis and Hamas. Later that Saturday afternoon, I drove to the Israeli Embassy and took pictures of the flowers left at the gate in respect for those killed in Israel during the massacre the week before. The eerie, grief-ridden silence at the embassy that day was unsettling.

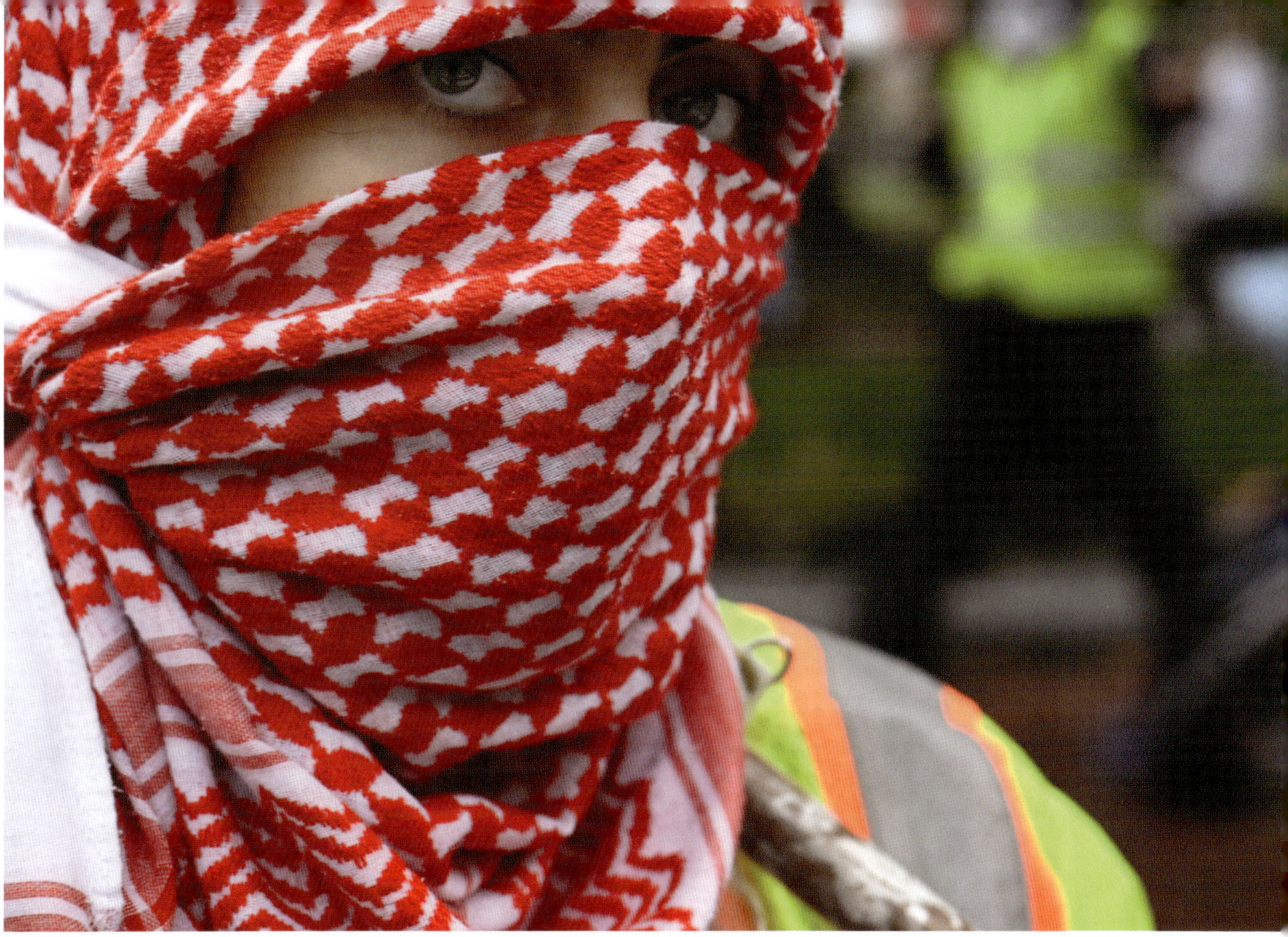

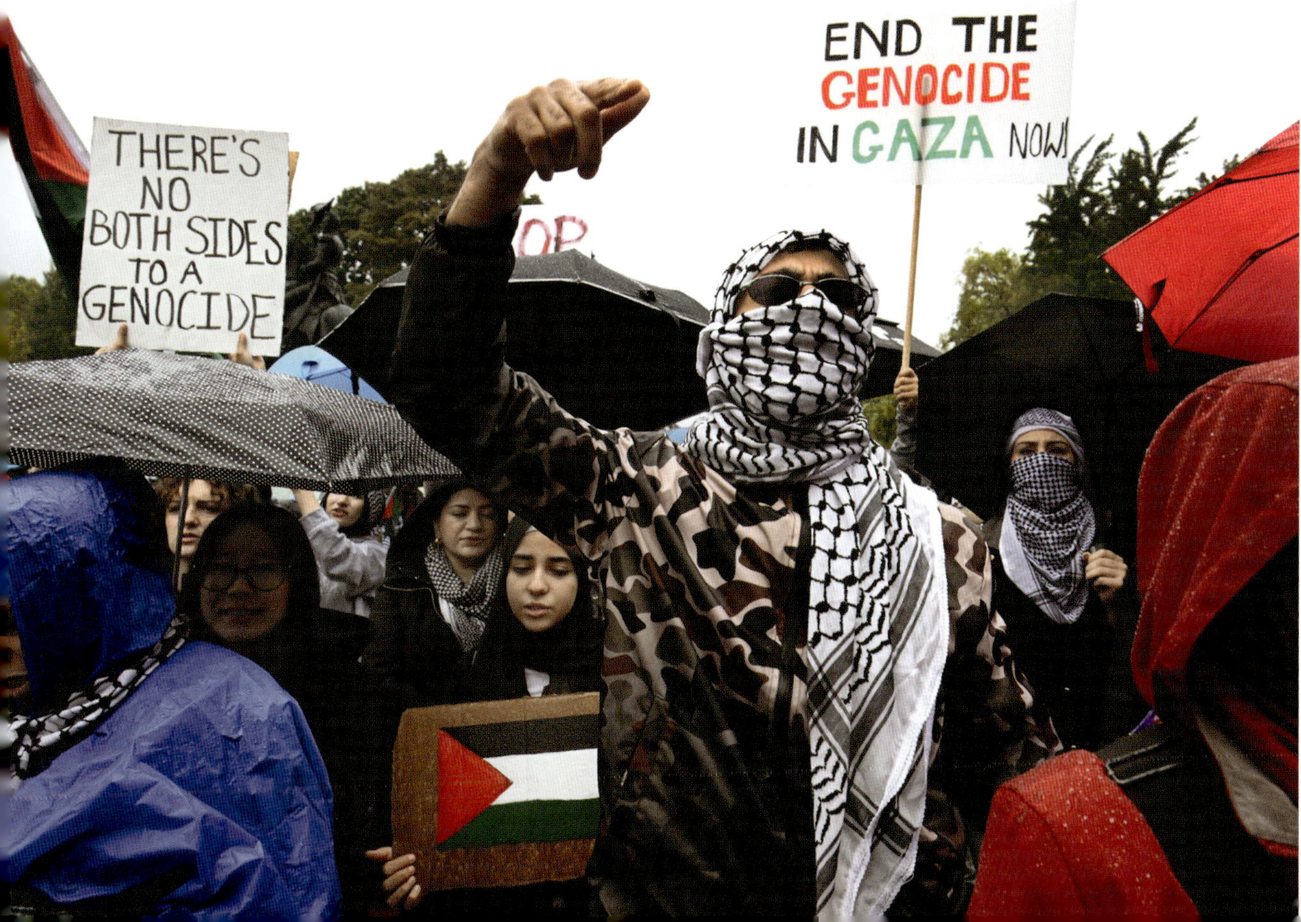

Palestinian protesters gather in Lafayette Park across from the White House to voice their opinion about the war in Israel and the slaughtering of people on the Gaza Strip, October 2023.

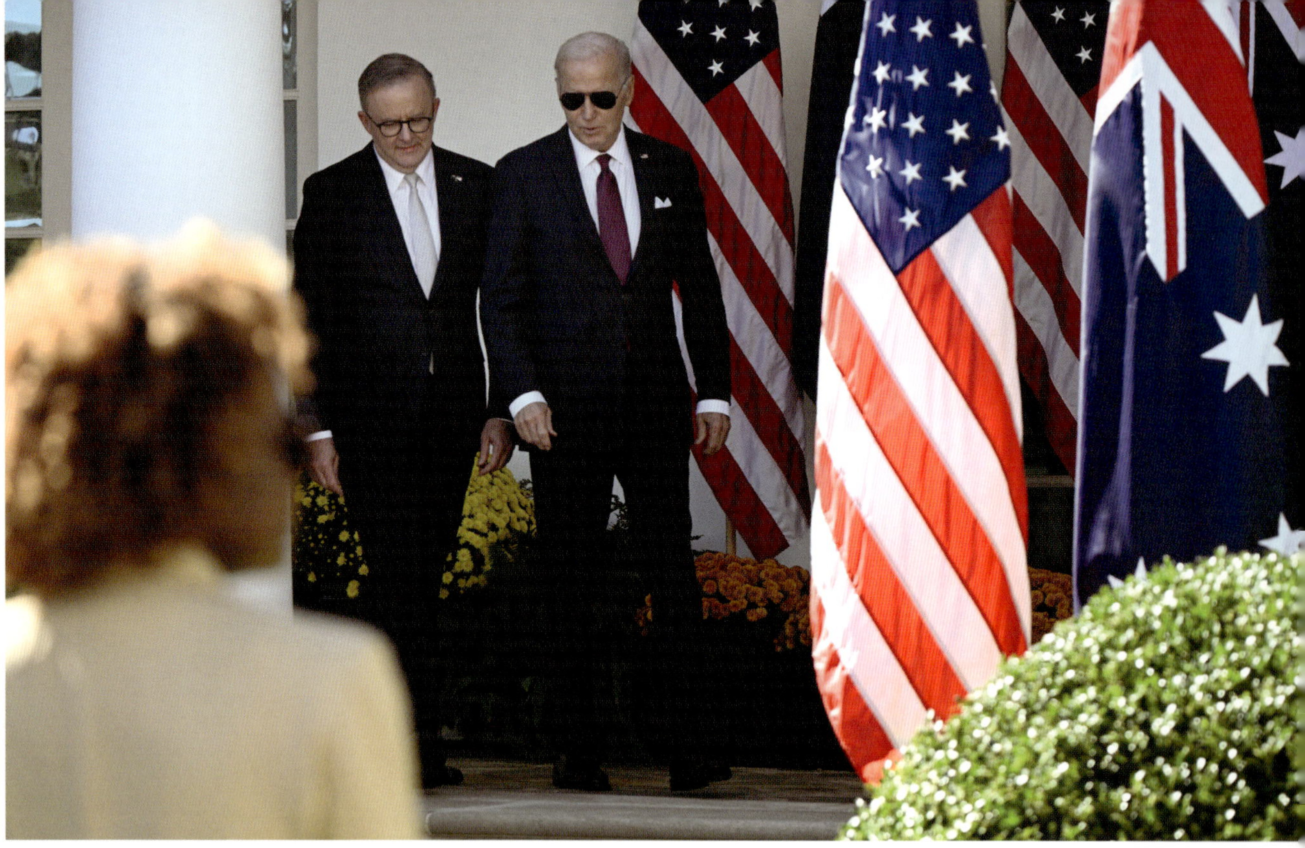

President Biden and Australian Prime Minister Anthony Albanese enter the Rose Garden during an official state visit, October 2023.

President Biden welcomed a second fellow Quad leader on October 25, 2023, when he held his fourth state arrival ceremony for Australian Prime Minister Anthony Albanese and his partner, Ms. Jodie Haydon. The two leaders held a brief joint press conference in the Rose Garden, where Biden was asked about the war in Israel. Even with these two powerful world leaders meeting, Representative Mike Johnson (R-LA) stole the spotlight when it was announced during the press conference that he'd been selected as the new Speaker of the House. After three weeks and hours of closed-door negotiations, Johnson beat out three other nominees to break the stalemate.

The last remaining Quad leader would not visit the White House until several months later, when President Biden and the first lady welcomed Prime Minister Fumio Kishida and Mrs. Yuko Kishida of Japan for an official arrival ceremony.

By the time of President Biden's third State of the Union address we were already in election season, and it was unbelievably down to a rematch of Biden versus Trump. In an effort to enhance security at the Capitol, protective riot fencing was put in place around the area prior to all the VIP politicians arriving.

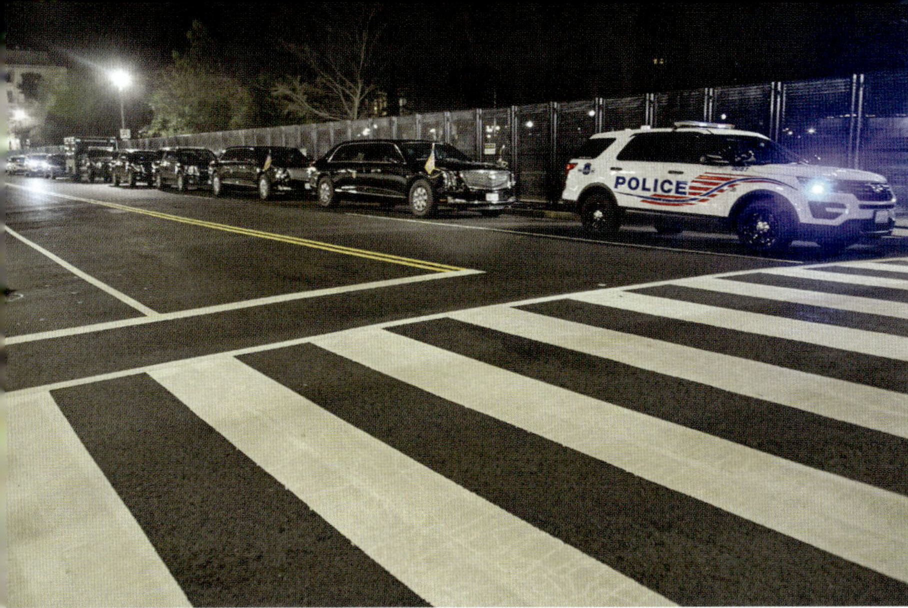

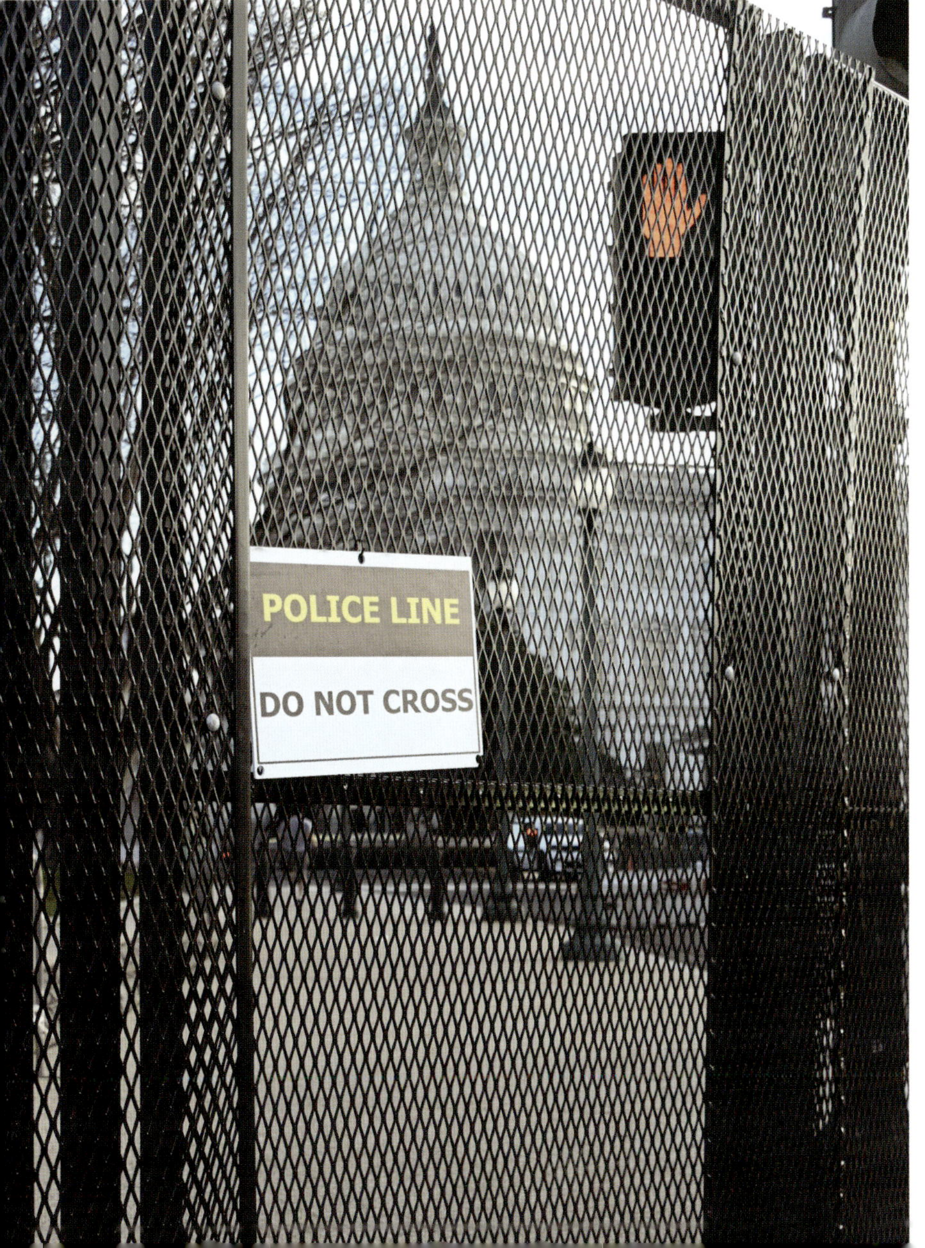

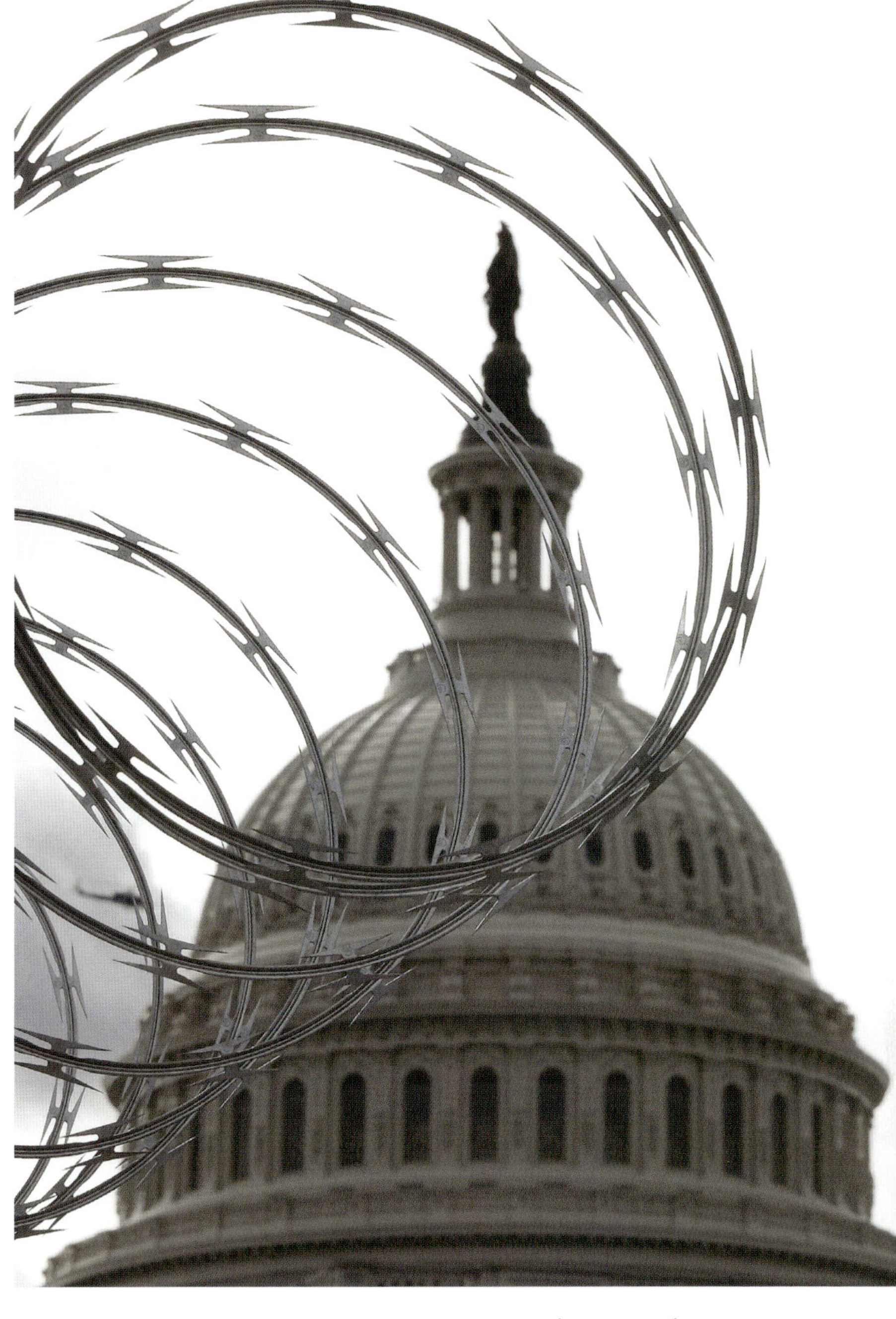

Since the January 6 insurrection, security at the Capitol has increased for big events, starting with razor wire installed soon after the insurrection (top) and kept up through the Biden inauguration in 2021. Riot fencing was even put in place around the Capitol as a protective measure for the 2024 State of the Union Address (left).

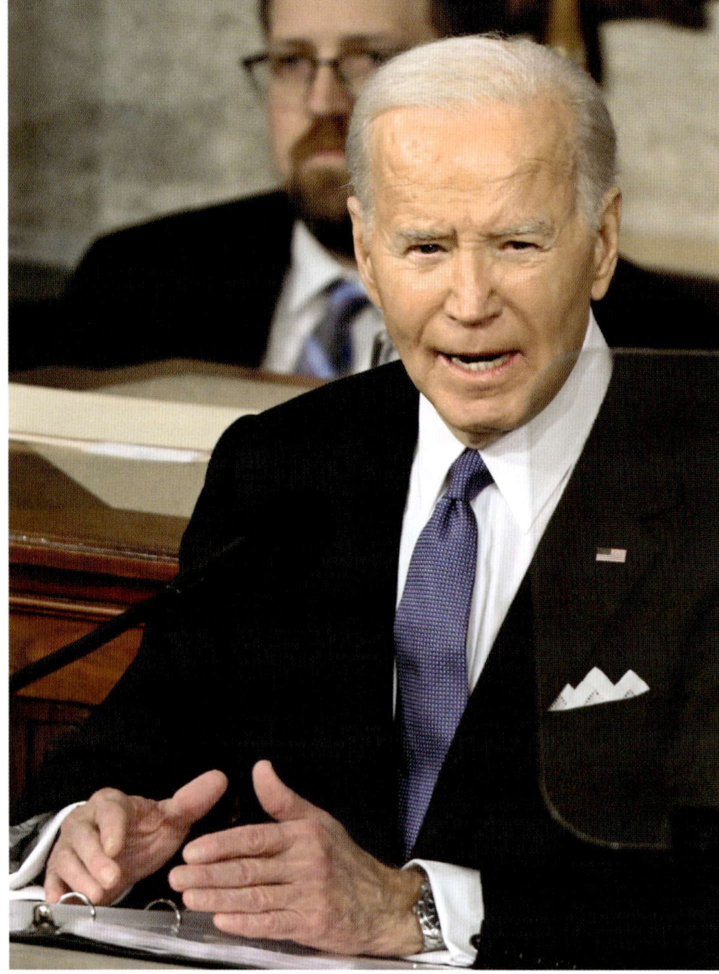

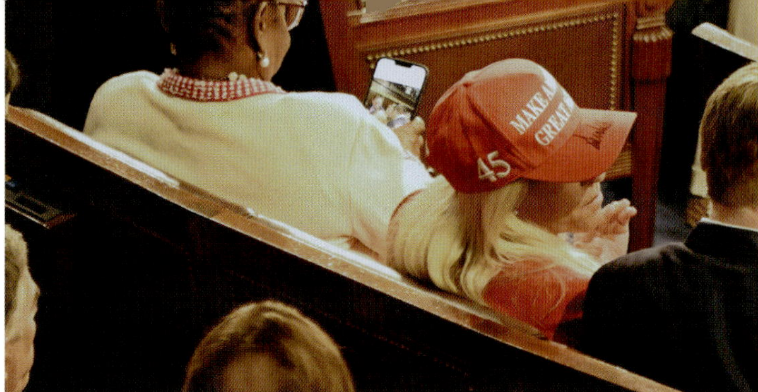

US Representative for Georgia Marjorie Taylor Greene talks with a colleague after shouting at President Biden during his March 2024 State of the Union Address.

President Biden speaks at the March 2024 State of the Union.

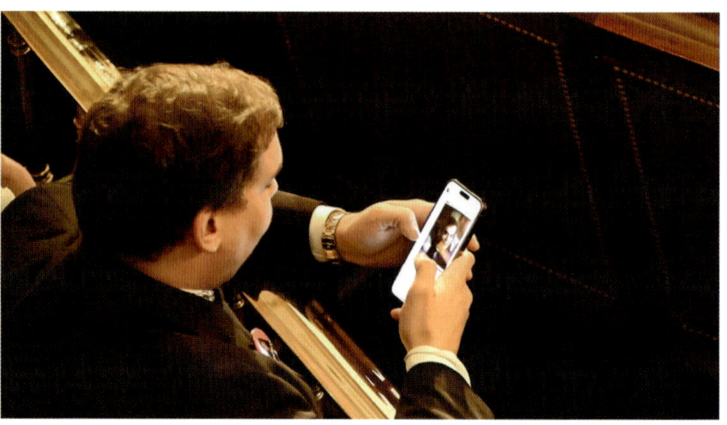

Former US representative George Santos reviews his selfie in the House Chamber during Biden's March 2024 State of the Union Address.

I am always so impressed by how President Biden demonstrates overcoming his childhood stuttering problem when courageously addressing the world about the state of the country—there could not be a bigger test than giving the State of the Union address. Even during that stressful speech, he was yelled at by a couple members of Congress who were ultimately unsuccessful at interrupting him. While photographing the event, directly below my position in the House Chamber, I spotted the disgraced Congressman George Santos taking selfies in the back of the room. I learned that apparently, even if you are kicked out of office, you still have privileges to attend events at the Capitol.

Most people considered Biden to have done a good job that night as he campaigned for reelection while giving his address, as other presidents have done.

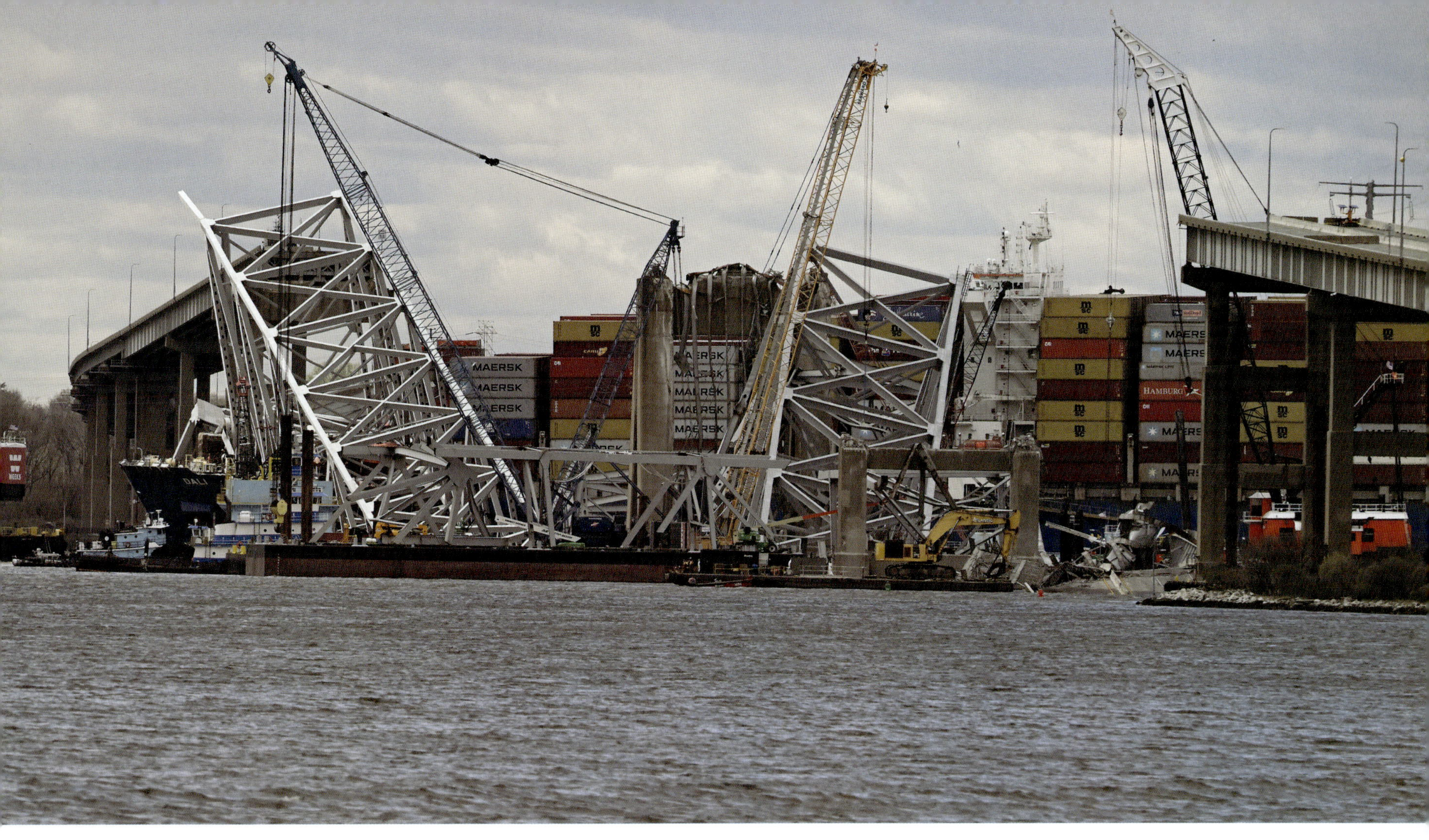

The collapsed segment of the Francis Scott Key Bridge following the crash of the Singapore cargo ship Dali, April 2024.

At the beginning of his term I photographed President Biden signing the big Infrastructure Bill that granted funding for the reconstruction of roads and bridges, so when the Singapore cargo ship, Dali, crashed into the Francis Scott Key Bridge in Baltimore, Maryland, help was on the way immediately. Six people were killed when the huge container ship lost power and destroyed the bridge, pinning the vehicles and their drivers under the massive structure as it collapsed into the river. The results of this tragedy were catastrophic, not only claiming civilian lives but also preventing cargo ships from making deliveries and disrupting the supply chain. I photographed President Biden as he visited the site of the crash, met with first responders and the families of those who were killed. Biden vowed to stand behind his word and help restore the bridge and shipping port.

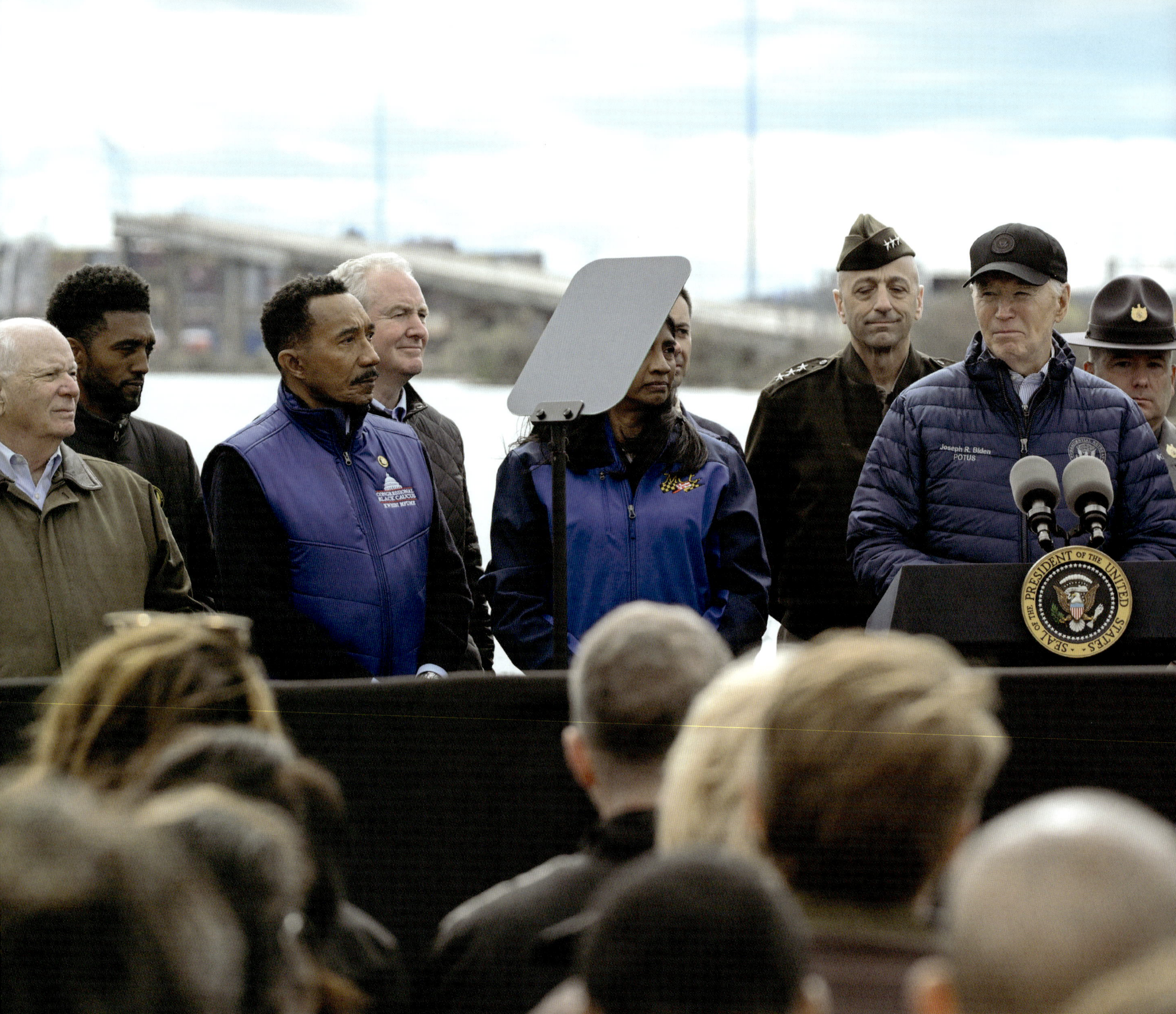

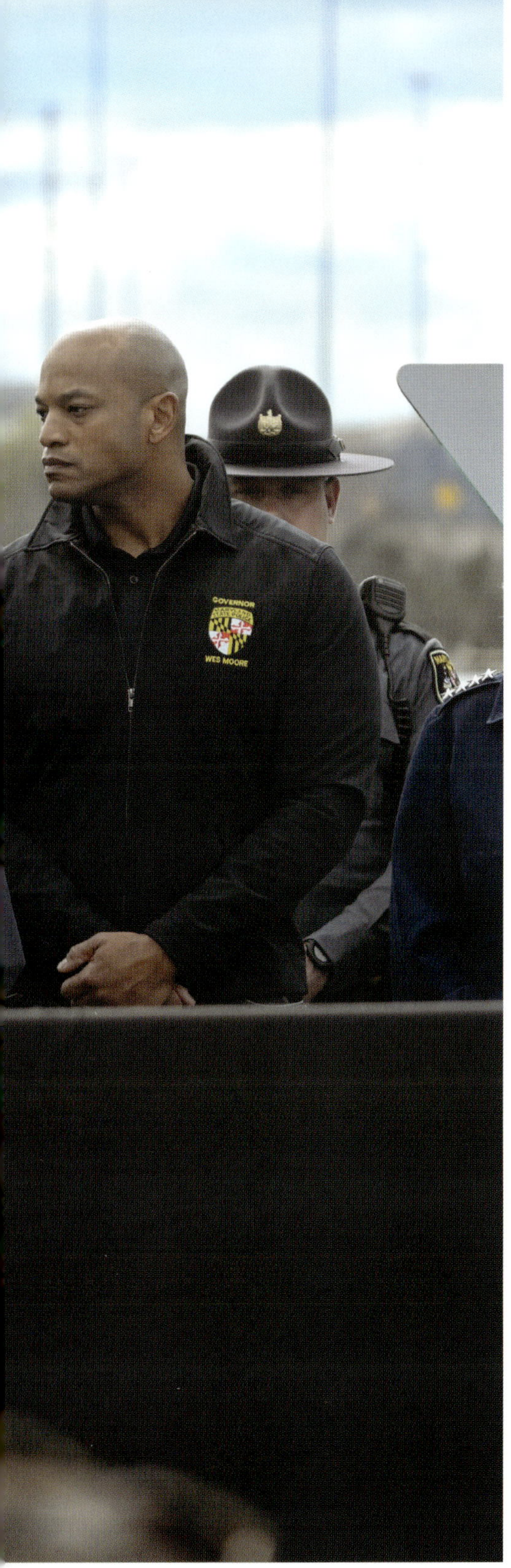

Surrounded by lawmakers, President Biden speaks to the media at the Maryland Transportation Authority in Baltimore after the Dali, a Singapore-flagged container ship, crashed into the Francis Scott Key Bridge, paralyzing the major Maryland shipping port. April 2024.

As the members of the press corps wait around for various events to begin, we talk among ourselves about how long it has been since any of us have been in the Oval Office. For those of us who were previously inside on a regular basis, the numbers range from four to ten years. I myself have not been allowed there since President Trump was in office—and even then, only once. I've attempted to get special permission to accompany the selected pool photographers (the only ones allowed in) on a couple of occasions but have been denied. Yet it is imperative that we have different points of view when covering the president; various perspectives help paint the full story as it truly happened. Without those photographed moments, there's a huge risk of creating a greater distance between the president and the people, which can foster a lack of trust.

Of the five presidents I have had the privilege to cover at the White House, I have had less opportunity and access in the Biden White House than ever before. In these unprecedented times, it is critical that there's a good working relationship between the press and the president.

The principle of cause and effect is real; we are living it. If we do not have more of an established relationship with our presidents, we cannot report accurately, and history cannot be fully recorded or captured. The American people deserve more.

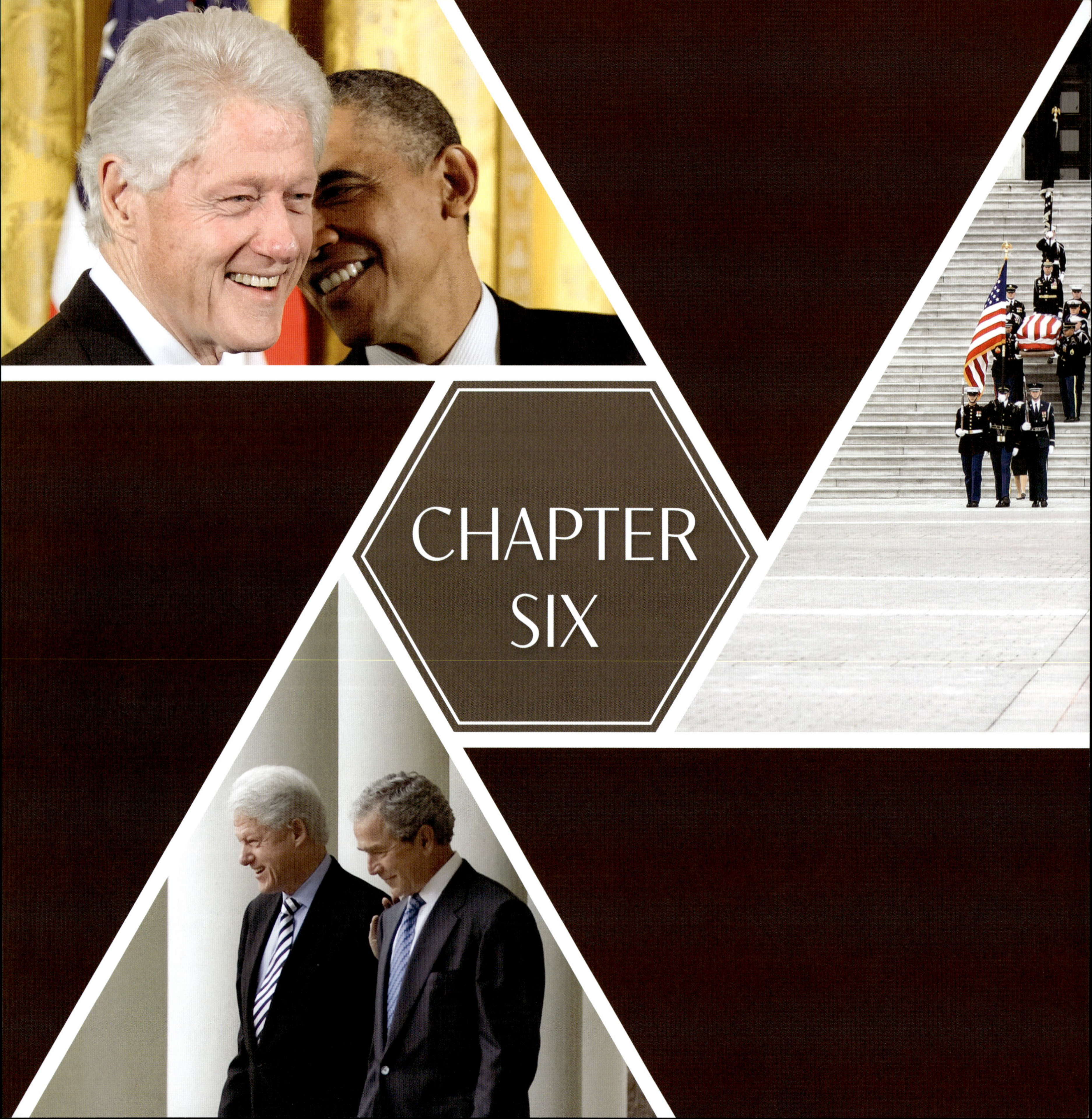

CHAPTER SIX

PRESIDENTIAL

LEGACIES

I always feel protective of each of our presidents. I respect what they give up in their personal lives—especially their privacy. Their Secret Service detail is always nearby, and the presidential photographers are around them much of the time as well.

There is an unofficial "special club" in which the current and former US presidents belong. No one else on earth knows what it is like to hold that position, to deal with the responsibilities that come with being the leader of the free world, and to be under the blinding glare of constant scrutiny. The sorrows and joyous times that are shared between the public and our presidents almost always make it into the news.

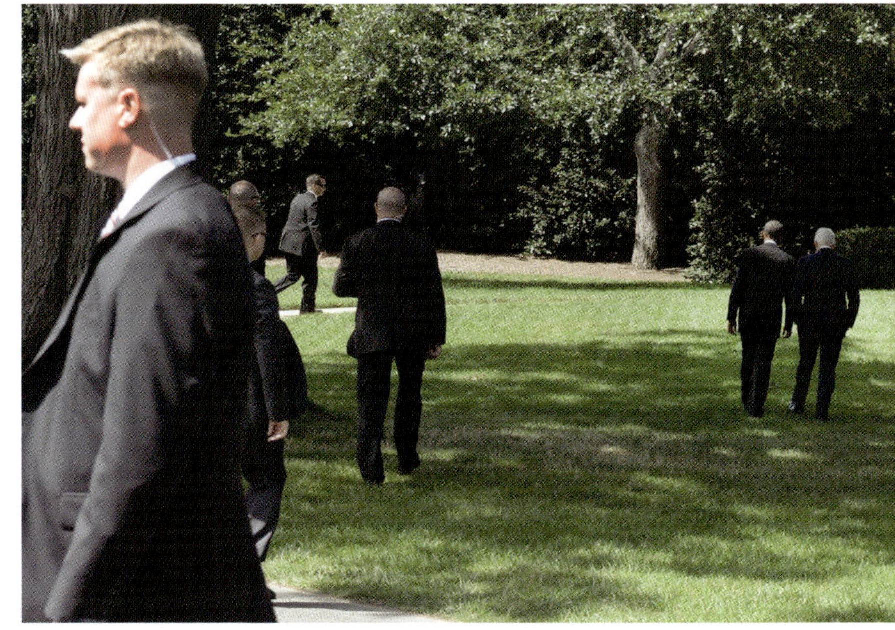

Presidents Obama and Clinton walk back to the Oval Office with plenty of security detail around them following an AmeriCorps Event, September 2014.

Witnessing our presidents get together and joke around with each other is a special treat for me. For instance, the friendship between Presidents Clinton and Obama was evident during the Presidential Medal of Freedom Ceremony in November 2013.

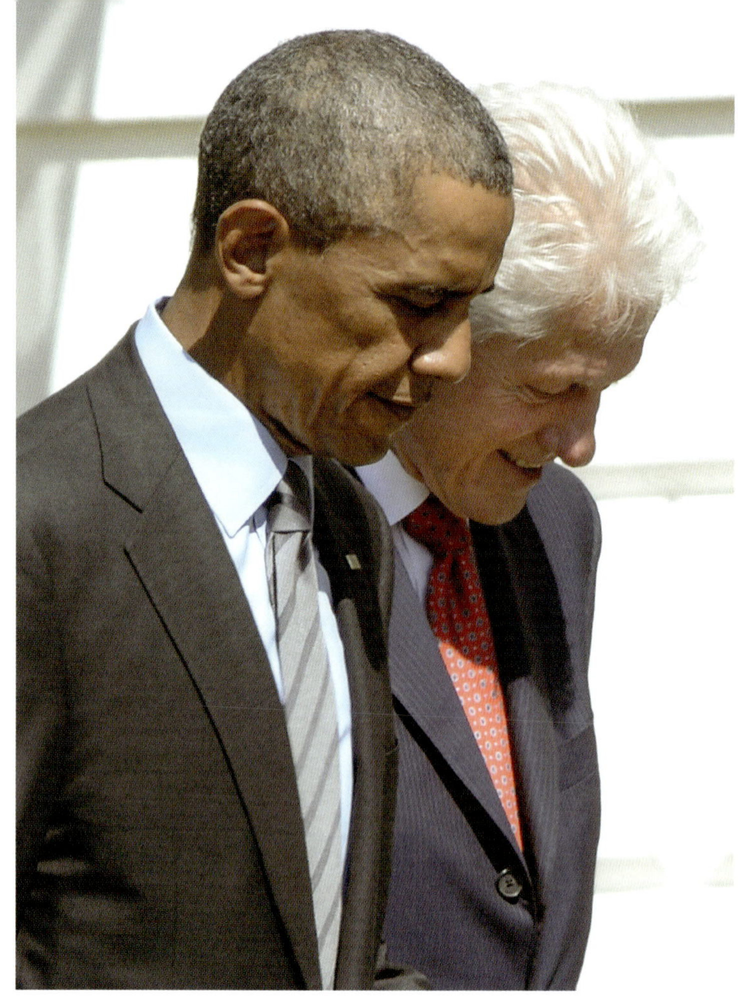

Presidents Obama and Clinton walk to the Oval Office surrounded by their US Secret Service protective detail, September 2014.

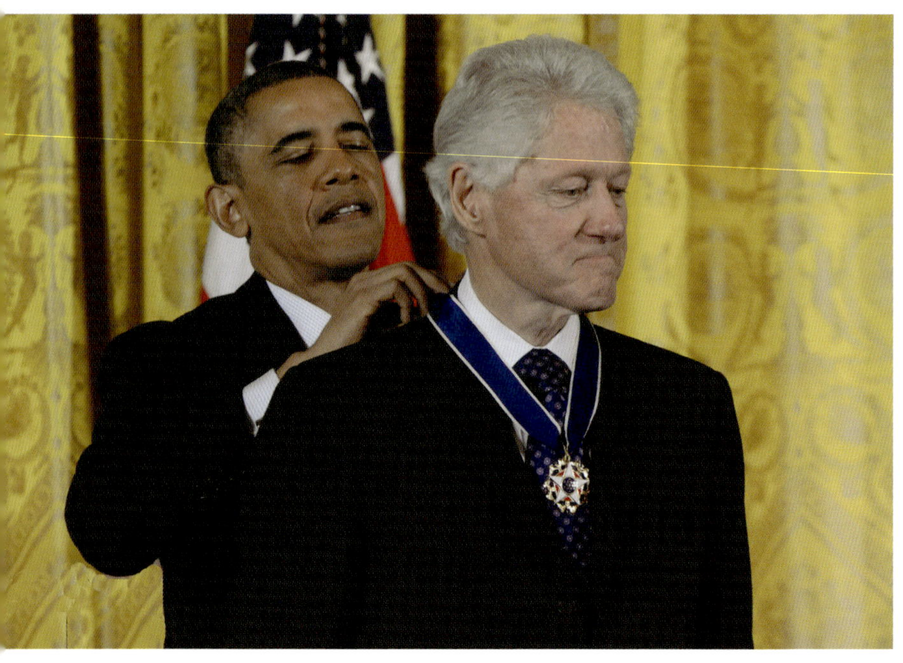

President Barack Obama awards the Presidential Medal of Freedom to former President William Jefferson Clinton, November 2013.

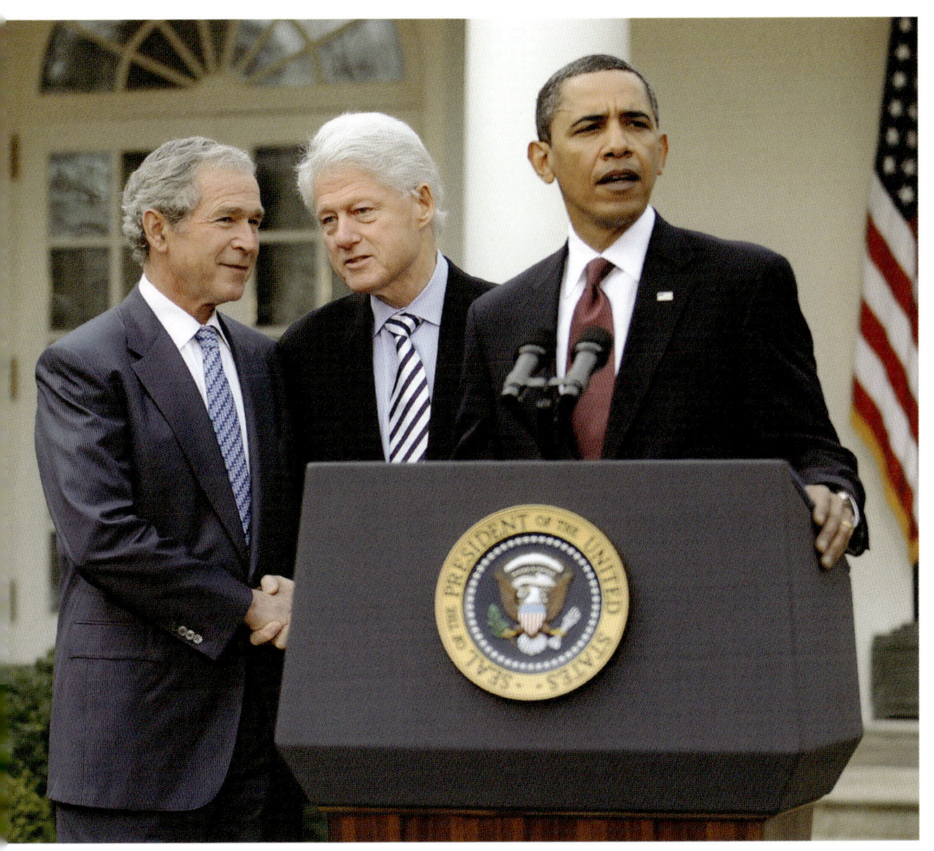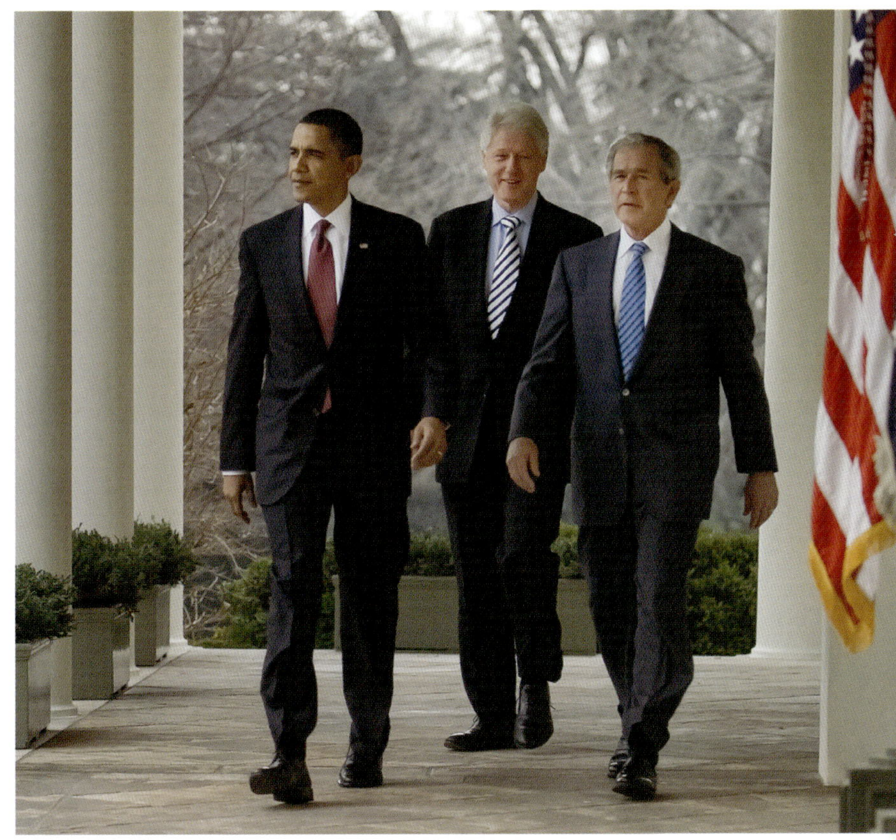

*In the Rose Garden of the White House, Presidents Obama, Bush, and Clinton unite
in helping the people of Haiti recover from a devastating earthquake. January 2010.*

President Obama awarded Clinton this honor as we all watched the two men playfully banter with each other just before the ceremony began. In January of 2010, Presidents Clinton, Bush, and Obama came together at the White House to help raise awareness for the people of Haiti following a devasting earthquake there. Although they were respectful of the serious situation, the comradery between the three men was obvious as I watched them display subtle gestures of respect and affection for one another.

But this kind of warmth doesn't always occur between presidents, as I found out for myself years earlier when photographing multiple presidents together at an event. In October 1995, I photographed Presidents Clinton, Carter, and Ford at a Truman Library fundraiser event at the National Building Museum in Washington, DC.

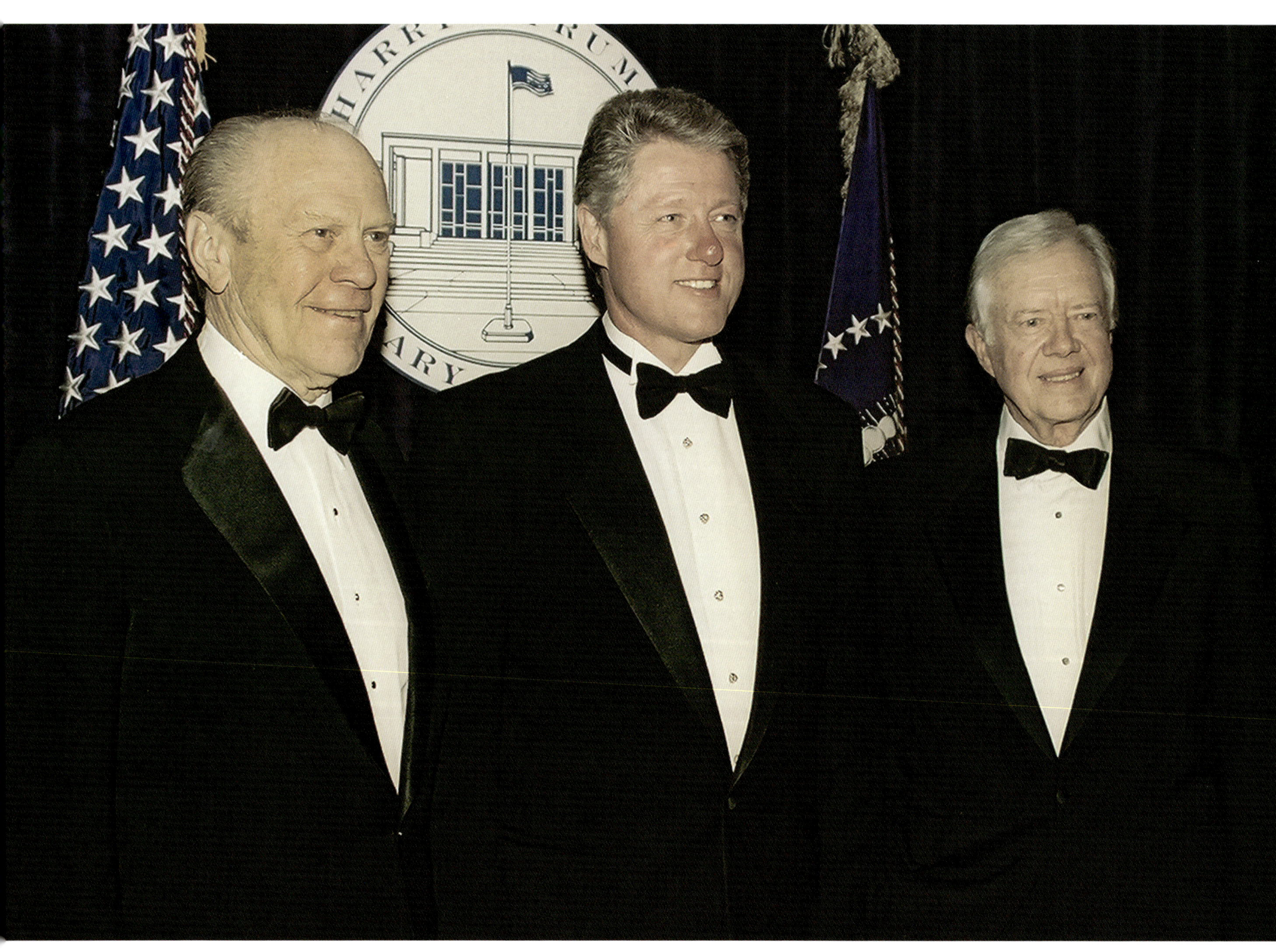

President Bill Clinton and former US Presidents Gerald Ford and Jimmy Carter pose for a picture at the National Building Museum during a fundraiser for the Harry Truman Presidential Library, October 1995.

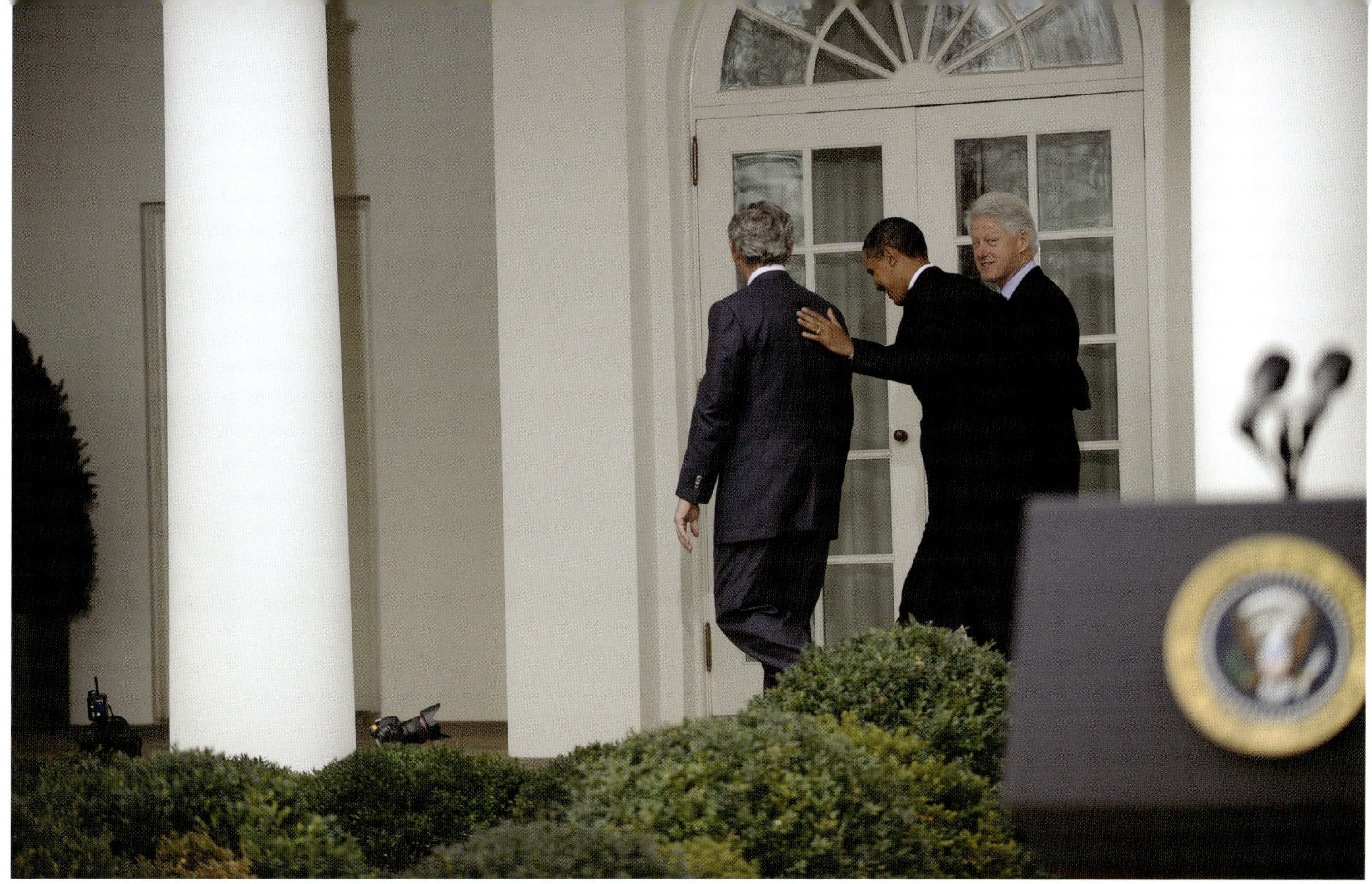

Presidents Obama, Bush, and Clinton walk back to the White House after speaking to
the press about their efforts in helping the people of Haiti recover after an earthquake.

I was grateful to have met the three of them with my bureau chief, Sarah McClendon. She had previously covered each of them, and they all had great respect for her. The journalist in me was able to convince the three of them to let me photograph them all with Sarah. I am happy to say that they complied, but it did not seem to me that they had much of a presidential bond with each other that evening. Of course, that could be attributed to one or more of them simply having an off day, like any of us. They are presidents . . . but they are also just people, with good days and bad.

There are certain cool traditions that take place when a new president comes into residency at the White House. One such tradition occurs when the outgoing president writes his successor a handwritten note on White House stationery and leave it in the drawer of the Resolute desk in the Oval Office. This is what President George H. W. Bush Sr. wrote for his successor, Bill Clinton:

Jan 20, 1993

Dear Bill,

When I walked into this office just now I felt the same sense of wonder and respect that I felt four years ago. I know you will feel that, too.

I wish you great happiness here. I never felt the loneliness some Presidents have described.

There will be very tough times, made even more difficult by criticism you may not think is fair. I'm not a very good one to give advice; but just don't let the critics discourage you or push you off course.

You will be our President when you read this note. I wish you well. I wish your family well.

Your success now is our country's success. I am rooting hard for you.

Good luck—

George

I have noticed throughout my coverage of five US presidents that there is one common denominator between them all. In having met and photographed eight of them over my lifetime, I've realized that no matter their political party, each of them is close with their family. They are protective and loving in their own ways.

Close bonds were well-known among members of the Bush family, starting with President Bush Sr., our forty-first president. The family was so comfortable with David Valdez, their presidential photographer, that they allowed him to photograph the president and first lady with some of their grandchildren piled in bed with them one morning while on vacation in Kennebunkport, Maine. I respect their openness and their willingness to let the public into their lives like that.

The long love story of President Jimmy Carter and his wife Rosalynn was also remarkable. They celebrated over 77 years of marriage: the longest marriage of a former presidential couple in history. Jimmy Carter wrote the poem "Rosalynn" in his book of poetry, *Always a Reckoning.* I am proud to have a copy of that book that they both signed for me.

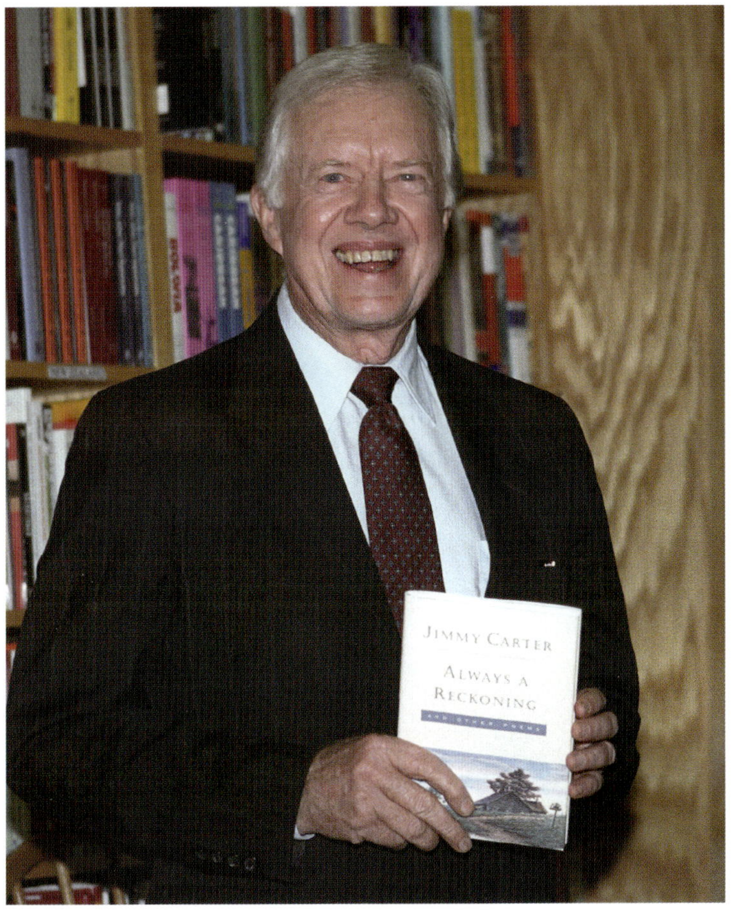

Former President Jimmy Carter releases his book Always a Reckoning, *a collection of poems for his wife Roselyn. Borders Books, Kensington, Maryland. November 1995.*

In 2009, as I was photographing the VIP arrivals at President Obama's inauguration, I was touched by the way President Carter held hands with his beloved wife as they arrived at the ceremony.

Although I did not photograph Carter when he was in office, I did photograph both him and his wife several times over the years. I believe that President Carter has made important contributions since he left office, most notably his passionate support for Habitat for Humanity.

Looking back on our presidents, I see what an enormous love story Ronald and Nancy Reagan lived. The Reagan presidency was before my time at the White House, and while I never photographed President Reagan during his lifetime, I did cover the portion of his funeral that was held in Washington, DC.

This funeral was so much more than our nation losing a leader; the Reagans' fairy tale relationship played out publicly. Nancy and her husband had shared a profound love for each other, and the entire world witnessed their final farewell. Nancy made sure that her husband was honored in the same grand fashion that she had loved him. As she wrote in her memoir, her "life didn't really begin" until she met the former president.[1]

I will always remember those couple of days covering Reagan's funeral. It was exceptionally hot on the June 2004 day that the former president's body arrived in DC. Both the media and onlookers waited in the stifling heat to see the procession approach the US Capitol, where the former president would lay in state. Streets were set up with barricades, confining tens of thousands of patriotic

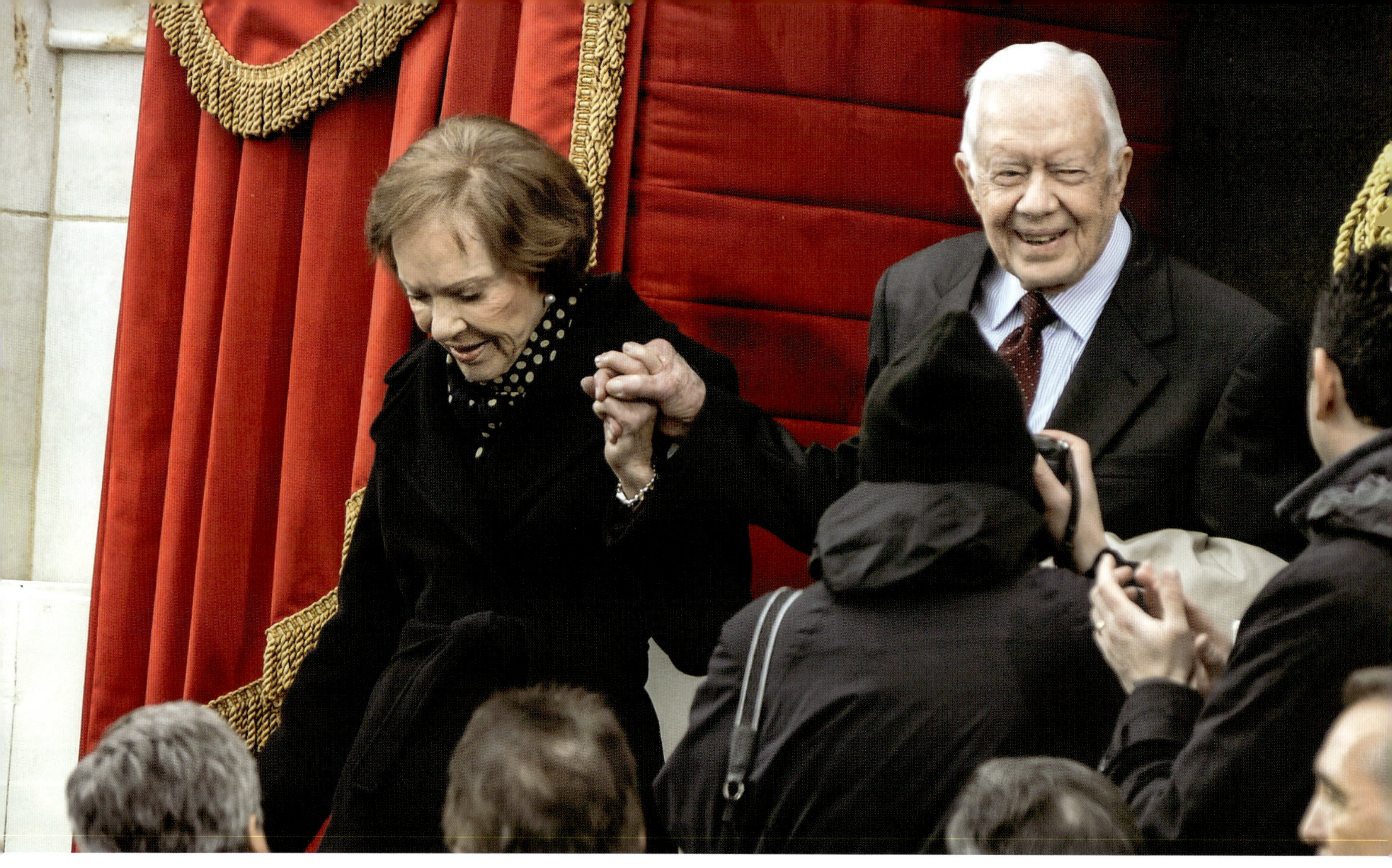

Jimmy Carter and Rosalynn Carter hold hands as they arrive at President Obama's 2009 inauguration.

Americans determined to witness the pageantry and say farewell to a beloved leader.

A disaster almost occurred that day. The small, misguided aircraft of a US midwestern governor unknowingly entered the restricted airspace around the Capitol. We were instructed by the police to vacate the area immediately, abandon our gear, and move quickly toward Union Station. Many people stampeded in a frantic effort to evade what many of us thought to be another terrorist attack. This evacuation caused the press corps photographers to forfeit our hard-earned positions along the route that we had secured six to ten hours earlier. Once the plane was successfully escorted away by military aircraft, we received the "all clear"

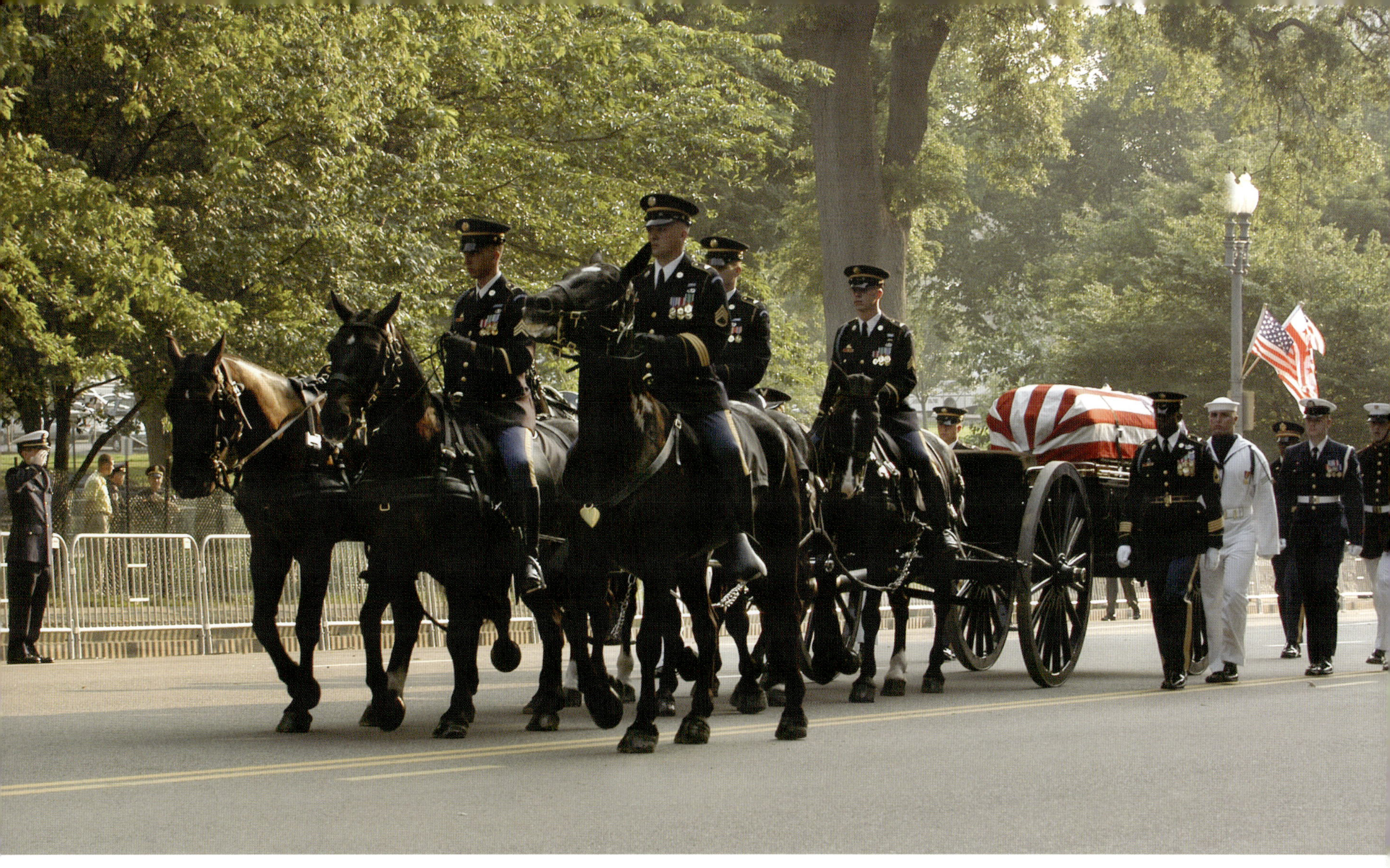

Ronald Reagan is carried by caisson to his funeral, June 2004.

signal and scrambled to reclaim our original vantage points. Months later I got a chance to speak with House Speaker Dennis Hastert as he was promoting his book, and he proudly informed me that the evacuation that day at the Capitol had occurred in record time, thanks to the internal practice drills carried out there since 9/11.

Finally, the parade of various military groups in dress uniform and the United States Marine Band began. They marched by with the formal precision you would expect of an event of this magnitude. The officers keeping guard along the parade route stood at attention in the heat for such a long period that some even fainted. Each was instantly carried off and replaced by another.

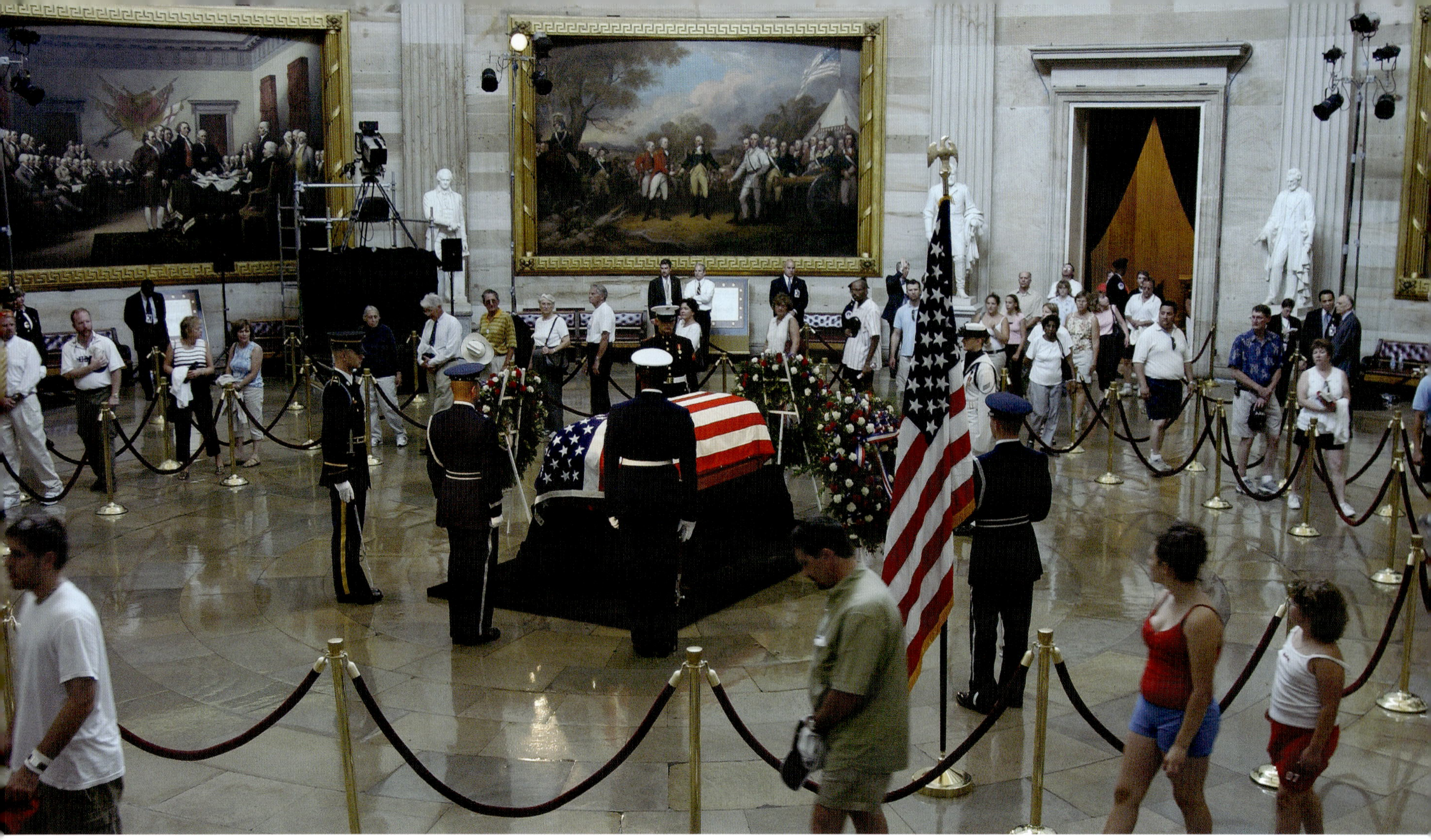

*The casket bearing former President Ronald Reagan lies in state at the US Capitol
as hundreds of mourners come to pay their final good-byes, June 2004.*

Off in the distance, the clip-clop of horse hooves could be heard. As the echoing sound grew louder and tensions mounted higher, the sea of bystanders fell into an eerie silence as the flag-draped casket ceremoniously passed by.

Once we were inside the Capitol, a presidential viewing protocol fell into place. Members of the military were vigilantly protecting the casket and stood on ceremony, changing the guard every fifteen minutes. A procession quickly formed, with thousands of citizens awaiting their turn to pay their final respects at the thirty-four-hour viewing. Periodically, the line was interrupted as various heads of state and members of Congress cut in with their official escorts.

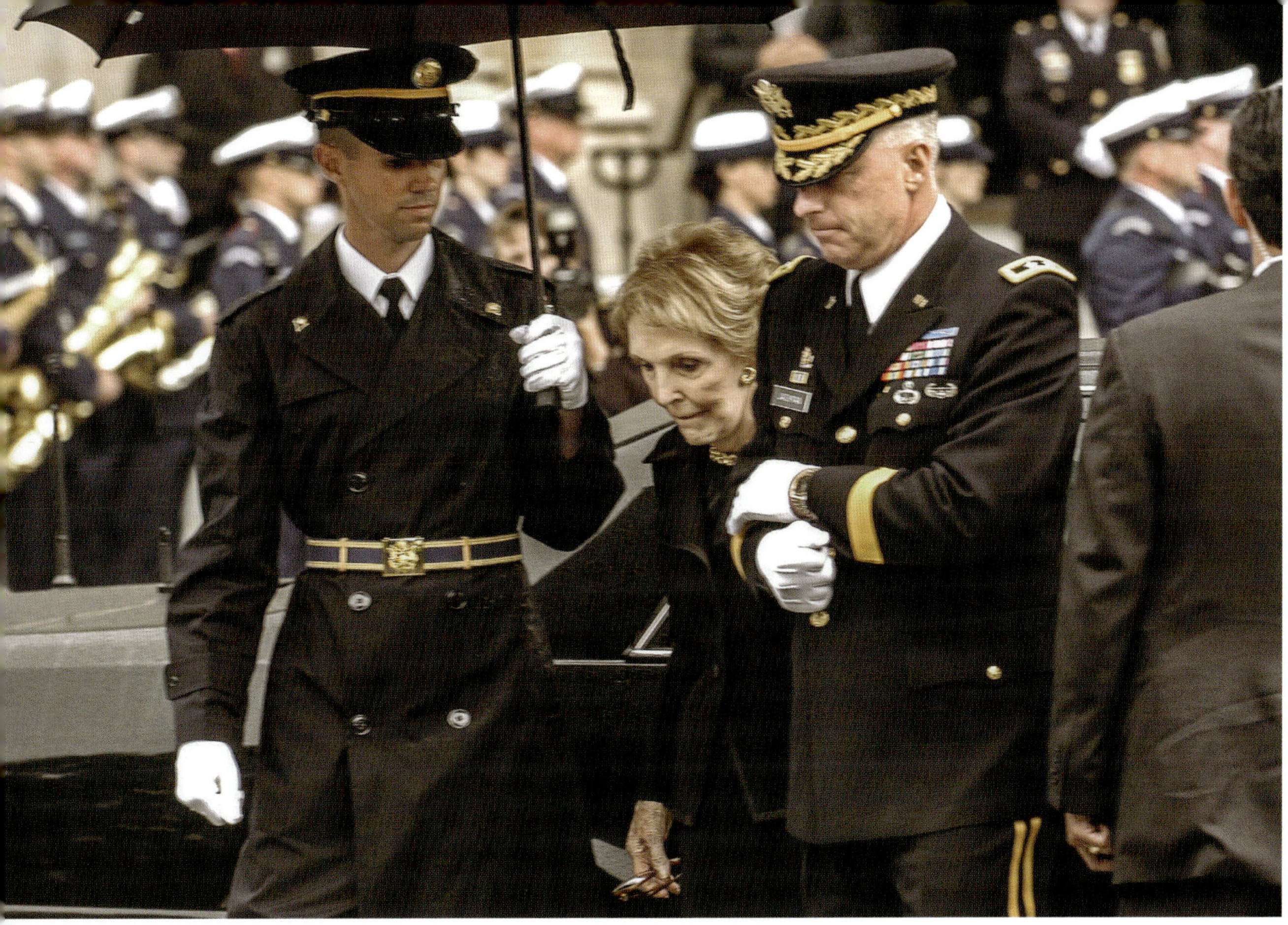

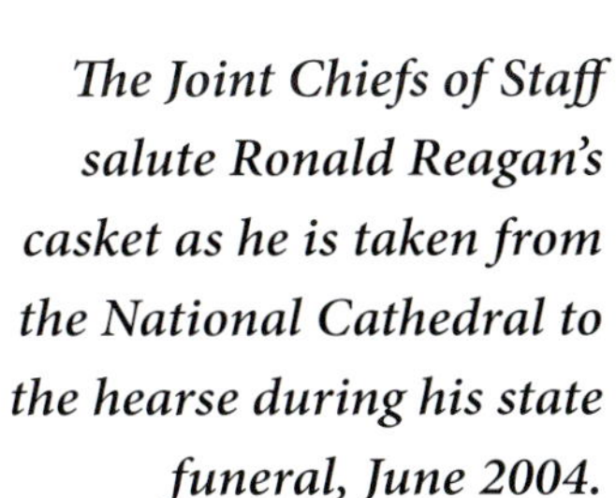

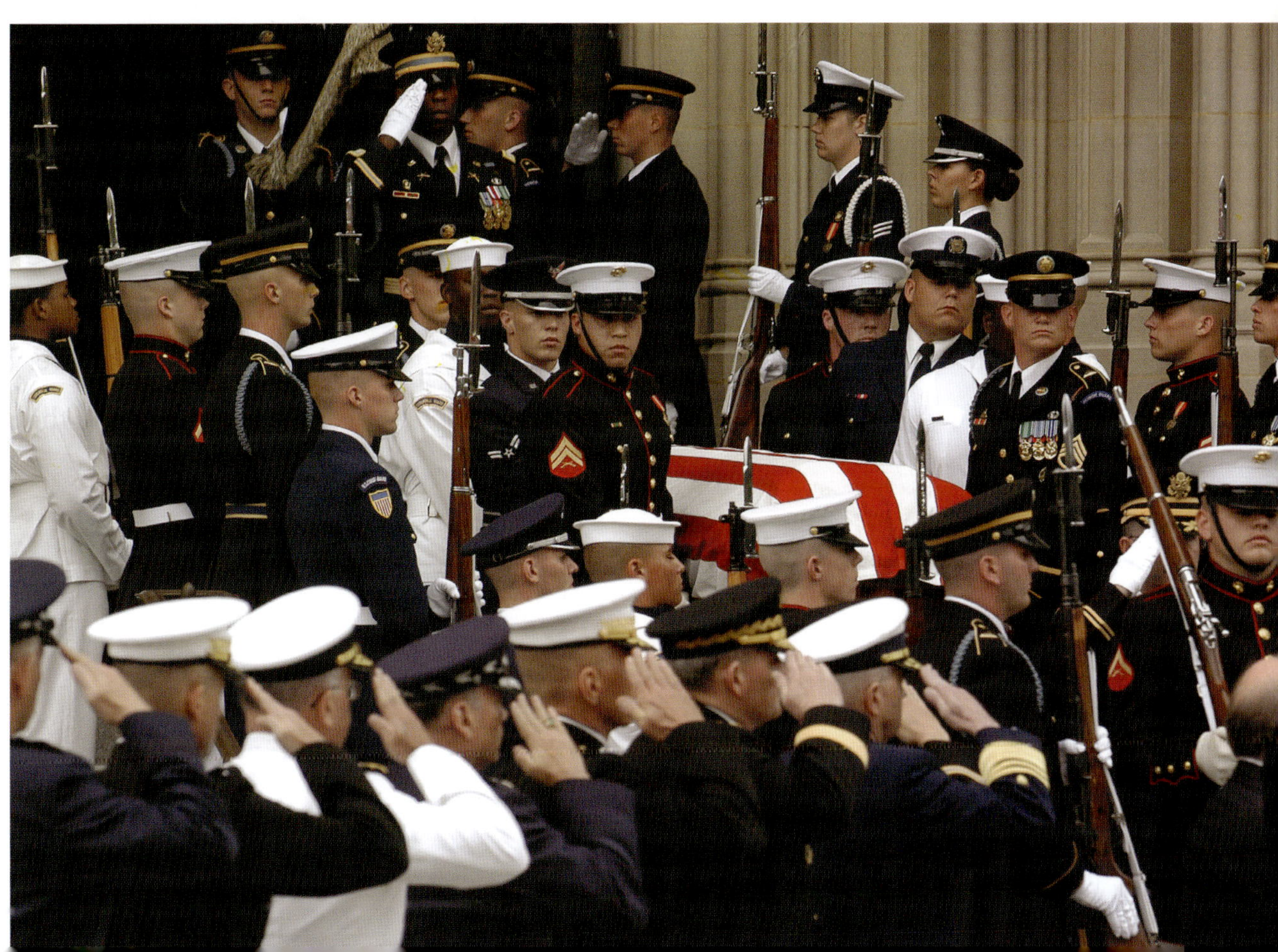

Former first lady Nancy Reagan arrives at the National Cathedral for the funeral of her husband former President Ronald Reagan, June 2004.

The Joint Chiefs of Staff salute Ronald Reagan's casket as he is taken from the National Cathedral to the hearse during his state funeral, June 2004.

The following day, I covered the ceremony at the Washington National Cathedral, the hallowed sanctuary that is the last stop for many dignitaries. As the funeral motorcade made its way through Washington, thousands of people lined the streets. Once inside the carefully secured grounds, there was a crowd mixed with celebrities, royalty, and various heads of state. A frail Nancy Reagan emerged from a limousine accompanied by a military escort and wound her way into the towering cathedral.

As we waited for the service to conclude, leaders from the different US military branches lined up and stood at attention to salute the casket as it was taken to the awaiting presidential hearse. Everyone seemed to have been deeply touched as the huge motorcade slowly pulled away from the cathedral. For the Reagan family, however, there was much more to come. They headed off to California for more services that would continue to honor President Reagan's memory and execute the final wishes both he and Nancy had planned so many years earlier.

We lost yet another of our former leaders on November 30, 2018. Less than a week later, I photographed former President George W. Bush saying good-bye to his father and friend, former President George H. W. Bush, forty-first president of the United States. This final good-bye felt much more personal to me since I had met and photographed both father and son over the years.

A lone drum was heard through the thick silence as the casket was brought down the stairs of the US Capitol. The traditional president's song, "Hail to the Chief," was played by the United States Marine Band as the forty-first president was placed in the presidential hearse.

> A lone drum was heard through the thick silence as the casket was brought down the stairs of the US Capitol. The traditional president's song, "Hail to the Chief," was played by the United States Marine Band.

As with any presidential funeral, the entire Bush family had to grieve in front of the world while suffering such a private loss. I could relate to this president losing his father; George W. Bush and his father were great friends, just as I was with mine.

I felt privileged to have had an inside glimpse into the human side of our forty-third president during his terms in office. George W. was one of the rare second-generation presidents to sit behind the desk in the Oval Office. I saw how much that meant to him.

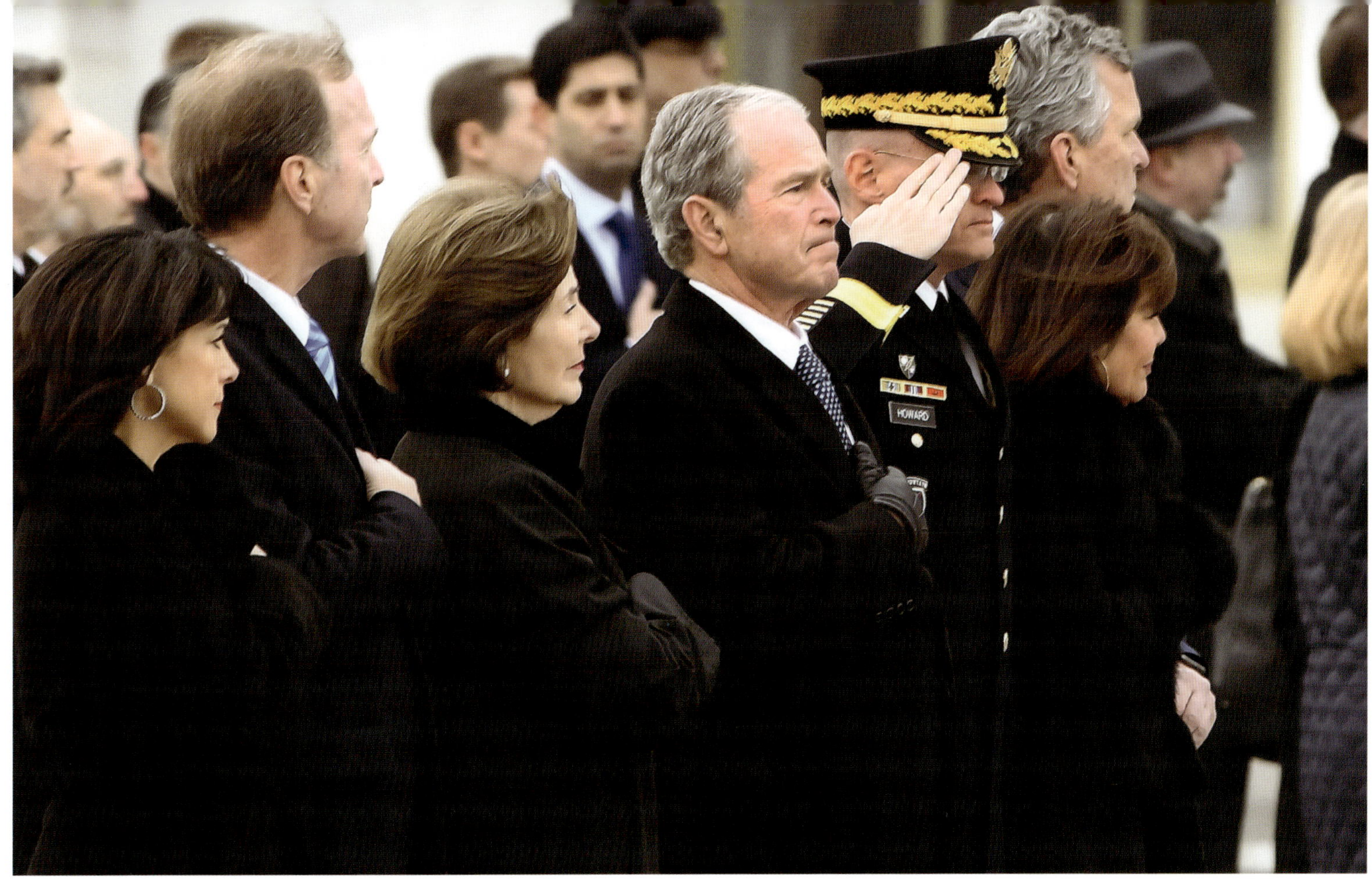

The casket of former President George H. W. Bush leaves the Capitol en route to his funeral service at the Washington Cathedral. President George W. Bush watches his dad's casket be moved from the building to the hearse as "Hail to the Chief" plays. December 2018.

Although I have always taken pride in being objective, I would like to share some of what I have learned from my years behind the camera.

Each president has been criticized for his faults, real or perceived, and often those mistakes take on a life of their own. Whether it's not speaking properly, having big ears or orange skin, falling off their bike, tripping on the stairs . . . the list goes on and on. But we need to remember that these presidents are still people with feelings, and everything they and their families do in their lives is always up for scrutiny. I know they all know this going in, but I am sure it gets to them over time. I hope that through my words, and especially my pictures, I am able to shed some light on the human side of our presidents to you.

Members of the press have been given the responsibility to act as the eyes and ears of the people as we document those who reside in the White House. I believe it is possible to do this job while keeping in mind that *all* of us are going to make mistakes along the way—even presidents, who come under the most intense examination of all.

The problem is that all of that scrutiny creates a barrier that leads to less and less access. In the time that I've been covering the presidents, somewhere along the way the public became accustomed to the norm of scandal, chaos, and political mudslinging; boosting ratings and increasing viewers and readership seems to have become the goal of papers and networks. Acts of kindness no longer appear to grab people's attention anymore.

I remember a time when candidates running for office would campaign on how they could make our country a *better* place, not on how much dirt they could dig up on their opponents and how dishonest their rivals' family members were. Controversy is now the everyday reality; it has become commonplace to see a sitting president impeached, charged with taking classified documents, misreporting income to the IRS, or watch a presidential candidate campaign outside the courtroom where they face felony charges. We are headed into a dangerous new normal.

Members of the media who cover our presidents need to devote a more mindful approach while rushing to meet deadlines. Today there is a steady stream of intense issues that happen on a regular basis. As we perform our jobs, we need to consider how we ourselves would like to be treated and presented in the press. There are often ways to subtly lean on the side of kindness while still holding our subjects accountable.

It comes down to having respect for one another. We are chronicling our leaders in both narrative and photographs for the generations to come. Without this, we cannot learn from history so that we do not repeat our mistakes.

We owe the presidents we cover that respect, and they owe us in the media the same.

At the end of the day, for those chosen few who lead our nation, the history books will decide how they are remembered . . .

Acknowledgments

Before all else, I owe a debt of gratitude to both the late Sarah McClendon and Helen Thomas for their guidance and friendship along the way.

To Warren Bowes, Father Jim Meyers, Dan Straub, and Mark Reinstein, many thanks to each of you for the time spent listening, bouncing ideas and inspiration.

I appreciate the encouragement from Betty Fraiser, Bill King, Joel Laurance, Greg Maitheson, Jon-Christopher Bau, and my other friends both in the White House press corps and those on the Photography Team at the National Press Club.

I offer the utmost appreciation for the support of my friends who are battling their own issues but still made time to be there for me: Priscilla Blackburn, Tom Crockett, and Susan Bainbridge.

I would like to honor Kristin Taylor for helping with my initial edits and the folks at Brown Books Publishing Group for their professionalism and dedication to my project, especially Tom Reale, Ben Davidoff, Jennie Knuppel, Mary Winzer, Brittany Griffiths, Danny Whitworth, and Amy Goppert.

Special thanks for the support of my friends, neighbors, and colleagues in Washington, DC; Bethesda and Chevy Chase, Maryland; and the Gardens of Ocean City, New Jersey.

As ever, I am grateful to God for the opportunities and experiences I have been allowed to witness over the years. My camera has been a unique passport to capture history as it has unfolded before my eyes.

Notes

Introduction: Still in the White House

1. Clinton Foundation, "Statement: Death of Sarah McClendon," press release, December 11, 2003, https://www.clintonfoundation.org/press-and-news/general/statement-death-of-sarah-mcclendon/.

2. "Salute to Journalist Sarah McClendon," aired May 25, 1995, on C-SPAN. https://www.c-span.org/video/?65368-1/salute-journalist-sarah-mcclendon#!.

3. "Citizen journalist," *Cape Cod Times*, January 9, 2003. https://www.capecodtimes.com/story/news/2003/01/09/citizen-journalist/50959705007/.

4. Maya Angelou, "Our Grandmothers," in *Maya Angelou: The Complete Poetry* (New York: Random House, 2015), 245.

Chapter 1: President William Jefferson Clinton

1. John F. Harris, "Alone, President Responds with Simple Apology," *Washington Post*, February 12, 1999. https://www.washingtonpost.com/archive/politics/1999/02/13/alone-president-responds-with-simple-apology/9a19fba1-1a4c-4122-a58f-bd9a99c1db1d/.

2. Ibid.

Chapter 2: President George W. Bush

1. Mary Bowerman, "George W. Bush: C students, you too can be president," *USA Today*, May 17, 2015. https://www.usatoday.com/story/news/nation-now/2015/05/17/george-w-bush-c-students-president-graduation/27488795/.

Chapter 3: President Barack Obama

1. NobelPrize.org, "The Norwegian Nobel Committee has decided . . .," press release, October 9, 2009, https://www.nobelprize.org/prizes/peace/2009/prize-announcement/.

2. Barack Obama, "Remarks on Winning the Nobel Peace Prize," Edited by Gerhard Peters and John T. Wooley, The American Presidency Project, October 9, 2009. https://www.presidency.ucsb.edu/documents/remarks-winning-the-nobel-peace-prize.

3. "Obama gives $1.4 million Nobel prize to 10 charities," *Reuters*, March 11, 2010. https://www.reuters.com/article/idUSTRE62A5EN/.

4. Wounded Warrior Project, "Soldier Ride." https://www.woundedwarriorproject.org/programs/soldier-ride.

Chapter 4: Donald J. Trump

1. Donald J. Trump (@realDonaldTrump), "When somebody challenges you unfairly, fight back – be brutal, be tough – don't take it. It is always important to WIN!" Twitter, June 27, 2015, 9:50 a.m., https://twitter.com/realDonaldTrump/status/614807981188710401.

2. "Brett Kavanaugh's Opening Statement: Full Transcript," *New York Times*, September 26, 2018. https://www.nytimes.com/2018/09/26/us/politics/read-brett-kavanaughs-complete-opening-statement.html.

3. Trump White House, "Remarks by President Trump at Swearing-in Ceremony of the Honorable Brett M. Kavanaugh as Associate Justice of the Supreme Court of the United States," October 8, 2018. https://trumpwhitehouse.archives.gov/briefings-statements/remarks-president-trump-swearing-ceremony-honorable-brett-m-kavanaugh-associate-justice-supreme-court-united-states/.

4. Morgan Chalfant, "Trump: 'The only way we're going to lose this election is if the election is rigged,' *The Hill,* August 17, 2020. https://thehill.com/homenews/administration/512424-trump-the-only-way-we-are-going-to-lose-this-election-is-if-the/.

Chapter 5: President Joseph R. Biden

1. Michael D. Shear, "Biden Has Held the Fewest News Conferences Since Reagan. Any Questions?" *The New York Times*, April 21, 2023. https://www.nytimes.com/2023/04/21/us/politics/biden-public-appearances-media.html.

2. Betty C. Monkman, "Pardoning the Thanksgiving Turkey," The White House Historical Association.

Chapter 6: Presidential Legacies

1. 1. Nancy Reagan, *My Turn: The Memoirs of Nancy Reagan*. New York: Random House Publishing Group, 2011.

About the Author

Before she jumped out of an airplane at 15,000 feet and earned her first-degree black belt in Tae Kwon Do, Christy Bowe, a third-generation Washingtonian, was thrown out of Catholic school in the ninth grade for refusing to conform. She briefly attended Montgomery College of Rockville, Maryland, and the University of Missouri Photo Workshop in Carthage, Missouri.

Most of her education has been "on the job."

In pursuit of her passion for photography, Christy earned her way into the small, elite circle of White House press photographers. With support from the late, widely celebrated White House reporter Sarah McClendon, Christy started ImageCatcher News Service. She is represented by Getty Images and Zuma Press.

Her corporate clients have included Harley–Davidson, the National Science Foundation, the National Press Club, the National Organization for Women, and the Hitachi corporation.

Christy is currently a member of the White House press corps, the House and Senate Press Photographers' Gallery, the White House Correspondents' Association, and the White House News Photographers Association. She has lectured at American University, Montgomery College, and George Mason University. Christy has ten images preserved in the George W. Bush Presidential Library. She resides in Bethesda, Maryland, and continues to work as a photojournalist, currently covering her fifth US president, Joseph R. Biden.

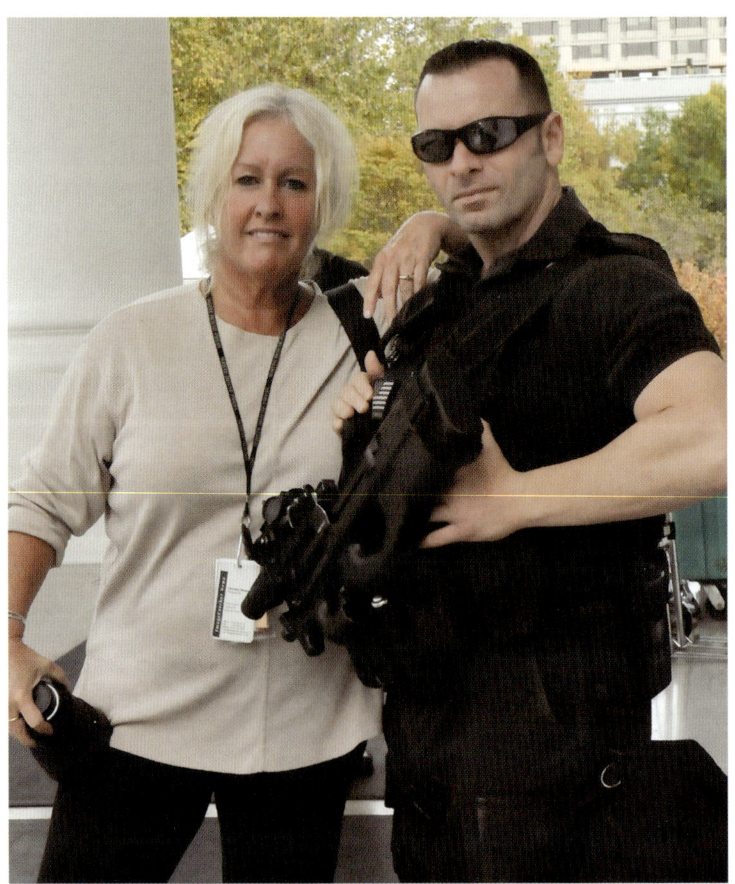

Barry Donadio, a member of the White House Secret Service Emergency Response Team, poses with me outside the North Portico.